The PROGRESSIVE APPROACH to READING

Kinder 1

(2ND EDITION)

HAZEL DOMINGO BABIANO

DONOVAN DOMINGO BABIANO
Authors

Complete with: teacher's guide, songs and games, and suggested activities for the different learning areas (THEMATIC)

PREFACE

Books are valuable teaching tools, and in some classrooms, regrettably, they are the only teaching tools. Books are a permanent and esteemed fixture in a teacher's arsenal, that is true. But books do have their limitations.

Our many years of teaching and of running a school have shown us that, though books are good and capable teachers, there are some things that can be taught faster and more effectively to some children when those same books are closed. We have witnessed the moment of realization spark in a child's eye during a game of "Letter Scrabble" when, under competitive and time pressure, he saw that "a," "p," and "t" could form either "tap" or "pat." We have witnessed children subtly learning the rules of subject-verb agreement — a complex lesson for preschoolers — by singing over and over again the songs that they enjoy. We have witnessed what some would call "difficult" or "reluctant" learners come out of their shells and participate with zeal once their books are closed and taken away from their hands, to be replaced by art paper, scissors, glue, and glitters. To a teacher such as ourselves, these moments are pure joy.

These and other moments have led us to an ongoing evolution in our series of books. Books should be alive and exciting. Books should interact with the class. Books should make teachers and pupils stand up, break sweat, shout, or sing at the top of their lungs. An atmosphere of deathly quiet, interrupted only by the rasping of pencil across paper, should not be the sum total of a child's classroom experience. Sometimes true learning can take place only in a classroom that's buzzing with activity and pulsing with energy.

This edition has included games, songs, class activities, and art projects to help the teacher put more life into the child's learning experience. Each lesson also has a teacher's guide which is meant not as an absolute command but as a supplement, an open suggestion, which the teacher may adapt to her own style and needs.

Let this book be a deep well of ideas from which the teacher can draw inspiration. And may the teacher experience, as we have, moments of pure joy in teaching.

Teacher Hazel & Teacher Dons

TABLE OF CONTENTS

FIRST QUARTER
PRE-READING SKILLS

Teacher's Objectives and Student Evaluation				
Lesson	*At the end of the activities, the child should be able to:*	**D**	**DD**	**WD**
1	1. develop left-to-right and up-down eye movements			
	2. improve eye-hand coordination			
	3. hold pencil correctly			
2	4. sort things that are alike and things that are different			
	5. note differences in size and in shape			
	6. identify similarities and differences in forms			
3	7. identify sounds made by animals and objects			
	8. recognize similarities and differences in sounds			
	9. tell whether a sound is loud or soft			
4	10. show the relationships between things			
	11. classify things according to use			
	12. identify then draw the missing parts of a picture			
5	13. identify the vowel letters and their phonetic sounds			
	14. name some objects whose names begin with the letters *a, e, i, o,* and *u*			
	15. develop sensory-motor skills by doing exercises such as encircling, connecting, checking, crossing-out, and coloring			

Legend:
D — Developing   DD — Developed   WD — Well-Developed

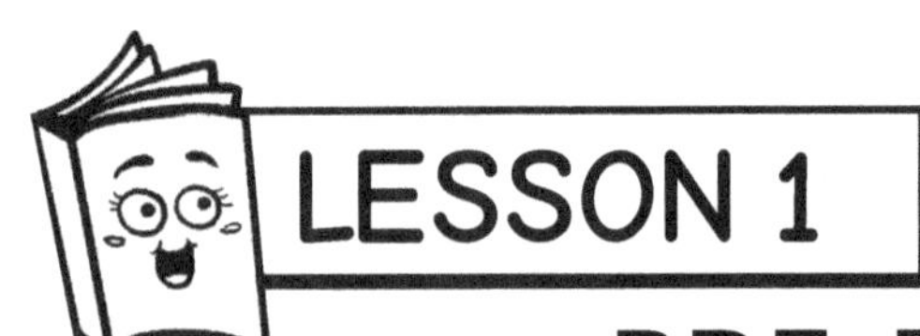

LESSON 1

PRE-READING SKILLS
Eye-Hand Coordination

Guide: Put different sets of broken lines across the classroom floor from left to right using masking tape. (The broken lines should be in different patterns: straight lines, zigzag lines, and curved lines.) Color the broken lines with the following: *straight*–red; *zigzag*–yellow; and *curved*–blue. Let the children walk along the broken lines, starting from the left going to the right.

Left-to-Right Eye-Hand Movement

ACTIVITY 1   SCORE:_______

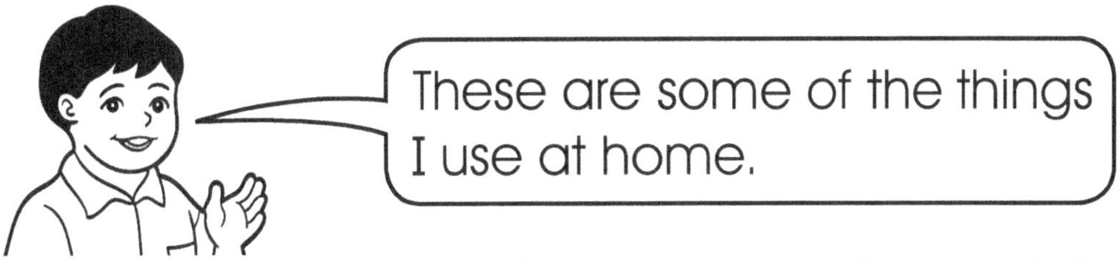

Connect the broken lines from the objects to their partners.

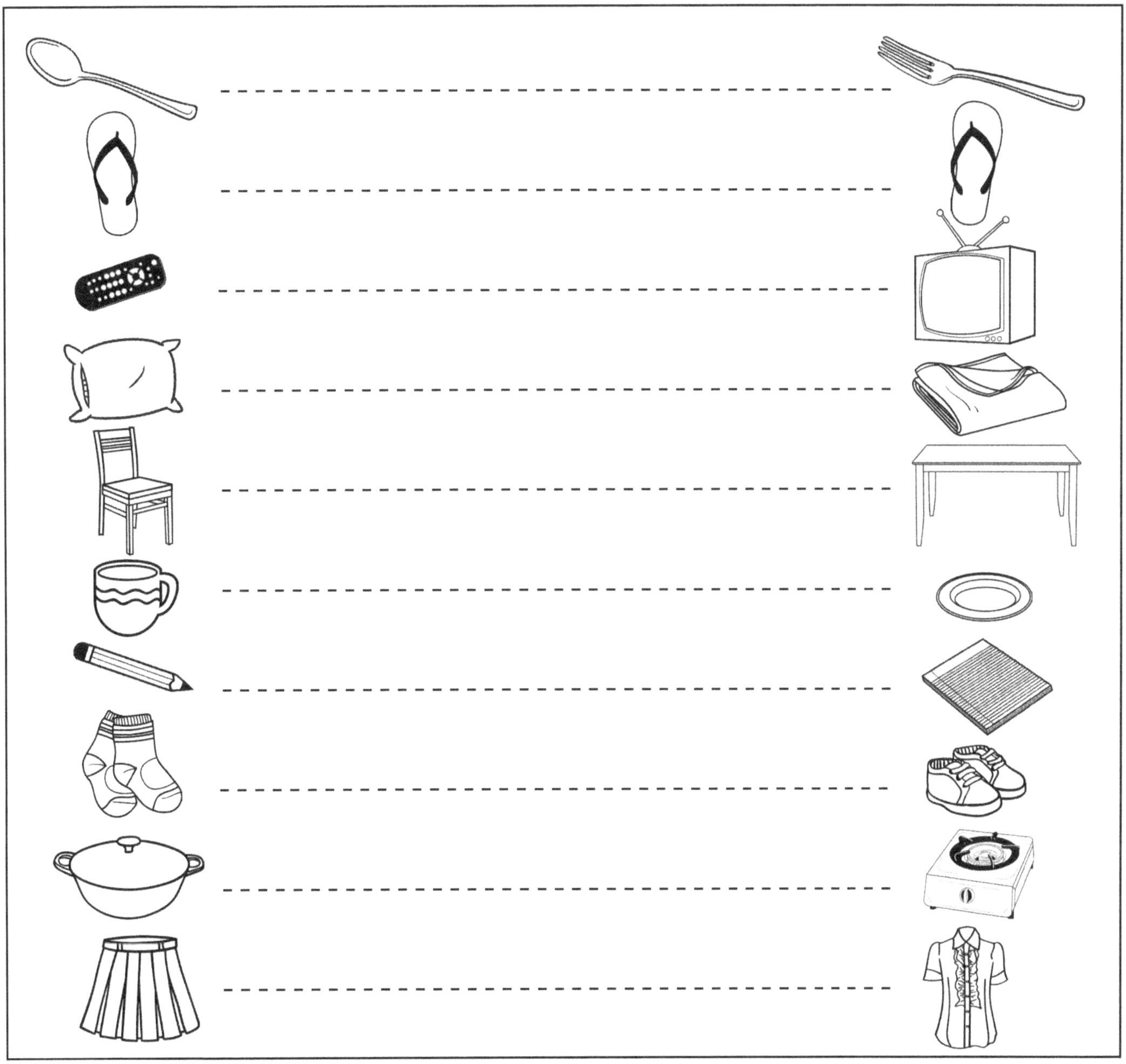

Up-Down Eye-Hand Movement

ACTIVITY 2   SCORE: _______

Connect the broken lines from top to bottom to complete the picture of the house.

# ACTIVITY 3

SCORE: _______

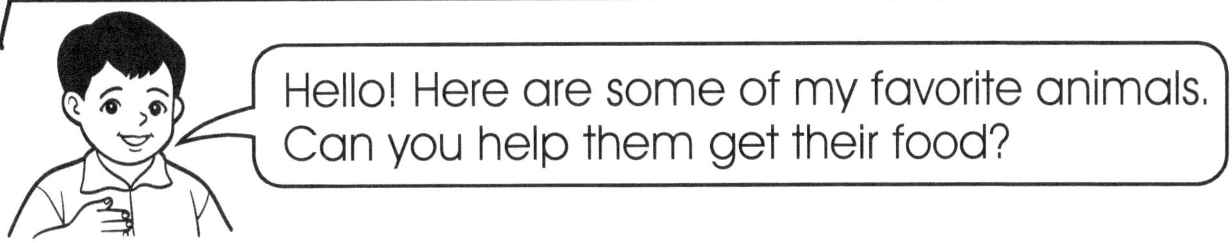

Connect the broken zigzag lines from the pictures of animals to their food.

ACTIVITY 4

SCORE: _______

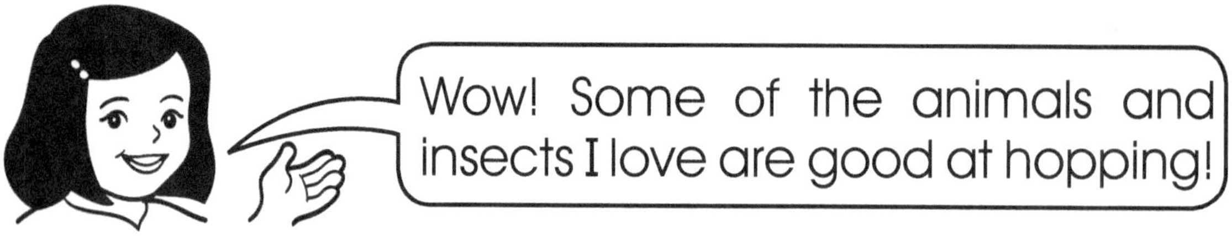

Connect the broken curved lines from the pictures of the baby animals to their mothers.

ACTIVITY 5   SCORE: _______

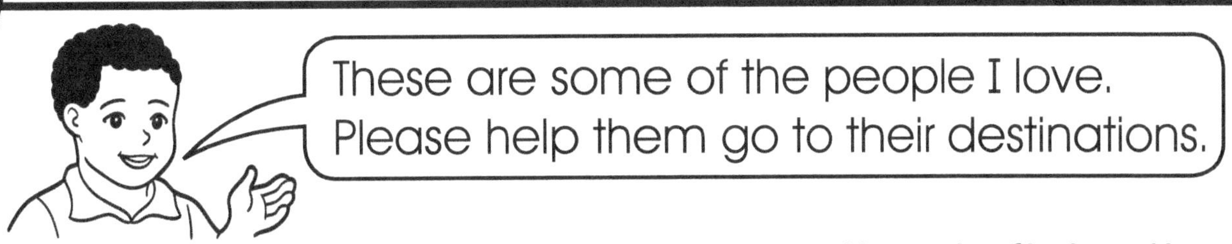

Draw lines from the pictures on the left to their destinations on the right.

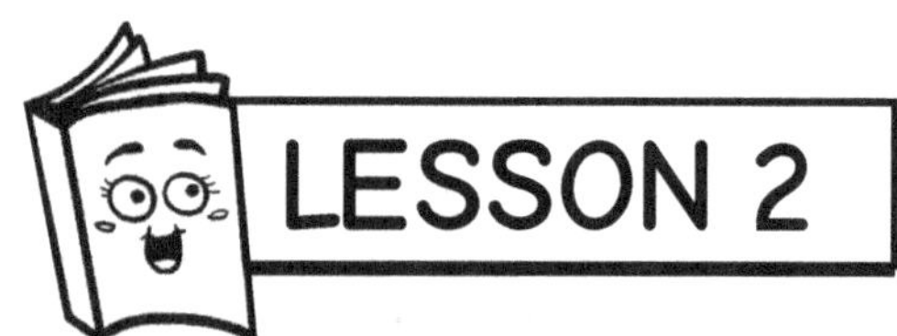

VISUAL DISCRIMINATION
Similarities and Differences

Guide: Put on a big tray pairs of things that are exactly alike. Have the children take turns in picking two things that are alike. Let them identify the objects. (You may also put pairs of things of different sizes and have the children pick those of the same size.) Later in the lesson, ask them to pick two things that are different.

Form, Size, and Shape

ACTIVITY 6   SCORE:_______

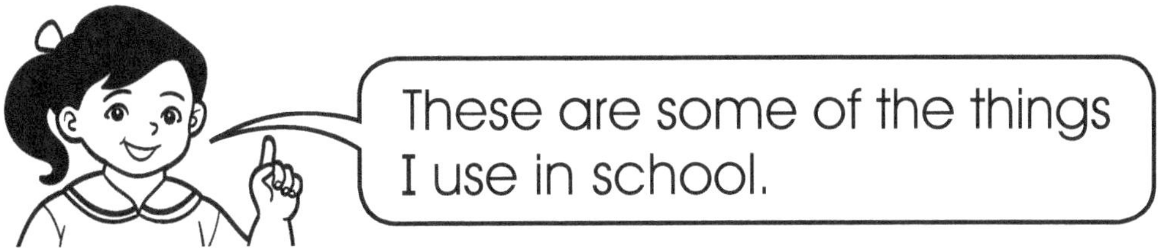

Color the pictures that are alike in each group.
Use a red crayon.

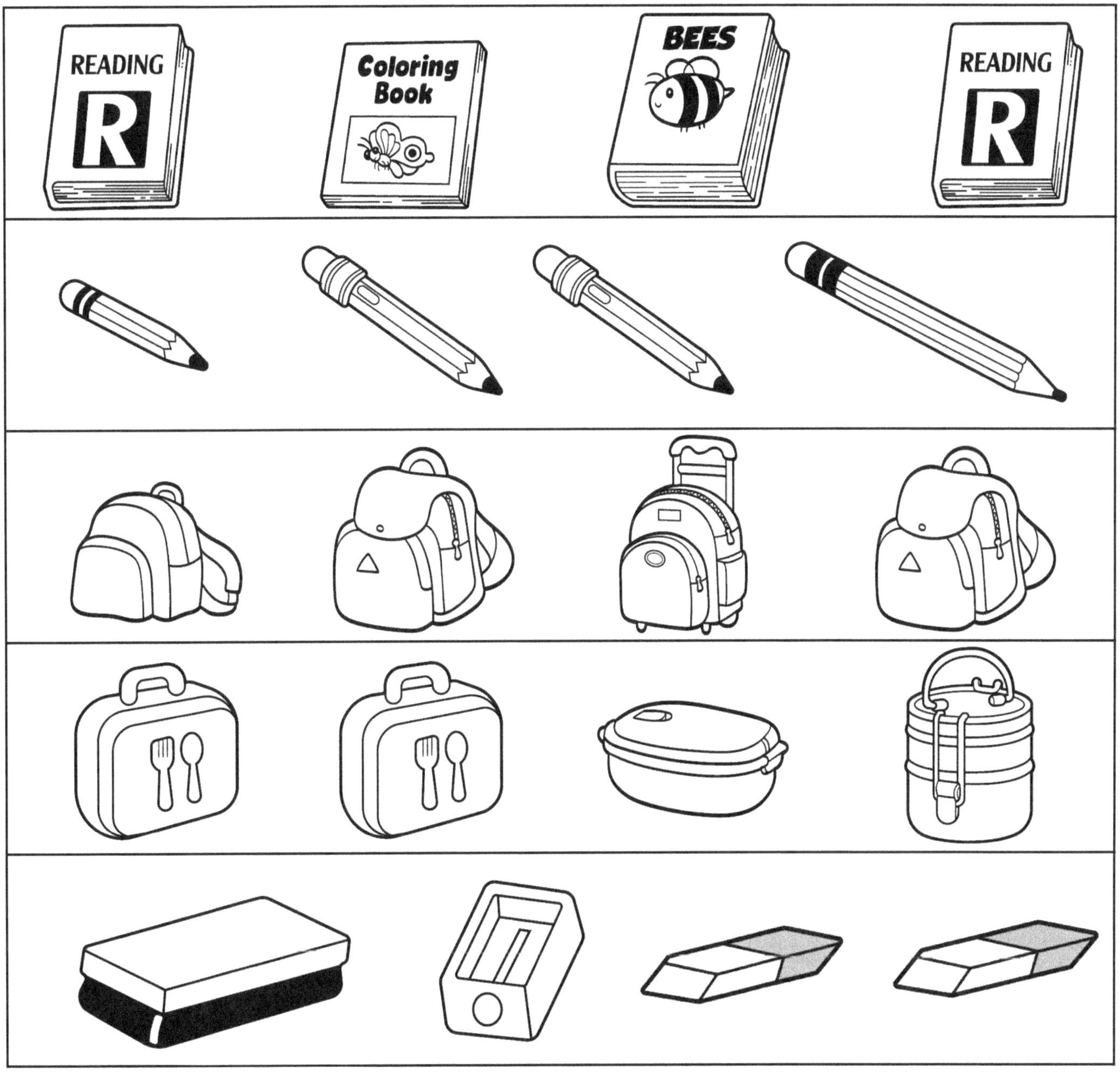

ACTIVITY 7

SCORE: _______

Encircle the picture that is different in each group. Use a blue crayon.

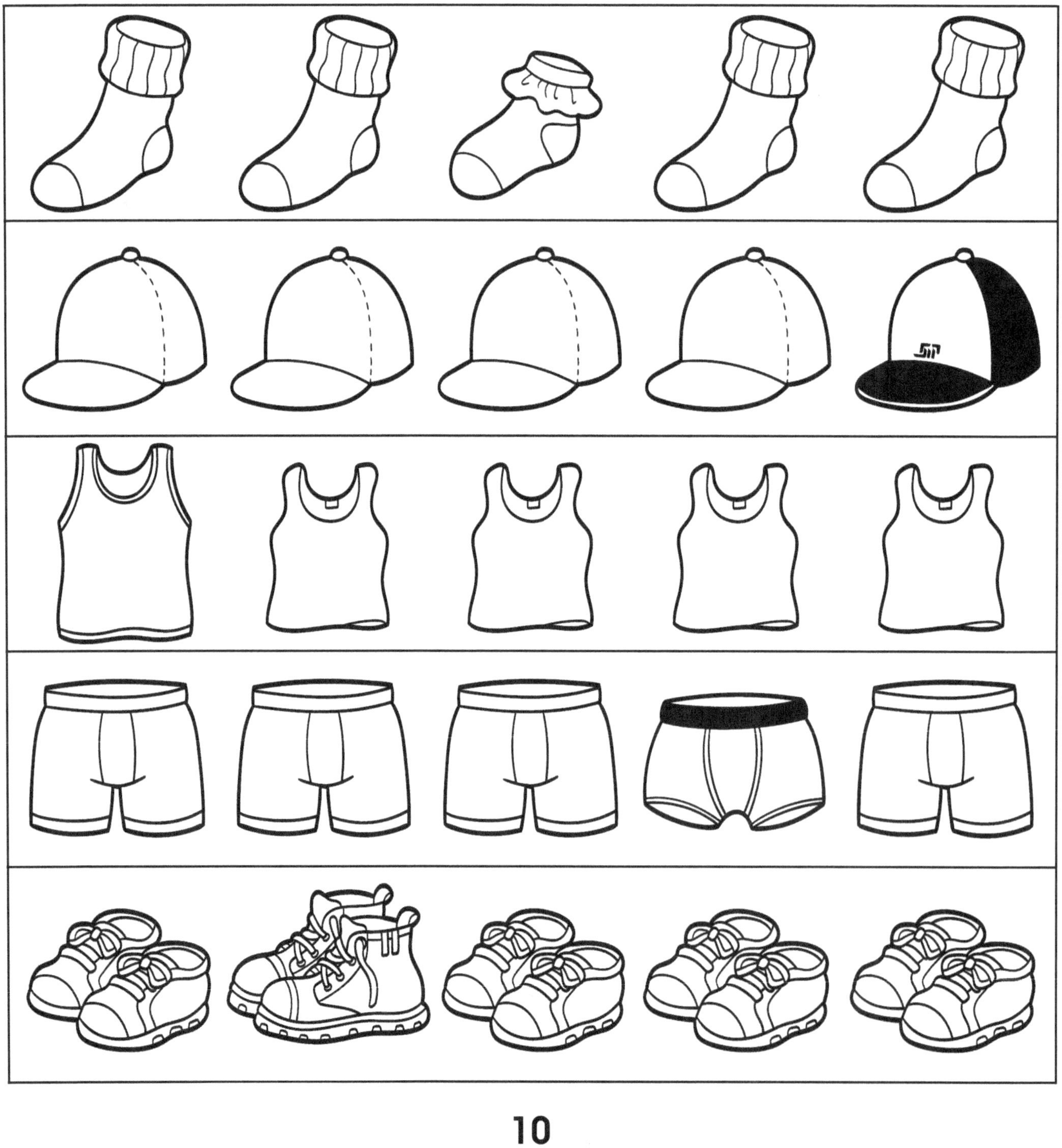

QUIZ NO. 1

SCORE: ________

Check (✓) the box with pictures that are alike. Cross out (✗) the box with pictures that are different. Use a yellow crayon.

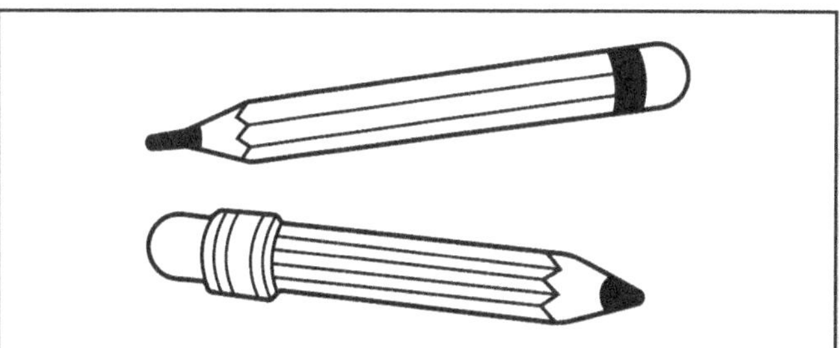

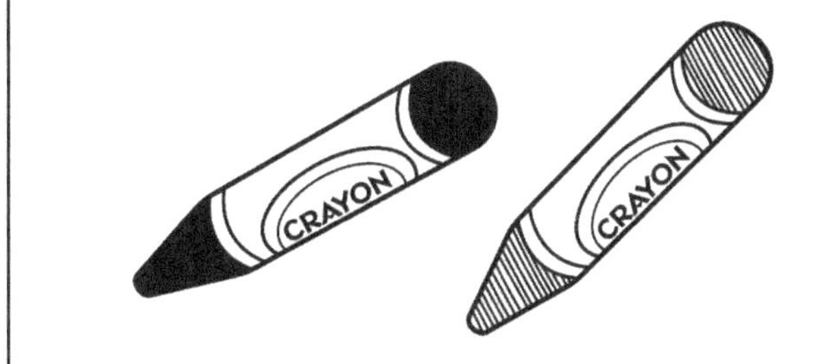

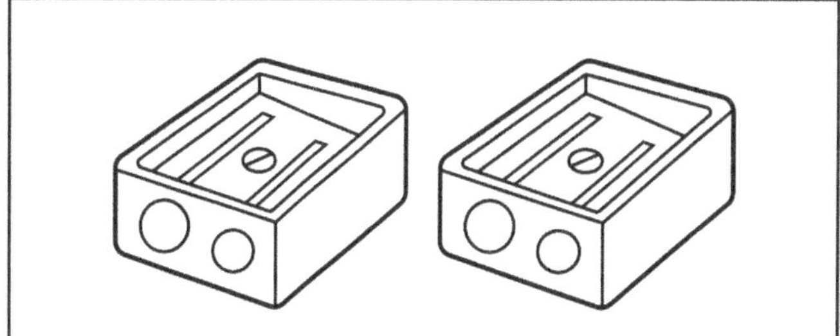

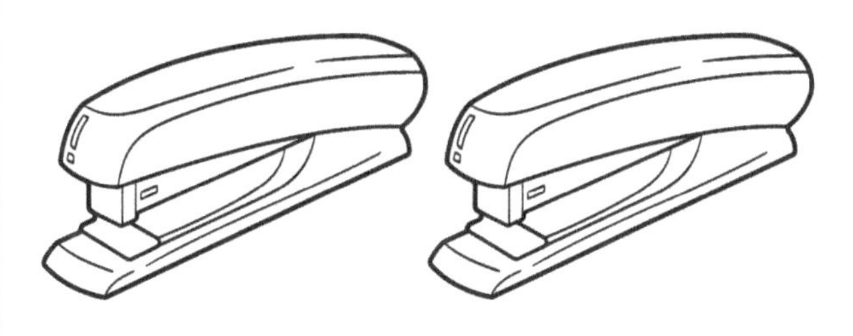

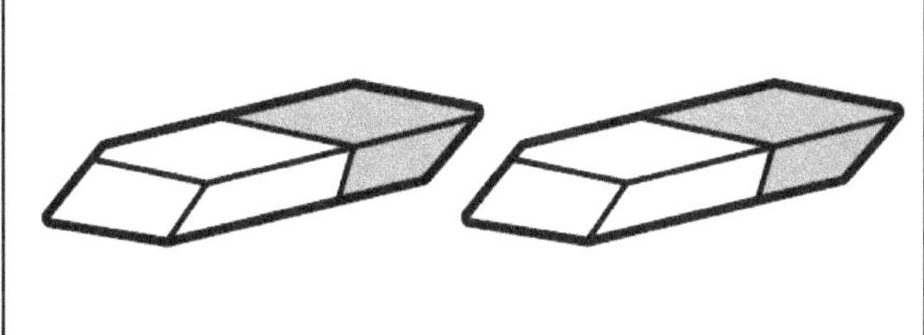

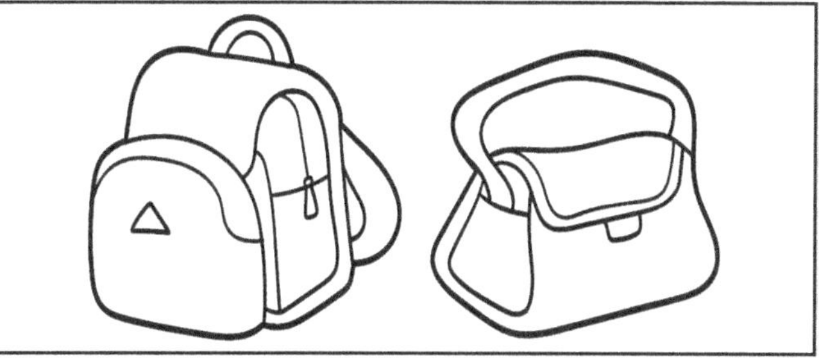

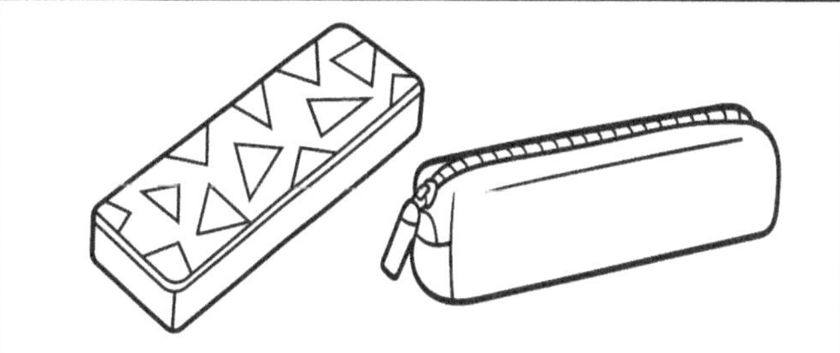

Missing Part

Cross out the picture that is different in each group. Use a green crayon.

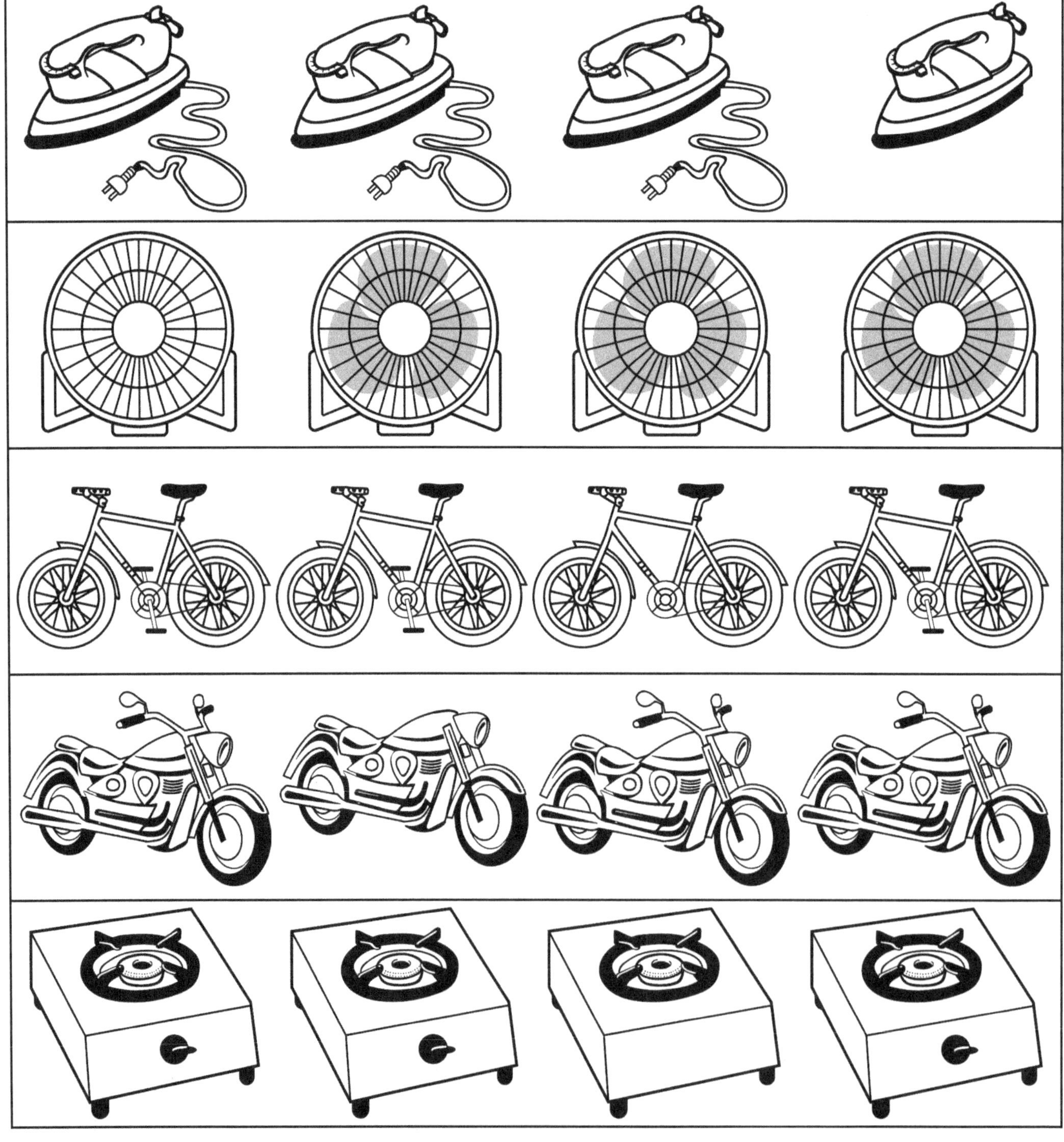

Function

Encircle the object that has a different use. Use an orange crayon.

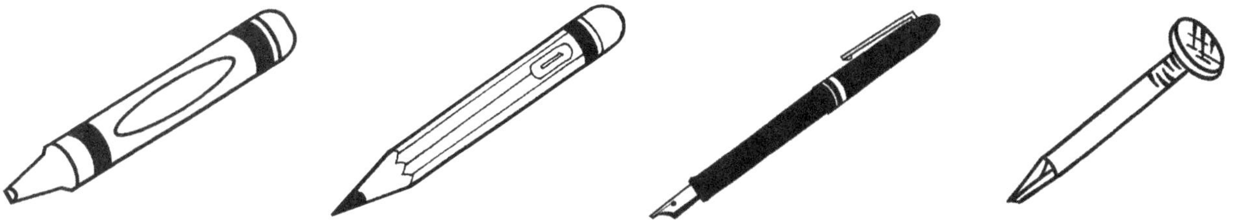

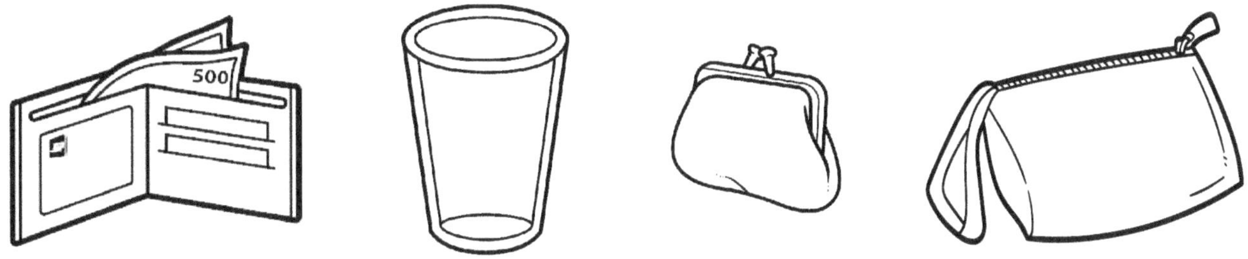

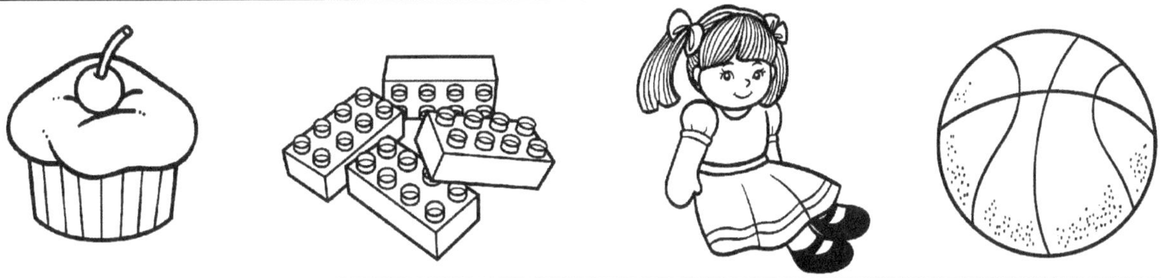

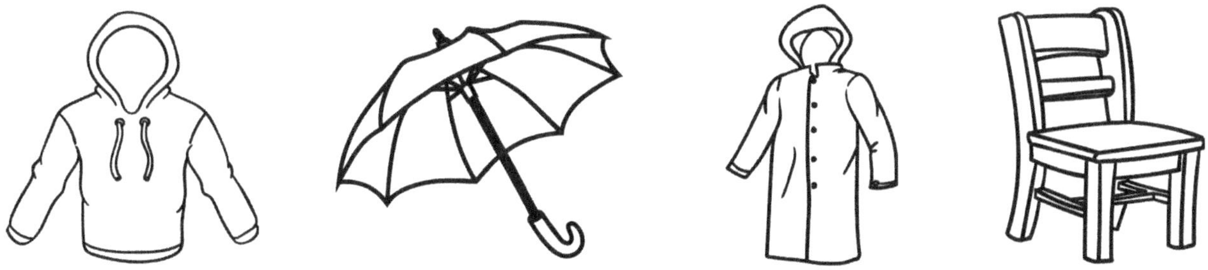

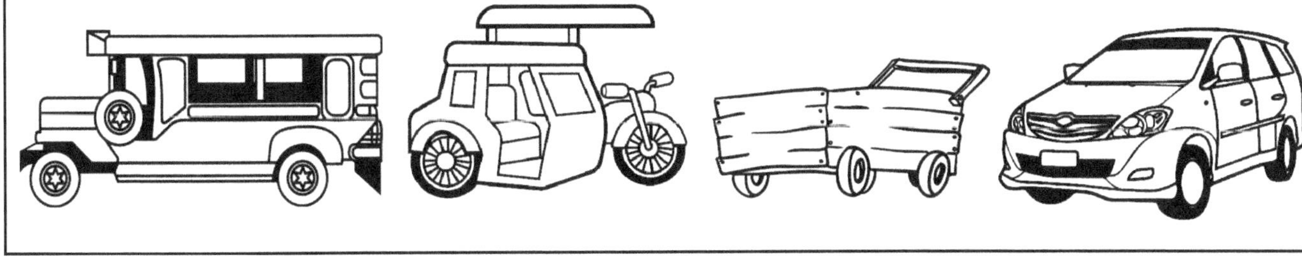

Form Perception

SCORE: _______

Box the form in each group that is the same as the one on the left. Use a green crayon.

Cross out the different letter in each group. Use a violet crayon.

q	g	q	q

E	E	E	F

b	d	d	d

P	P	R	P

W	M	W	W

Word Configuration

Draw a star (☆) on the word that is the same as that on the left.

pot	pop	top	pod	pot
bed	led	bet	fed	bed
fin	fin	fit	bin	tin
hum	sum	bum	hum	lum
tag	tap	tag	lag	rag

Underline the word that is different in each group. Use a brown crayon.

bad	bad	dab	bad

tree	free	tree	tree

mine	mind	mind	mind

bald	bulb	bald	bald

frame	frame	frame	flame

ADVANCED GROUP

Draw a sun (☼) in the box if the pictures in each group are alike. Draw a moon (☾) if they are different.

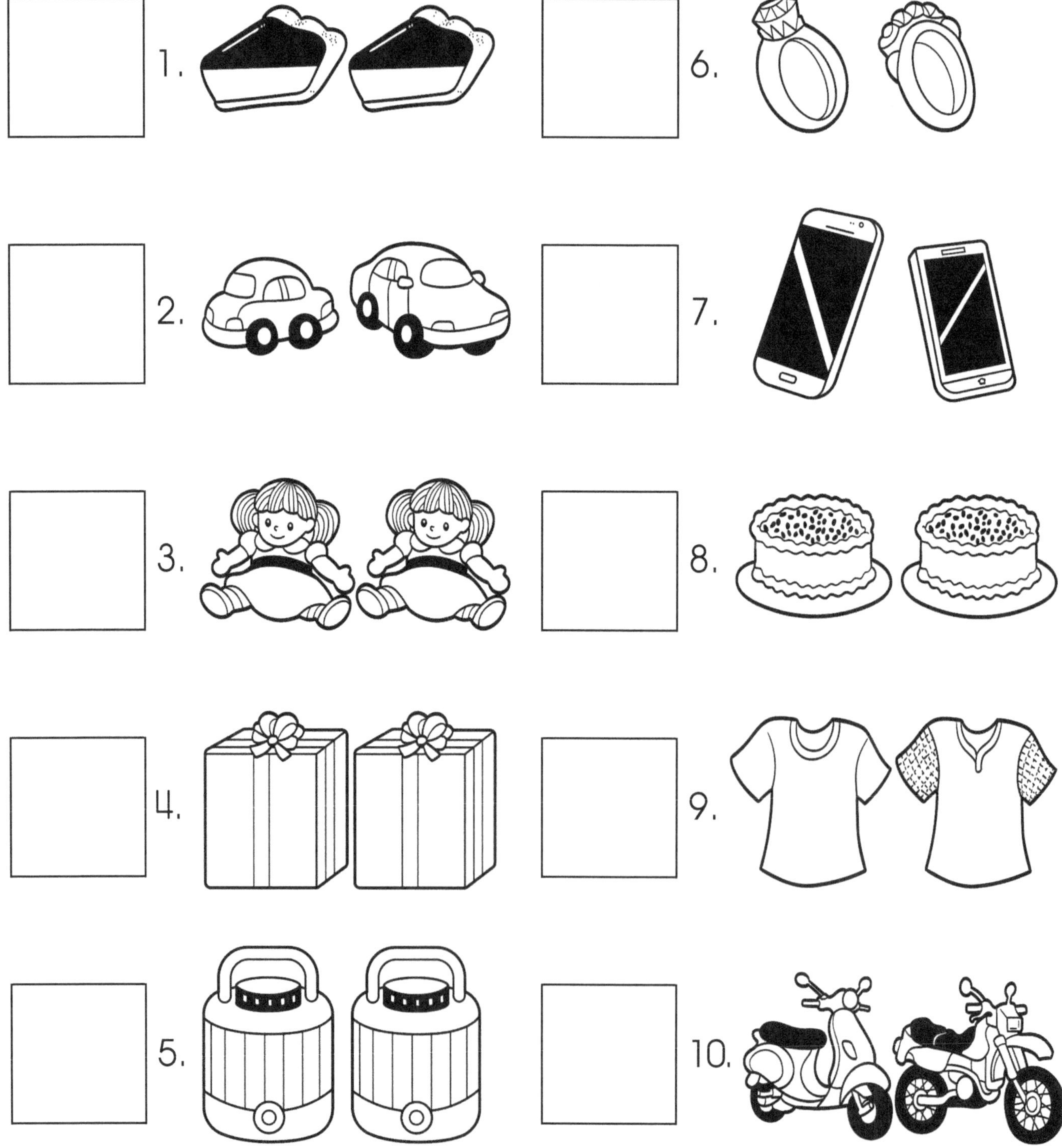

AUDITORY DISCRIMINATION
Things that Produce Sounds

Guide: Have the children sit in a circle. Ask them to close their eyes. Walk to a corner of the room and use a musical instrument to make sounds. Have the children point to the direction of the sound they hear. You may also play a guessing game with the children. Put objects such as mongo seeds, rice grains, thumbtacks, nails, or pins inside small canisters. Have the children guess the objects as you shake each canister.

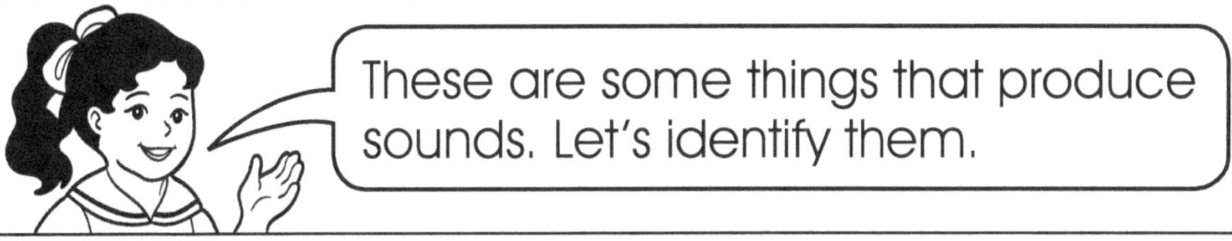

television

whistle

cellphone

piano

flute

trumpet

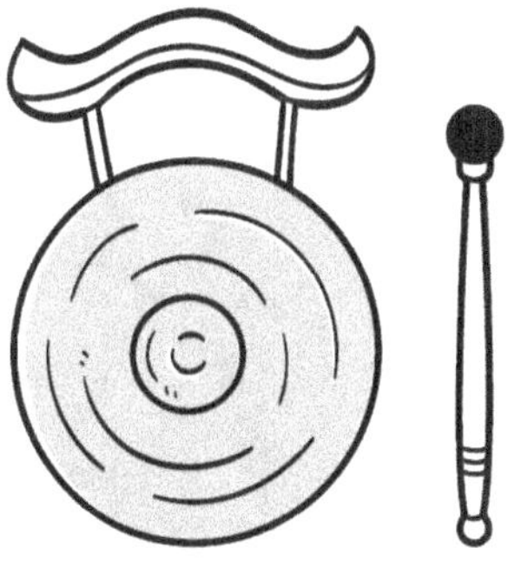

gong

bell

radio

alarm clock

Put a check (✓) beside the objects that produce sounds. Put a cross (✗) beside those that don't make sounds.

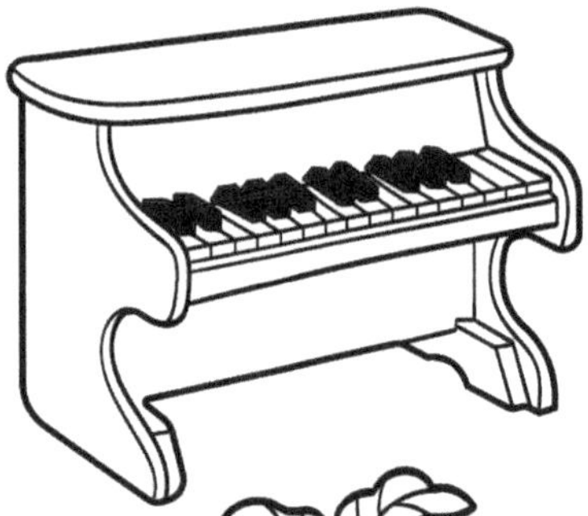

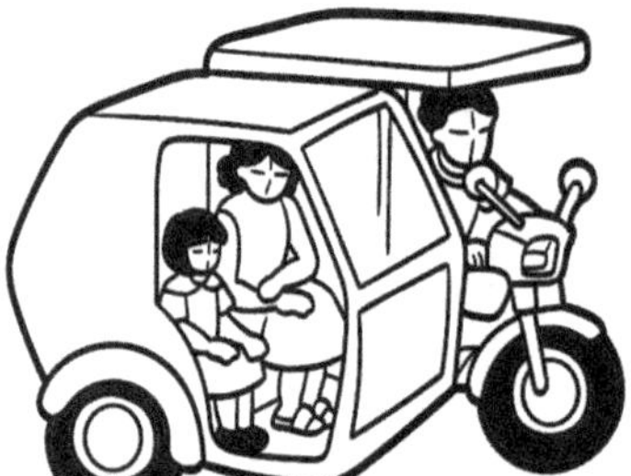

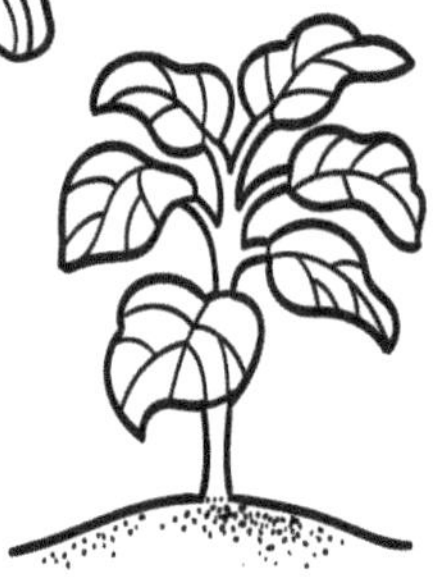

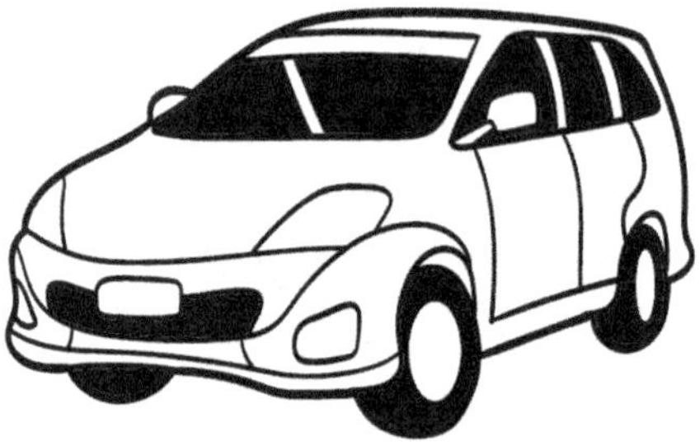

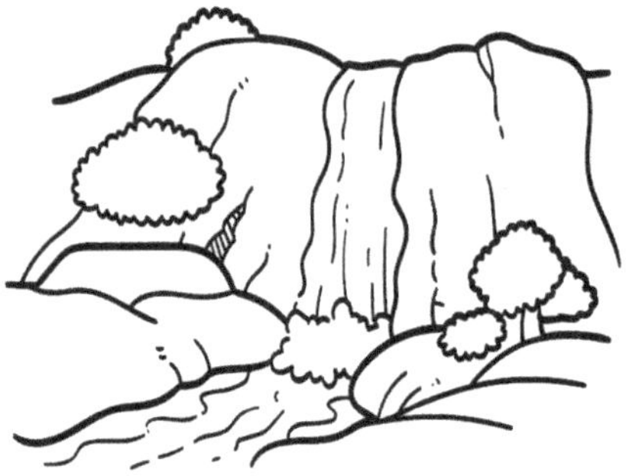

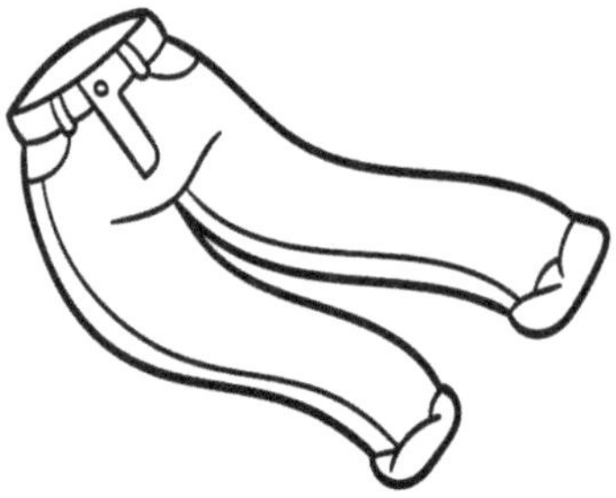

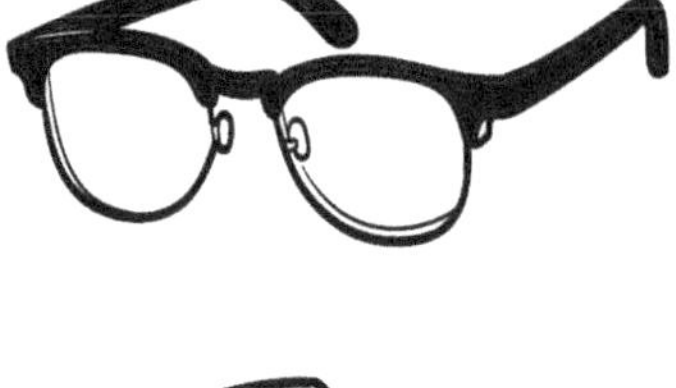

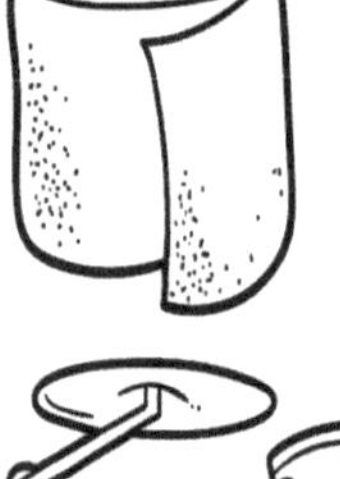

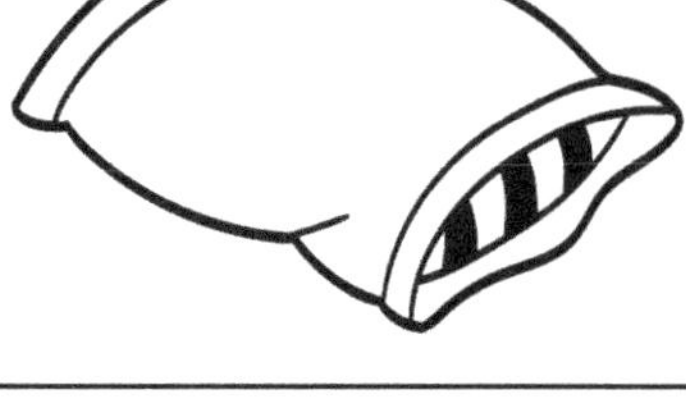

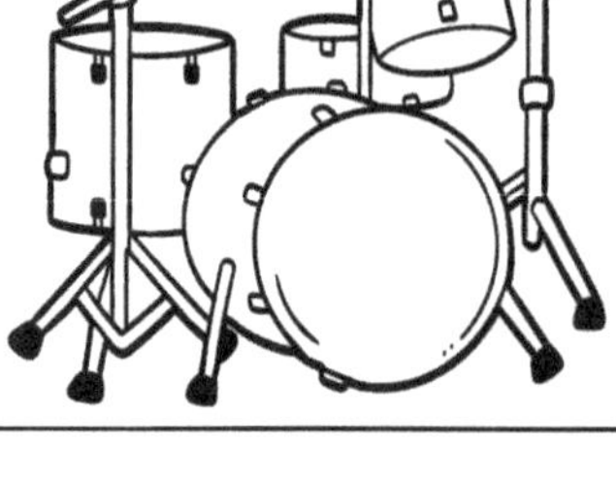

Animals that Make Sounds

<table>
<tr><td><u>Guide</u>:</td><td>Record animal sounds on a mobile phone or another sound recording device. Provide the children with plastic animals or animal pictures. Challenge them to identify the recorded sounds they hear by matching each sound with the correct plastic animal or animal picture.</td></tr>
</table>

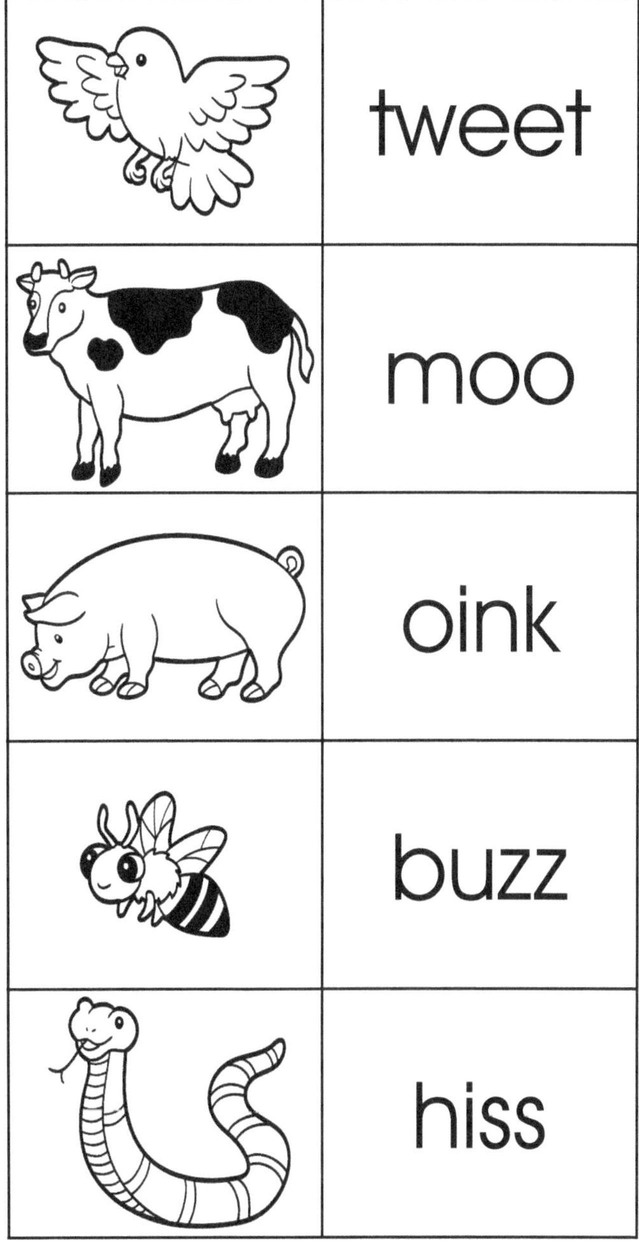

cat	meow	bird	tweet
dog	woof	cow	moo
duck	quack	pig	oink
horse	neigh	bee	buzz
sheep	baa	snake	hiss

Pet Talk

My pet is a dog and he says, "Arf! Arf!"
He says, "Arf! Arf!" He says, "Arf! Arf!"
My pet is a dog, and this is how we talk:
"Arf, arf, arf, arf arf, arf, arf!" (2x)

My pet is a cat and she says, "Meow!"
She says, "Meow!" She says, "Meow!"
My pet is a cat, and this is how we talk:
"Meow, meow, meow, meow,
meow, meow, meow!" (2x)

Name some other animals and the sounds they make.

Examples:

My pet is a bird and she says, "Tweet! Tweet!"…
My pet is a cow and she says, "Moo! Moo!"…
My pet is a goat and he says, "Mee! Mee!"…

QUIZ NO. 7

SCORE: _______

Connect the pictures of animals to the sounds that they make. *(5 points)*

moo

meow

quack

tweet

oink

woof

hiss

neigh

baa

buzz

ASSOCIATION AND REASONING
Things that Go Together

Guide: During circle time, scatter on the floor pictures or real objects that go together. Have each child pick up a pair and show it to the class. Have him or her name the pictures or objects.

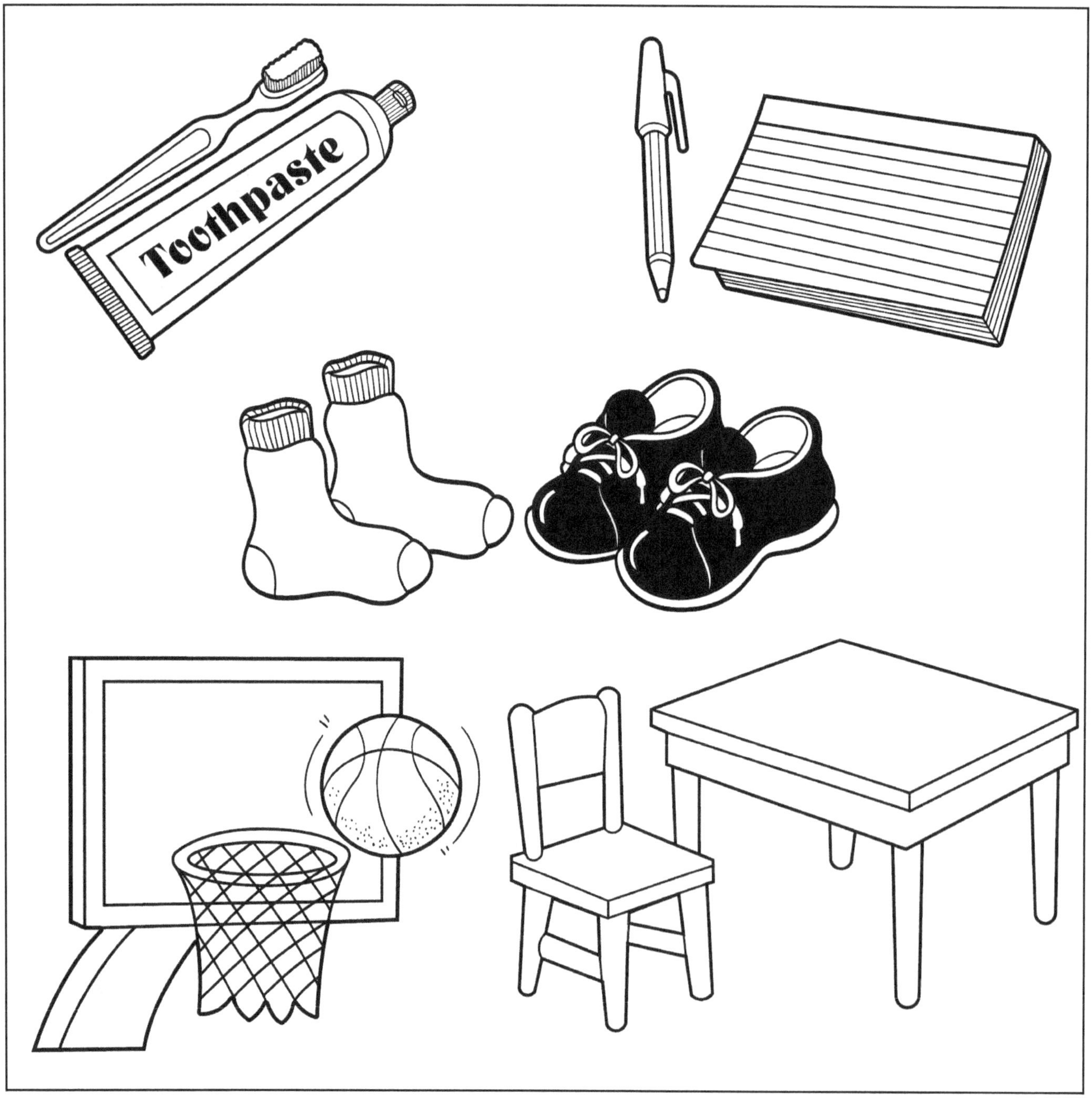

ACTIVITY 9

SCORE: _______

Connect the objects that go together using a line.

1. 	•	• 
2. 	•	• 
3. 	•	• 
4. 	•	• 
5. 	•	• 
6. 	•	•
7. 	•	• 
8. 	•	• 
9. 	•	•
10. 	•	•

QUIZ NO. 8

SCORE: _______

Put a check (✓) in the box if the objects in each group go together. Put a cross (✗) if they don't go together.

1.

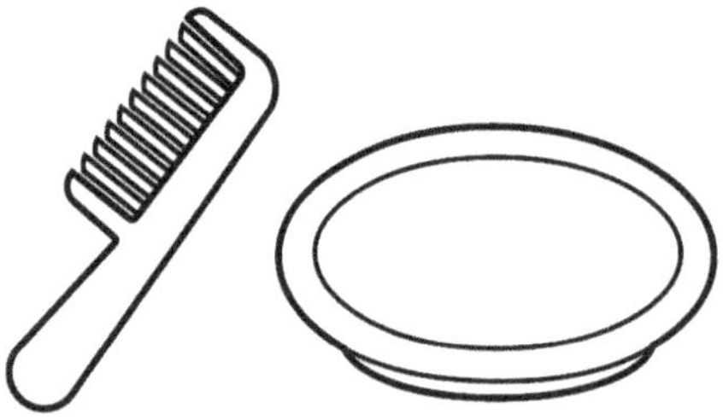

2.

3.

4.

5.

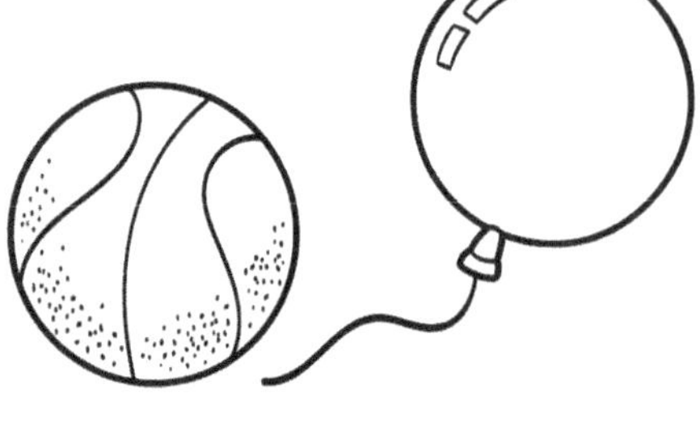

6.

7.

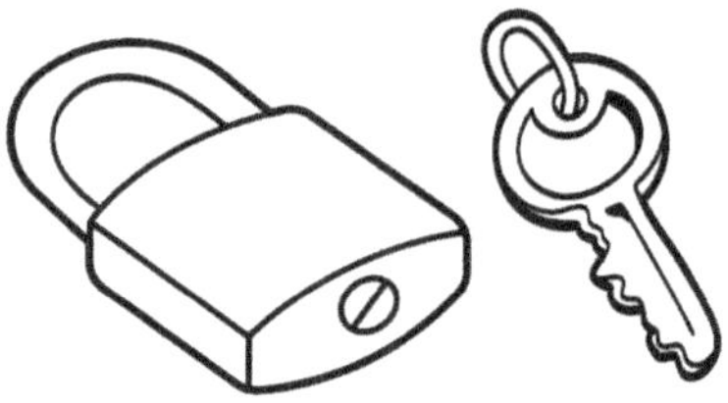

8.

9.

10.

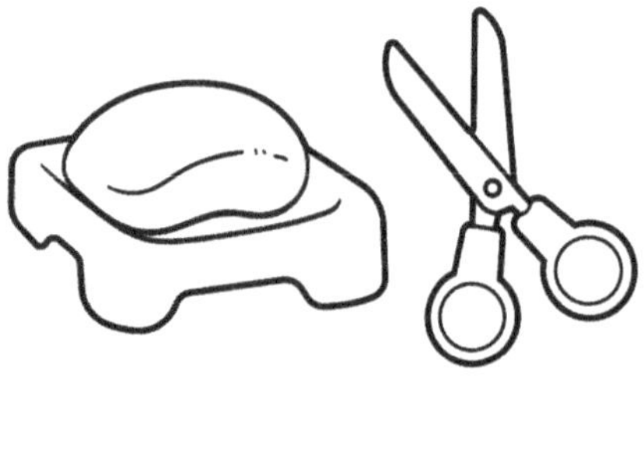

Classifying Things

Guide: Put a group of similar objects in a box, with one object not belonging to the group. Have the children identify the object that does not belong to each group.

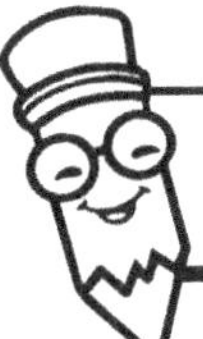

ACTIVITY 10 SCORE: ______

Encircle the object that does not belong to the group.

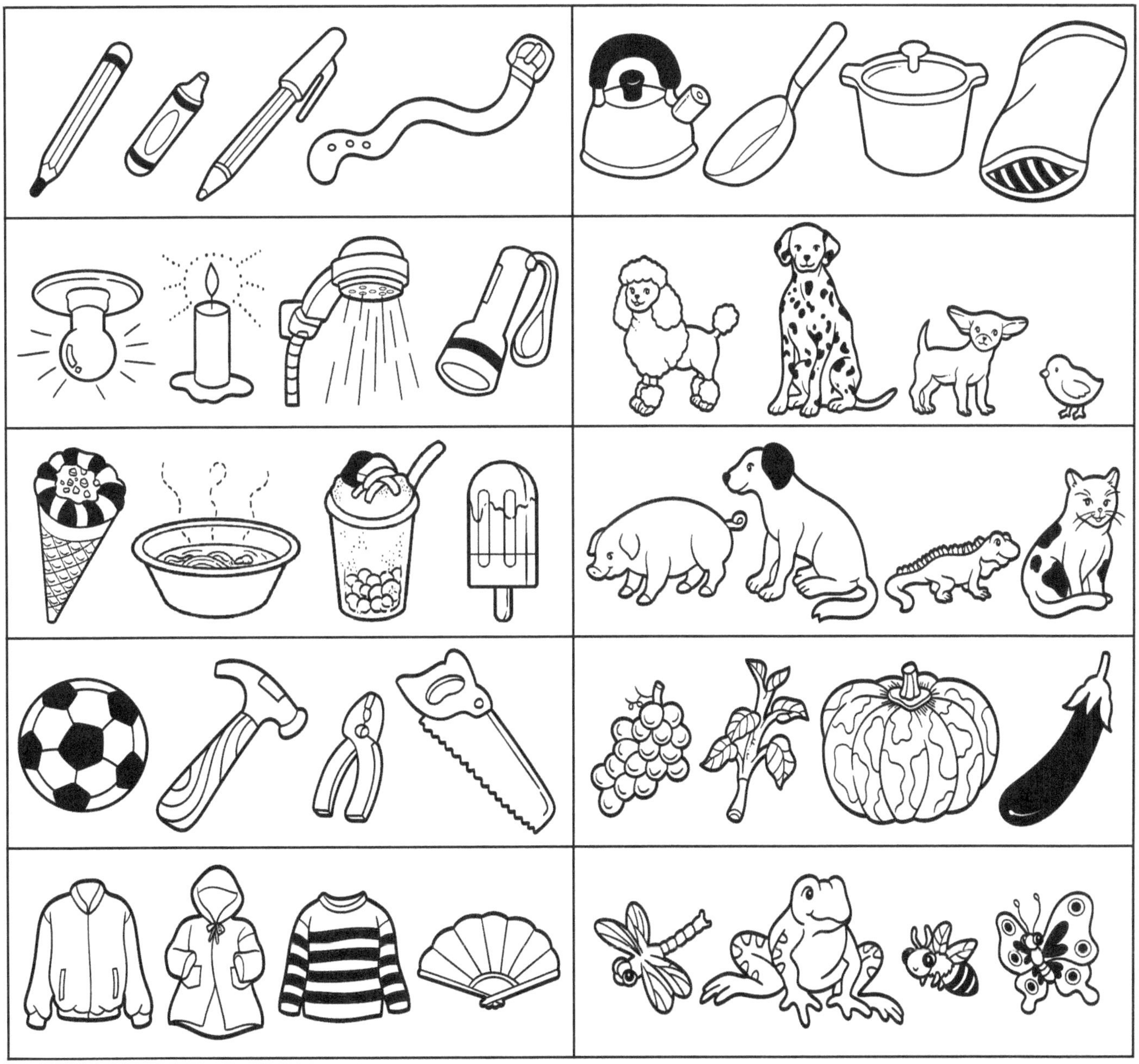

Things Needed for Different Activities

Guide: Play a guessing game with the children. Perform some motions such as "brushing your teeth," "cooking," "sweeping the floor," etc. Have the children guess what you are doing. Then ask them what things are needed for these activities.

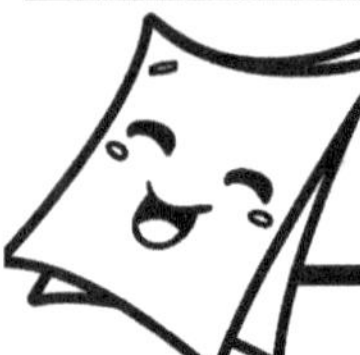

QUIZ NO. 9 SCORE: ______

Connect the person to the thing that he or she needs.

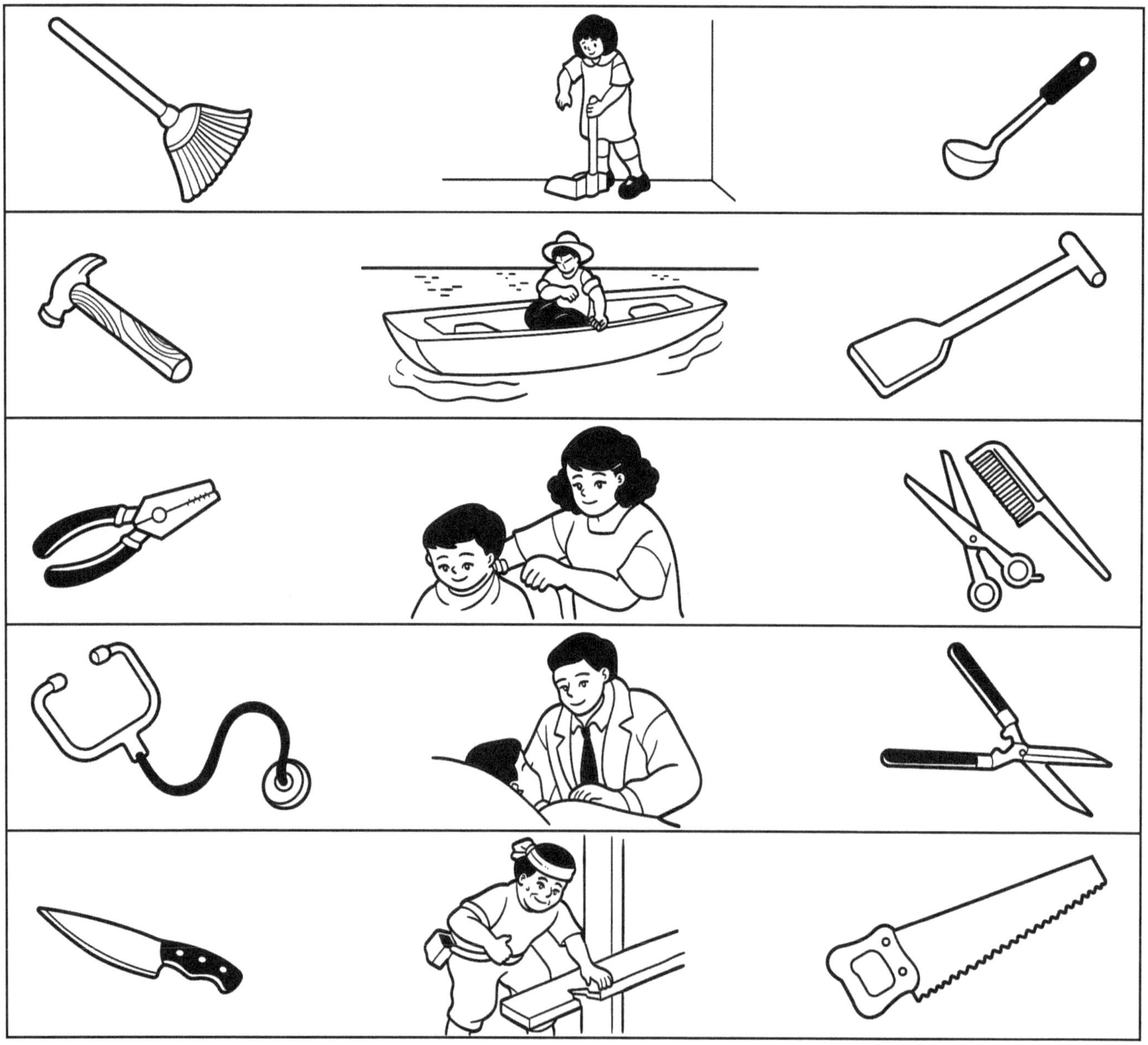

Part-Whole Relationship

SCORE:_______

Guide: Invite the children to solve name puzzles. Write their names on strips of tag board, leaving enough spaces between letters. Cut the letters apart, jigsaw-style. Have the children put their names together. Later, provide them with lots of opportunities to solve jigsaw puzzles, as these reinforce the concept of part-whole relationships.

Color the picture to which the part belongs.

Noting Details

Guide: Show real objects with missing parts (e.g., a mug with broken handle, an eyeglasses frame without lens, a flower without stem, etc.). Have the children identify the missing parts.

Draw the missing part to complete each picture.

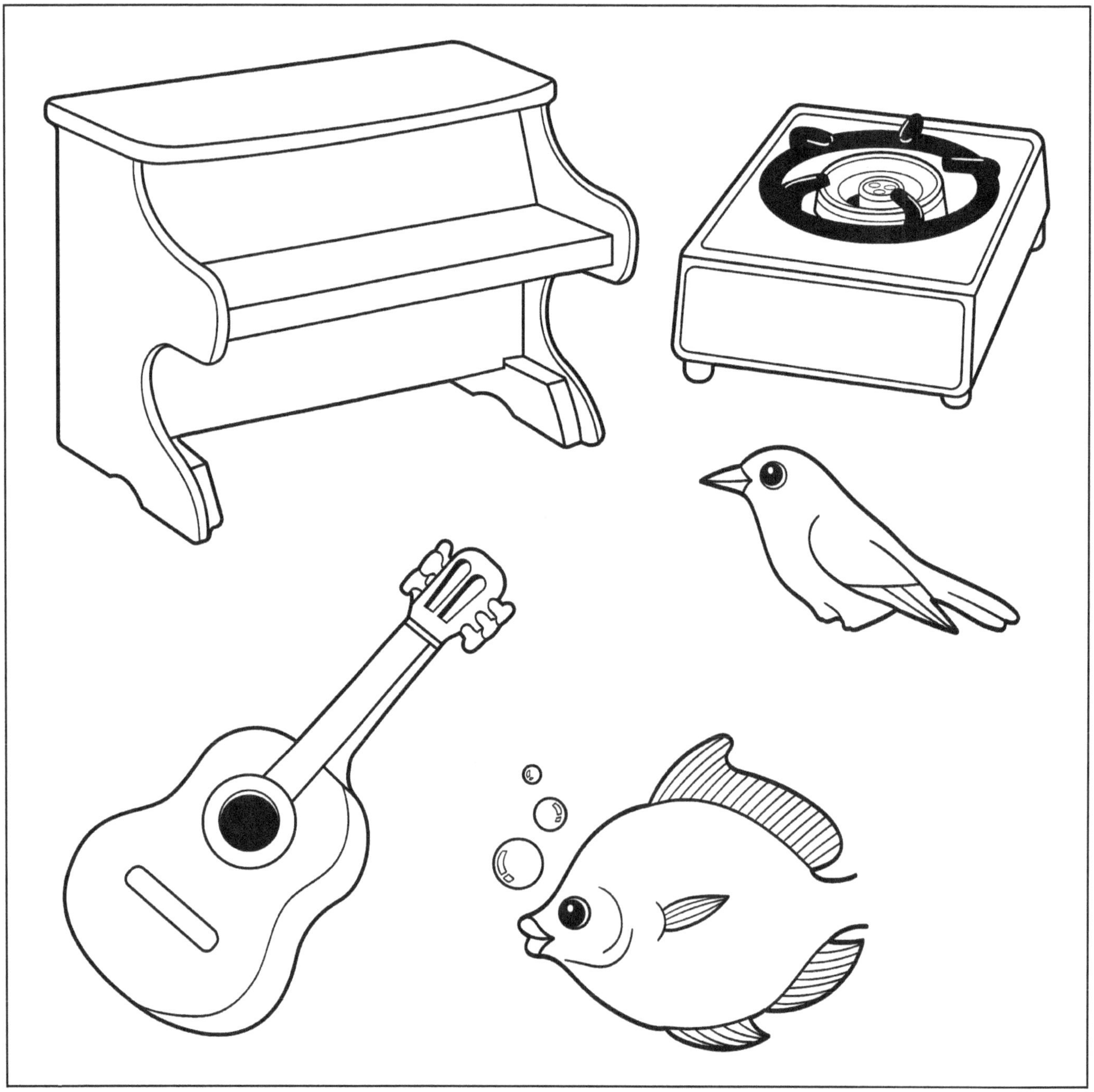

THE VOWEL FAMILY

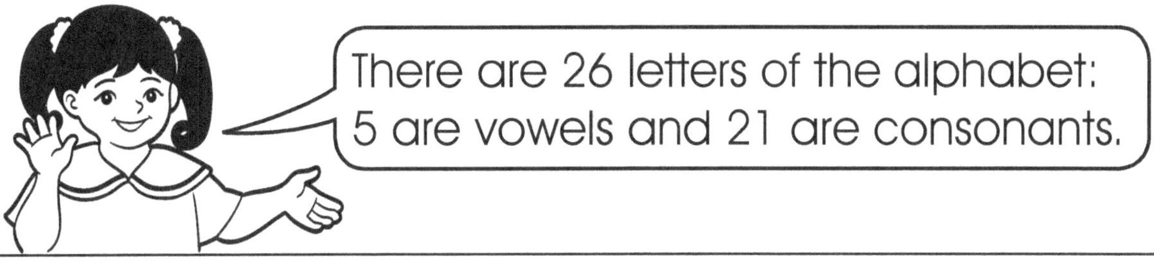

Aa

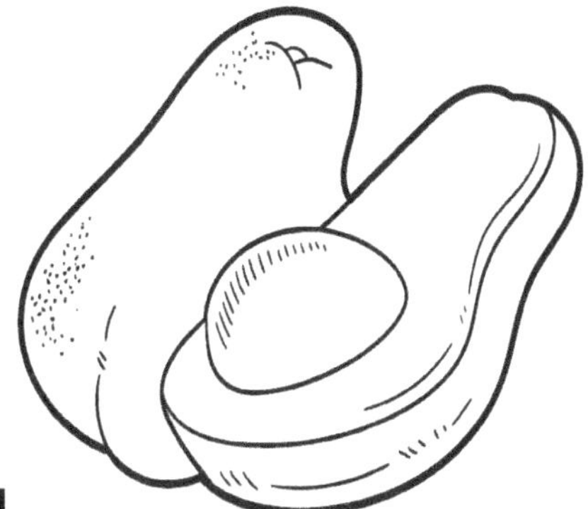

Ee

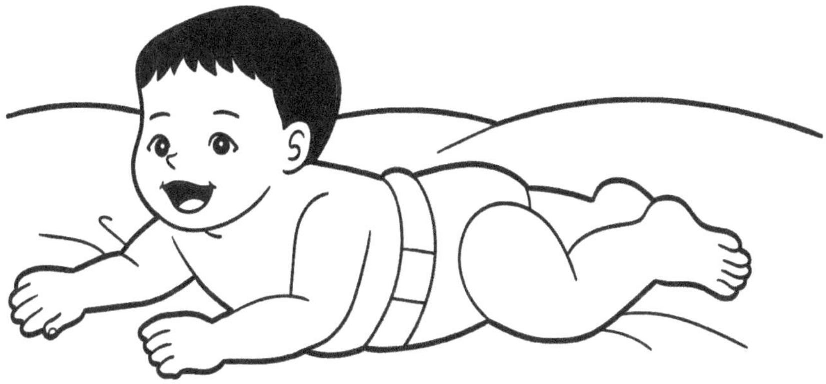

Ii

Oo

Uu

LESSON 5

Aa
/æ/ as in **cat** /aː/ as in **arm**

Guide: Provide a "Magic Box." Put pictures or real objects whose names begin with the letter **A** in it. Have the children take turns getting and identifying the objects.

ax

arm

alligator

album

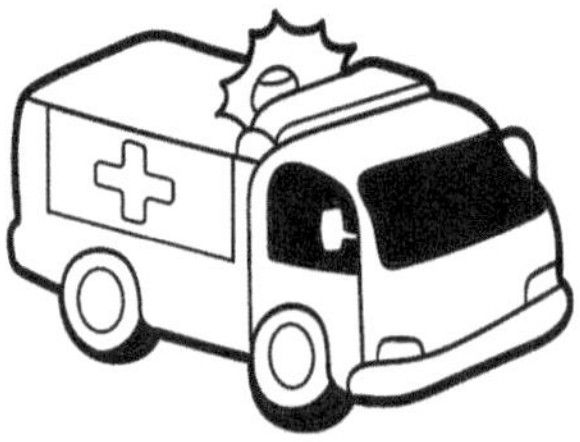

ambulance

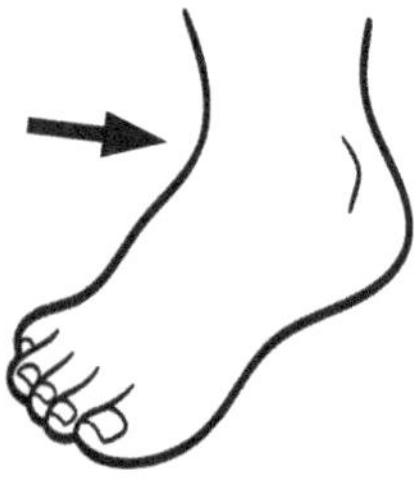

ankle

astronaut

ant

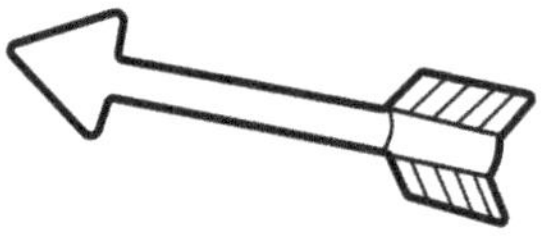

arrow

apple

Practice writing the letter **Aa**.

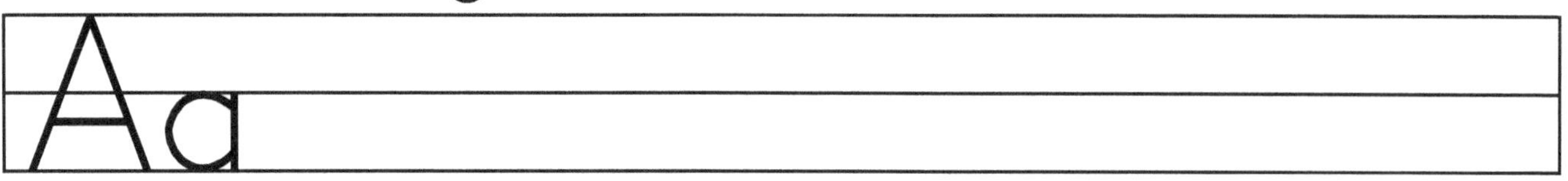

ACTIVITY 12

SCORE: ______

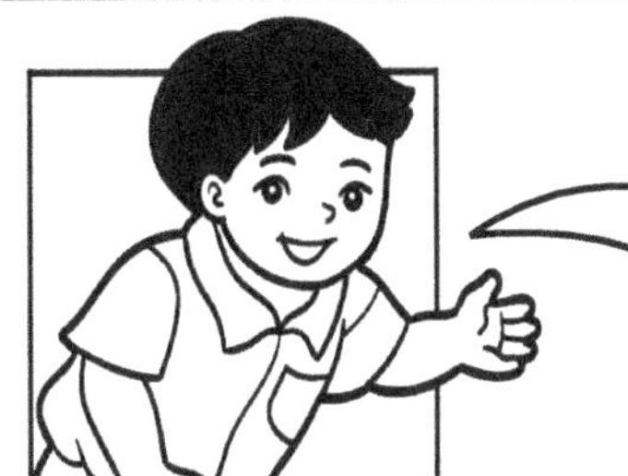

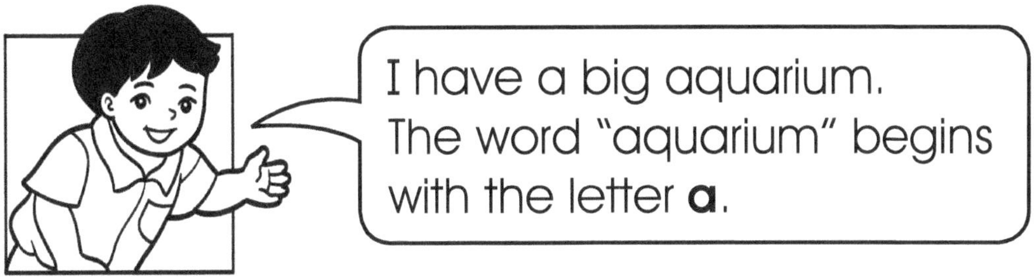

Check the pictures whose names begin with **Aa**.

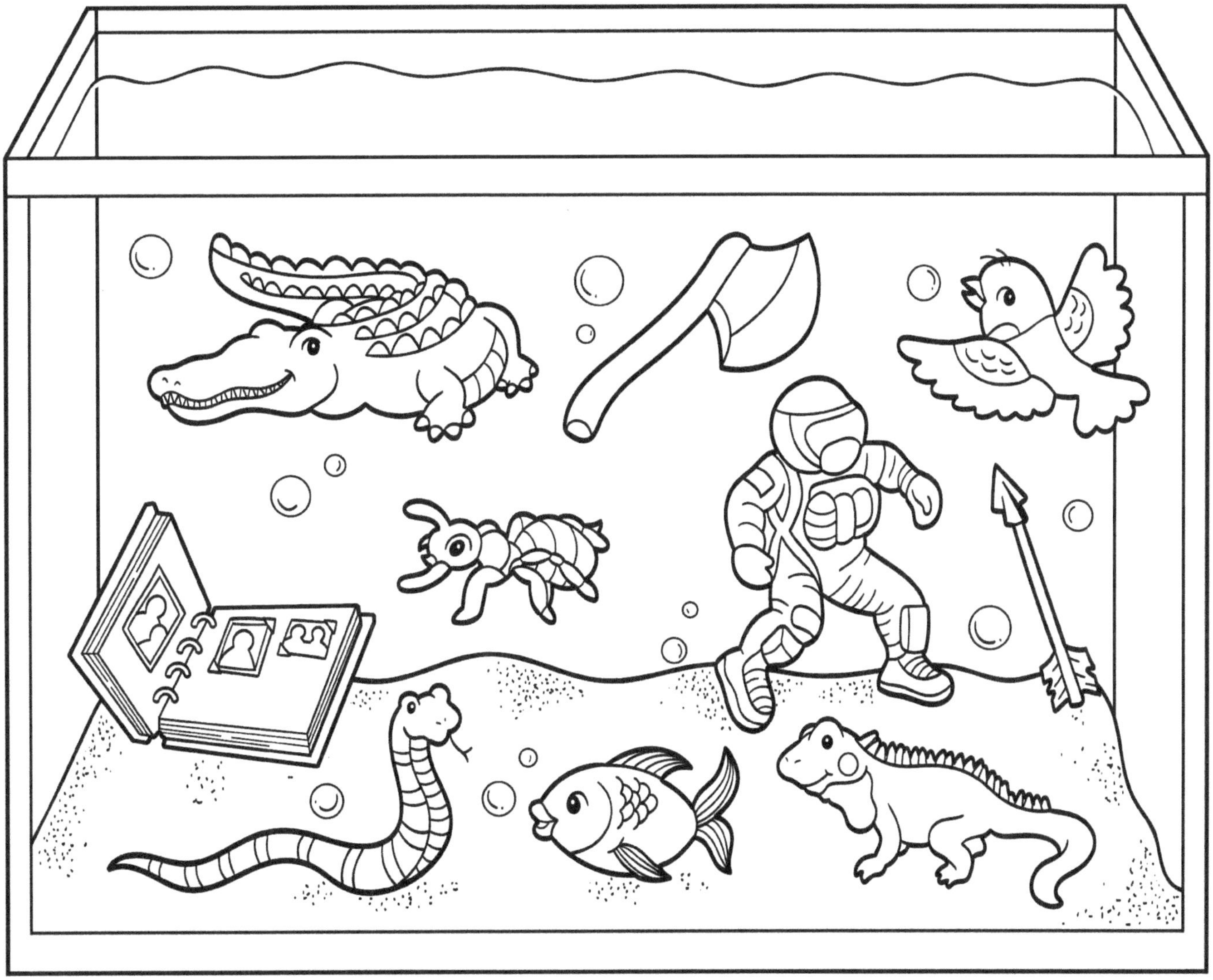

Encircle the letter **Aa**'s.

A e a V a A V

A a A u E c A

Letter *A* Rhyme

Way up high in the apple tree,
(Stretch both arms above your hands, hands open.)
Two little apples smiled at me.
(Keep arms above head, close hands into fists.)
I shook that tree as hard as I could,
(Keep arms above head, "shake" tree.)
Down came the apples,
(Bring fists down toward stomach.)
Mmmm, they were good!
(Rub stomach.)

Guide: Have the children check all the letter **Aa**'s they can find in the rhyme.

POEM

A's Everywhere

A's, A's everywhere,
"I see A's," said the Bear.
A's on the curtains,
A's on the door.
A's on the table,
A's on the floor.

Guide: Have the children check all the letters **Aa**'s they can find in the poem.

Guide: Draw a simple picture of a living room scene, with a table, a door, curtains, and a floor. Make copies of the picture for the children. Have the children mark **A**'s on the appropriate items in the scene using markers or crayons.

SONG

A Marching Army Ant

(Tune: "If You're Happy and You Know It")

Oh, I wish I was a marching army ant,
Oh, I wish I was a marching army ant.
Oh, I'd march way up high,
Until I could touch the sky.
Oh, I wish I was a marching army ant.

Guide: Have the children check all the letter **Aa**'s they can find in the song.

SUGGESTED ACTIVITIES FOR THE DIFFERENT LEARNING AREAS

> **Guide**: Have a special "letter of the week" each week. During the week, make crafts and do activities that feature the "letter of the week" and have the children practice writing the upper and lower cases of the letter. You may also have a "book of the week" featuring the letter of the week. Using fasteners and half-sized folders and bond paper, have the children make books. (The featured letter should be written on the book's cover.) Have the children fill their books with pictures whose names begin with the featured letter. Assign the "alphabet books" activity as homework.

Language

A Mail

1. Set out a mailbox (cardboard shoe box).
2. Tape an index card on the box with a big letter **A** on it.
3. Take twelve small envelopes and write different names on them, including seven that begin with the letter **A**, such as *Angie*, *Andy*, *Amelia*, *Angelo*, and *Abby*.
4. Give a child a small bag and have her or him "deliver" only the **A** mail to the box.

Science and Math

Make your *arms* as the body part for **A** week. Do simple exercises with your arms and work on telling which your right arm is and which your left arm is. You may also count all the boys' arms and all the girls' arms with the children.

Values Education and Social Studies

During **A** week, try taking the children to the *amusement* park. While you're there, have the children find things whose names begin with the letter **A**. Inculcate the value of not littering in public places.

Physical Education and Health, Music, and Arts

A Necklace

1. Print out a number of small **A** patterns.
2. Cut them into small squares.
3. Have the children color the letter **A**'s or glue on some glitters.
4. Punch two holes at the top of the square shape.
5. Have the children string some yarn through the holes to make an **A** necklace.

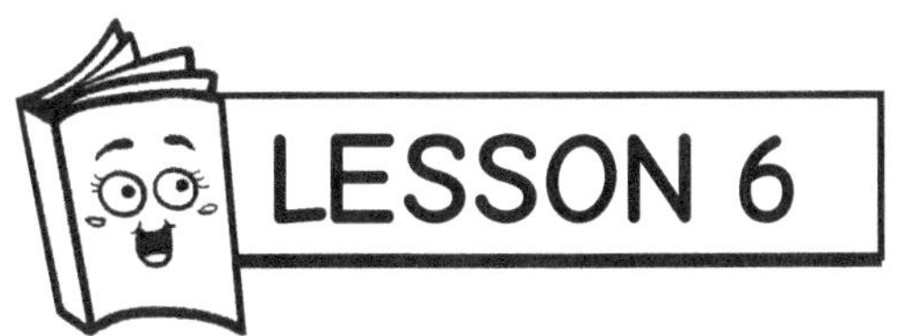

LESSON 6

Ee

/ɛ/

Guide: Collect two to three small objects or pictures of objects whose names begin with the letter ***E***. Place the objects inside large plastic eggs along with some objects whose names do not start with the letter "***E***." Have the children choose an egg, open it, and tell if the object in their egg starts with the letter ***E***.

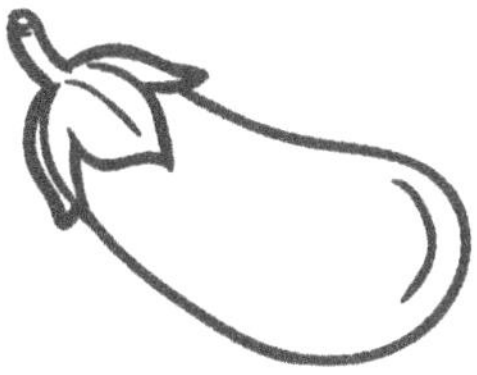

eggplant

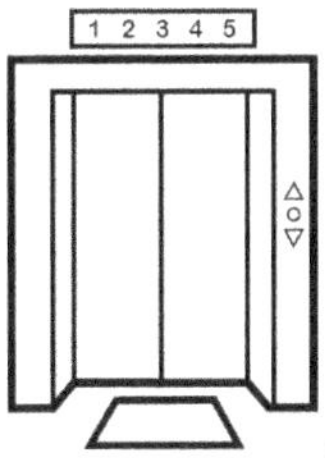

elevator

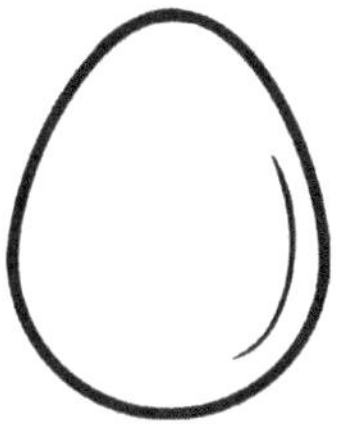

egg

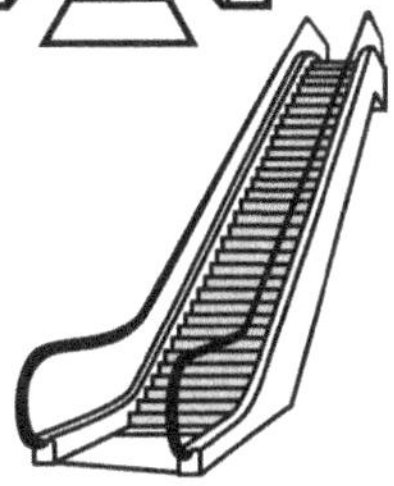

escalator

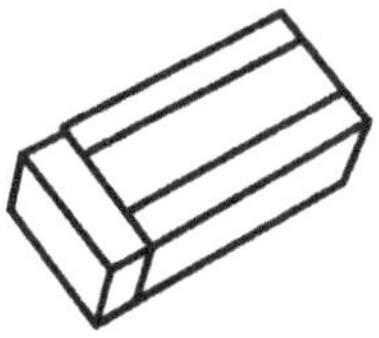

eraser

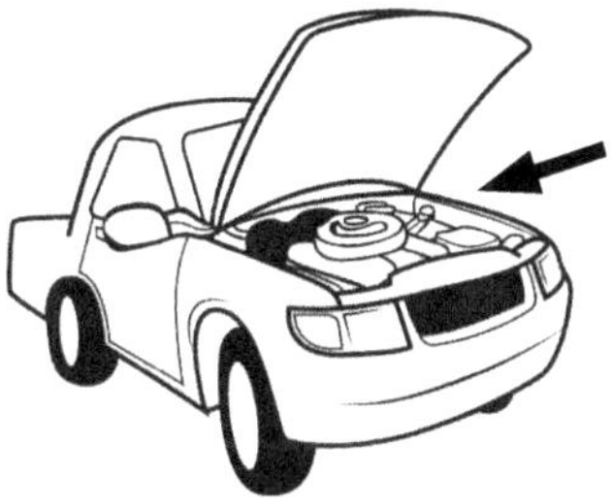

engine

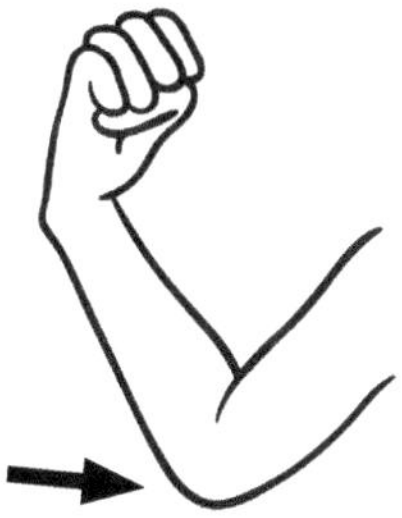

elbow

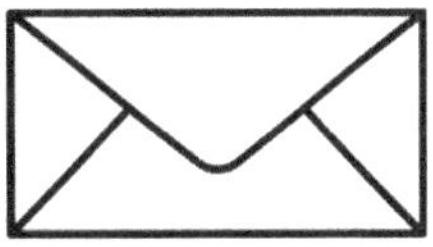

envelope

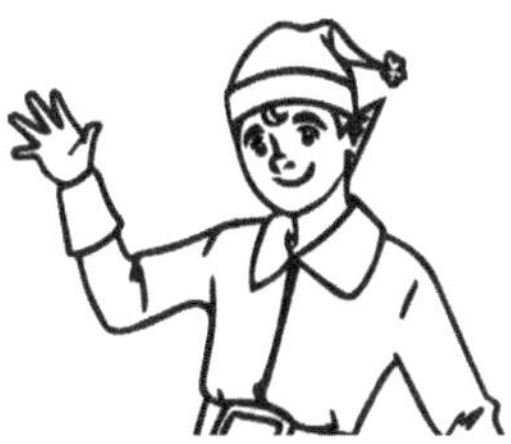

elf

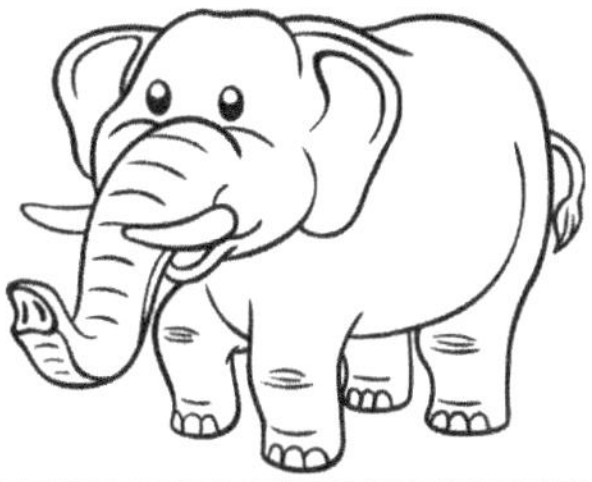

elephant

Practice writing the letter **Ee**.

Ee

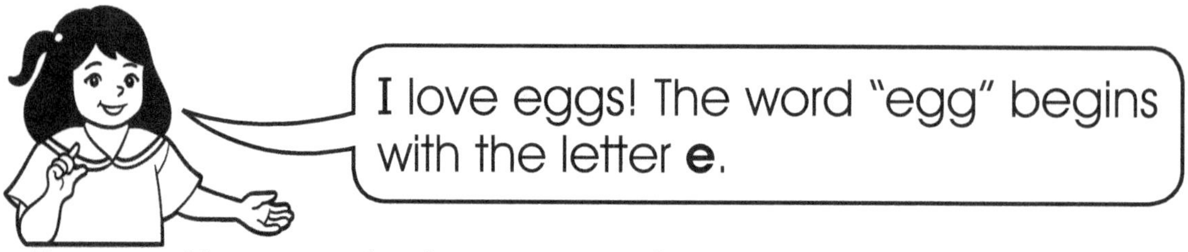

Underline the pictures whose names begin with **Ee**.

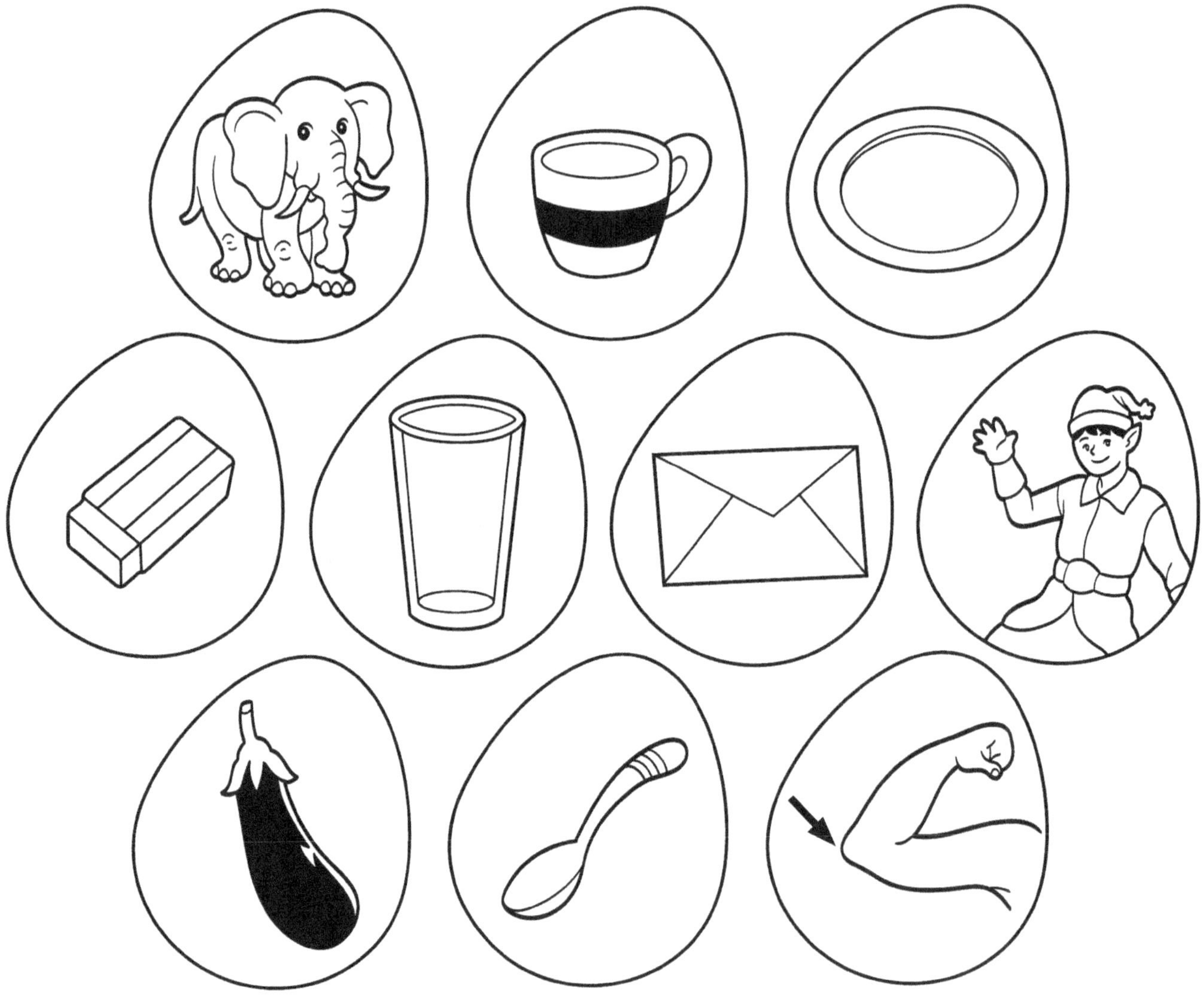

Check the letter **Ee**'s.

a   e   o   B   e   E   F
E   f   e   E   c   E   e

QUIZ NO. 10

SCORE: _______

Check the pictures whose names begin with the letters on the left.

E is for *Eggs*

(Tune: "Are you Sleeping?")

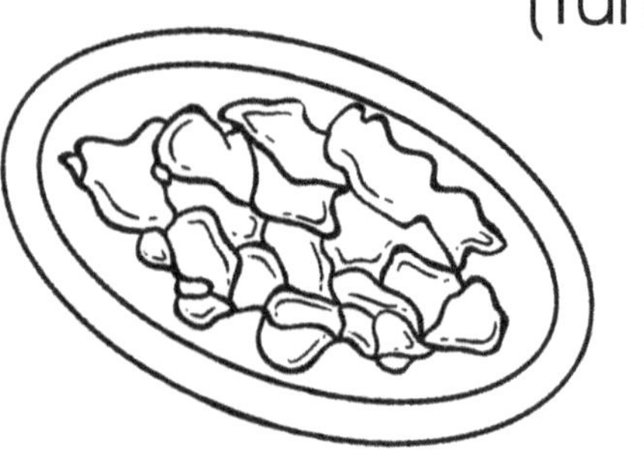

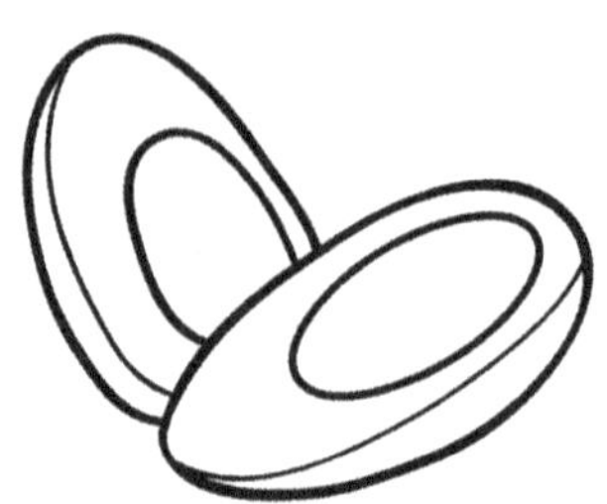

I love eggs,
I love eggs,
Yum, yum, yum!
In my tum!
Scrambled, boiled, or fried,
Any way I've tried,
Yum, yum, yum!
Yum, yum, yum!

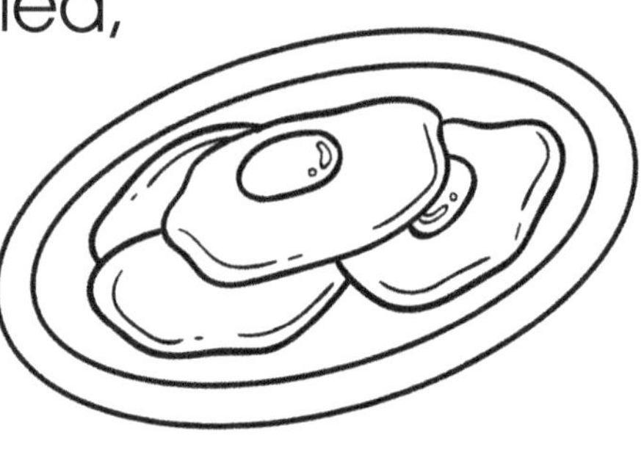

E is for *Echo*

Be my echo,
Be my echo,
/ɛ/ says E,
/ɛ/ says E,
Elephant and *e*nter,
Eggs and *elevator*,
/ɛ/, /ɛ/, /ɛ/,
/ɛ/, /ɛ/, /ɛ/!

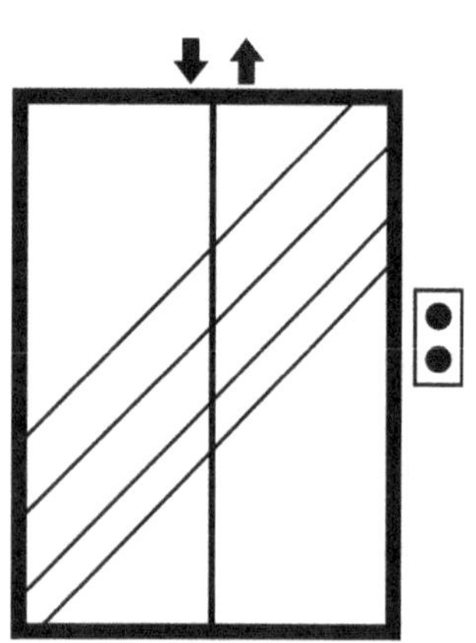

Guide: Teach the songs to the children. Let them underline all the letter **Ee**'s they can find in the songs.

SUGGESTED ACTIVITIES FOR THE DIFFERENT LEARNING AREAS

Guide: During the week, make crafts and do activities that feature the letter **Ee** which is the "letter of the week" and have the children practice writing its upper and lower cases.

Activity	Learning Areas
• Have fun cooking! *Eggs* are the best food for this since you can try a few different preparations with them. (They can be hard-boiled, scrambled, or fried, or made into omelettes, egg rolls, and egg sandwiches.) Make sure you let the children crack an egg themselves. Have them take turns beating eggs and putting egg spread on sandwiches. Discuss the nutritional value that we get from eggs. Also, help them discover which animals hatch from eggs: birds, fish, chickens, snakes, etc.	* Values Education and Social Studies * Science * Language * Physical Education and Health, Music, and Arts
• Set out some colored plastic eggs. Let the children count the eggs. (You may also ask them to sort out the plastic eggs according to color.) Remove or add eggs while interest in the game lasts.	* Science * Mathematics
• Make *egg shakers* for instruments! • Decorate with *eggshells*! Wash them and use the white *eggshells* as "clouds" or dye them to make a colored mural. • *Exercise!* Make your *elbow* as the body part for *E* week. Do exercises with your elbows by wiggling, shaking, swinging, and moving them up and down.	* Physical Education and Health, Music, and Arts * Science * Language
• Make six-page blank books for the children by folding three pieces of bond paper in halves and stapling the spine. Write "**My *E* Book**" on each cover. Each day for five days, have the children cut and paste different *E* objects on a page of their book.	* Language * Values Education and Social studies

Paper Plate Elephant Craft

Materials:

- gray paint and paint brush
- paper plate
- template pieces
- scissors
- glue

Directions:

1. Paint the bottom of the paper plate gray.
2. Color the template pieces.
3. Cut the craft templates.
4. Glue the pieces to the plate to make an elephant face.
   - Glue the trunk on the bottom of the face.
   - Glue the tusks on either side of the trunk.
   - Glue the ears on either side of the head.
   - Glue the hair onto the center of the head.
   - Glue the eyes onto the face above the trunk and under the hair (or cut out holes for eyes to turn it into a mask).
   - Glue the eyebrows above the eyes.

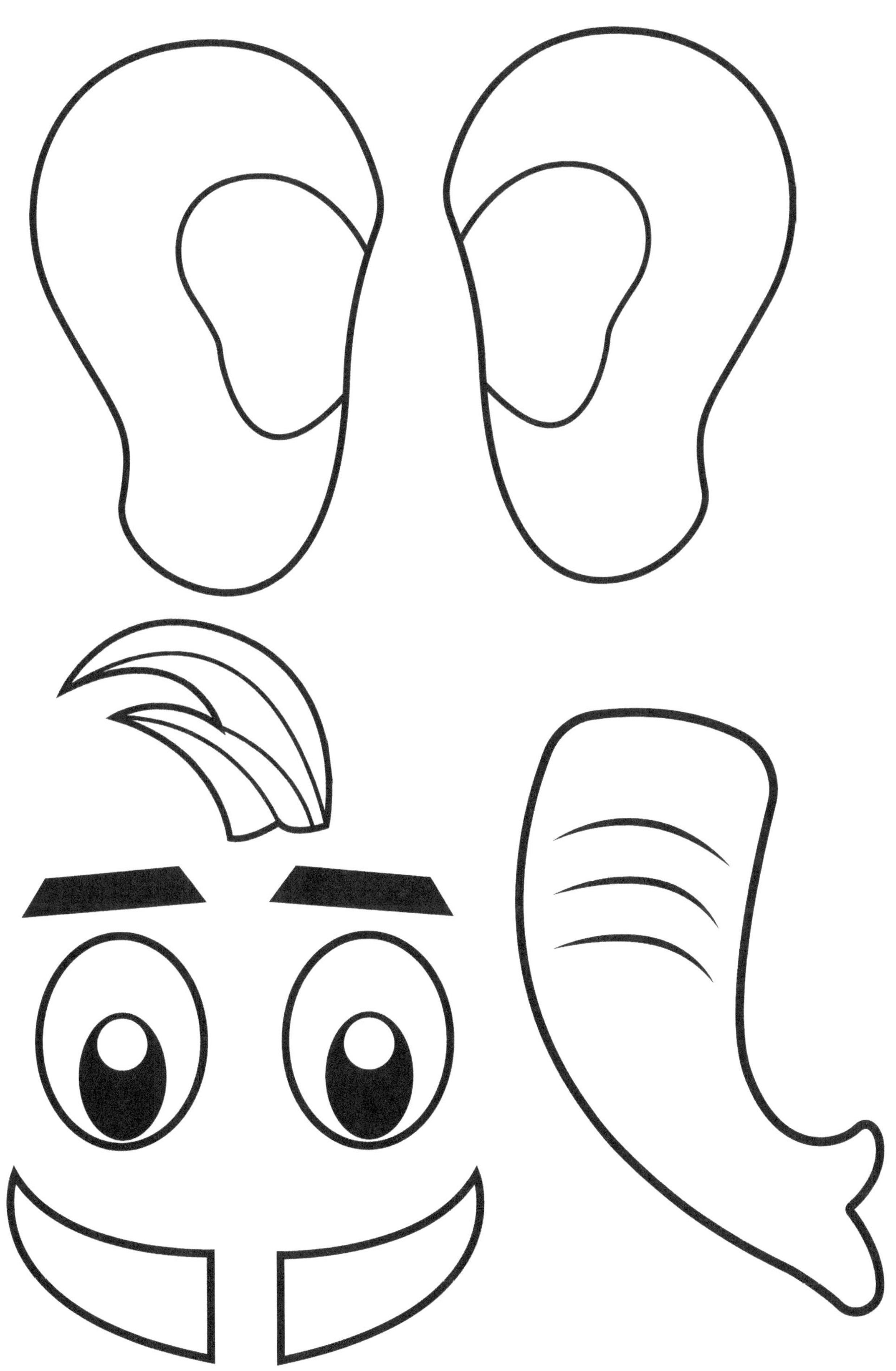

Ii
/I/

Guide: Prepare small plastic insects for a bingo-type game. Using a permanent marker, draw a bingo board on a piece of construction paper and write a different number in each square. Have the children fill their bingo cards as you call a number at random. Discuss other things that begin with the letter *I*.

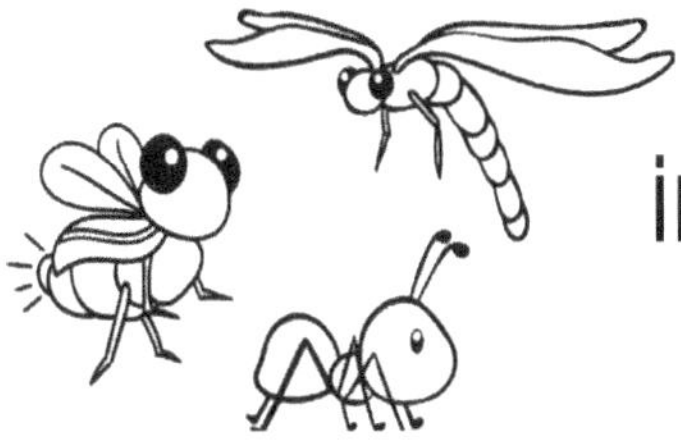

insects

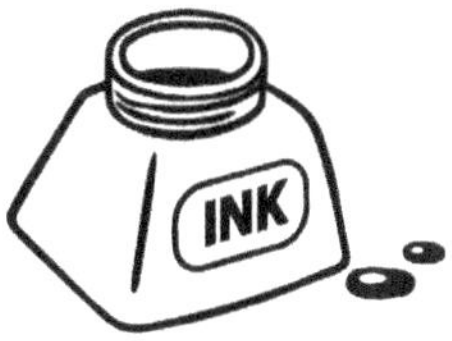

ink

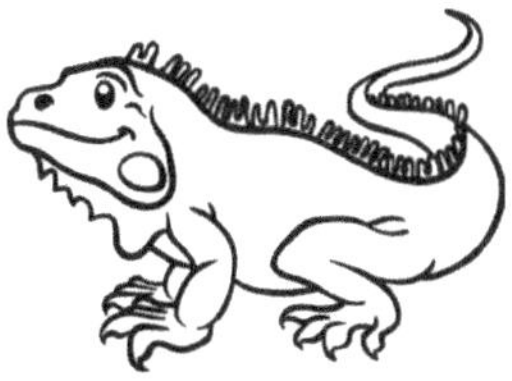

iguana

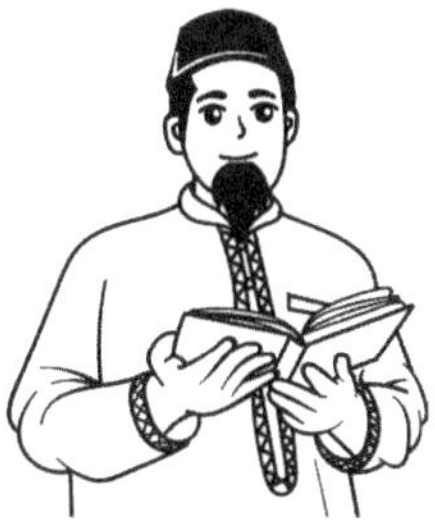

Imam

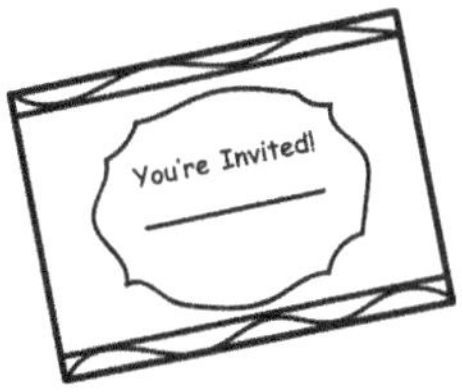

invitation

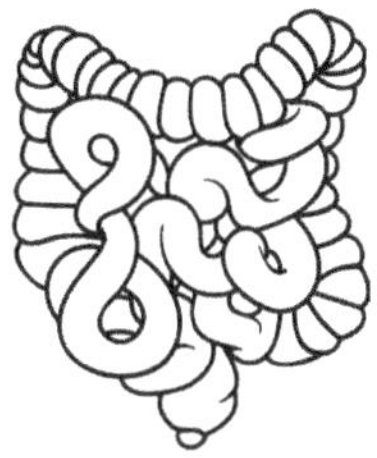

intestines

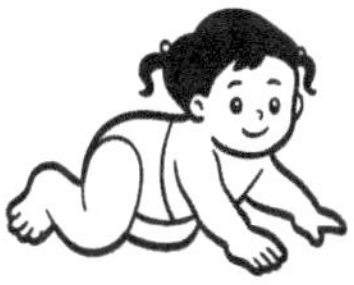

infant

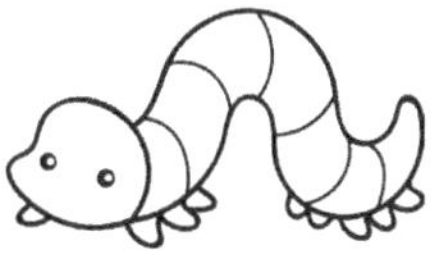

inchworm

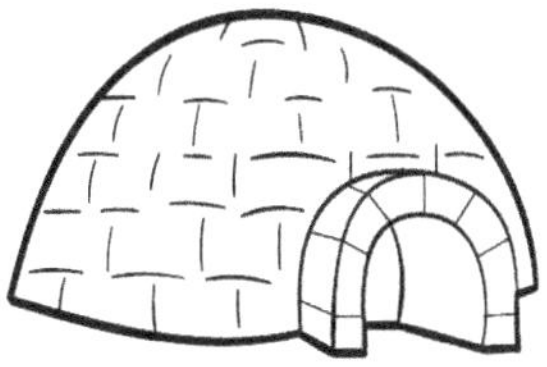

igloo

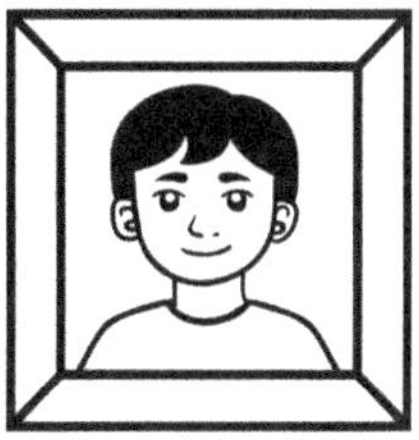

image

Practice writing the letter **Ii.**

ACTIVITY 14 SCORE:______

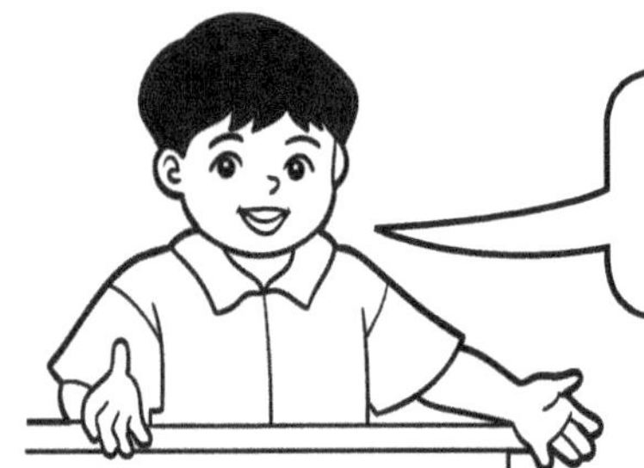

Encircle the pictures whose names begin with **Ii**.

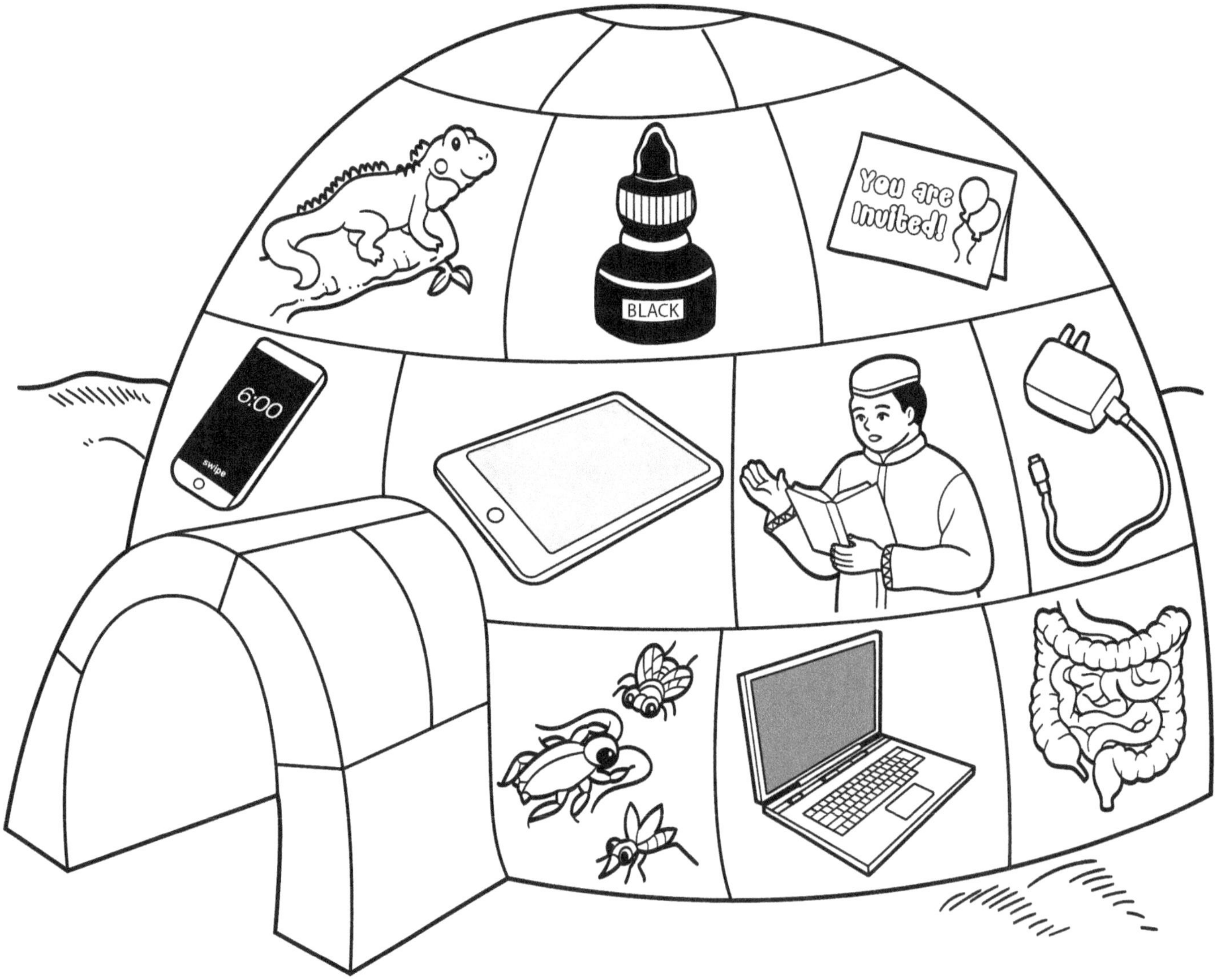

Underline the letter **Ii**'s.

T	i	I	I	t	l	I
f	I	i	i	T	i	L

ACTIVITY 15

SCORE: _______

Box the letter of the beginning sound for each picture on the left.

	i	a	e
	e	i	a
	i	e	a
	a	i	e
	a	e	i
	e	a	i
	i	a	e
	a	i	e
	i	a	e
	e	i	a

A Big, Green Iguana
(Tune: "If You're Happy and You Know It")

Oh, I wish I was a big, green iguana,
Oh, I wish I was a big, green iguana.
Oh, I'd itch and I'd scratch,
And I'd find a leafy patch.
Oh, I wish I was a big, green iguana.

Guide: Have the children box all the letter **Ii**'s they can find in the song.

Guide: Take the children out in the school garden or in the neighborhood for an insect-hunting activity. Discuss with them the insects' body parts, number of legs, movements, etc.

Encourage them to tell stories about their encounter with insects in their own houses. Don't forget to have them identify the insects they find. Have fun!

3-D Inchworm

Materials:

- two toilet paper tubes
- green crayon or watercolor
- scissors
- stapler
- paper punch
- white and black construction paper
- drinking straw

Directions:

1. Cut two toilet paper tubes into rings. (4 rings each for a total of 8 rings)

2. Fold 7 of the rings and then cut them in half. One ring needs to be left whole to use as the inchworm's head.

3. Have the children color the inchworm pieces.

4. Staple the inchworm together so that the back is formed of little arches.

5. Use a paper punch to put holes at the top of the worm's head. Insert 1/4 of a drinking straw into the holes to use as antennas.

6. Add googly eyes or eyes made of white and black construction paper.

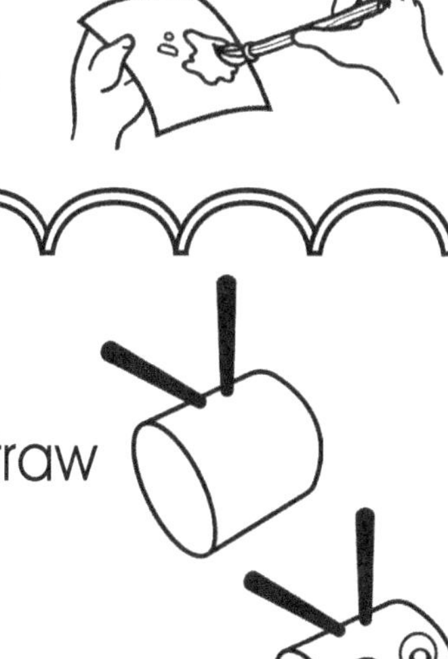

7. Staple all the parts together.

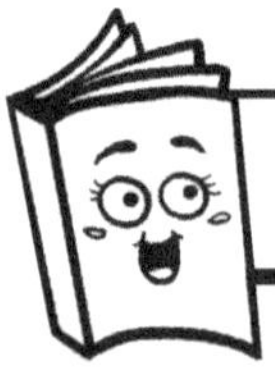

Oo

/ɔ/ as in **oven** /oʊ/ as in **ocean** /ɒ/ as in **ox**

Guide: Play a hunting game. Have the children go on an orange hunt around your classroom. You may have them look for real objects that are colored orange, or you may place small orange paper shapes around for them to find. Then have the children "hunt" for the objects whose names begin with the letter **O**.

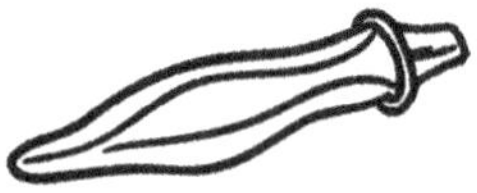

okra

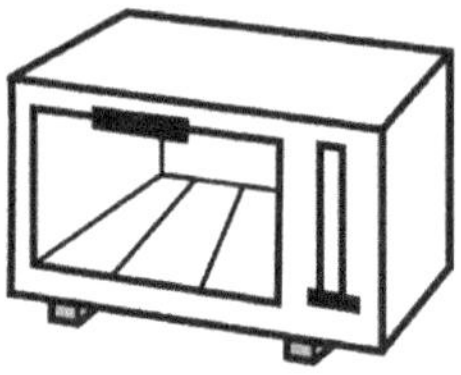

oven

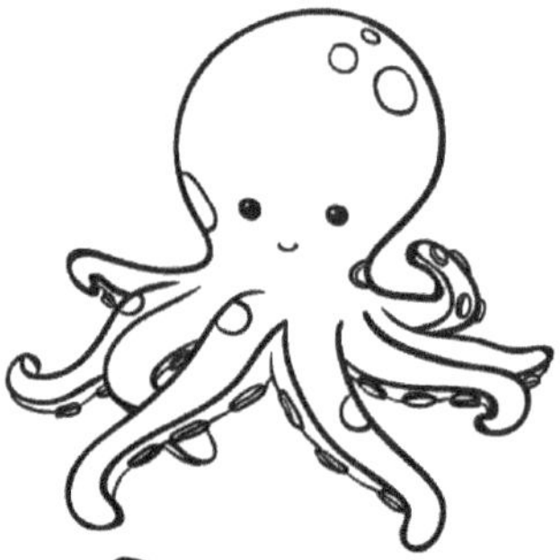

octopus

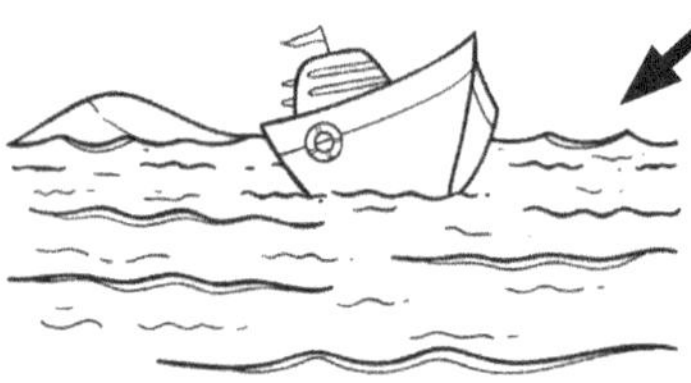

ocean

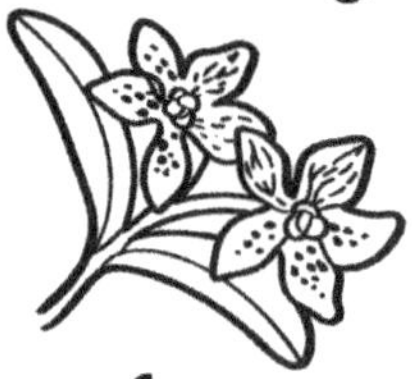

orchid

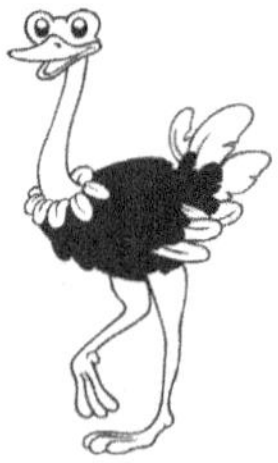

ostrich

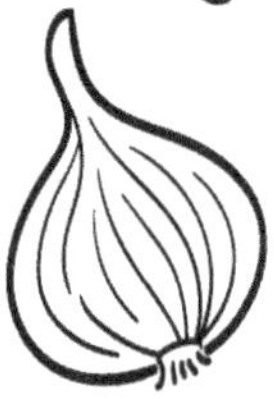

onion

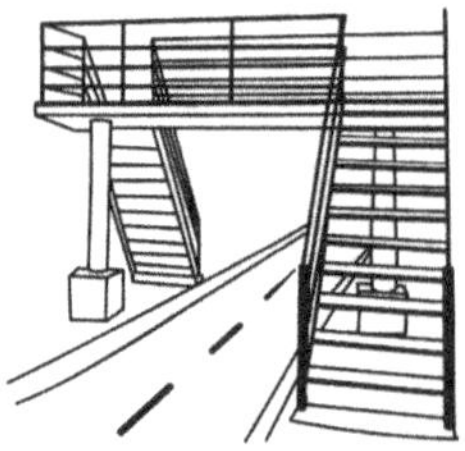

overpass

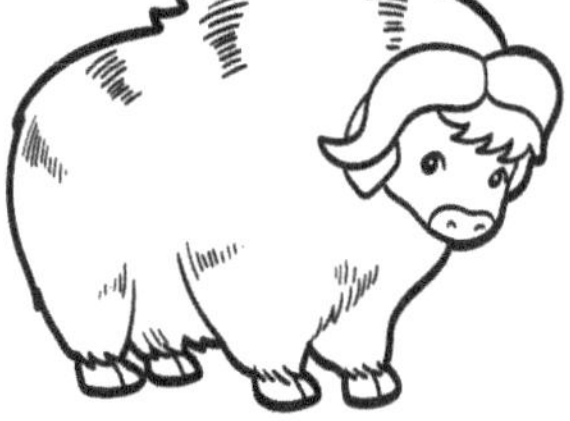

ox

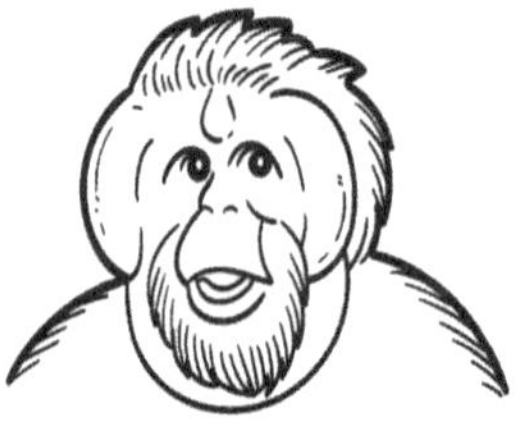

orangutan

Practice writing the letter **Oo**.

ACTIVITY 16

SCORE:_______

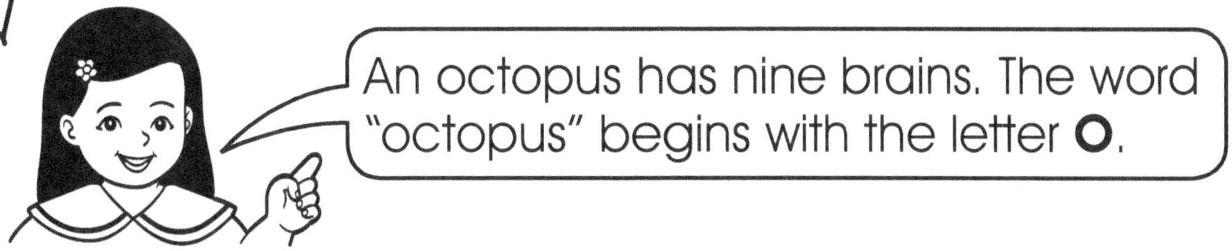

Color with an orange crayon the pictures whose names begin with **Oo**.

Box the letter **Oo**'s.

O	c	o	e	o	O	b
D	o	P	o	O	c	o

Orange Octopus

(Tune: "If You're Happy and You Know It")

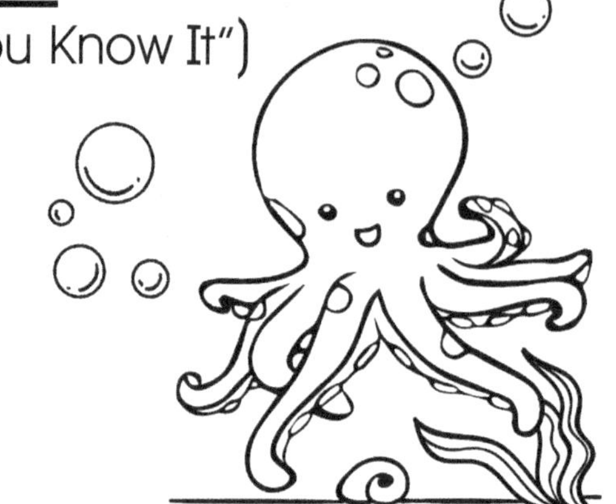

Oh, I wish I was an orange octopus,
Oh, I wish I was an orange octopus.
Every day, I would explore
All across the ocean floor.
Oh, I wish I was an orange octopus.

Guide: Have the children box all the letter **Oo**'s they find in the song.

Octopus Toilet Paper Roll Craft

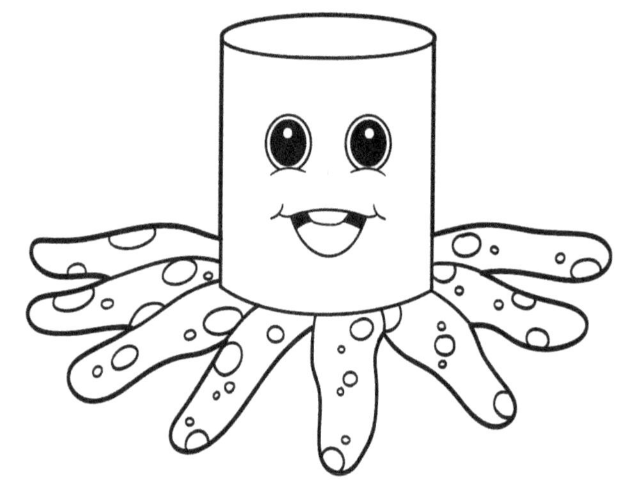

Materials:

- toilet paper roll
- template pieces
- scissors
- glue

Directions:

1. Color and cut out the template pieces.
2. Glue on the large rectangular piece first to cover the tube. (A toilet paper roll is a bit too tall for the octopus, so cut it down a bit. Use the height of the rectangle as a guide.)
3. Bend about 1/4 inch of each tentacle and glue to the inside of the tube. (Let them count the tentacles.)

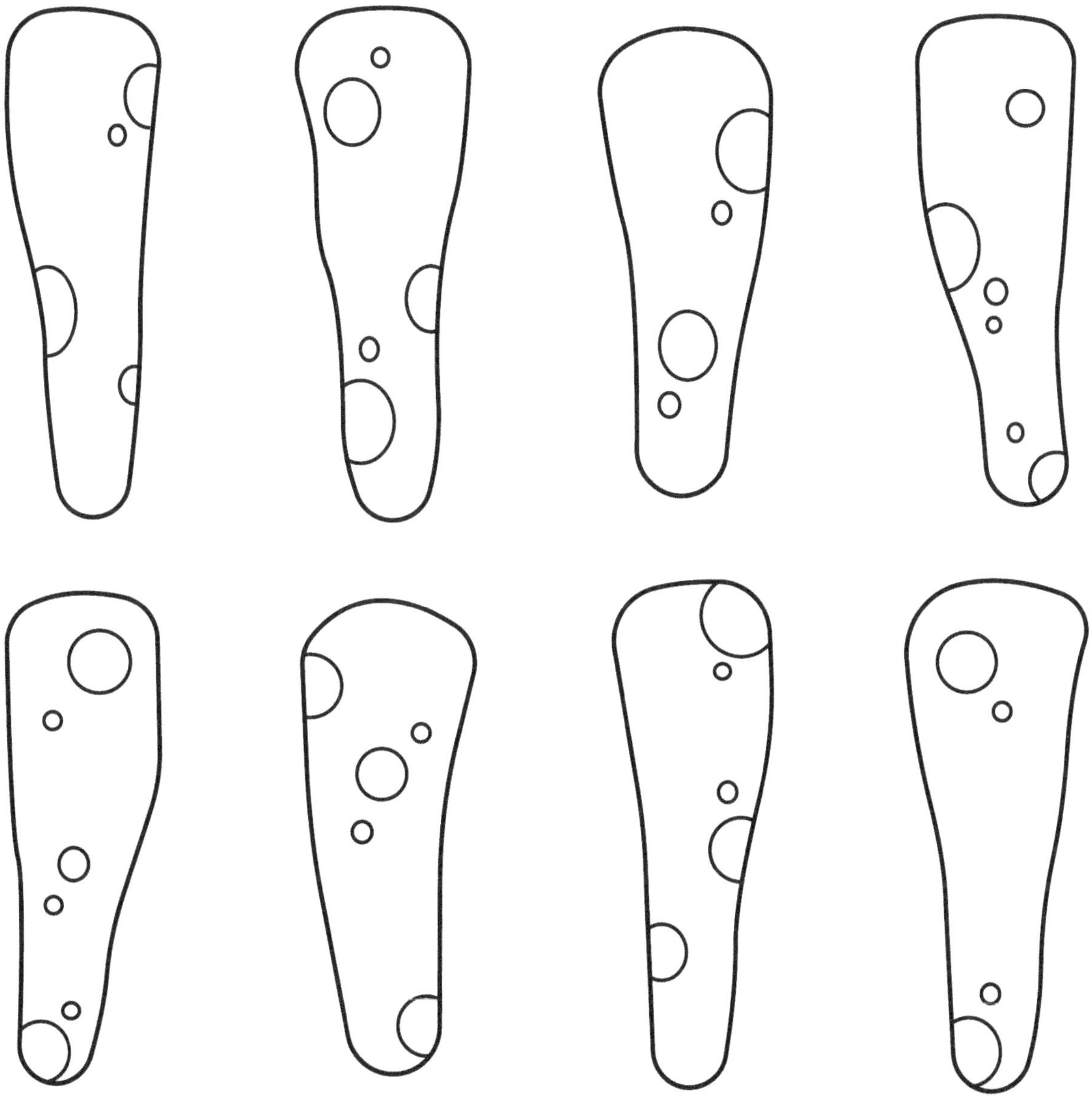

Connect the pictures to their initial sounds.

 •   • 

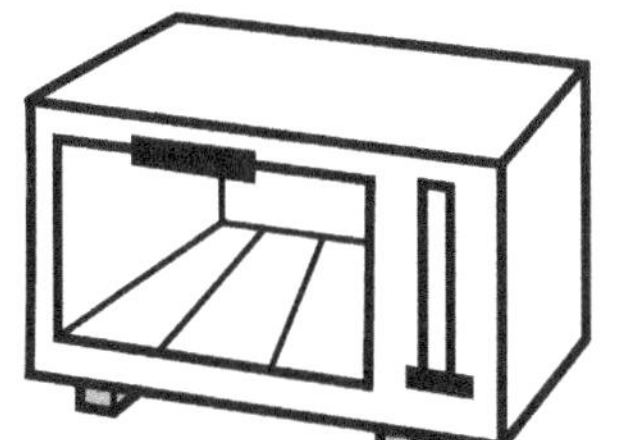 •  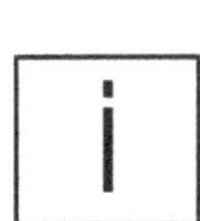 • 

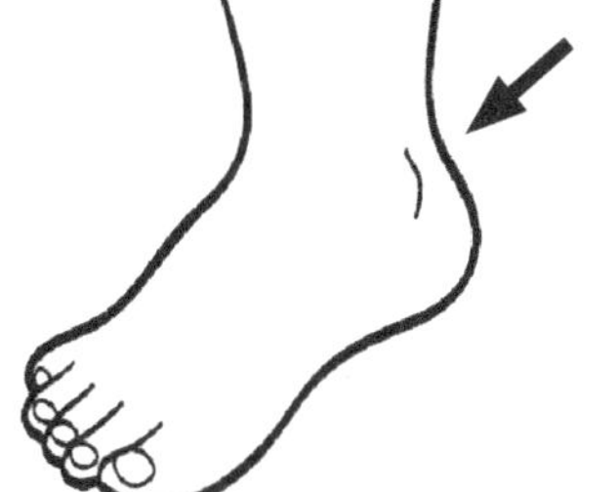 •   • 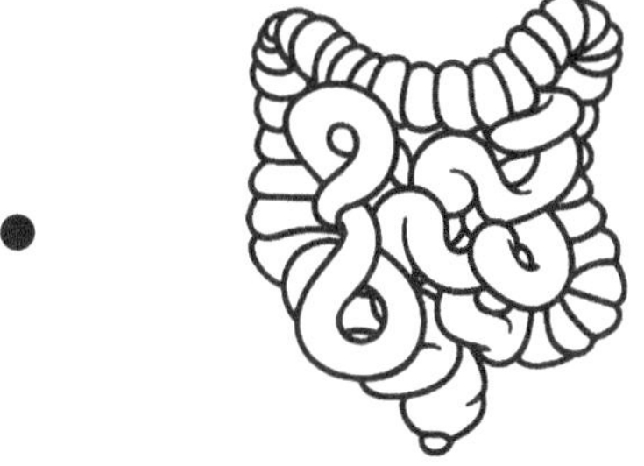

 •   • 

 •  • 

LESSON 9

Uu

/ʌ/

Guide: Give each child an inflated balloon. Have the children bat the balloon *up* and continue to tap it so that it doesn't fall down. The child who keeps his balloon *up* the longest is the winner. After this activity, show the children pictures or real objects whose names begin with the letter ***U***.

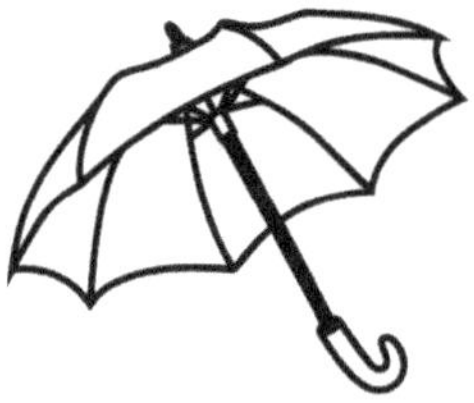
umbrella

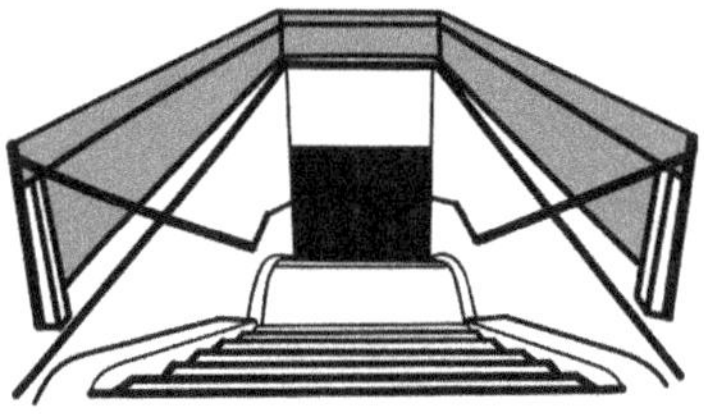
underpass

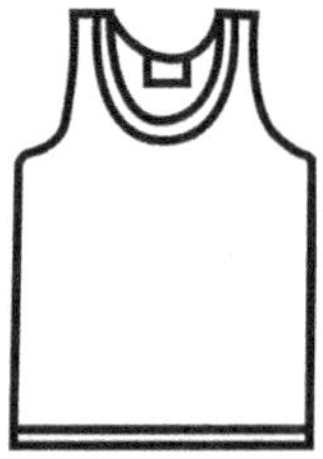
undershirt

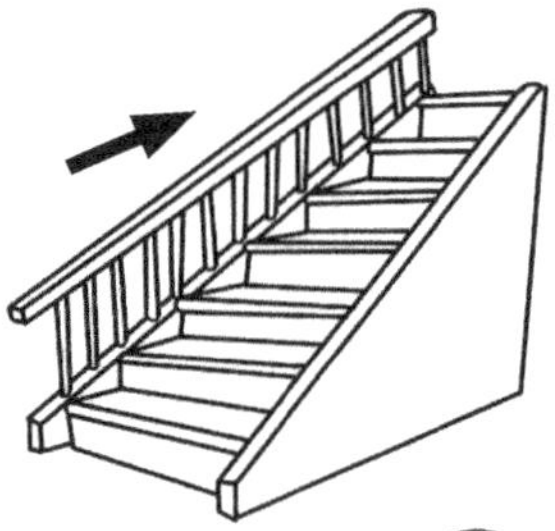
upstairs

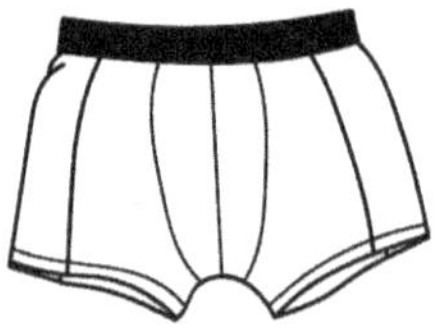
underpants

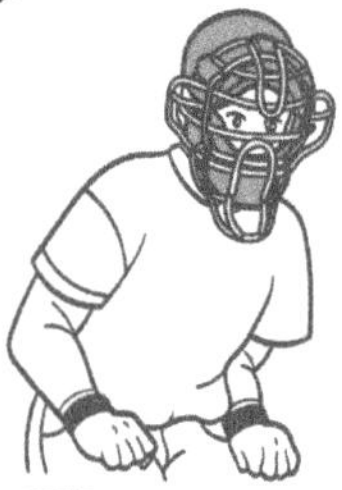
umpire

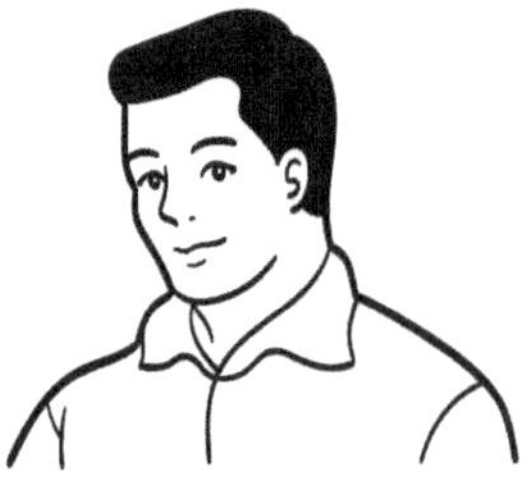
uncle

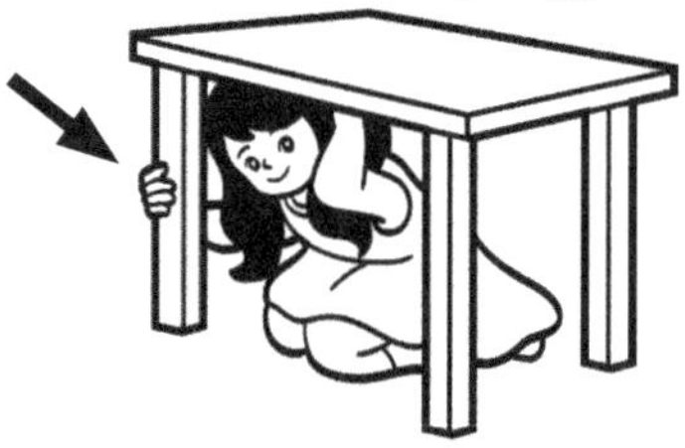
under

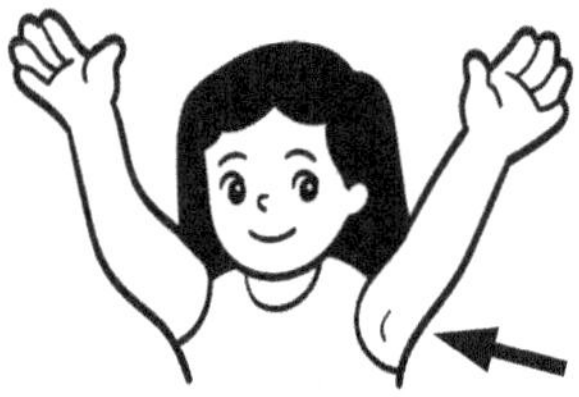
underarm

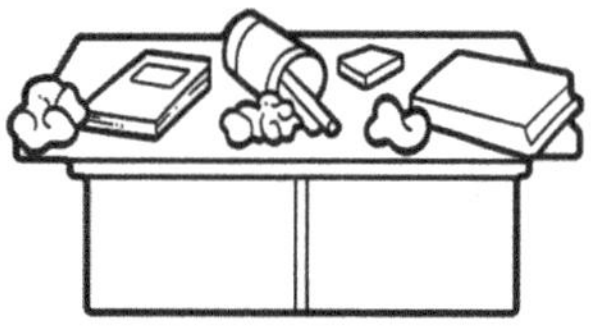
untidy

Practice writing the letter **Uu**.

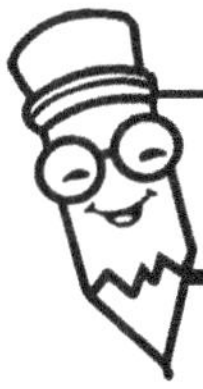

ACTIVITY 17 SCORE:______

I wear an undershirt at home.
The word "undershirt" begins with the letter **u**.

Box the pictures whose names begin with **Uu**.

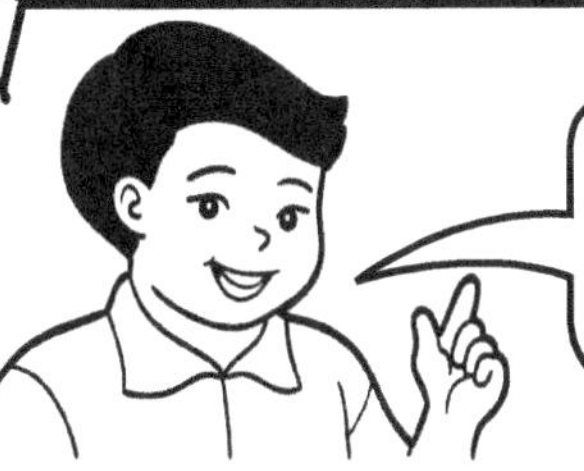

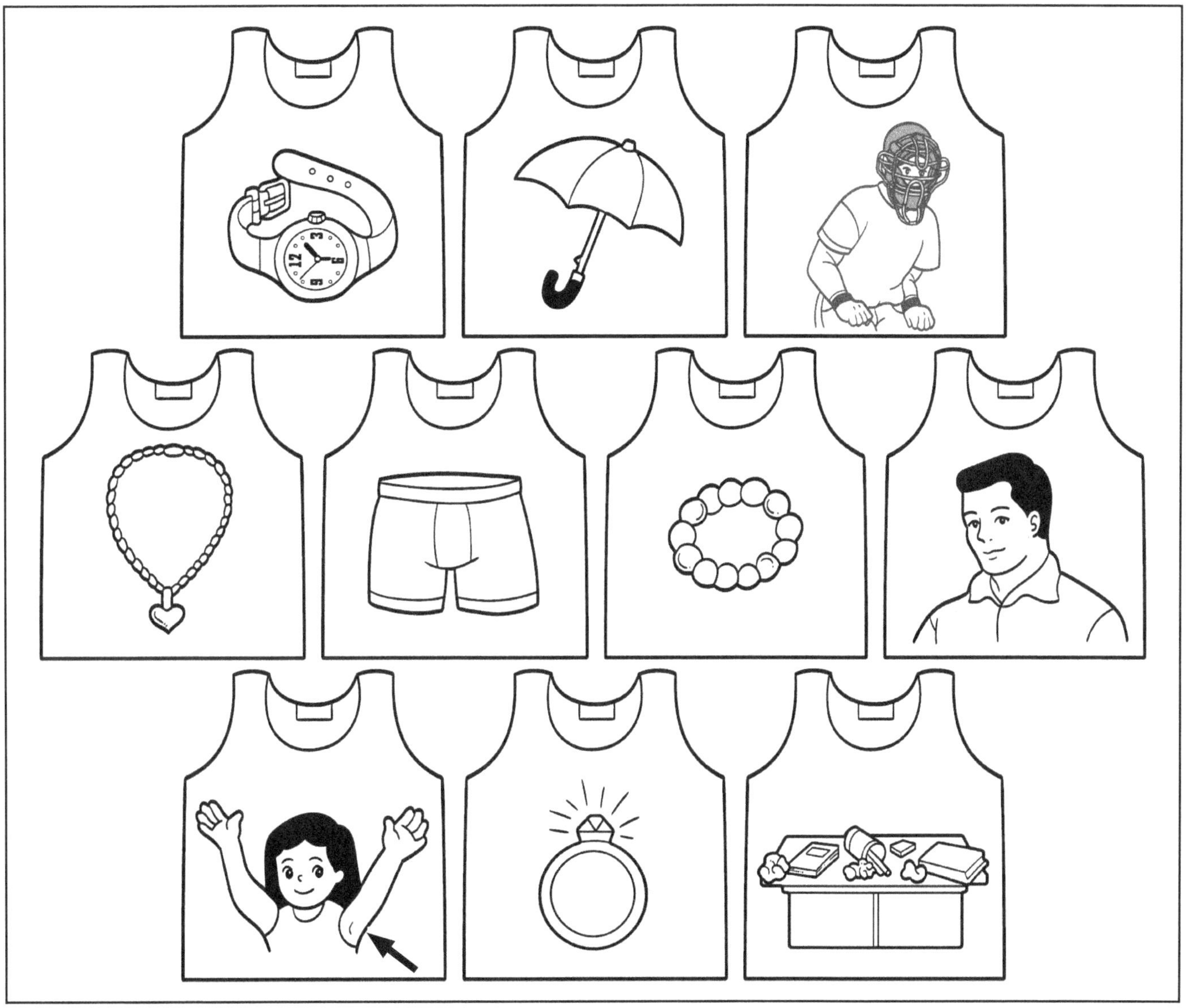

Draw a triangle around the letter **Uu**'s.

u U u p u U o

v a U V U n u

ACTIVITY 18   SCORE:______

Encircle the pictures in each group whose names begin with the letter on the left. (10 points)

e				
u				
i				
a				
o				

ACTIVITY 19   SCORE:______

Underline the correct partner of the letter on the left.

I	e	o	i	u
U	i	u	o	a
E	u	a	e	o
A	a	u	i	e
O	e	i	a	o

Cross out the picture in each set whose name does not begin with the letter in the middle.

	a	
	i	
	o	
	e	
	i	
	e	
	u	
	a	
	o	
	u	

Box the correct beginning sound of each picture.

	i	e	a	u	o
	o	a	e	i	u
	a	i	o	e	u
	e	u	i	o	a
	i	o	u	e	a
	a	o	i	u	e
	o	e	u	i	a
	a	e	i	u	o
	e	i	u	o	a
	u	e	i	a	o

FIRST QUARTERLY TEST

(Review Guide for Parents and Teachers)

Name: _______________________________   **Score:** _________

Level: _________   **Date:** _________

I. Follow the directions.

1. Box the letters. Encircle the numbers.

2. Check three animals that live on land.

3. Encircle the things we don't use when eating.

4. Underline three things that we eat.

5. Draw a star on the things needed for bathing.

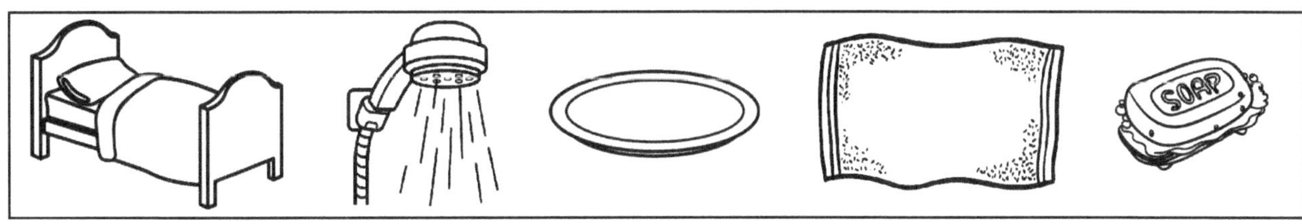

II. Draw a flower (❀) in the box if the pictures are alike. Draw a leaf (🍃) if they are different.

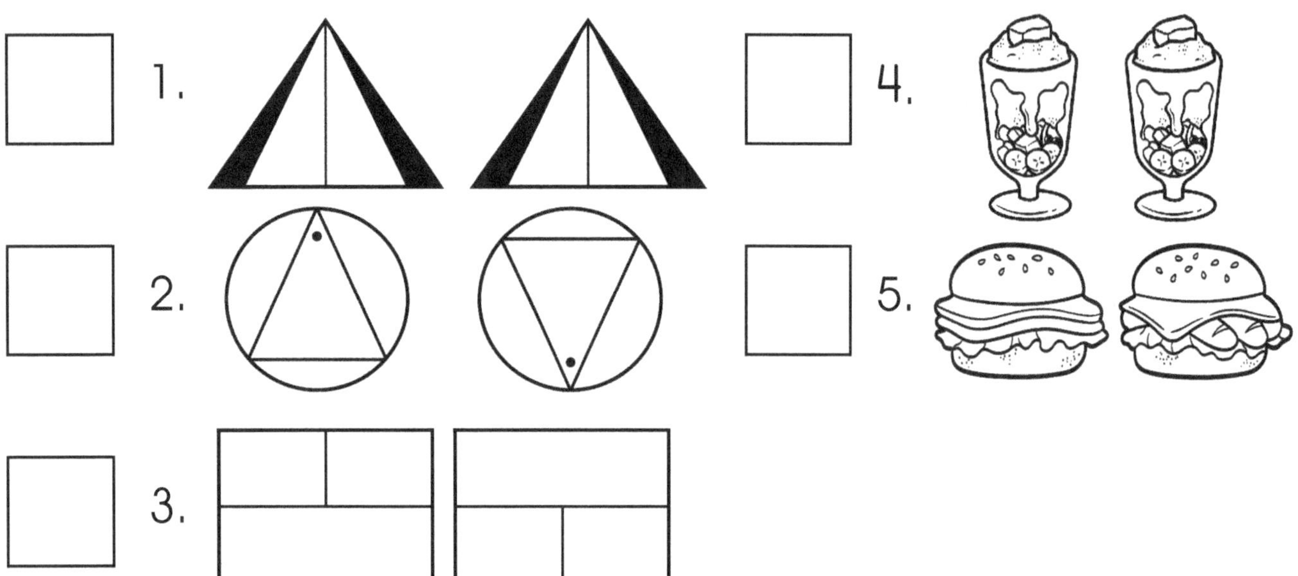

1.

2.

3.

4.

5.

III. Check the picture in each group that is the same as the one on the left.

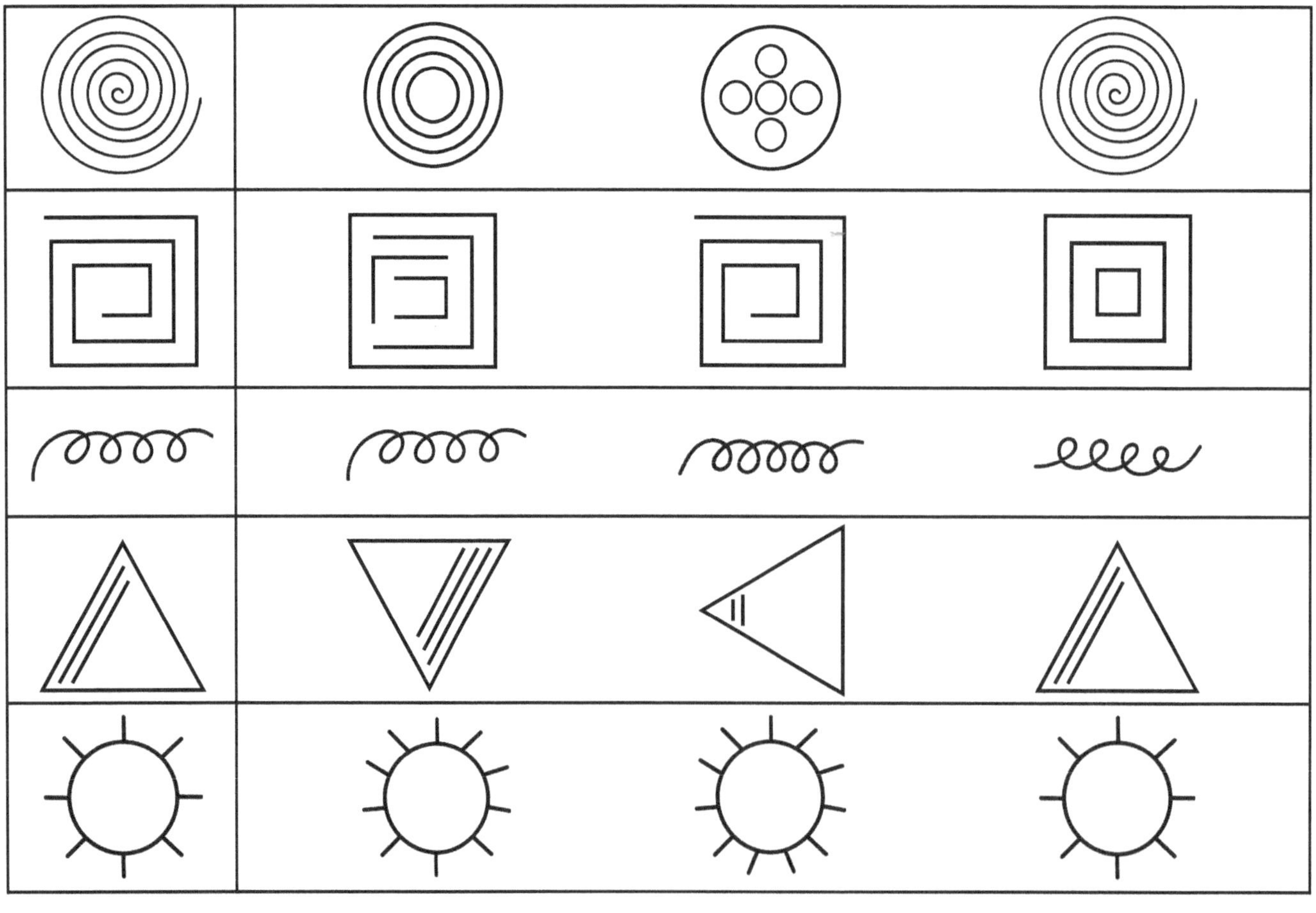

IV. Cross out the picture which does not belong to the group.

V. Box the word in each group that is the same as the one on the left.

bill	bell	bull	ball	bill
gum	mug	gum	gun	hum
net	net	ten	nut	not
box	fox	bus	box	bow
jam	jar	gun	jaw	jam

<u>VI</u>. Underline the letter in each group that the teacher will sound out.

1. a o u e   4. i u e o

2. o e a u   5. e o i a

3. i o u a

<u>VII</u>.

A. Write the lowercase letters of the following:

1. A _____   4. O _____

2. U _____   5. E _____

3. I _____

B. Write the uppercase letters of the following:

1. _____ a   4. _____ e

2. _____ o   5. _____ u

3. _____ i

VIII. Write the correct beginning sound.

1. ___nderpass   6. ___mbrella

2. ___lephant   7. ___mbulance

3. ___ctopus   8. ___ntestines

4. ___lbum   9. ___ngine

5. ___guana   10. ___verpass

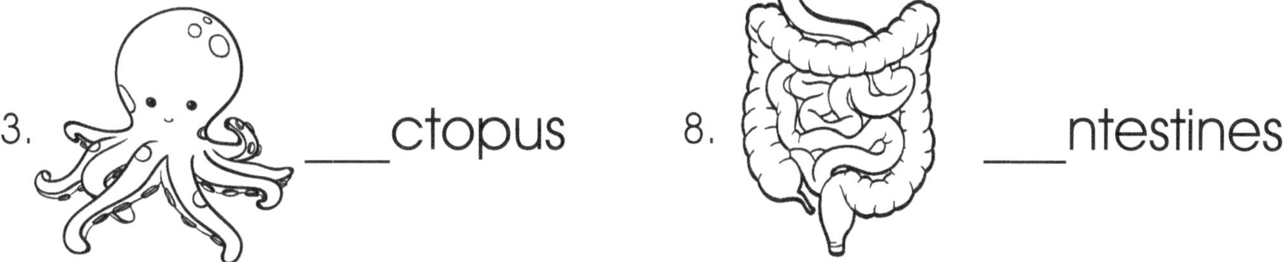
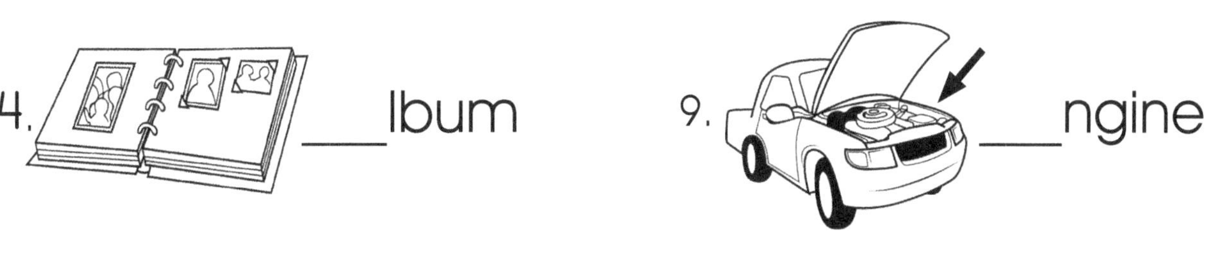
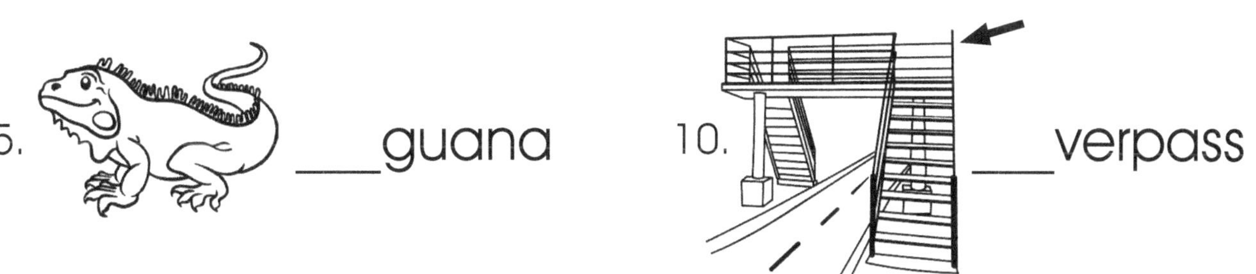

PROGRESS CHART
FIRST QUARTER

Name: _________________________________   Level: ___________

ACTIVITY	No. of Items	My Score	HOME ACTIVITY	No. of Items	My Score	QUIZ	No. of Items	My Score
1	10		1	5		1	10	
2	5		2	5		2	5	
3	5					3	5	
4	5					4	5	
5	5					5	5	
6	5					6	10	
7	5					7	5	
8	5					8	10	
9	10					9	5	
10	10					10	10	
11	5					11	10	
12	10					12	10	
13	10					13	10	
14	10							
15	10							
16	10							
17	10							
18	15							
19	5							
TOTAL	150		TOTAL	10		TOTAL	100	

___________________________   ___________________________
Parent's/Guardian's Signature   Teacher's Signature

SECOND QUARTER
THE CONSONANT FAMILY

Teacher's Objectives and Student Evaluation			
Lesson	*At the end of the activities, the child should be able to:*	D	DD	WD
1	1. identify the letter *Bb* and tell its phonetic sound			
2	2. identify the letter *Cc* and tell its phonetic sound			
3	3. identify the letter *Dd* and tell its phonetic sound			
4	4. identify the letter *Ff* and tell its phonetic sound			
5	5. identify the letter *Gg* and tell its phonetic sound			
6	6. identify the letter *Hh* and tell its phonetic sound			
7	7. identify the letter *Jj* and tell its phonetic sound			
8	8. identify the letter *Kk* and tell its phonetic sound			
9	9. identify the letter *Ll* and tell its phonetic sound			
10	10. identify the letter *Mm* and tell its phonetic sound			
11	11. identify the letter *Nn* and tell its phonetic sound			
12	12. identify the letter *Pp* and tell its phonetic sound			
13	13. identify the letter *Qq* and tell its phonetic sound			
14	14. identify the letter *Rr* and tell its phonetic sound			
15	15. identify the letter *Ss* and tell its phonetic sound			
16	16. identify the letter *Tt* and tell its phonetic sound			
17	17. identify the letter *Vv* and tell its phonetic sound			
18	18. identify the letter *Ww* and tell its phonetic sound			
19	19. identify the letter *Xx* and tell its phonetic sound			
20	20. identify the letter *Yy* and tell its phonetic sound			
21	21. identify the letter *Zz* and tell its phonetic sound			
22	22. name objects whose names begin with the consonant letters			
	23. write the letters of the alphabet in their sequence			
	24. identify the missing letters of the alphabet			
	25. tell the letter that comes after a given letter			

Legend:

D — Developing   D — Developed   WD — Well-Developed

THE CONSONANT FAMILY

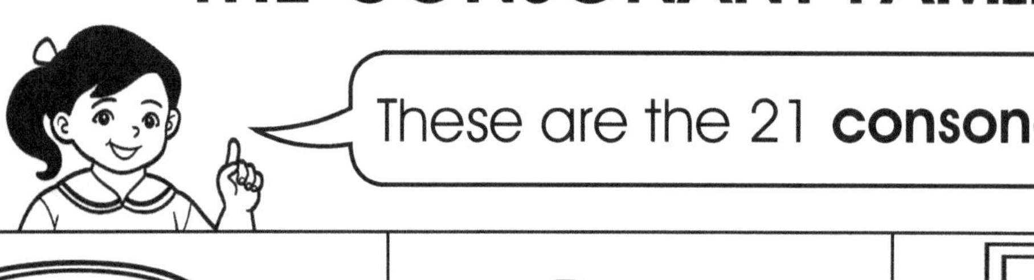

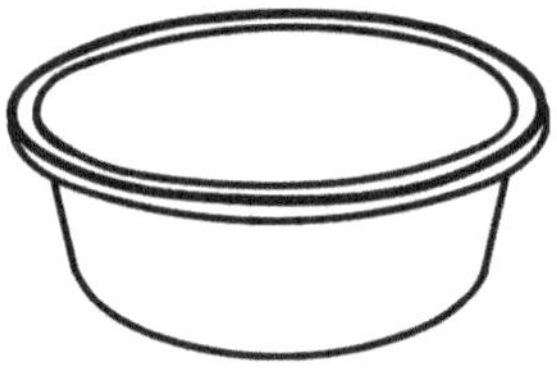 Bb	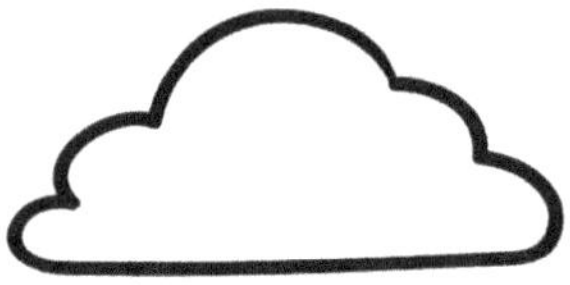 Cc	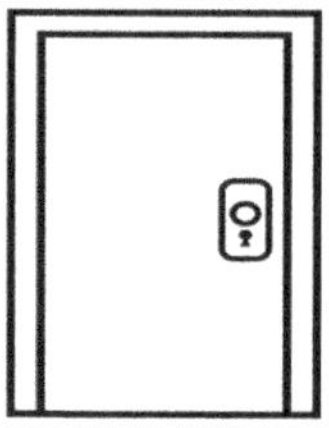 Dd
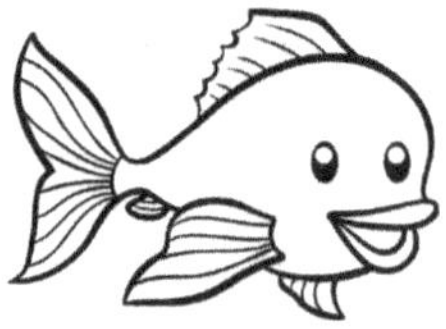 Ff	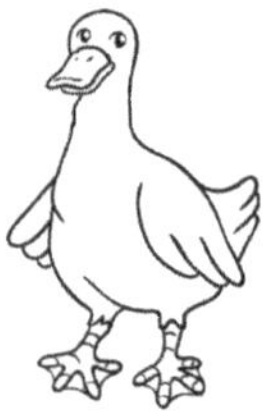 Gg	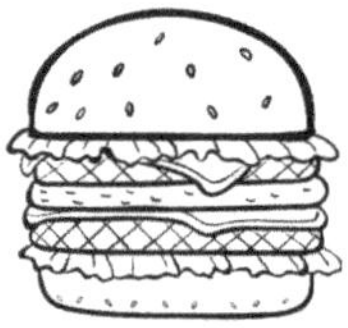 Hh
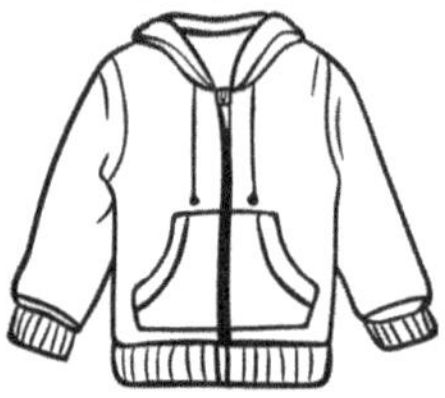 Jj	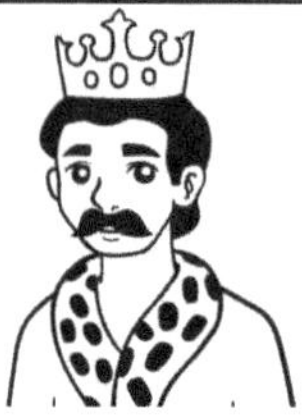 Kk	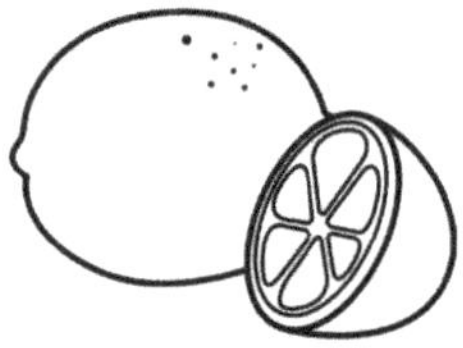 Ll
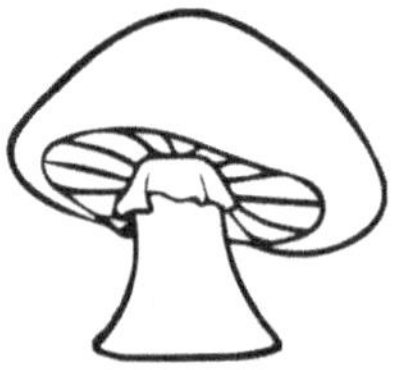 Mm	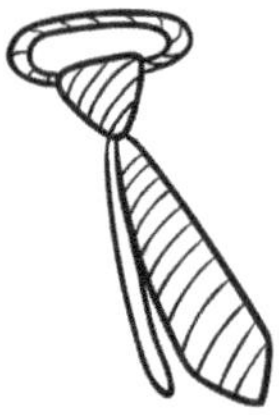 Nn	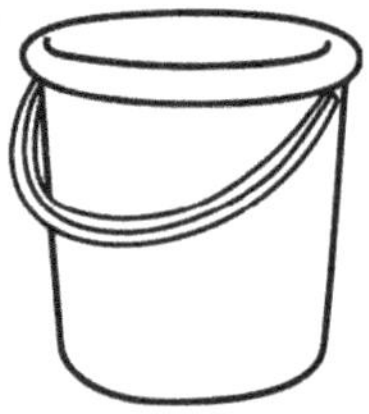 Pp
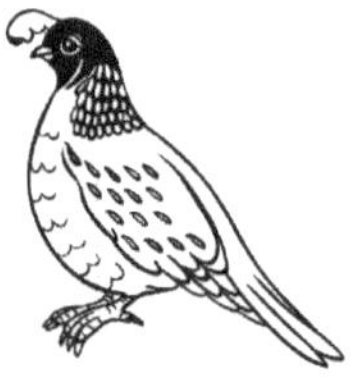 Qq	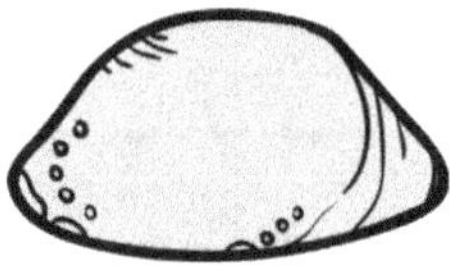 Rr	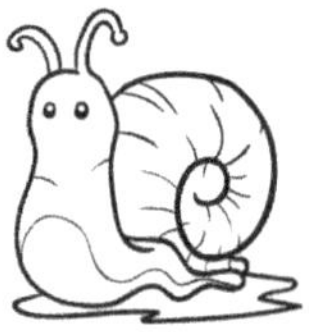 Ss
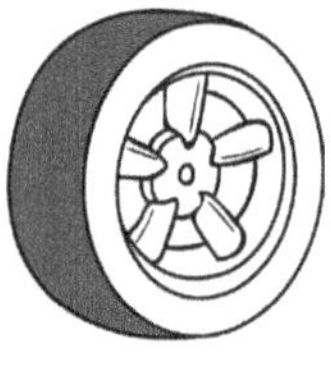 Tt	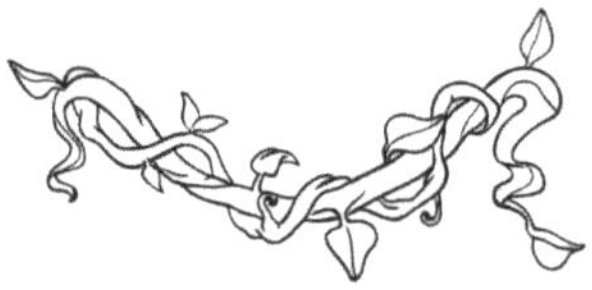 Vv	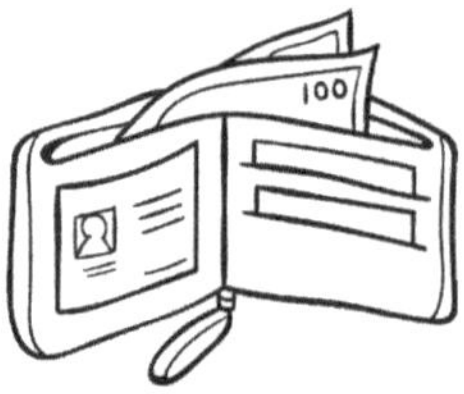 Ww
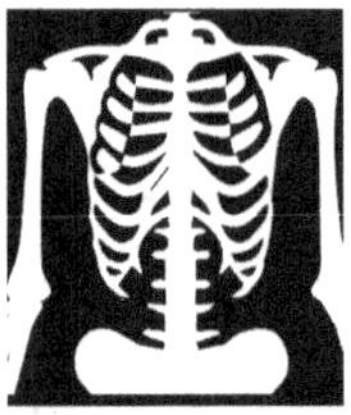 Xx	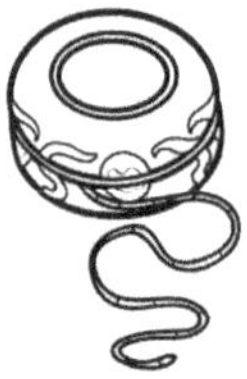 Yy	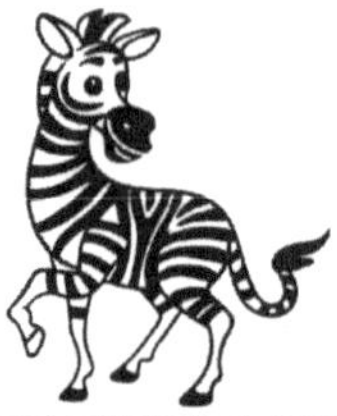 Zz

LESSON 1

Bb
/b/

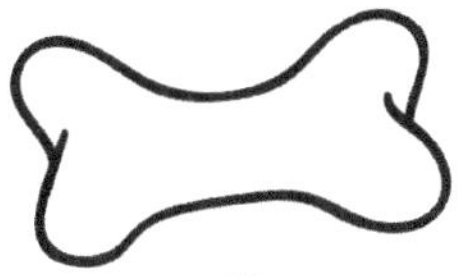

bone

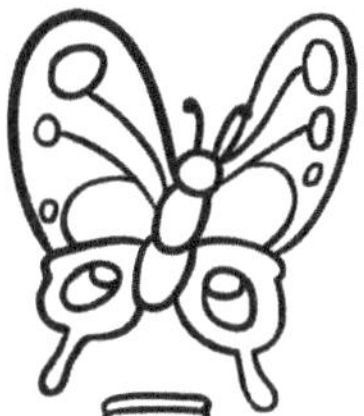

butterfly

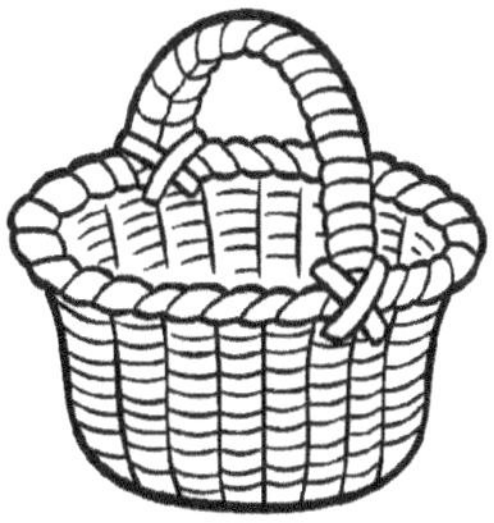

basket

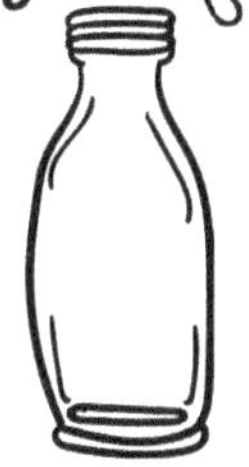

bottle

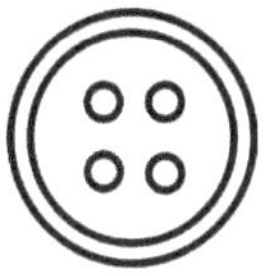

button

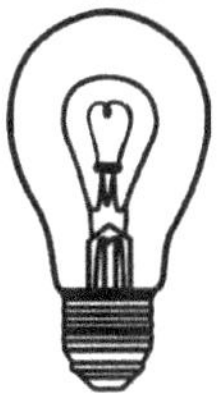

bulb

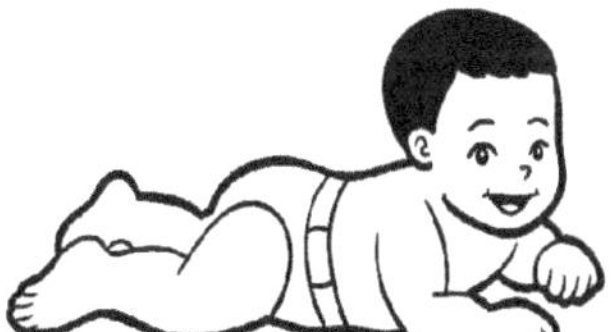

baby

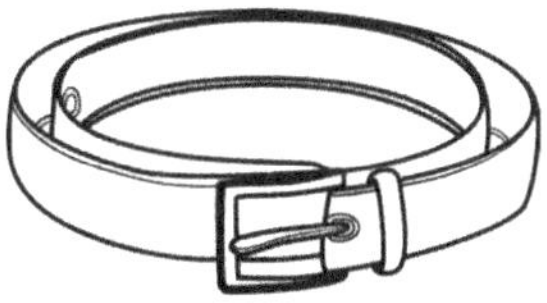

belt

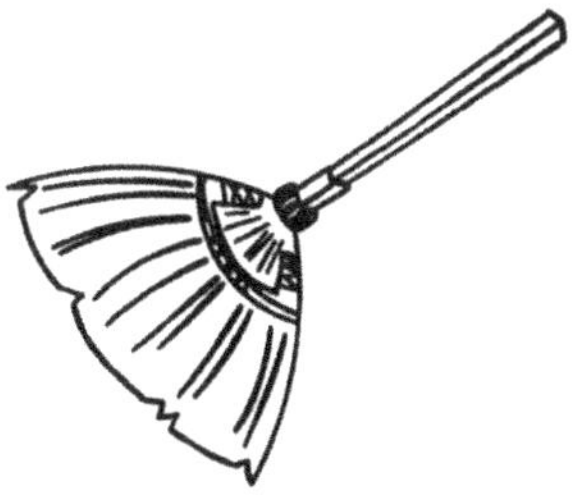

broom

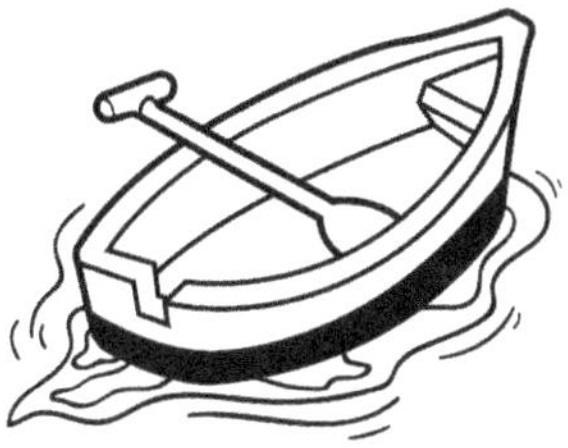

boat

Practice writing the letter **Bb**.

Bb

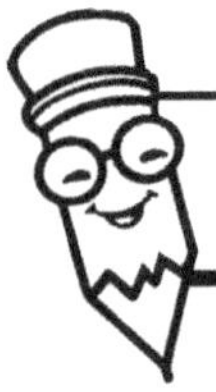

ACTIVITY 1 SCORE:______

My family celebrates birthdays with balloons.
The word "balloon" starts with the letter **b**.

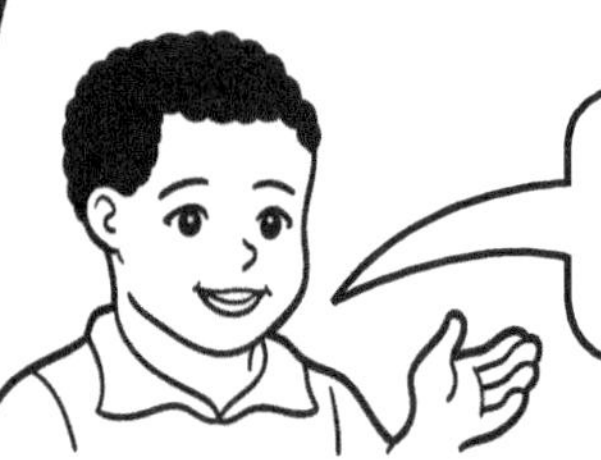

Color the balloons with pictures whose names begin with **Bb**.

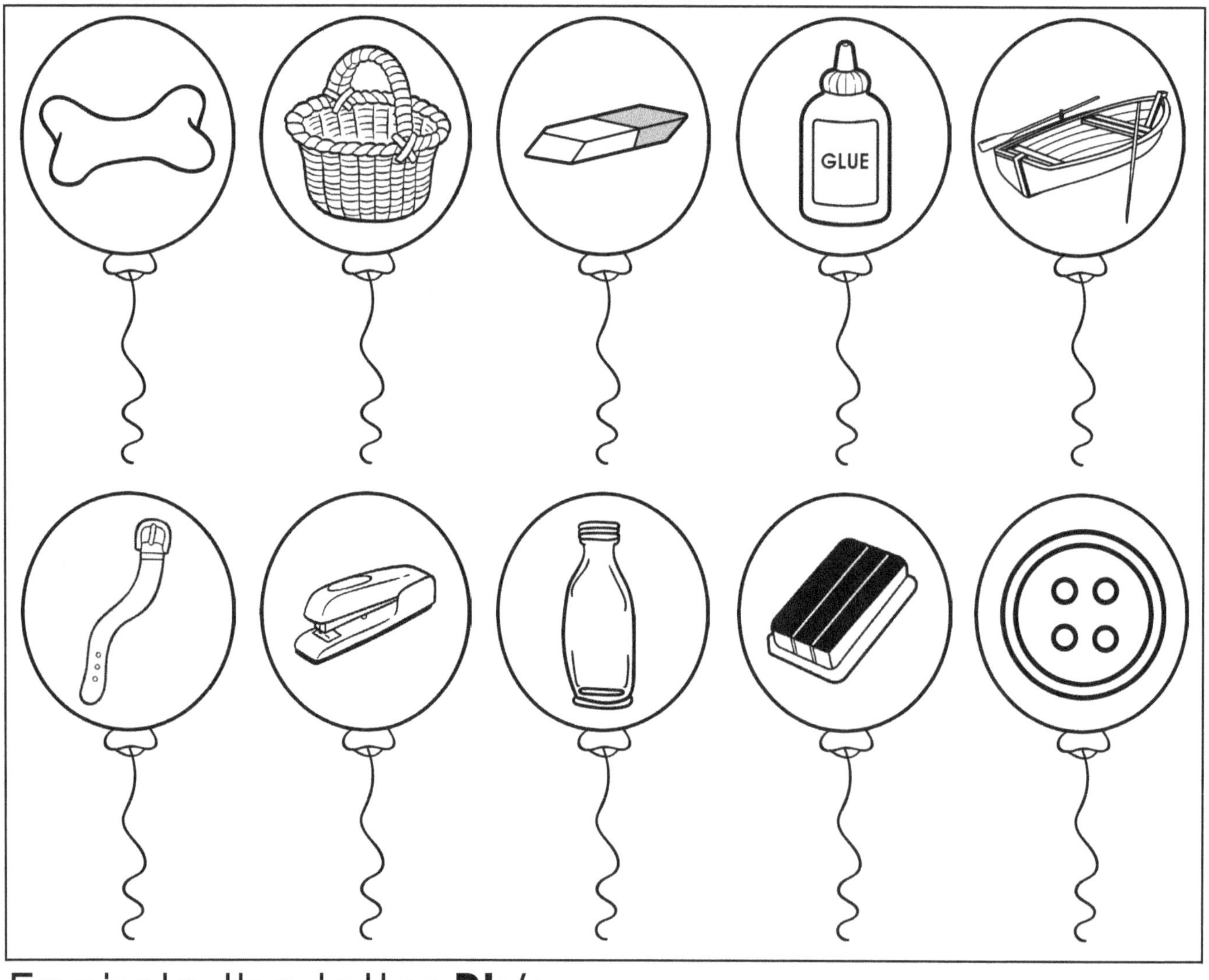

Encircle the letter **Bb**'s.

t	b	g	b	q	B	B
D	B	b	q	B	P	b

GAMES and ACTIVITIES

Game/Activity	Learning Areas
Baby Day Invite parents with babies to come with their babies. The following day, let your students pretend to be babies. Bring some baby bottles for the children to use at snack time. Let the children crawl around. Sing lullabies for babies.	* Language * Physical Education and Health, Music, and Arts * Science * Values Education and Social Studies
Birthday Party Decorate the room with **B** things such as balloons, banners, baseball hats, etc. Place **B** cutouts on straws for drinks. Serve cupcakes with **B's** printed on top with blue icing. Play baseball or other ball games. Let the children help plan the party. Take pictures of the party and later see how many **B** things they can find in the pictures.	* Physical Education and Health, Music, and Arts * Language * Mathematics * Science * Values Education and Social Studies
Moving Like _B_'s Have the children move like butterflies, bubbles, bugs, and bumblebees. Have them ride bikes, walk on balance beams, bounce balls, or play a bowling game.	* Physical Education and Health, Music, and Arts * Science * Language
Snack Time with _B_ Make buttered biscuits with the children for snacks. Serve broccoli or green beans. Don't forget bread and bananas, too. Have the children count bread, bananas, and beans.	* Physical Education and Health, Music, and Arts * Language * Mathematics * Science * Values Education and Social Studies

Cc
/k/

candle

cotton

corn

can

cow

comb

crab

clown

cake

coin

Practice writing the letter **Cc**.

Cc

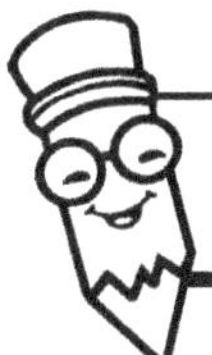

ACTIVITY 2

SCORE: ______

Coconuts are rich in vitamins.
The word "coconut" begins with the letter **c**.

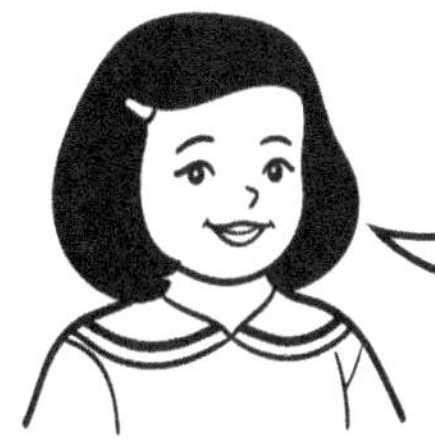

Box the pictures whose names begin with **Cc**.

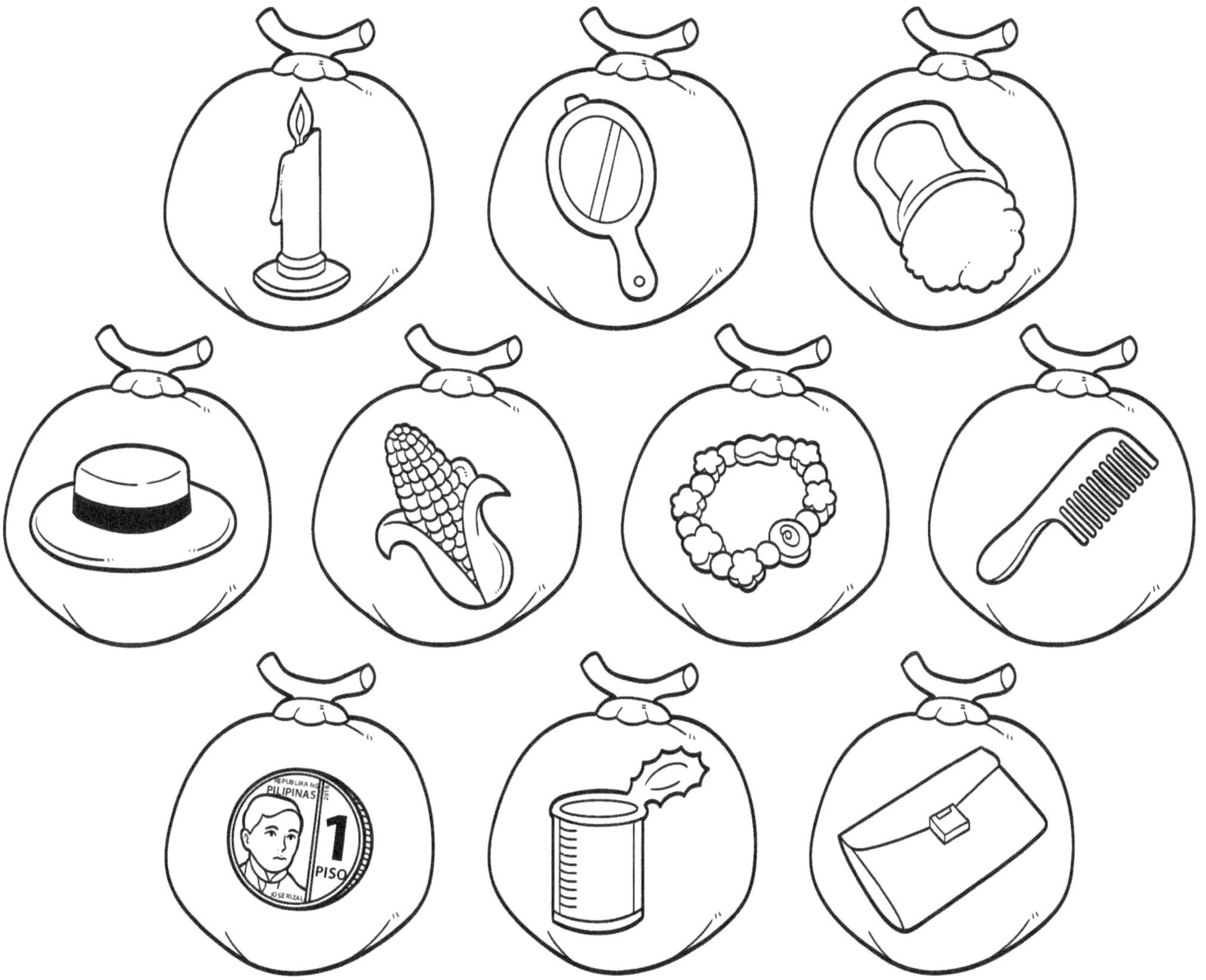

Check the letter **Cc**'s.

C	c	c	a	C	O	D
c	d	C	D	c	C	o

ACTIVITY 3

SCORE:______

Connect the pictures whose names begin with **Bb** to the ball. Connect those whose names begin with **Cc** to the computer.

Dd
/d/

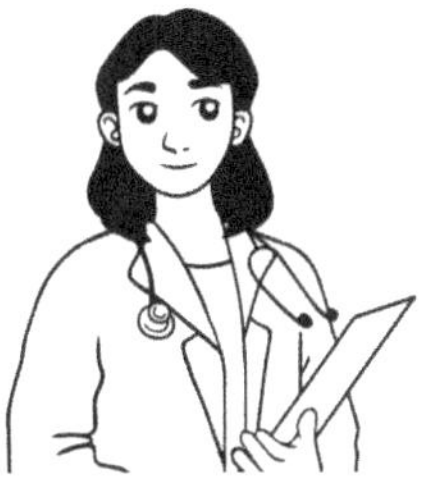

doctor

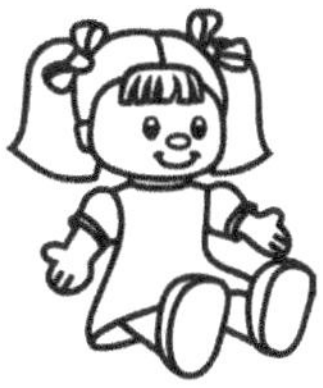

doll

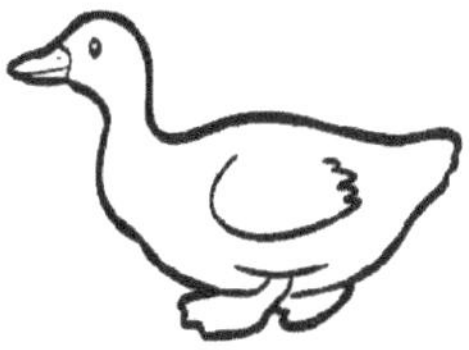

duck

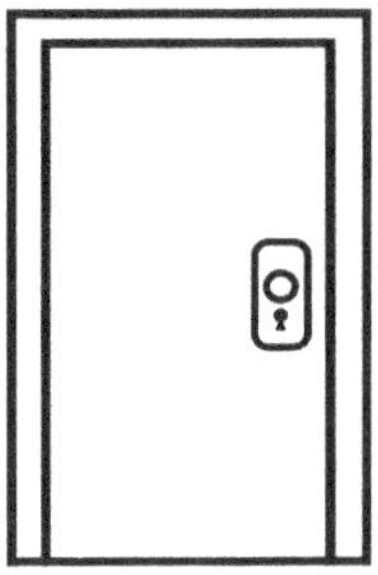

door

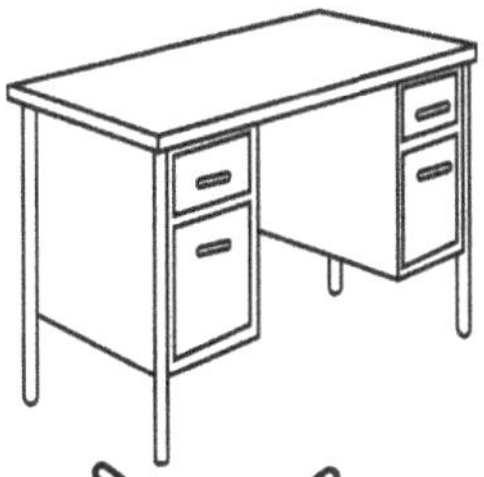

desk

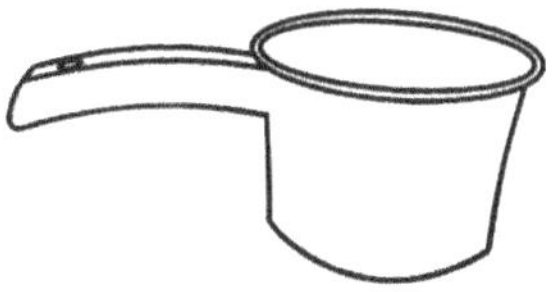

dipper

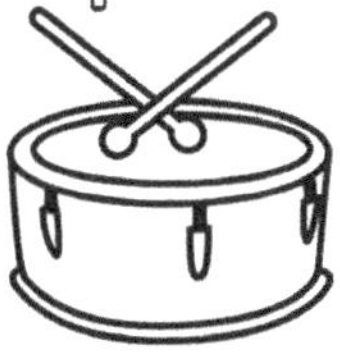

drum

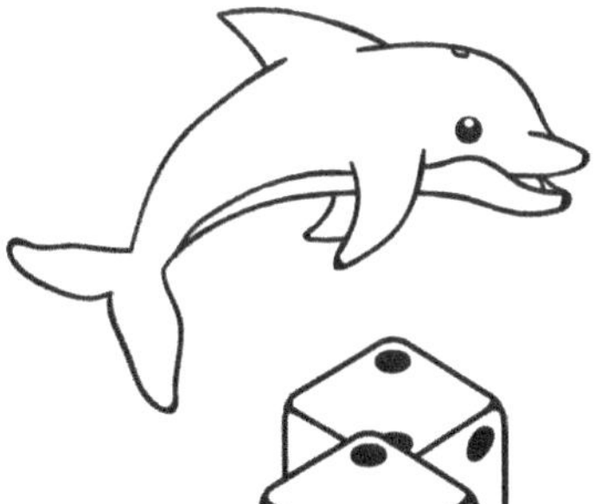

dolphin

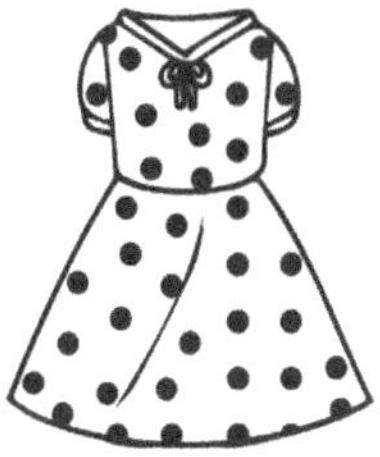

dress

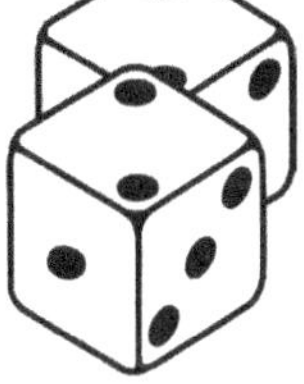

dice

Practice writing the letter **Dd**.

Dd

ACTIVITY 4   SCORE:_______

Encircle the pictures whose names begin with **Dd**.

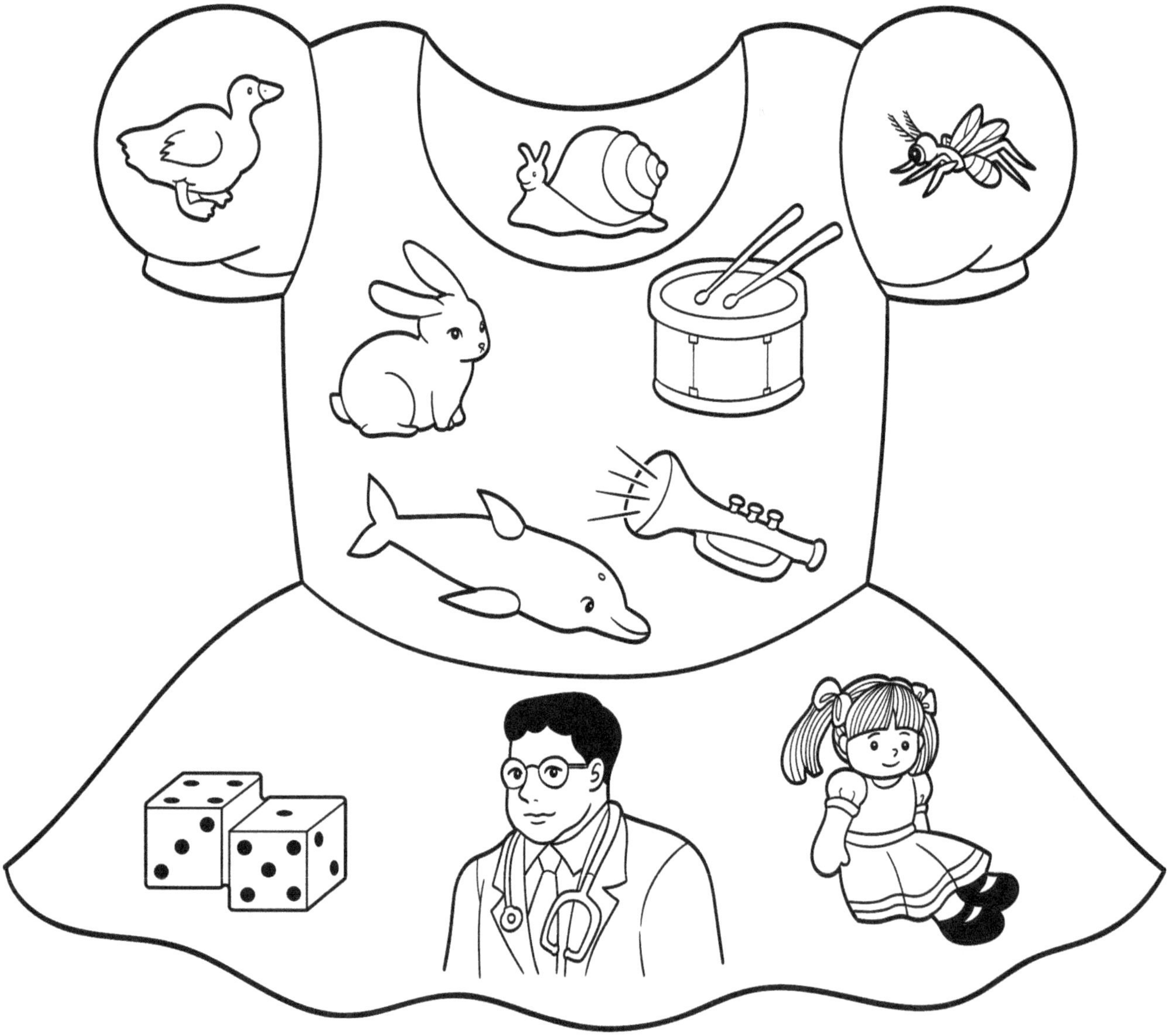

Underline the letter **Dd**'s.

d   g   d   D   P   D   B

D   P   O   d   D   d   b

Dickle, Dickle, Derry

Dickle, Dickle, Derry,
Dickle, Dickle, dee.
Come walk around the mango tree.
Dickle, Dickle, Derry,
Dickle, Dickle, dee.
Are you ready? 1, 2, 3!

Guide: Have the children underline all the words that begin with the letter **D**.

Guide: Have the children form a circle. Have one pupil be the "it" to act as the mango tree. The "it" stands and sways in the middle, while the other children sing and walk around the "mango tree." You may later substitute "walk" with other action words, and the "mango tree" with other kinds of trees.

Guide: Have the children sound out each letter.

1.	b	e	a	c
2.	d	u	b	e
3.	c	o	i	d
4.	d	o	a	b
5.	c	u	b	i

Connect the pictures to their correct initial sounds.

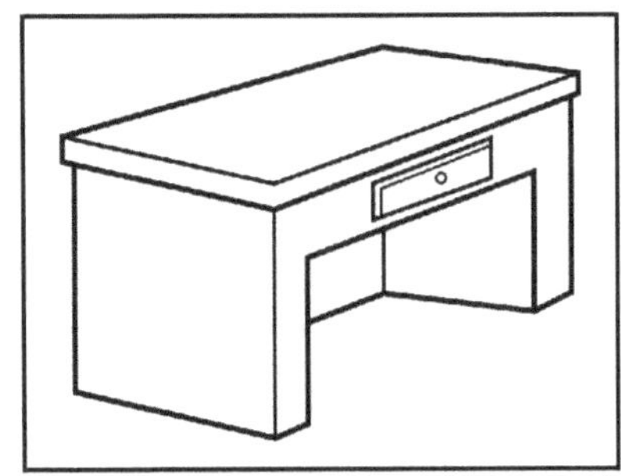

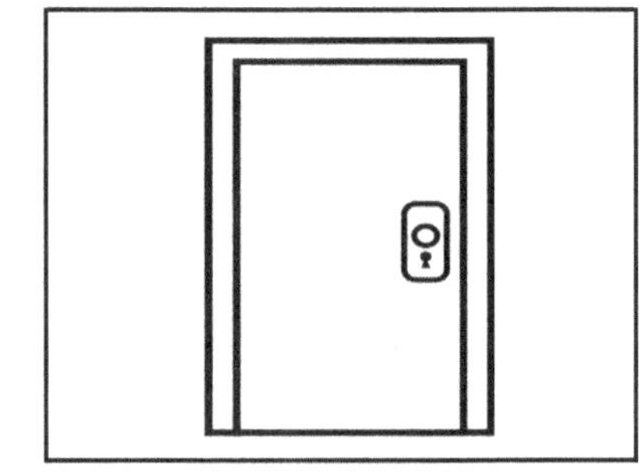

LESSON 4

Ff
/f/

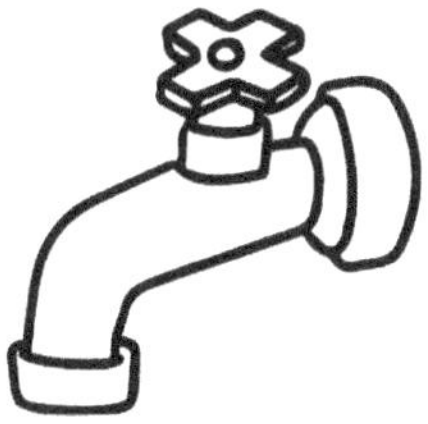

faucet

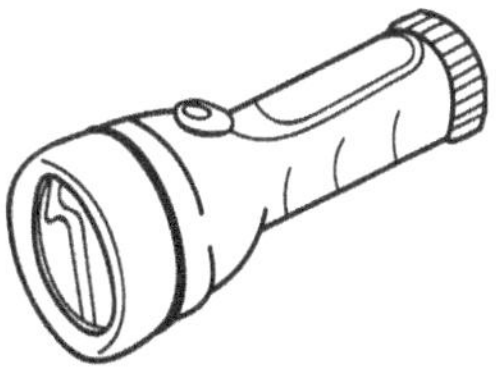

flashlight

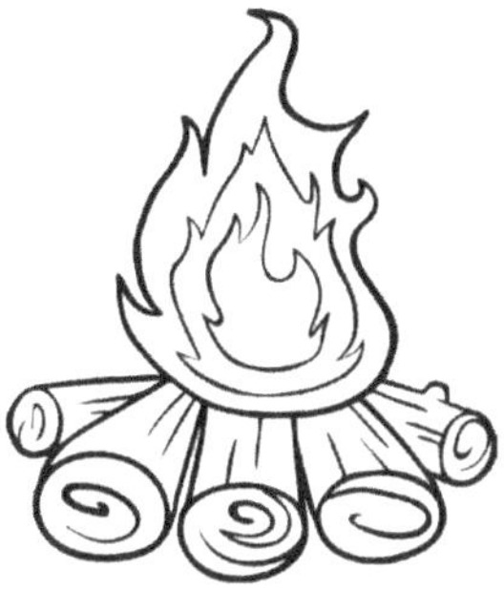

fire

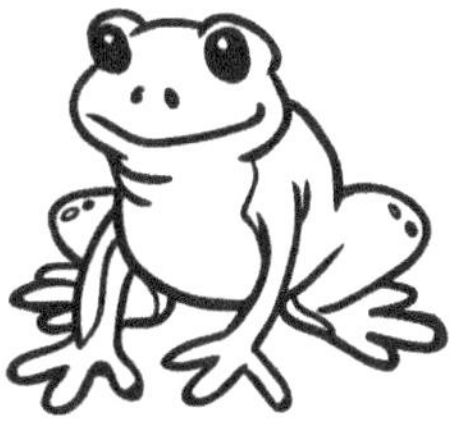

frog

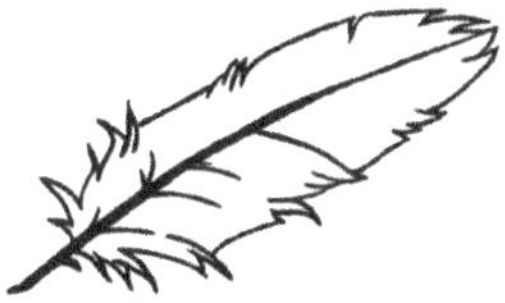

feather

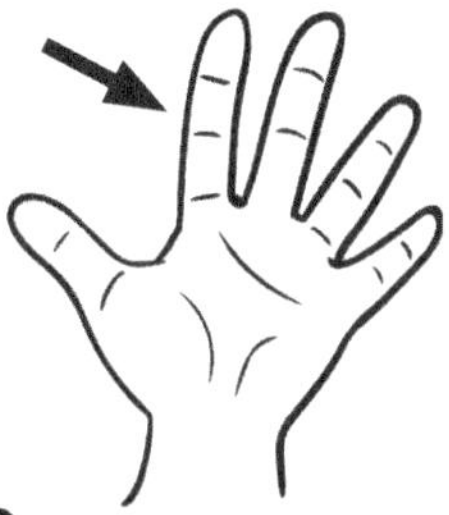

finger

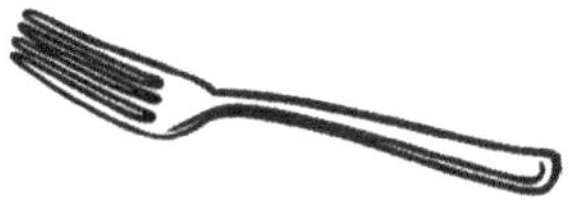

fork

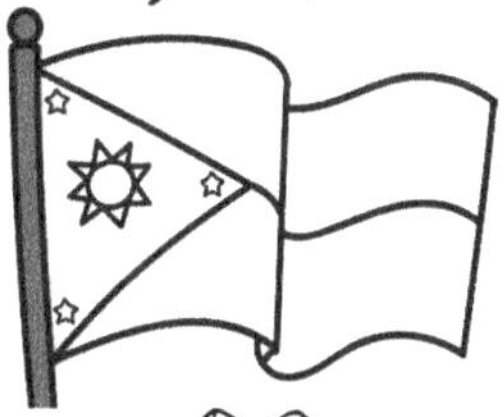

flag

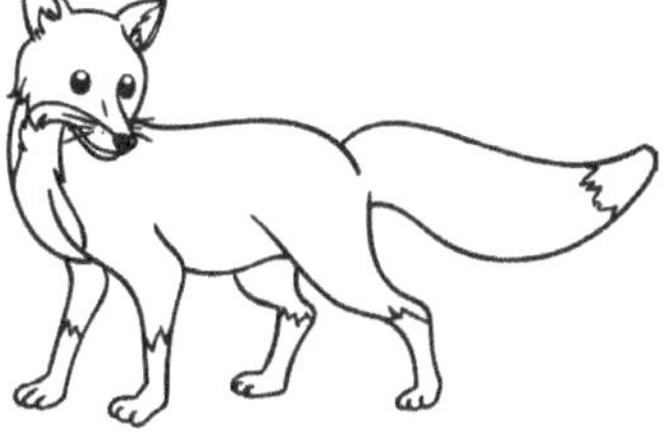

fox

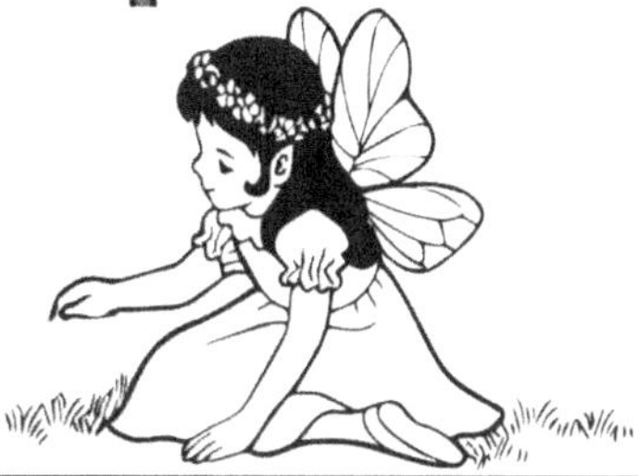

fairy

Practice writing the letter **Ff**.

Ff

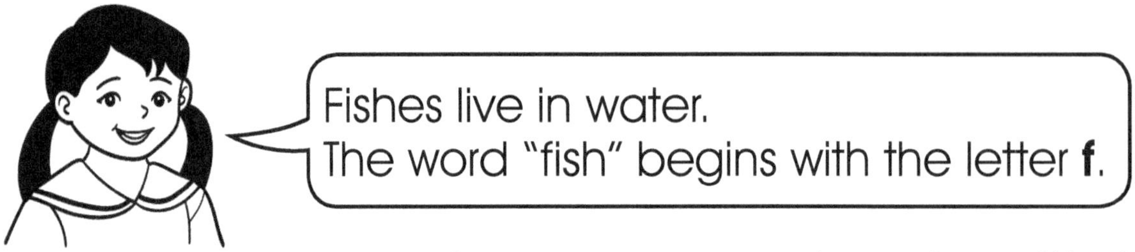

Check the pictures whose names begin with the letter **Ff.**

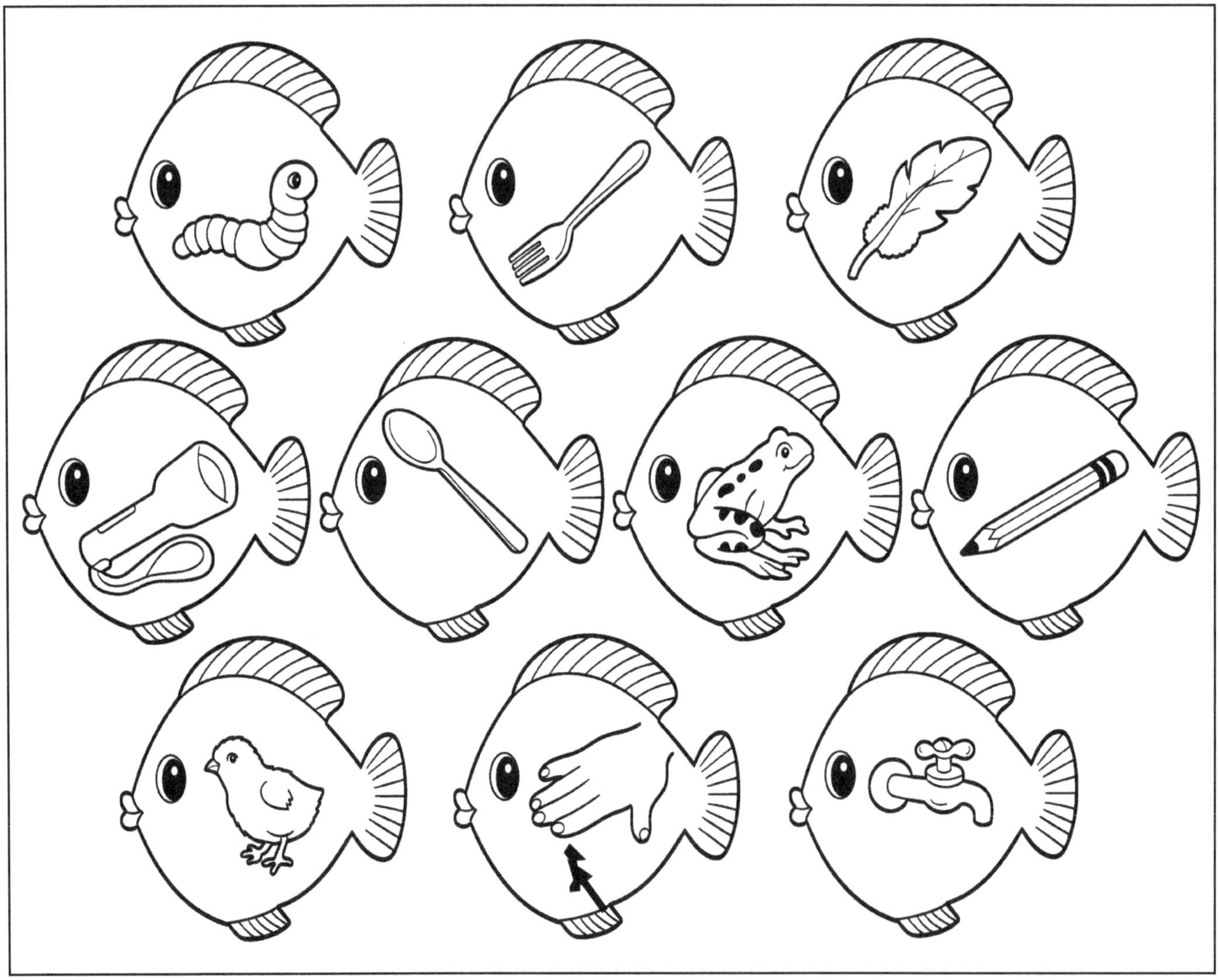

Box the letter **Ff**'s.

P	B	f	F	f	L	b
F	f	t	E	F	f	F

GAMES and ACTIVITIES

Game/Activity	Learning Areas
Feeling Game Have the children close their eyes one at a time and give them an object to feel. See if they can identify the object by only feeling it. (Suggestions: a small rubber ball, a large crayon, an orange or an apple, a small rock, a bitter gourd, a ruler, or a small piece of wood.) Count how many objects each child is able to identify.	* Language * Science * Mathematics
Individual Footprint Puzzles Have the children take off one shoe. Then, have them stand on a piece of folder or cartolina. Draw around their foot with a pencil. Cut out the foot shapes and write the child's name on the back of the shape, at the top and at the bottom. On the toe part of the foot, write an uppercase **F**; on the heel part, write a lowercase **f**. Then cut out each footprint in half with a different puzzle cut across the middle of the foot. Let the children put their foot shape back together. (Variation: You could take all the feet puzzles and mix them up. Have the children make name matches by looking at the back of the feet puzzles.)	* Physical Education and Health, Music, and Arts * Language * Science * Values Education and Social Studies
Movement Time Have the children pretend to: - fly like fairies - float like a feather - be fishing - fall like a falling leaf - fight fires - hop like a frog	* Language * Physical Education and Health, Music, and Arts, * Science * Language
Snack Ideas - fruit bars - fruit juice - fruit cups - french fries - finger foods - fish sticks/fishballs (Have the children count french fries and fish sticks.)	* Physical Education and Health, Music, and Arts * Language * Mathematics * Science * Values Education and Social Studies

Gg
/g/

Guide: Add some **G** items to your housekeeping or dramatic play area such as globes, guitar, glasses, garbage can, guava, garden gloves, etc. Have the children identify the objects whose names begin with the letter **G**.

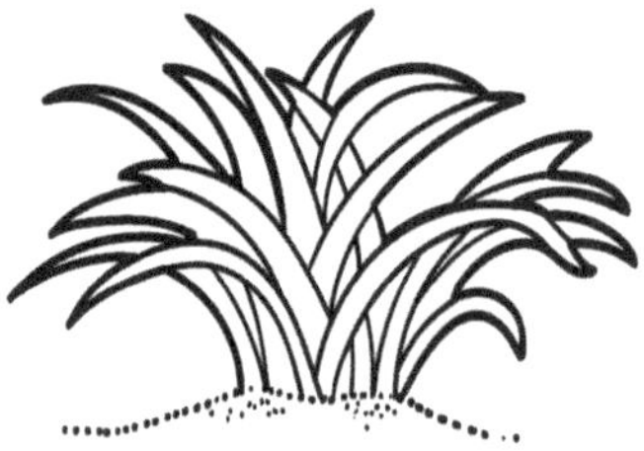

grass

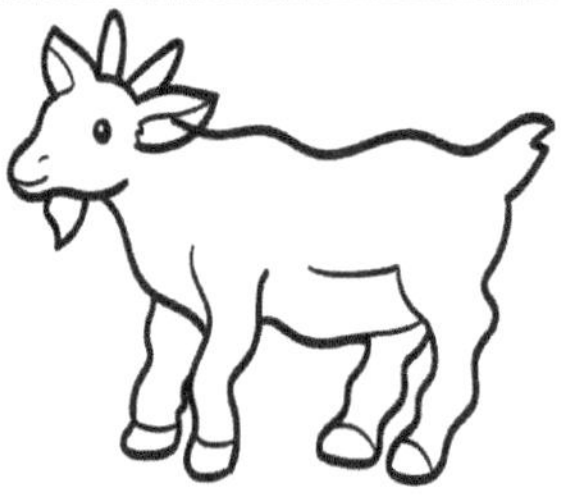

goat

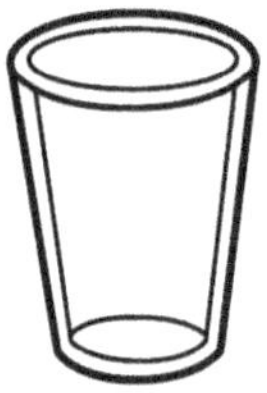

glass

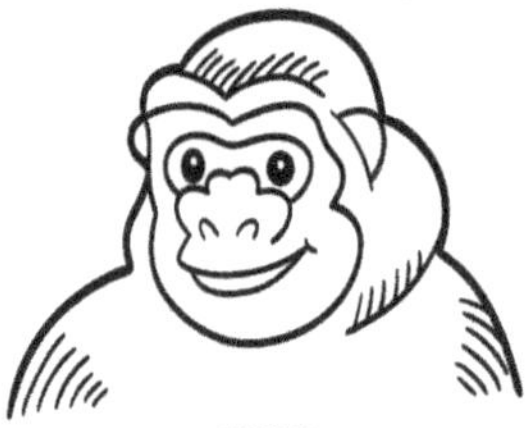

gorilla

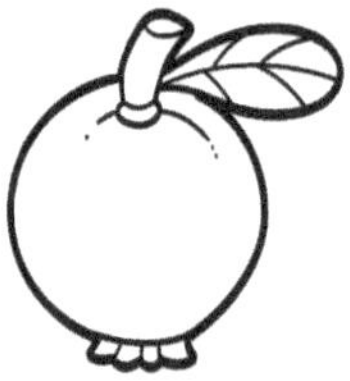

guava

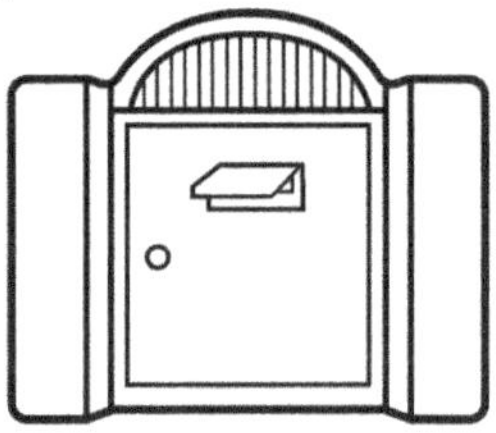

gate

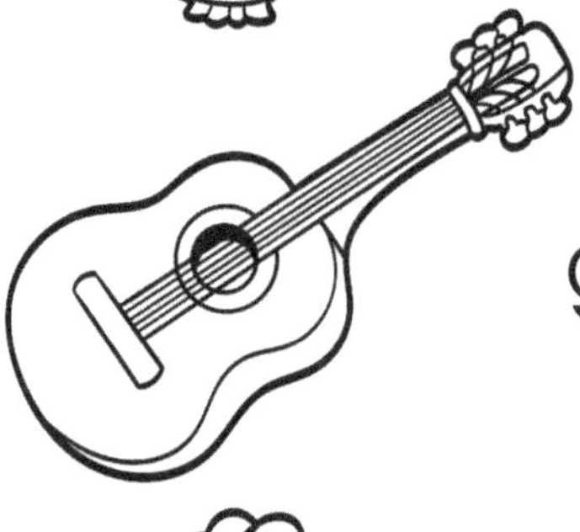

guitar

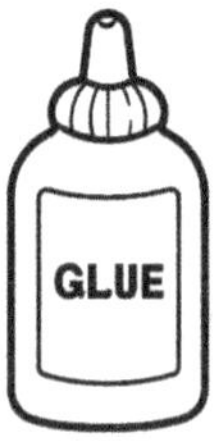

glue

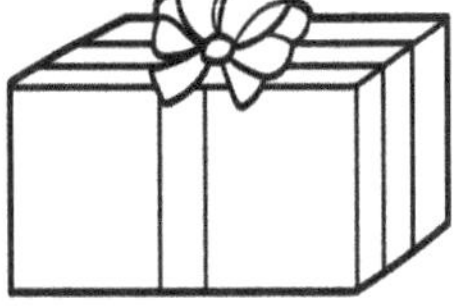

gift

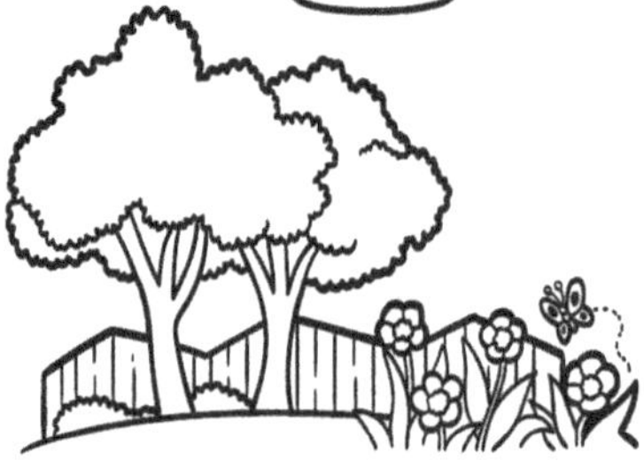

garden

Practice writing the letter **Gg**.

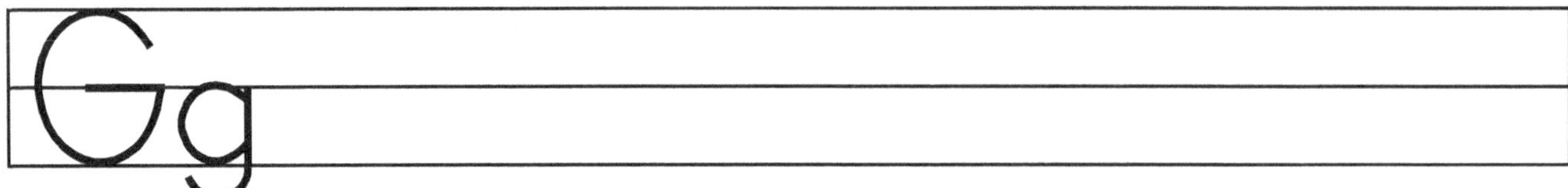

ACTIVITY 6 SCORE: ______

We have a globe at home.
The word "globe" starts with the letter **g**.

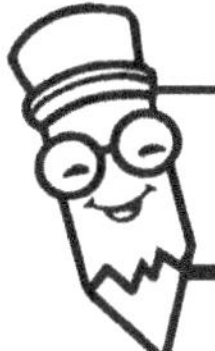

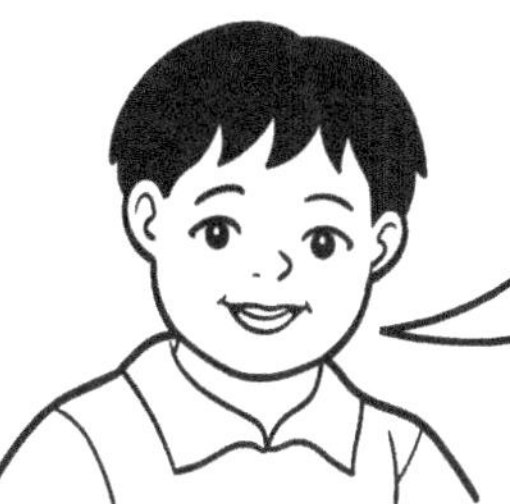

Box the pictures whose names begin with **Gg**.

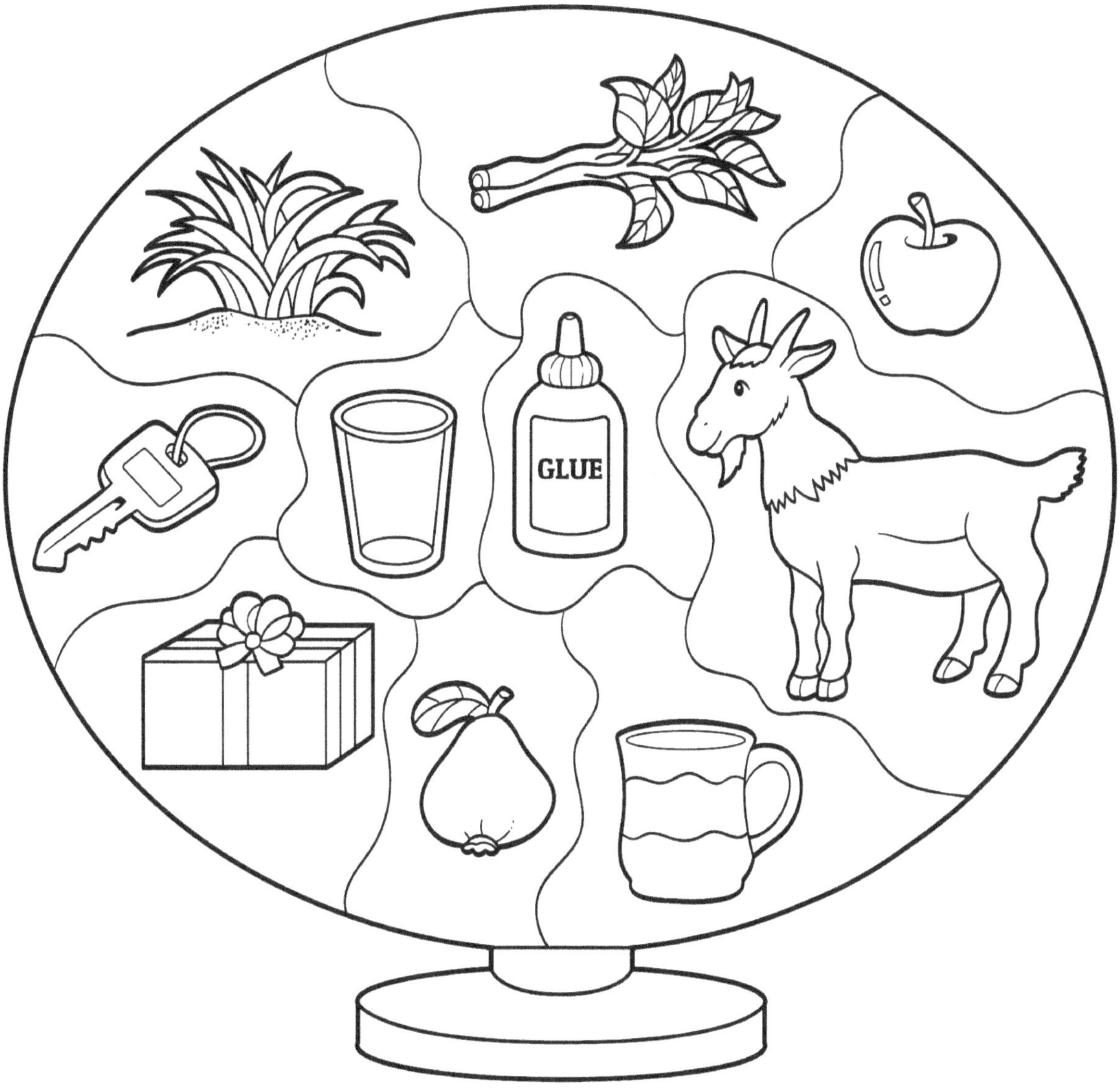

Draw a star on the letter **Gg**'s.

g	q	d	G	d	G	C
g	G	O	b	G	g	g

Little Pretty Mary

Where, oh, where is little pretty Mary? (3x)
Up in the guava tree.
Picking some guavas, putting in the basket (3x)
From up in the guava tree.

Match the small letters with their capital letters by connecting them with lines.

f •	• D	C •		• U
g •	• G	u •		• E
a •	• F	i •		• C
d •	• A	e •		• O
b •	• B	o •		• I

HOME ACTIVITY 1   SCORE:______

Shade the box beside the correct beginning sound for each picture.

 ☐ g ☐ f	 ☐ g ☐ f
 ☐ f ☐ g	 ☐ g ☐ f
 ☐ f ☐ g	 ☐ g ☐ f
 ☐ f ☐ g	 ☐ f ☐ g
 ☐ g ☐ f	 ☐ g ☐ f

Connect the pictures to the initial letters of their names.

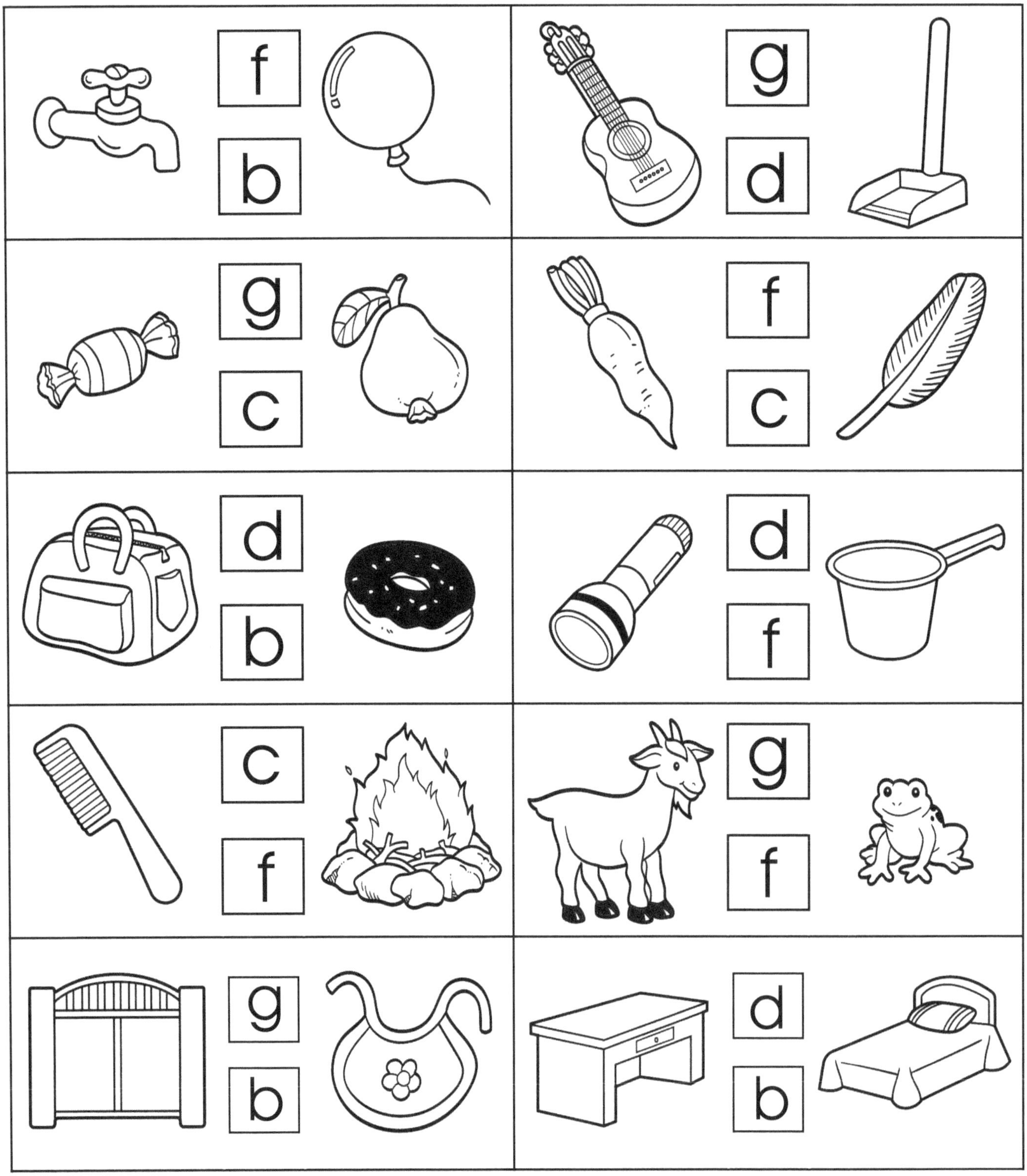

A. Check the letter that your teacher will tell you.

1.	b	f	d	c	g
2.	c	g	f	d	b
3.	b	f	g	c	d
4.	f	b	d	c	g
5.	c	d	g	f	b

B. Encircle the letter that your teacher will sound out.

1.	b	d	c	f	g
2.	g	d	f	c	b
3.	d	g	c	b	f
4.	d	b	g	f	c
5.	b	c	d	g	f

LESSON 6

Hh
/h/

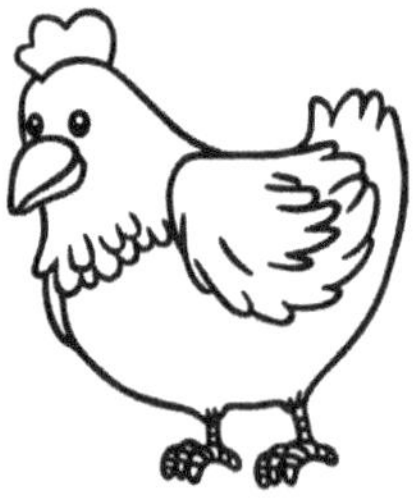

hen

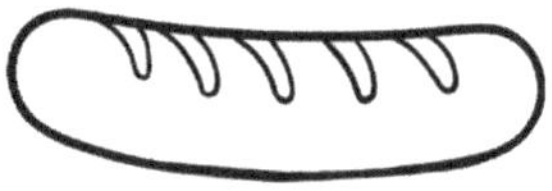

hotdog

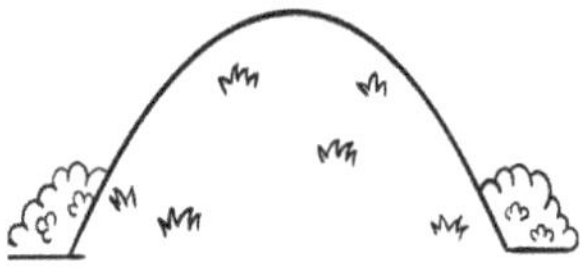

hill

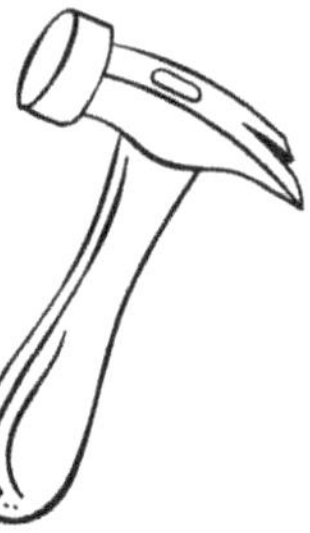

hammer

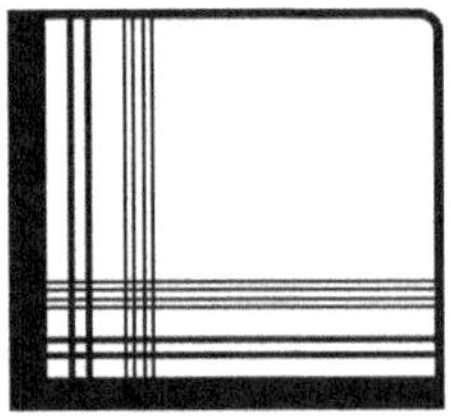

handkerchief

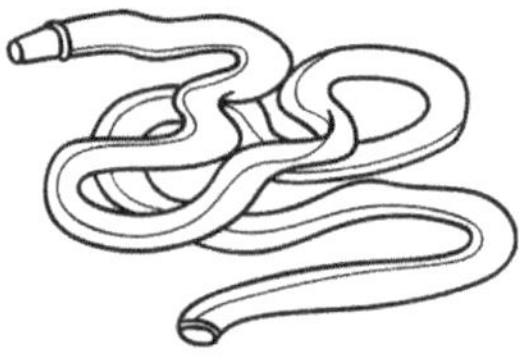

hose

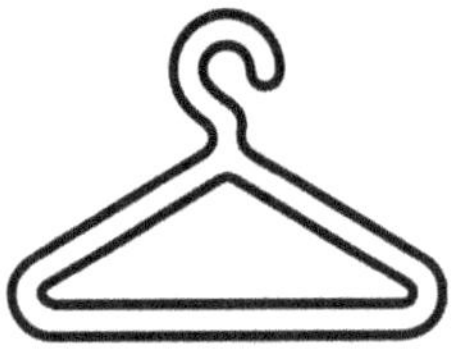

hanger

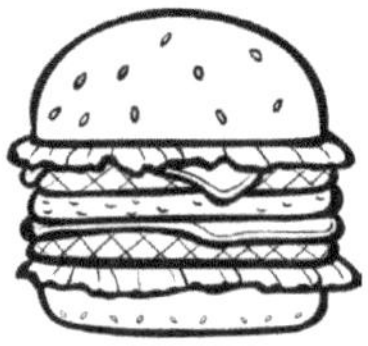

hamburger

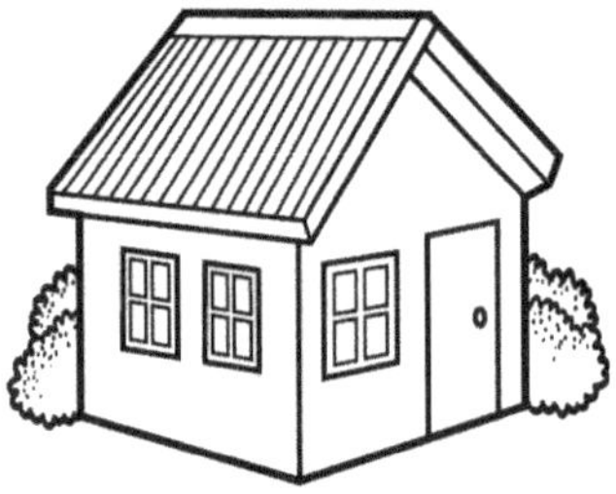

house

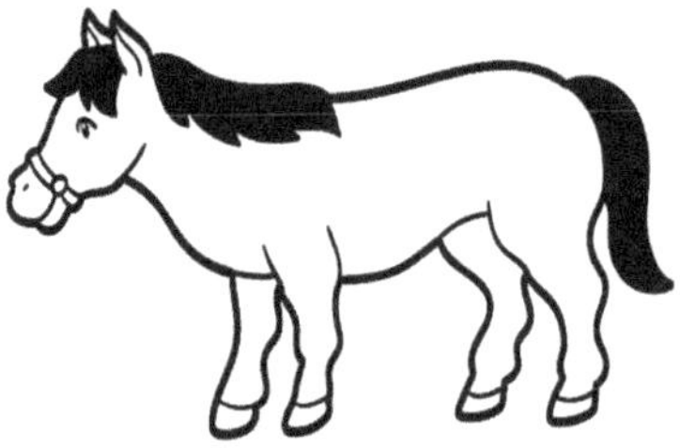

horse

Practice writing the letter **Hh**.

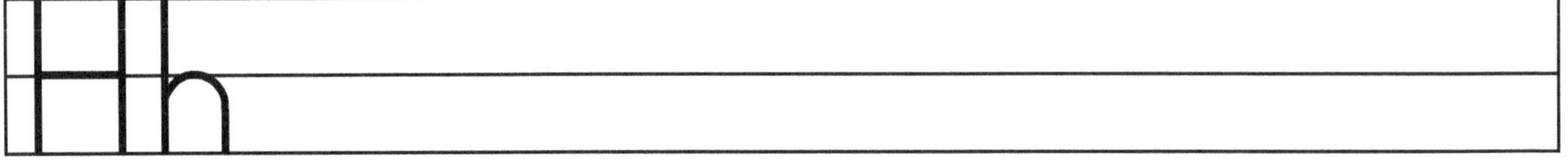

ACTIVITY 8

SCORE:_______

Check the pictures whose names begin with **Hh**.

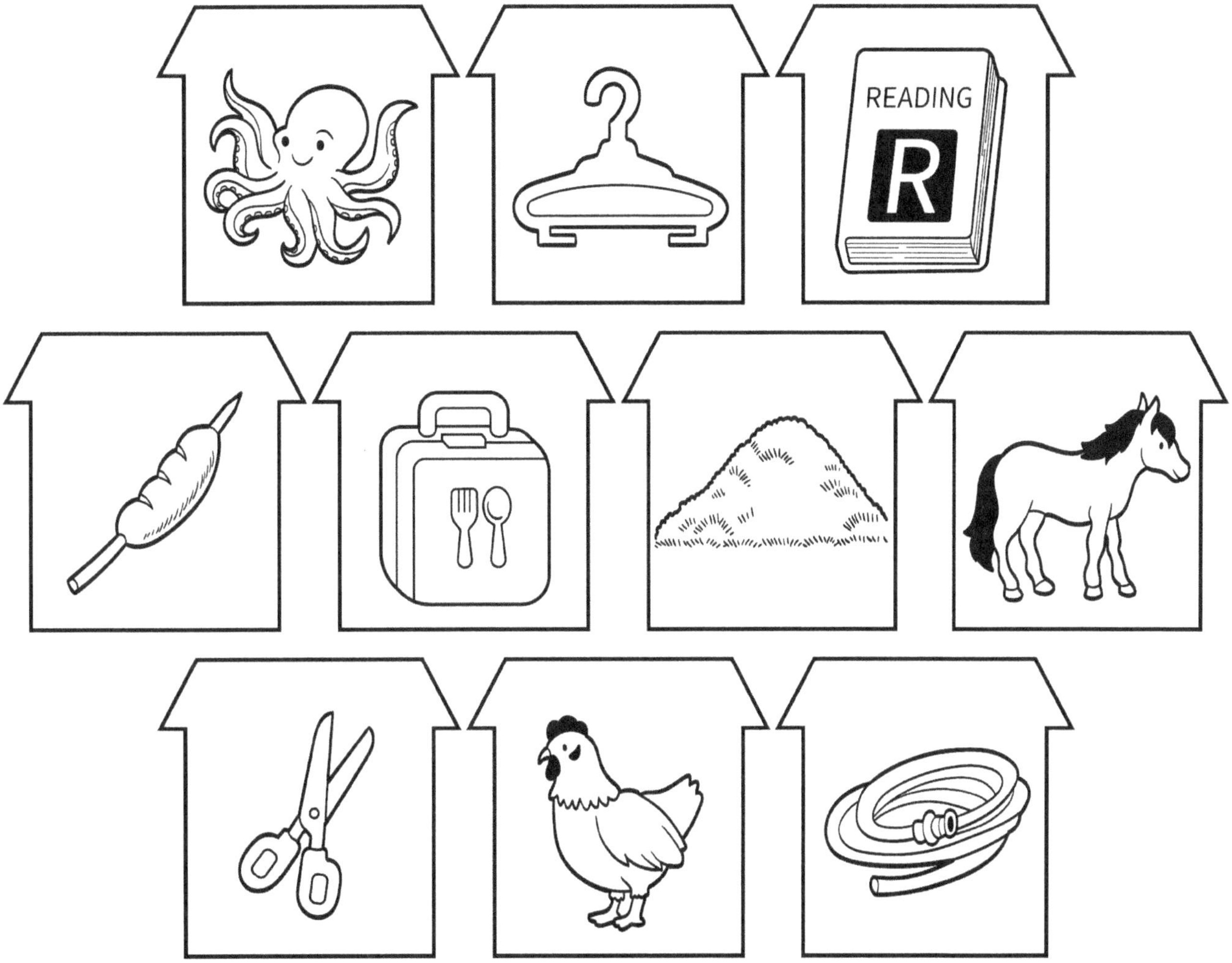

Encircle the letter **Hh**'s.

h   T   h   F   H   L   H

h   H   E   H   d   h   b

ACTIVITY 9

SCORE: _______

Match the pictures with the beginning letters of their names by connecting them with lines.

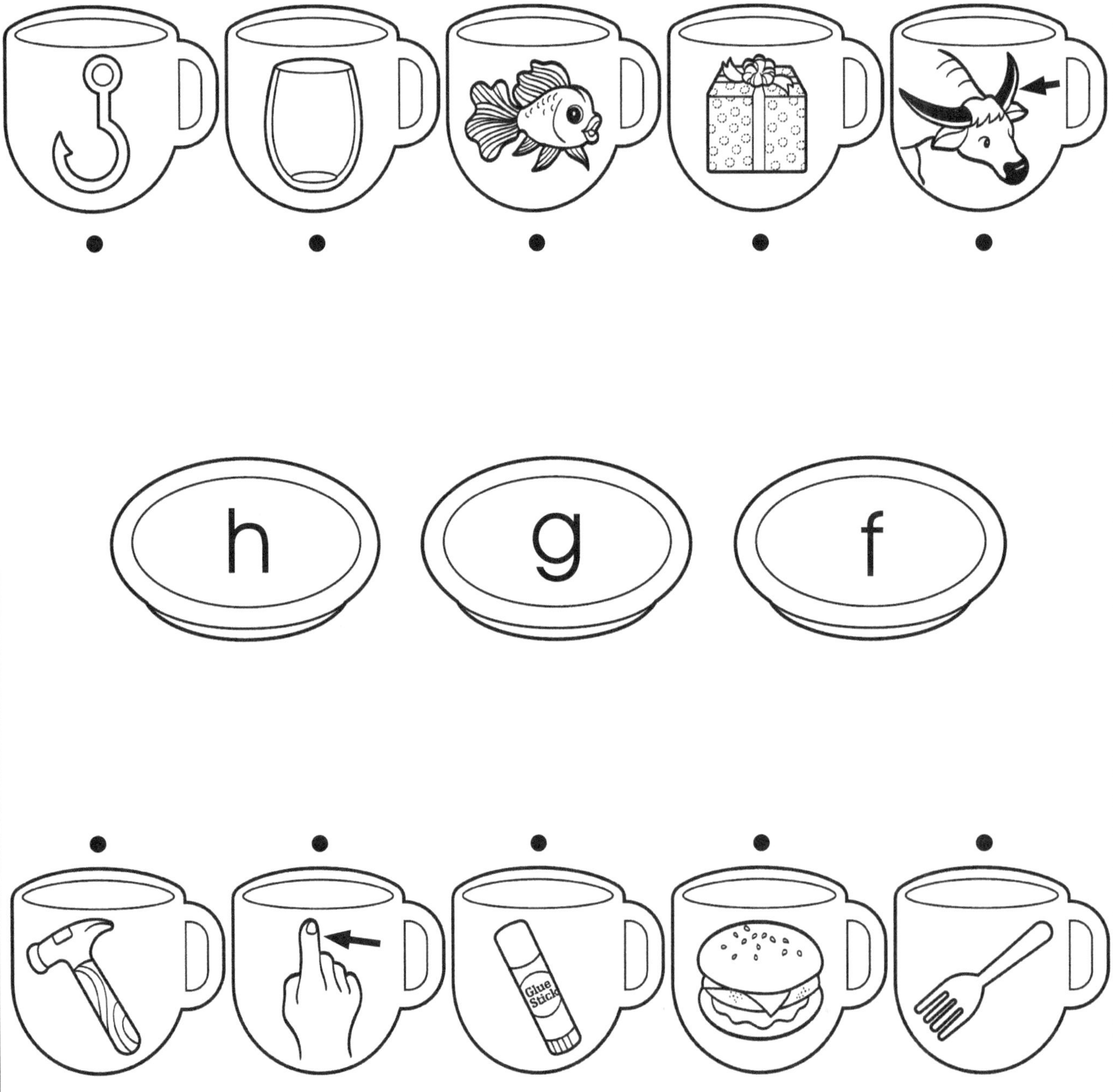

HOME ACTIVITY 2   SCORE:_______

Match the pictures with the beginning letters of their names by connecting them with lines.

Jj
/dʒ/

Guide: Set out some identical glass jars on a plastic dish pan. Have the children experiment by pouring different amounts of water into each jar. Then have them lightly tap each jar with a spoon. Observe and ask what they notice. (Guide questions: Do they notice anything different about the sounds the jars make? Why do they sound different? How can they make them sound the same?) After this activity, discuss other things whose names begin with the letter **J**.

jet

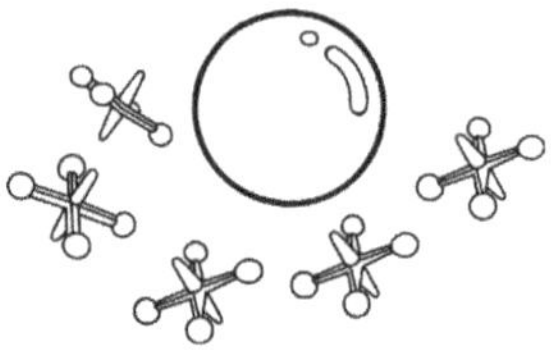

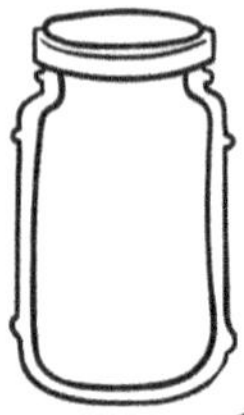

jar

juice

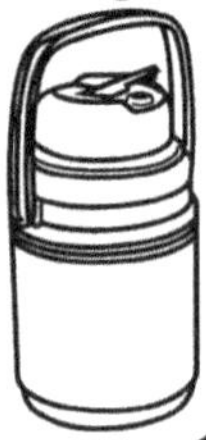

jacket

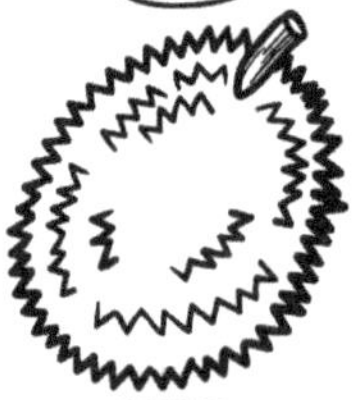

jeep

jackstones

jellyfish

jug

jackfruit

jam

Practice writing the letter **Jj**.

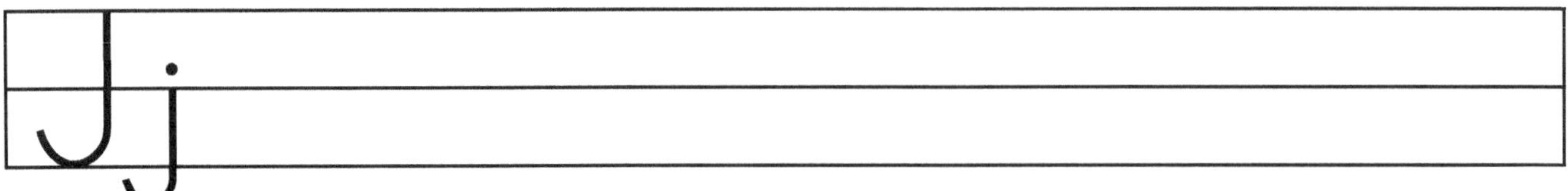

ACTIVITY 10 SCORE: ______

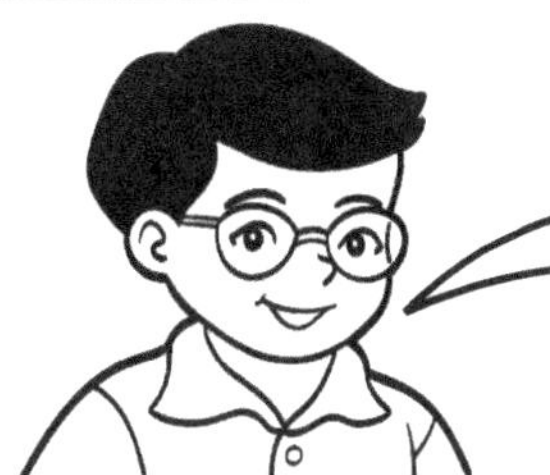

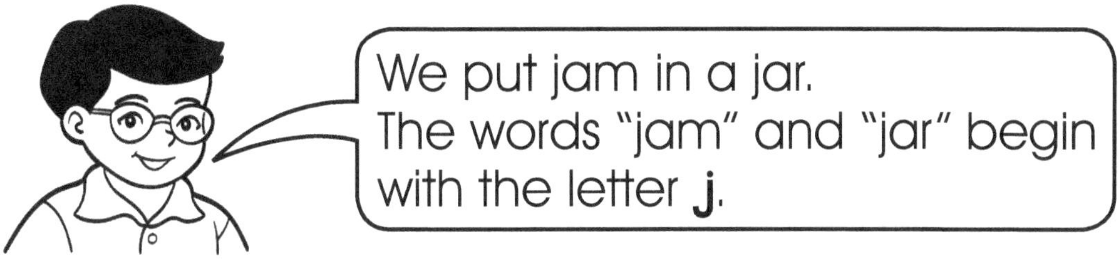

Underline the pictures whose names begin with **Jj**.

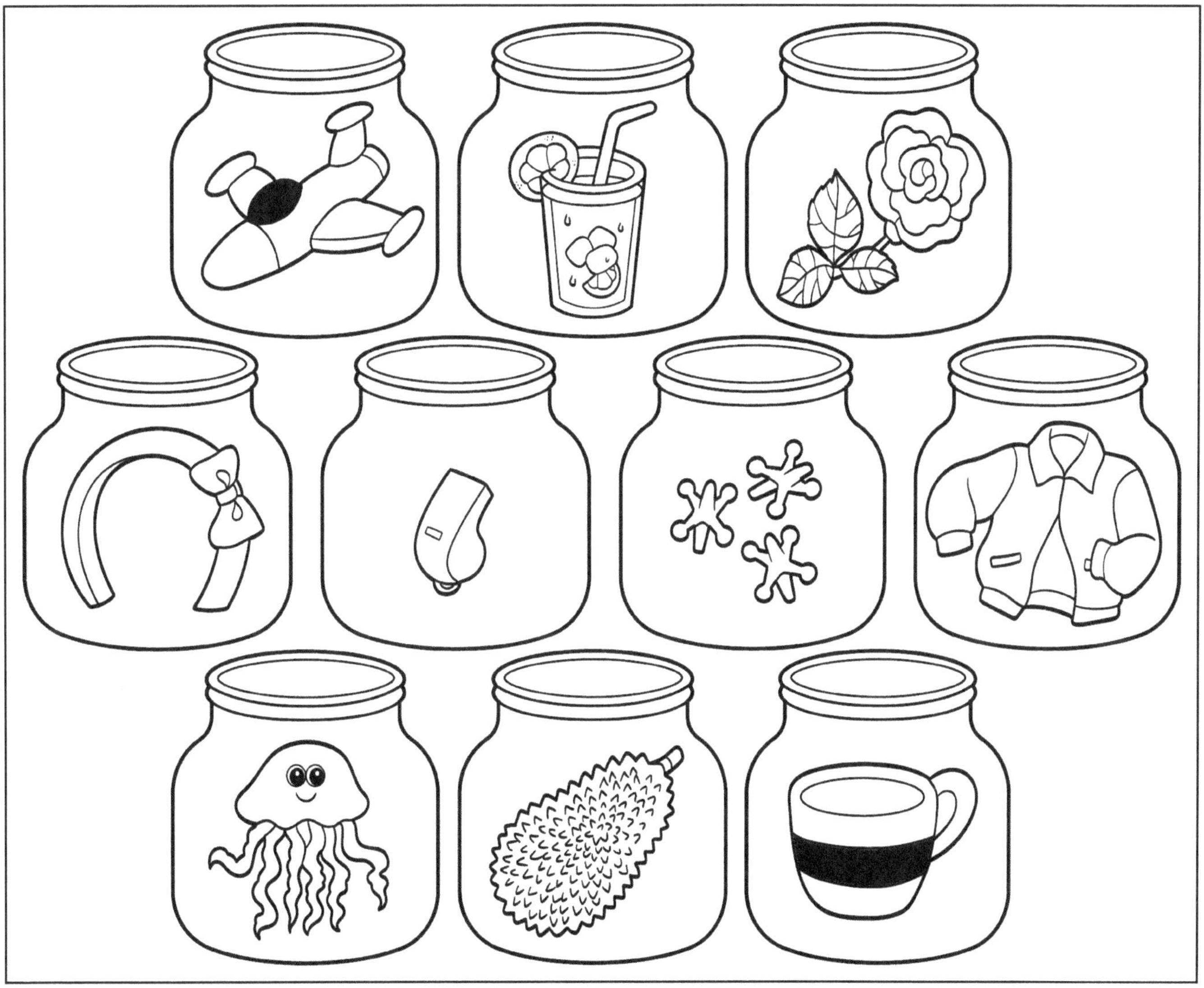

Check the letter **Jj**'s.

g	j	J	D	J	j	g
J	j	P	L	J	j	i

ACTIVITY 11 SCORE:_______

Cross out the word in each group that does not begin with **Jj**.

jackstones	jail	jet	blackboard	jackfruit
jellyfish	jaguar	jar	jeep	quail
goose	jewel	juice	jump	jungle
jug	yarn	pocket	jam	jacket

ACTIVITY 12 SCORE:_______

Encircle the picture in each group whose name does not begin with the letter at the top.

h	d	f	g	j

Compare the sounds of **b**, **d**, **g**, and **j**. Box the correct beginning sound for each picture.

b d g j	g d b j	j g d b
d g j b	b j d g	j d g b
b d j g	j g d b	d b j g
g j d b	b d g j	j b d g
g d b j	d b j g	g j b d

Kk
/k/

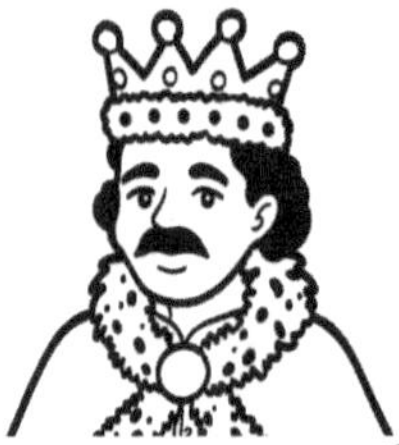

king

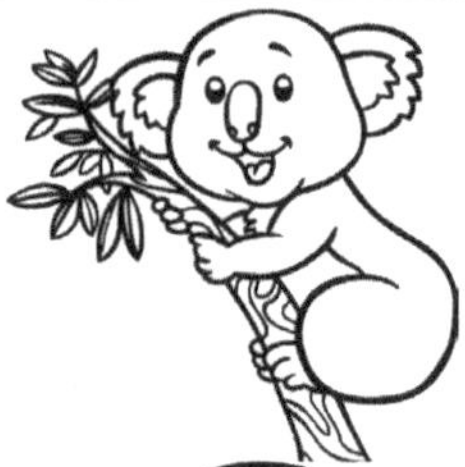

koala

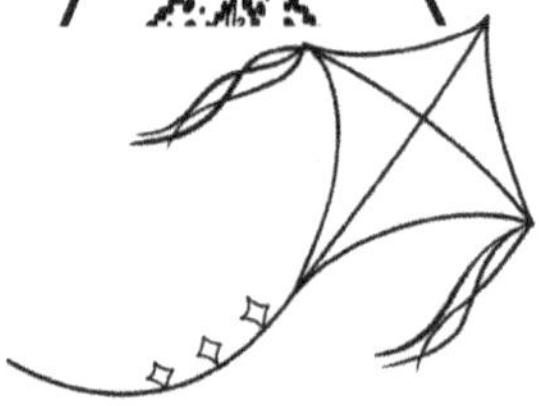

kite

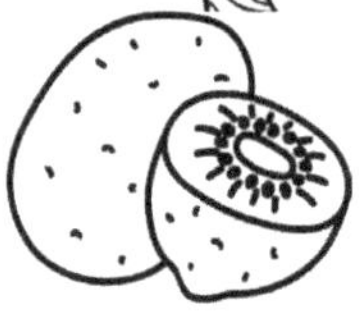

kiwi

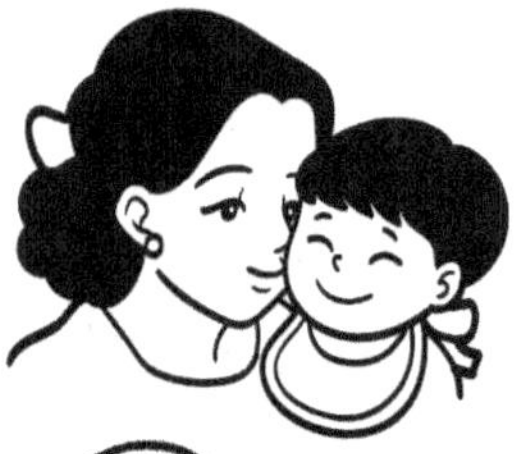

kiss

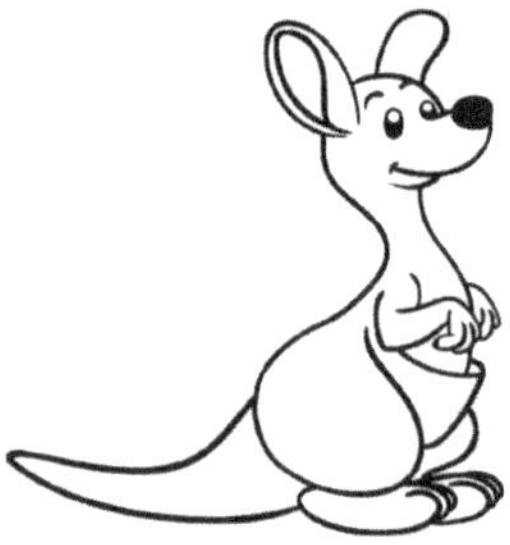

kangaroo

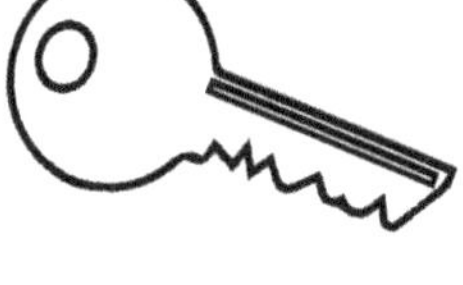

key

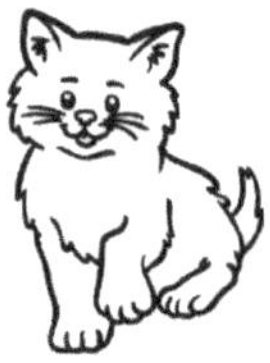

kitten

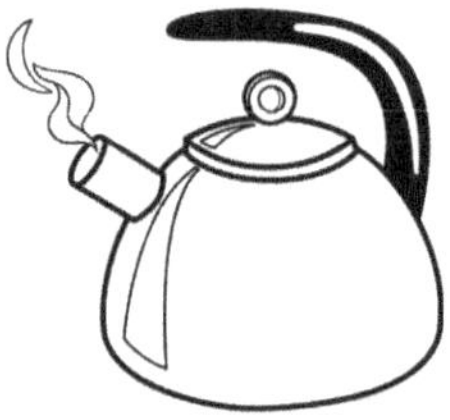

kettle

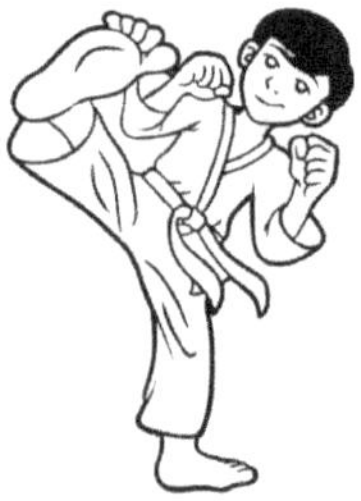

kick

Practice writing the letter **Kk**.

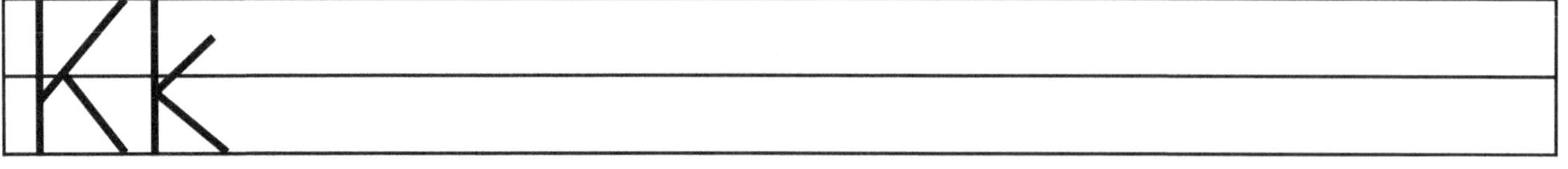

ACTIVITY 14 SCORE: ______

My father and I love to fly kite together.
The word "kite" begins with the letter **k**.

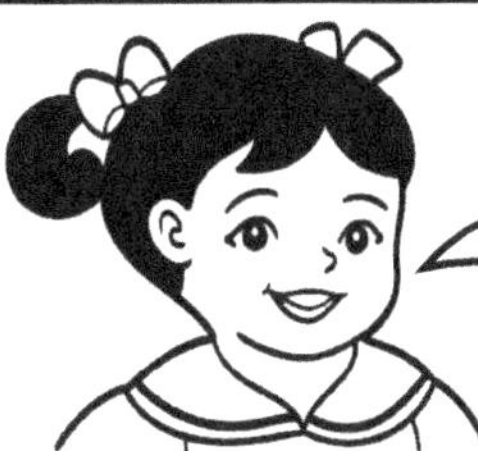

Encircle the pictures whose names begin with **Kk**.

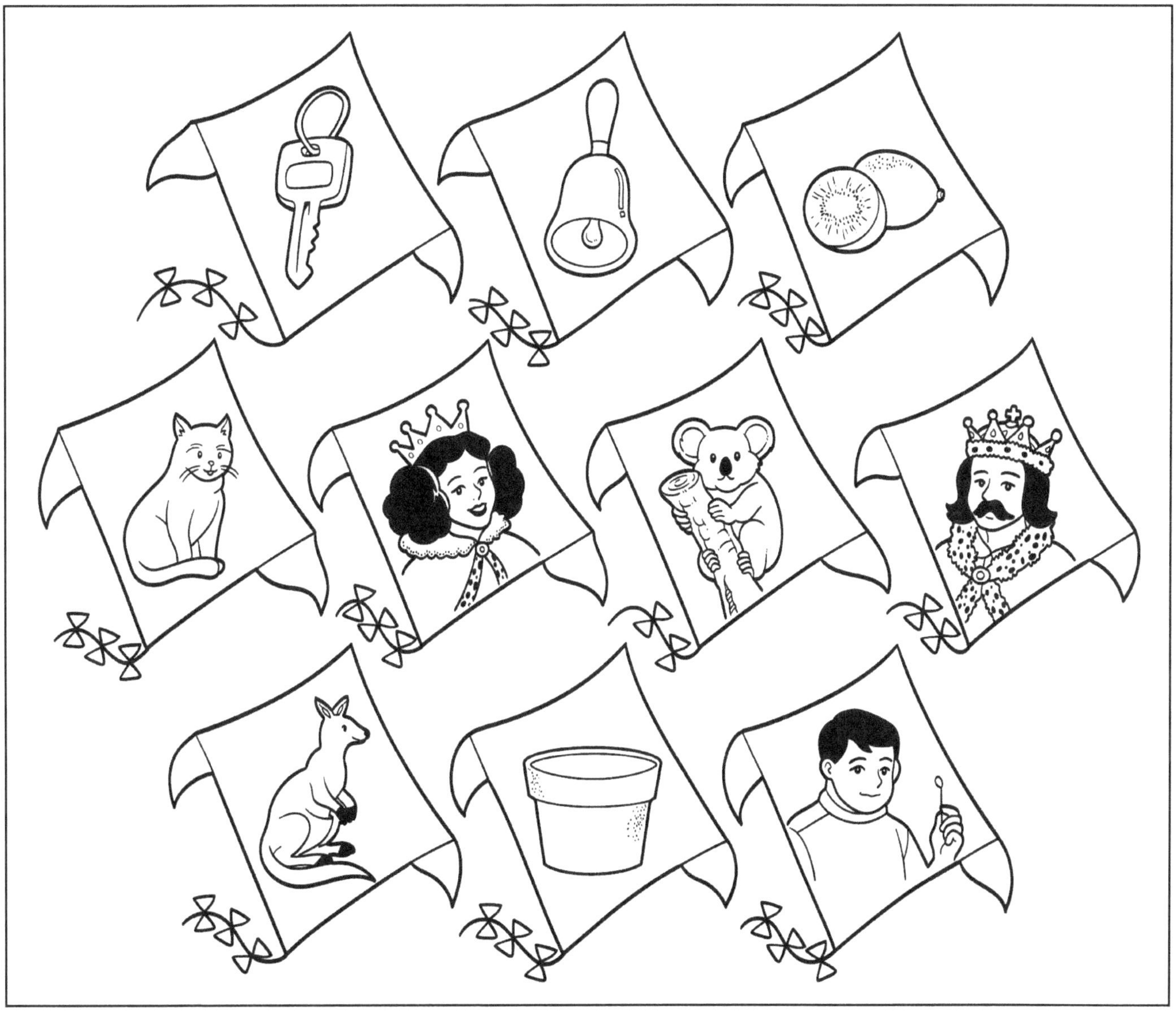

Underline the letter **Kk**'s.

t	k	f	K	h	K	k
K	B	k	R	k	b	K

Encircle and then write on the blank the correct letter that completes the name of each picture.

1.  j   k   h   __ iss

2.  k   j   h   __ uice

3.  h   k   j   __ eep

4.  h   j   k   __ ammer

5.  j   h   k   __ ite

6.  k   h   j   __ ouse

7.  j   k   h   __ ettle

8.  h   k   j   __ ey

9.  k   h   j   __ otdog

10.  j   k   h   __ et

GAMES and ACTIVITIES

Game/Activity	Learning Areas
Kicking Contest Go outside with the children. Let each child have a turn kicking a ball. Then place a marker where each ball lands. Give a king's crown to the child whose ball went the farthest.	* Physical Education and Health, Music, and Arts * Values Education and Social Studies * Mathematics
K **Movement** - Have the children pretend they are karate kids. - Have them hop and kick like kangaroos. - Have them kick different balls.	* Physical Education and Health, Music, and Arts * Language * Science * Values Education and Social Studies
Crowns for Kings Prepare pieces of construction paper and cut a zigzag through the middle of the paper lengthwise. Tape the two strips together. Let the children decorate their king's crowns by gluing on triangular shapes of glossy paper (to represent jewels). When done, wrap the crowns around their heads and tape them to fit. Let a child be the king for a day and wear his or her crown.	* Physical Education and Health, Music, and Arts * Values Education and Social Studies * Language
Flying Kites Make kites with the children. Go out and fly kites with them. Have fun!	* Physical Education and Health, Music, and Arts * Values Education and Social Studies
K **Snacks** - kiwi - kidney beans - kettle corn	* Language * Science * Mathematics
K **Sounds** Play a game with the children by having them search for words in magazines and papers that start with the letter *K*. Have the children underline/encircle the words.	* Language * Mathematics

LESSON 9

Ll

///

> **Guide**: Go out to the nearest park or neighborhood garden and pick leaves from different kinds of plants. (Ask permission from the park or garden keeper.) Put these leaves in a box and have the children group the leaves according to their kind. You may also have them group the leaves according to color, size, and shape. Counting the leaves is another fun activity! Discuss other things whose names begin with the letter *L*.

leaf

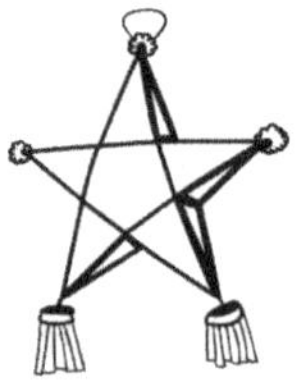

lantern

lollipop

lion

lock

lamp

lizard

lemon

line

ladybug

Practice writing the letter **Ll**.

ACTIVITY 15 SCORE: ______

My mother and I love to collect different kinds of leaves.
The word "leaf" begins with the letter l.

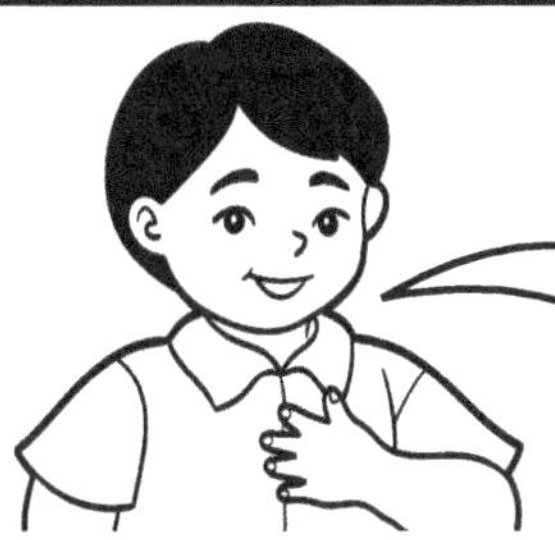

Draw a star (☆) on the pictures whose names begin with **Ll**.

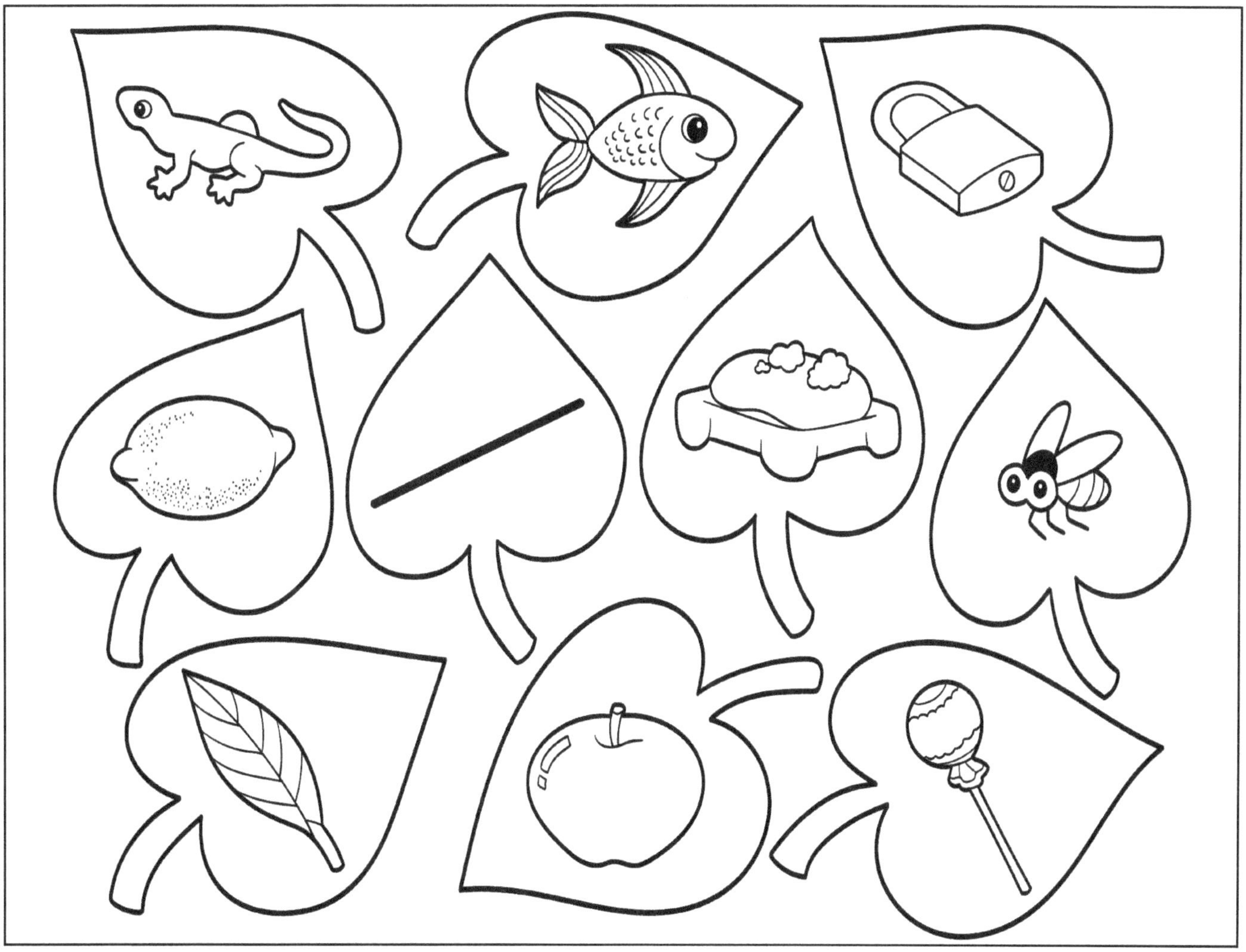

Box the letter **Ll**'s.

F l T L l i L

l f L l t L I

ACTIVITY 16

SCORE:_______

Match the pictures to their correct initial sounds.

c

h

l

j

k

 **LESSON 10**

Mm
/m/

Guide: Celebrate the letter **M** with masks. Cut paper plates in half. Cut out eye and nose half-circles along the straight edge. Have the children decorate their masks with marking pens, glitters, colored paper scraps, etc. Lead the children to look at themselves in the mirror. Discuss other things whose names begin with the letter **M**.

mask

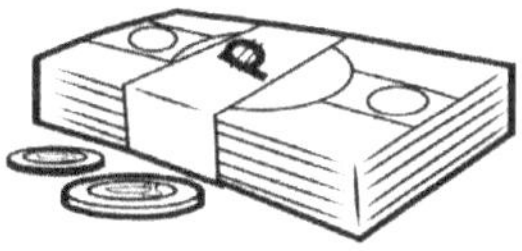

money

match

mountain

monkey

mosquito

mushroom

magnet

mirror

moon

Practice writing the letter **Mm**.

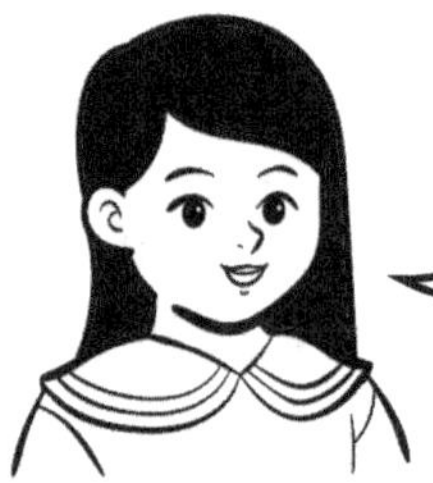

ACTIVITY 17 SCORE:______

My relatives live near the mountains.
The word "mountain" begins
with the letter **m**.

Color the pictures whose names begin with **Mm**.

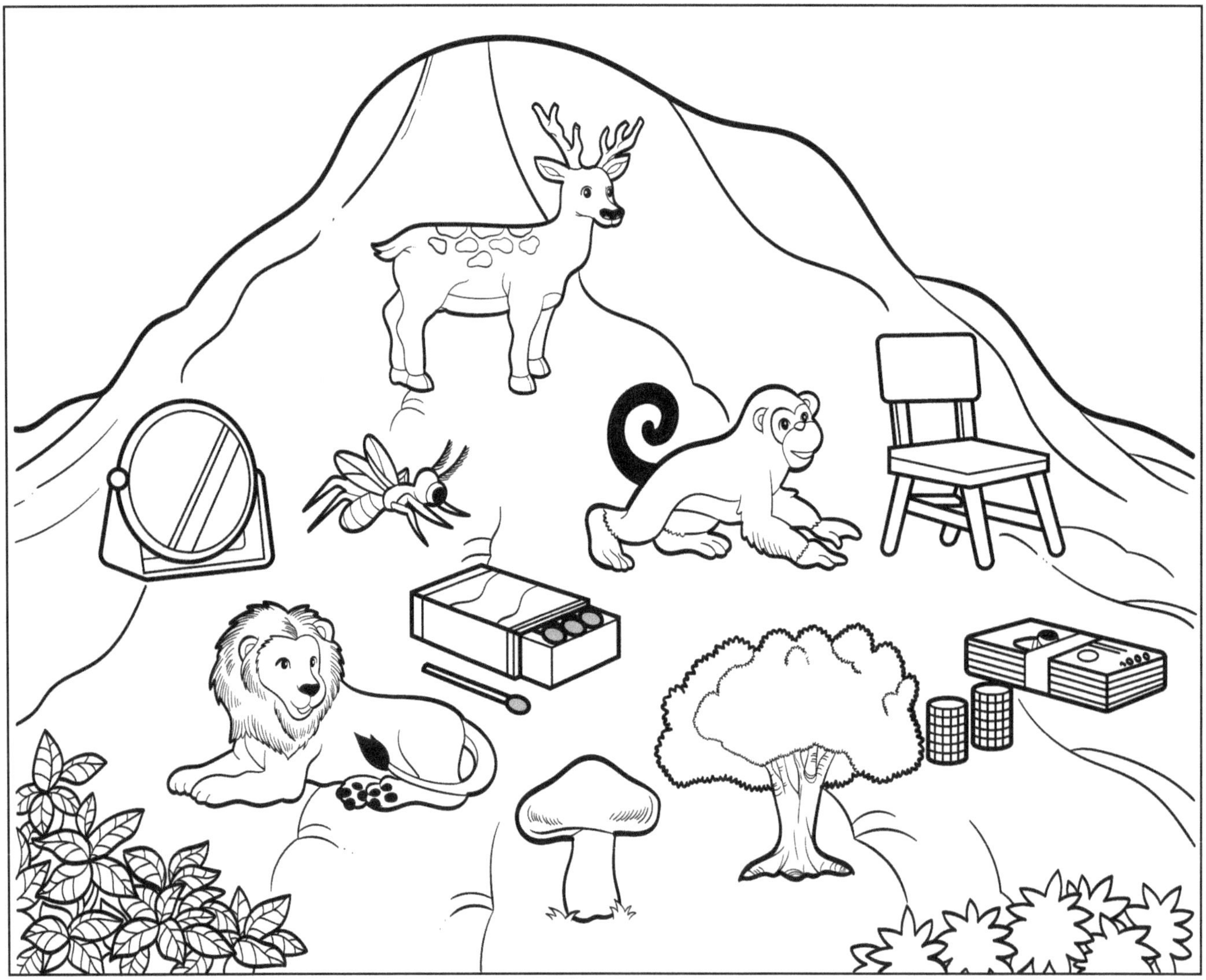

Draw a star on the letter **Mm**'s.

M	w	N	m	u	M	m
P	m	M	W	M	n	m

ACTIVITY 18   SCORE:______

Draw a sun (☼) on the blank beside the correct uppercase letter for each lowercase letter on the left.

i	__L	__T	__I
b	__B	__D	__P
g	__J	__O	__G
k	__F	__R	__K
d	__D	__B	__P
j	__J	__I	__L
h	__B	__H	__P
m	__M	__W	__N
c	__B	__C	__D
f	__E	__L	__F

Write the correct beginning sound of each picture.

1.  ________

2. ________

3.  ________

4.  ________

5.  ________

6.  ________

7.  ________

8.  ________

9.  ________

10.  ________

QUIZ NO. 6   SCORE: _______

Write the small letters of the following:

B ___   L ___   D ___   F ___   J ___

C ___   G ___   M ___   K ___   H ___

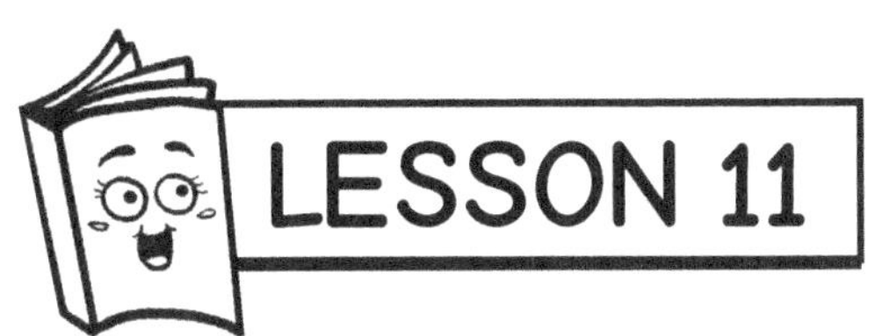

Nn
/n/

<table>
<tr><td>Guide:</td><td>Give the children sheets of newspaper and have them look for the letter N's. Give them colored pens to circle the upper and lower cases of N. Then see how many N names you all can think of such as Nelifel, Nonie, Natasha, Nida, Nilo, etc. Discuss other N objects such as necklace, nest, necktie, nuts, nurse, etc.</td></tr>
</table>

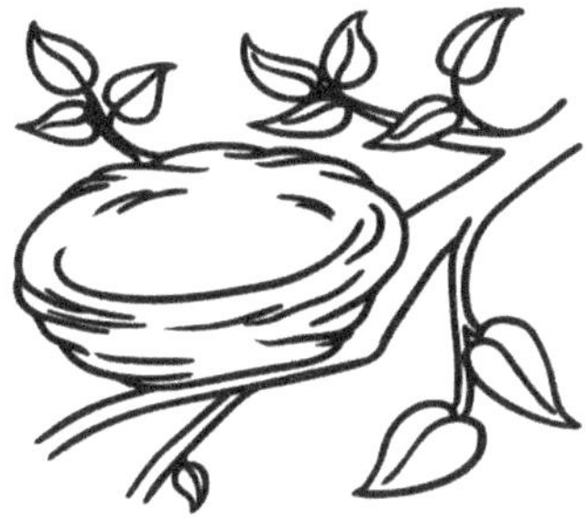

nest

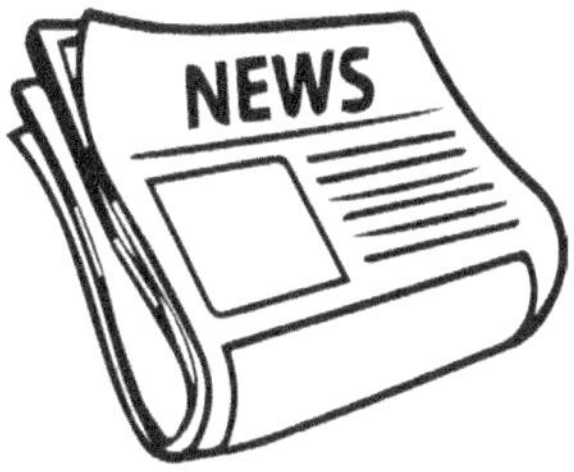

newspaper

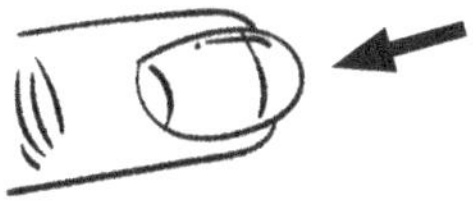

nail

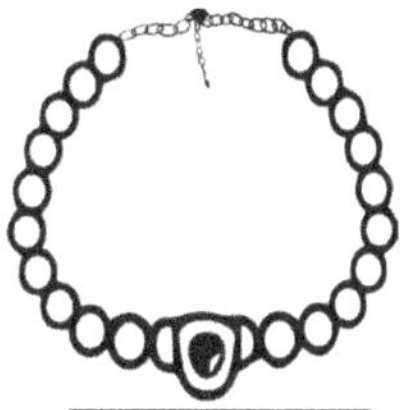

necklace

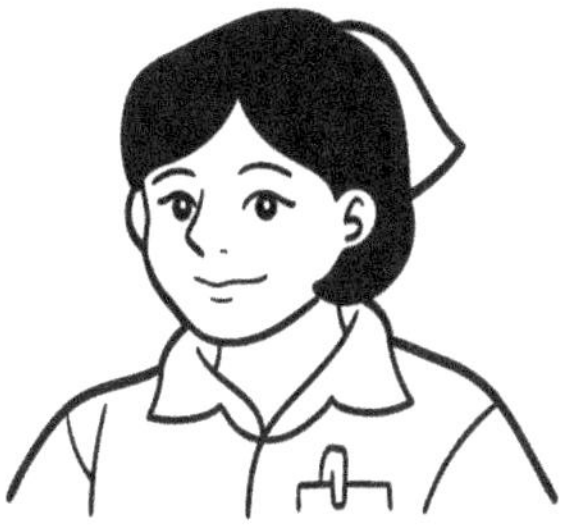

nurse

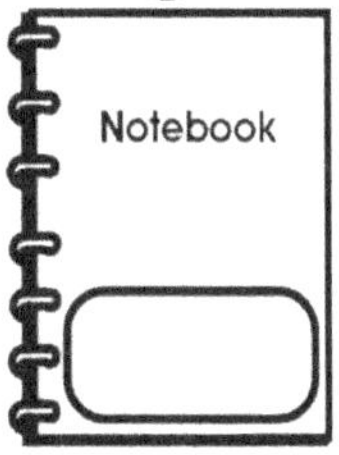

notebook

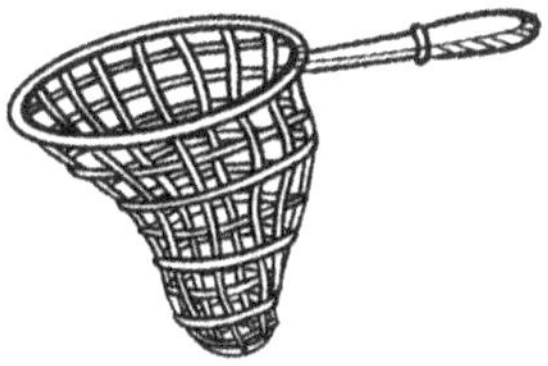

net

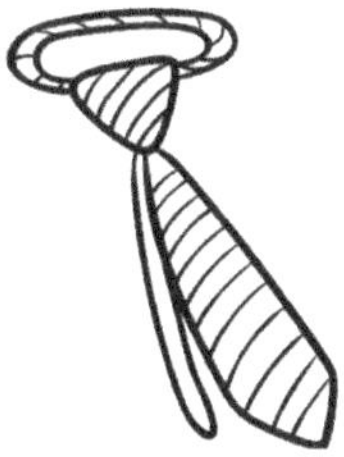

necktie

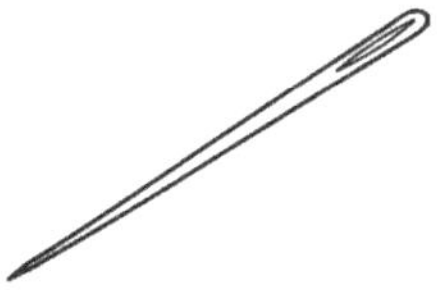

needle

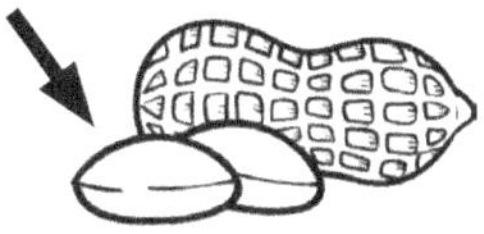

nuts

Practice writing the letter **Nn**.

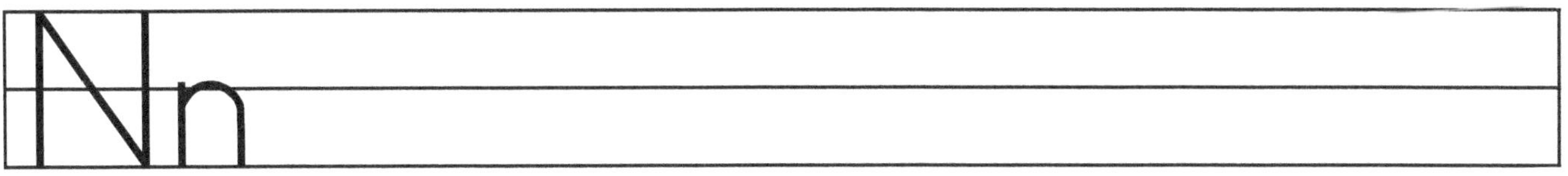

ACTIVITY 19 SCORE: ______

My sister copies lectures on her notebook.
The word "notebook" begins with the letter **n**.

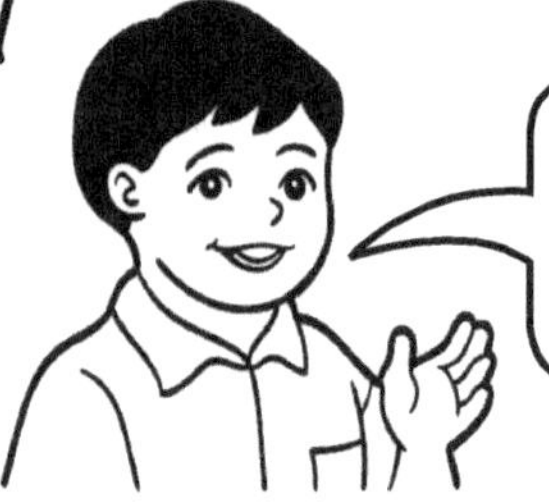

Check the pictures whose names begin with **Nn**.

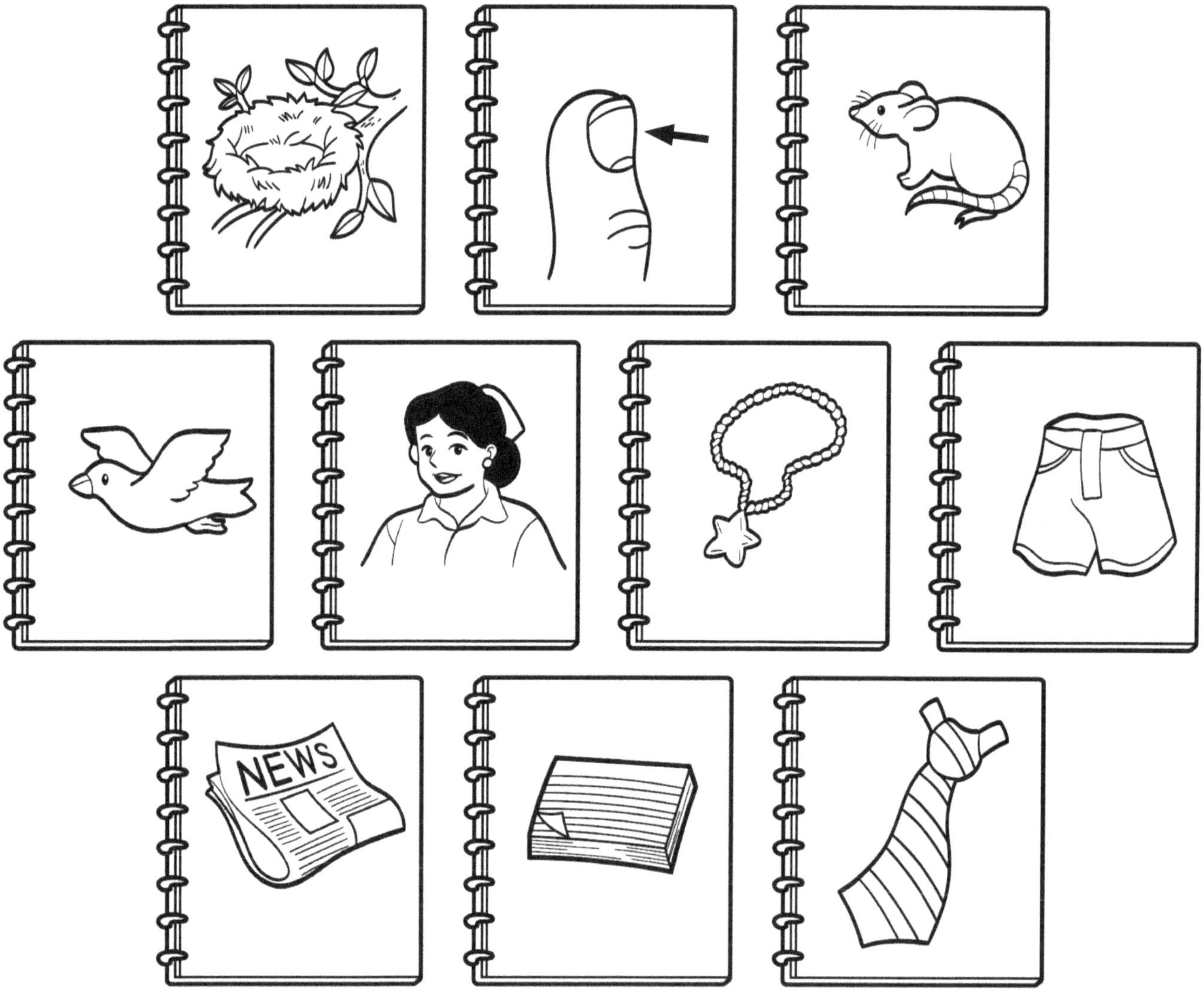

Encircle the letter **Nn**'s.

N m n W a N n

n p N M N u n

ACTIVITY 20

SCORE: _______

Connect each picture to the first letter of its name.

109

Necktie Paper Craft

Materials:

- scissors
- glue
- sheet of cartolina (any color) or gift wrapper
- construction paper
- markers or crayons
- ruler
- buttons (optional)

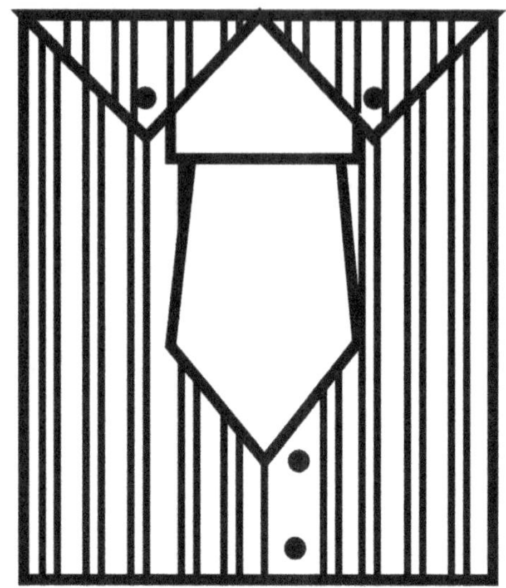

Directions:

1. For the basic part of the shirt, cut out one piece of cartolina five inches wide and eight inches long. Gift-wrapping paper with a design on it also makes a good material for this.

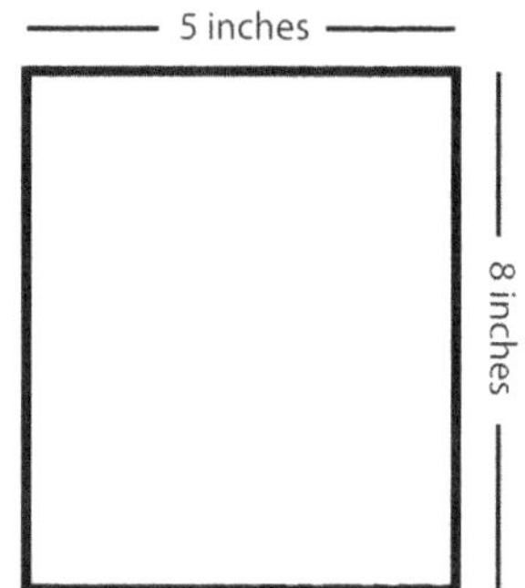

2. Cut two squares that are two inches long by two inches wide from the same paper as the shirt. Fold in half to make triangles. These will be your collar. Open them to be squares again, and glue 1/2 of them to the back of the shirt paper so that when you fold them over, the triangles form a collar.

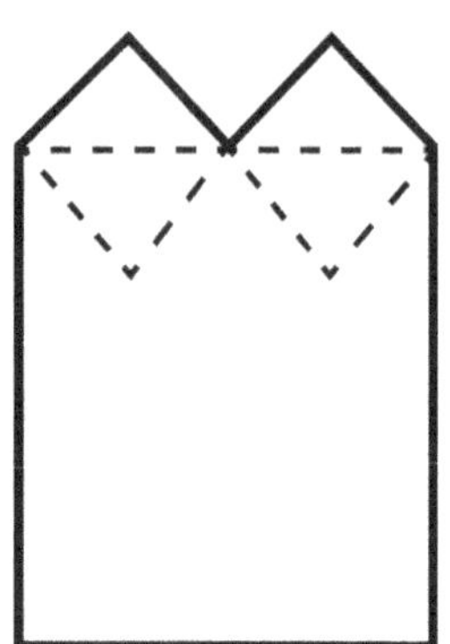

3. Cut a square that is about two inches by two inches out of construction paper. Fold it in half to make a rectangle. This will go under the collar to make the "knot" part of the tie.

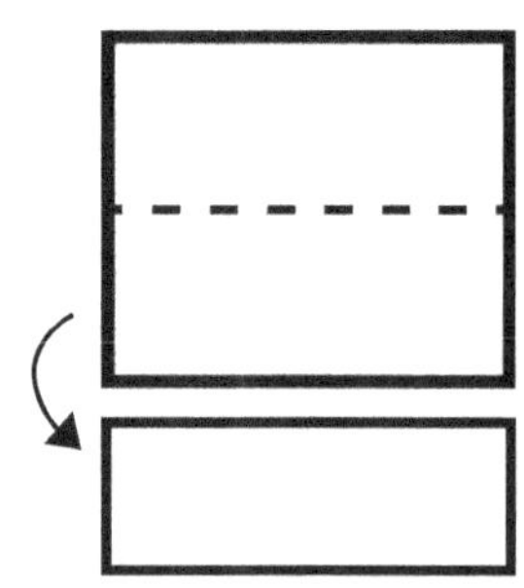

4. Cut a rectangle about seven inches long
   and three inches wide. Fold the bottom
   two corners up to make creases in your tie.
   Mark the top of the rectangle into three (3)
   equal parts (1 inch each) and draw a line
   from those marks to the lower corners
   to make a tie shape. Trim off the sides
   to form an upside-down pentagon.

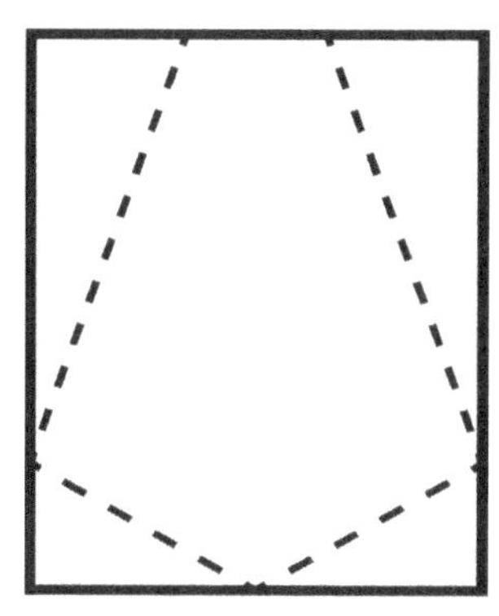

5. Put your "tie" together by sliding
   the hanging part under the knot part
   and gluing it. Position the tie at the top
   of the card. Glue it in place at the "knot."

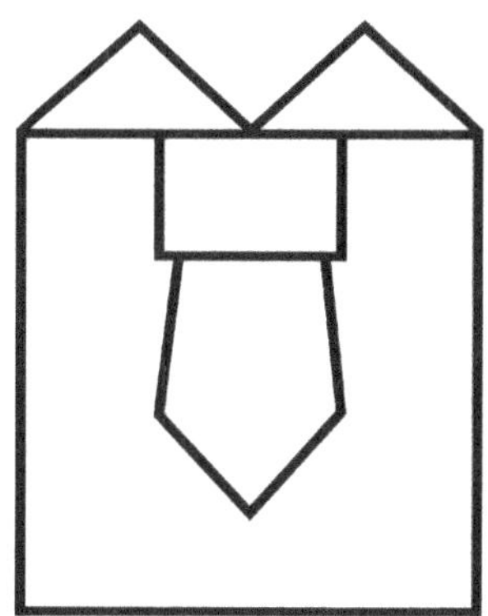

6. Fold the collar down. Now add a line
   of glue under the collar at the very top
   of the card to hold the collar down
   over the tie.

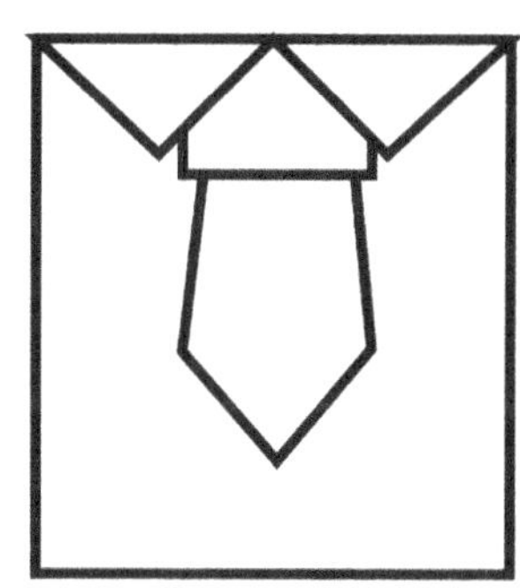

7. Use your markers or crayons to decorate
   the shirt. Lift the tie and draw a straight line
   down the middle for the front of the shirt,
   and add buttons. You can use real buttons,
   or you can use markers or cut out
   from construction paper.

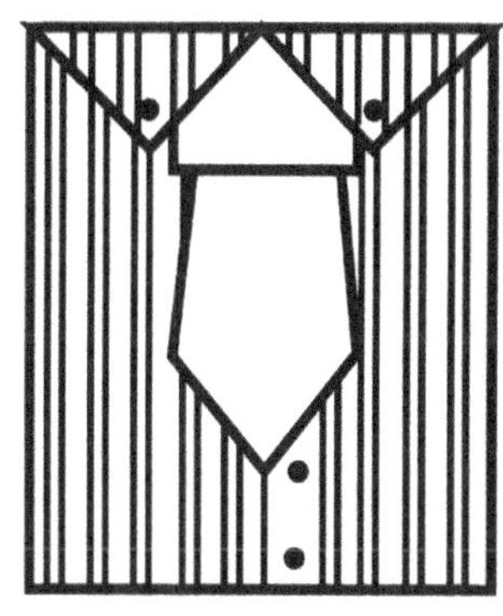

LESSON 12

Pp
/p/

potato

pineapple

pillow

piano

peanut

pie

pencil

pants

pail

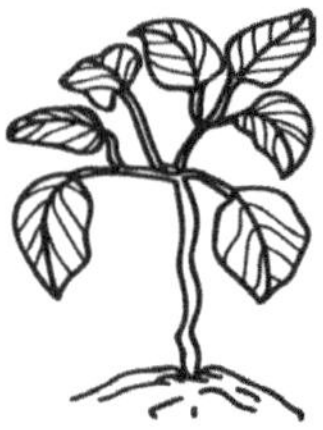

plant

Practice writing the letter **Pp**.

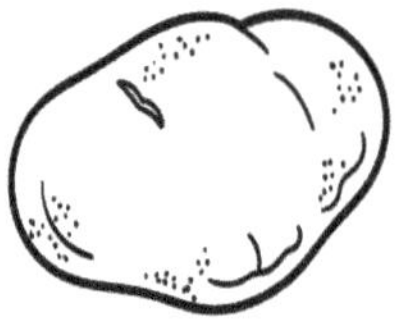

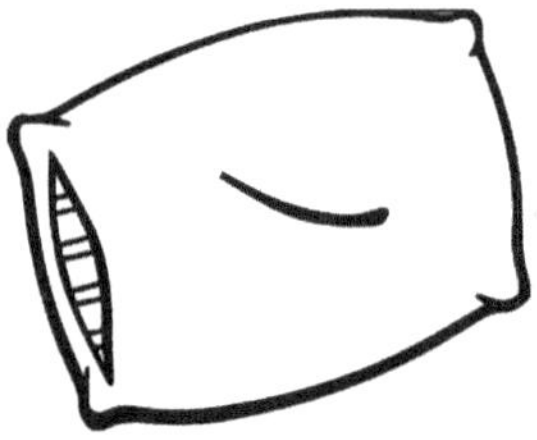

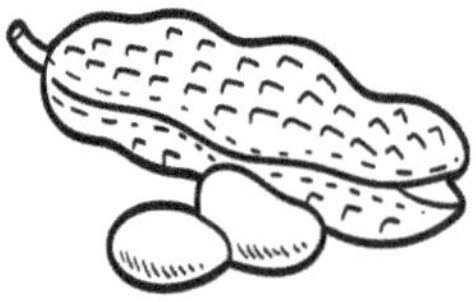

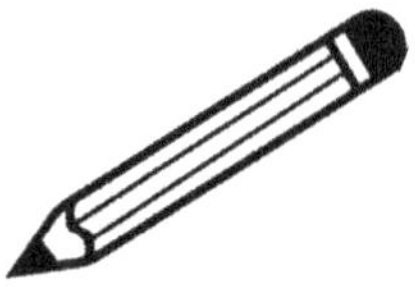

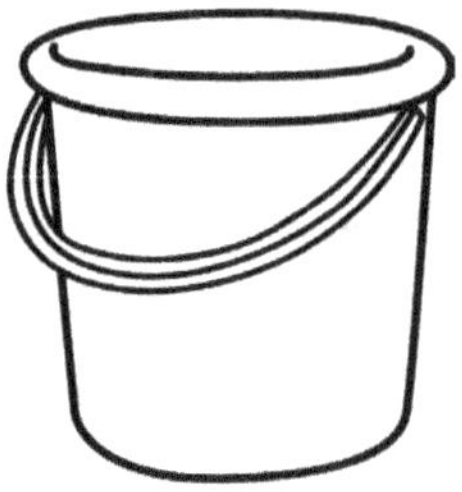

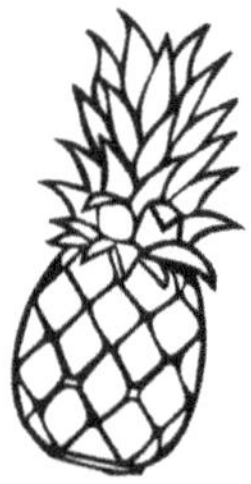

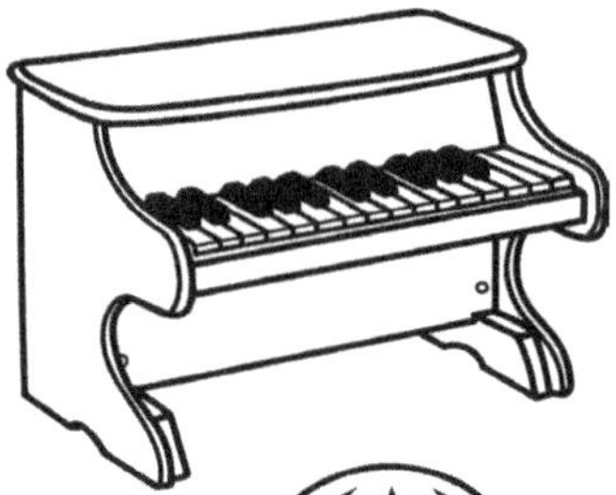

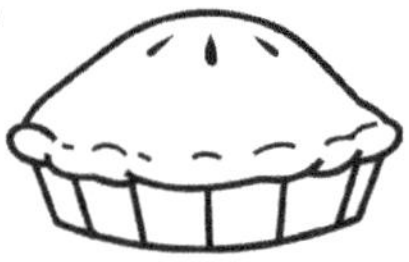

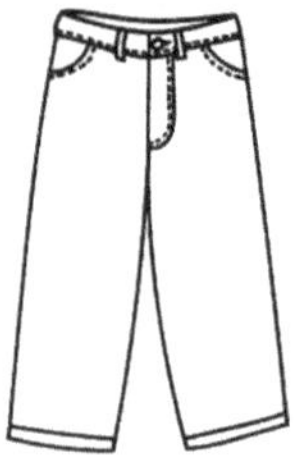

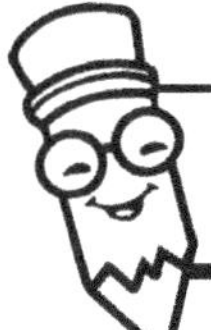

ACTIVITY 21 SCORE: ______

My brother's favorite snack is pizza.
The word "pizza" begins with the letter **p**.

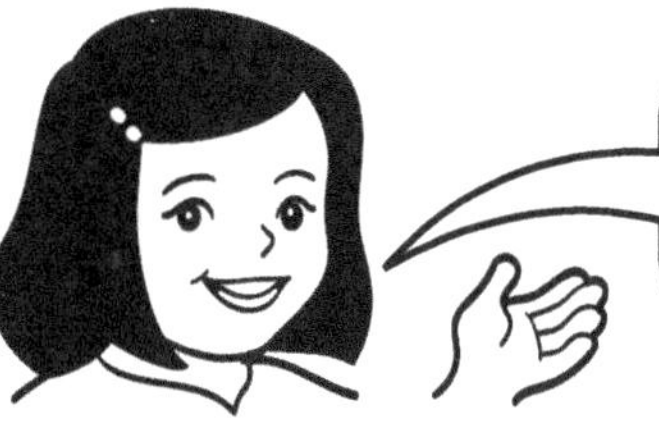

Connect the pictures whose names begin with **Pp** to the ***P***.

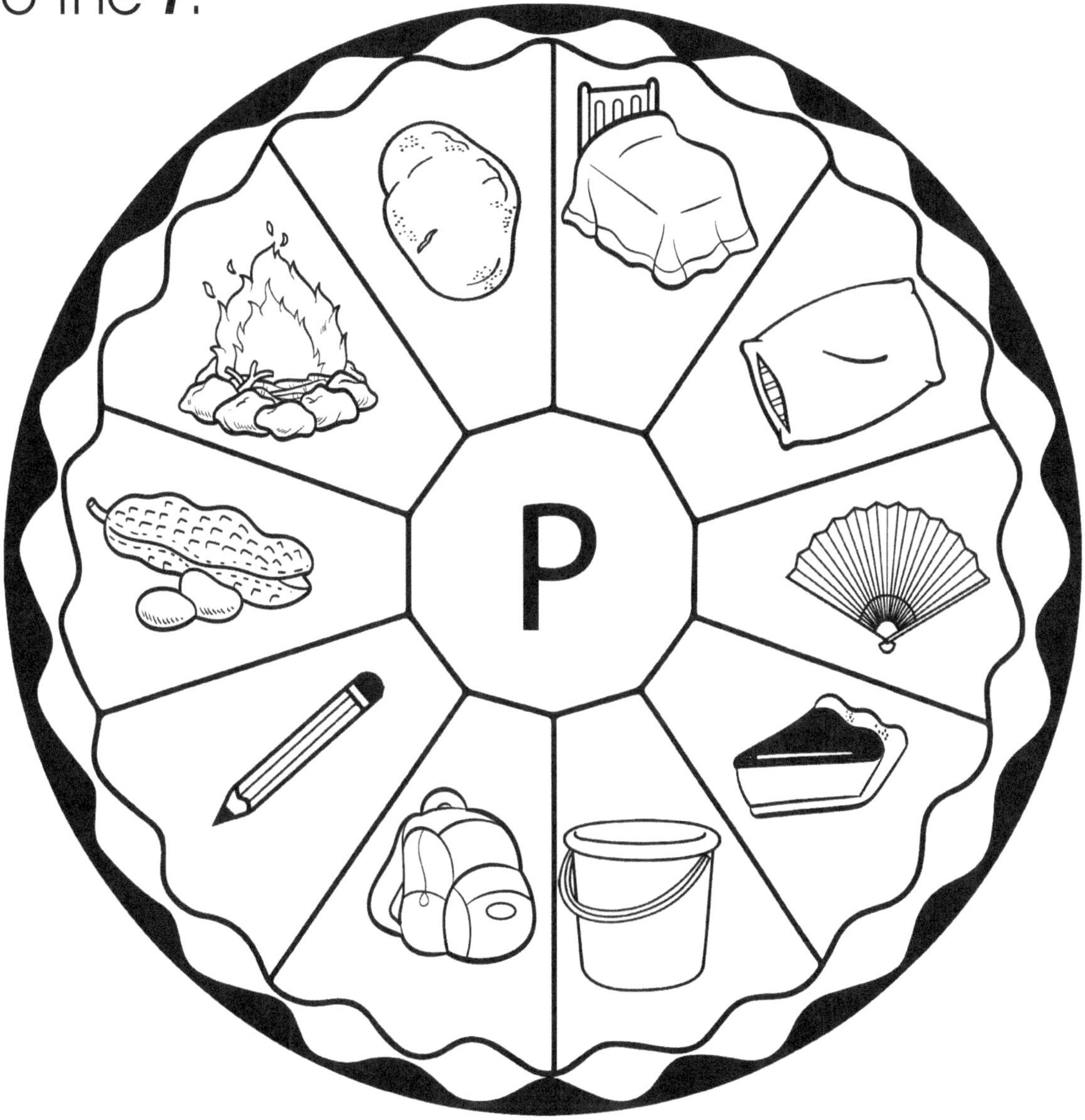

Check the letter **Pp**'s.

p	P	d	q	p	P	g
P	B	p	P	D	b	p

Write the missing letters in the boxes to complete the names of the pictures.

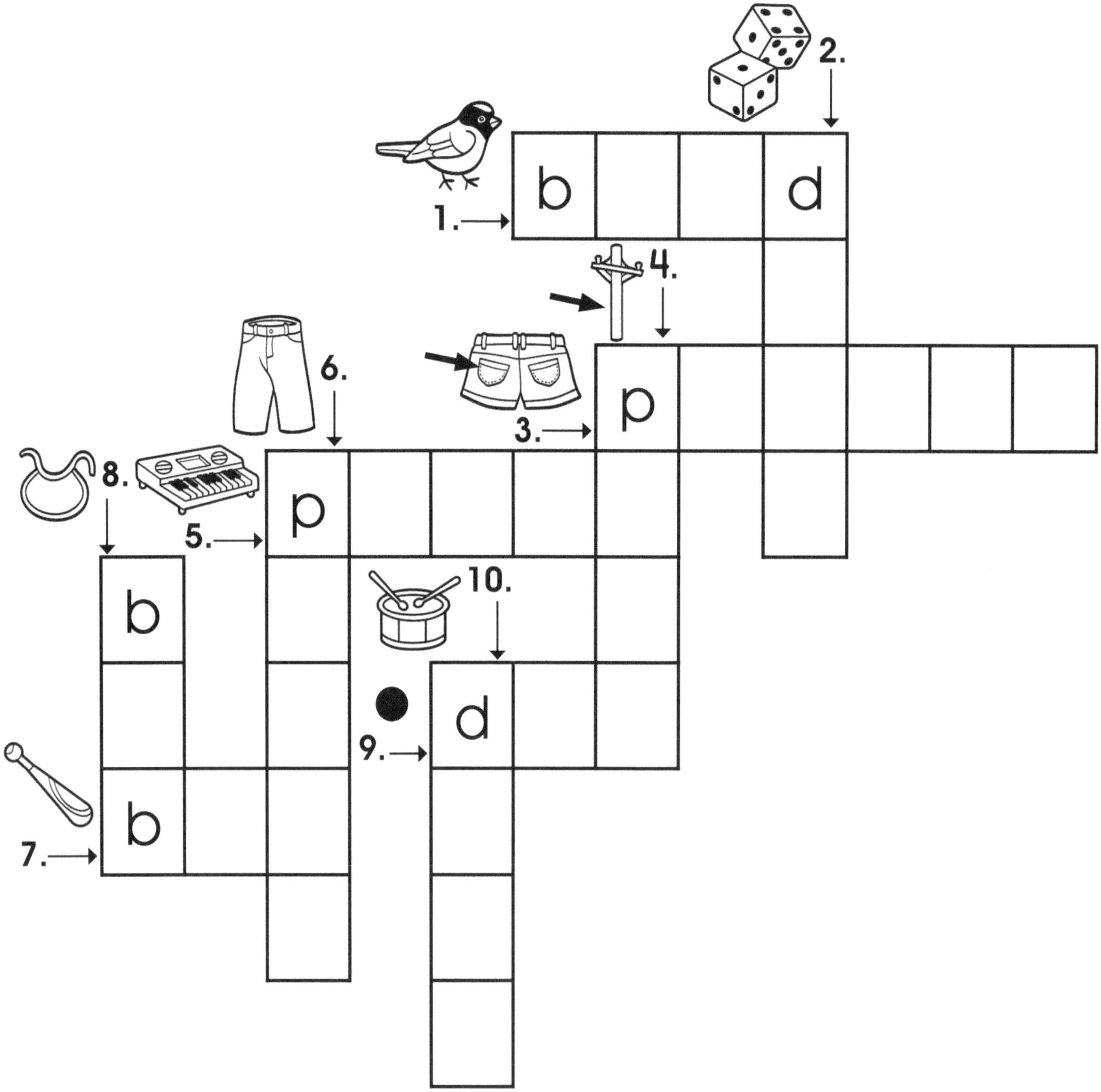

ACTIVITY 22

SCORE: _______

Box the letter of the correct initial sound for each picture.

1. | d | p | b |

2. | b | d | p |

3. | d | b | p |

4. | p | b | d |

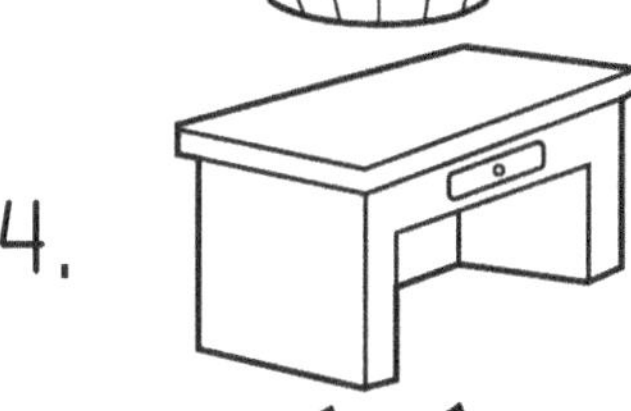

5. | d | p | b |

6. | b | p | d |

7. | p | d | b |

8. | d | p | b |

9. | p | b | d |

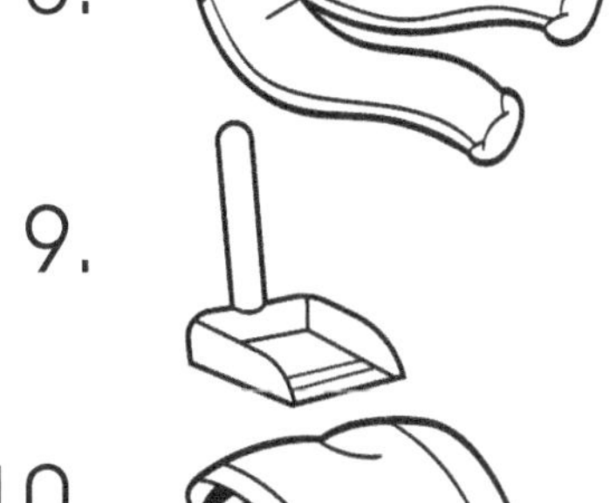

10. | d | b | p |

LESSON 13

Qq
/k/

quail

quilt

queen

quill

quiver

question mark

quarter

quarrel

quiet

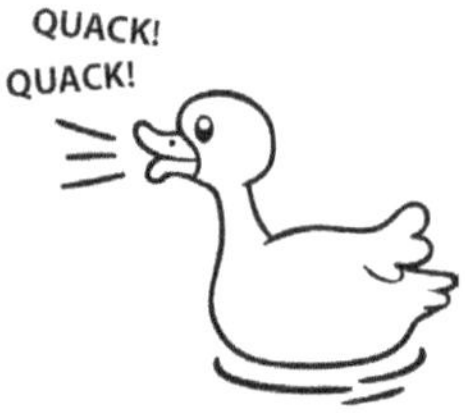

quack

Practice writing the letter **Qq**.

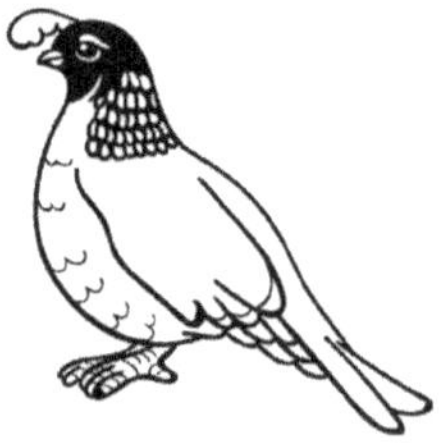

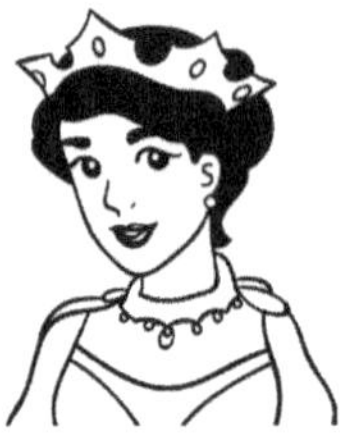

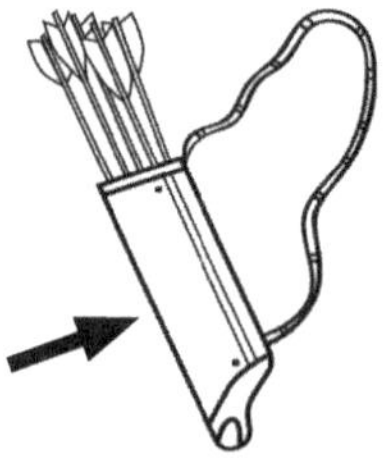

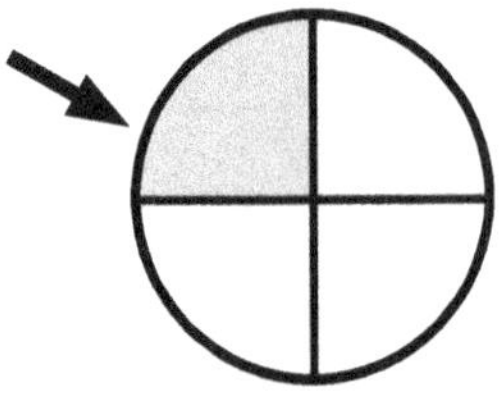

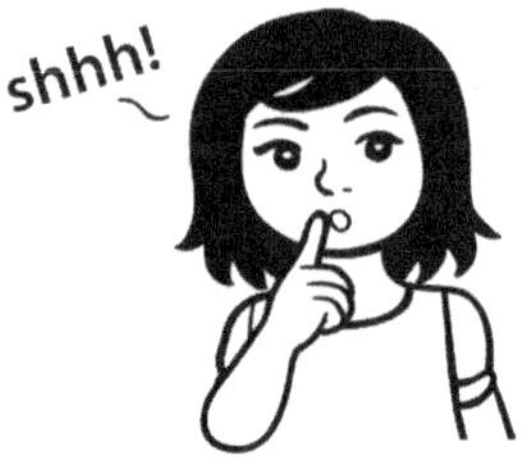

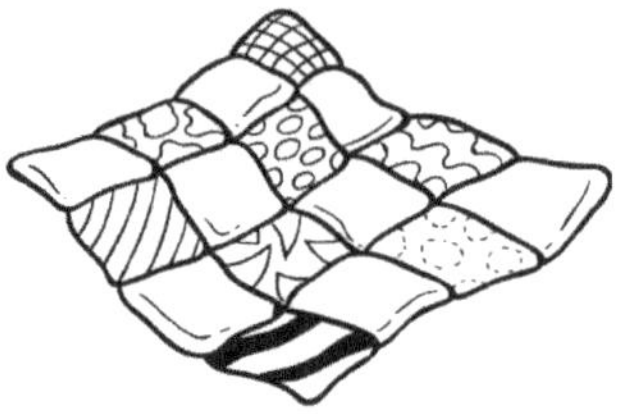

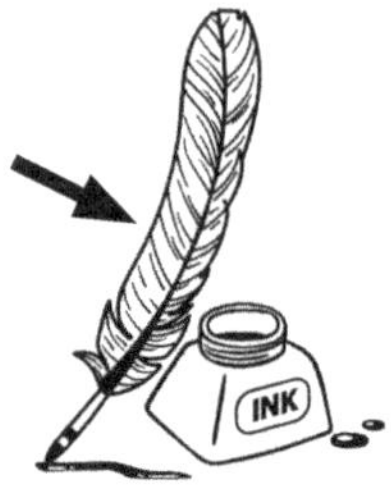

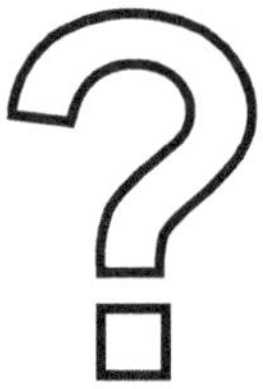

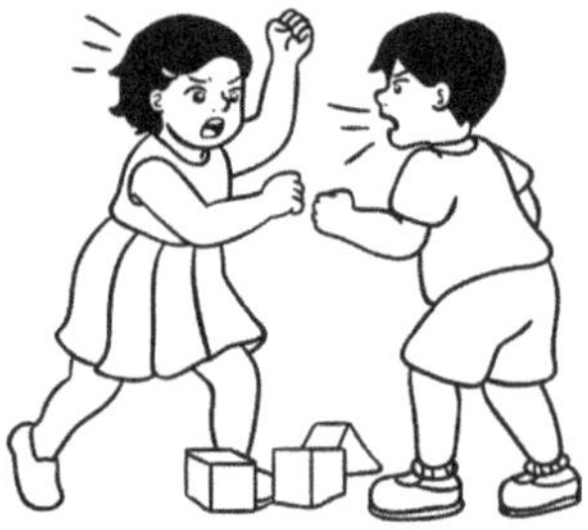

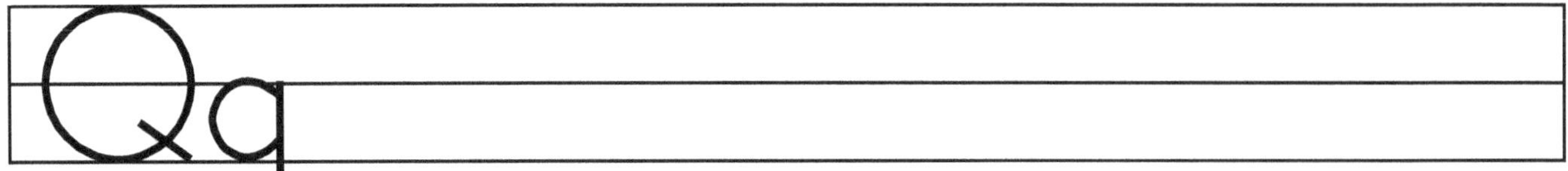

ACTIVITY 23

SCORE:______

Encircle the pictures whose names begin with **Qq**.

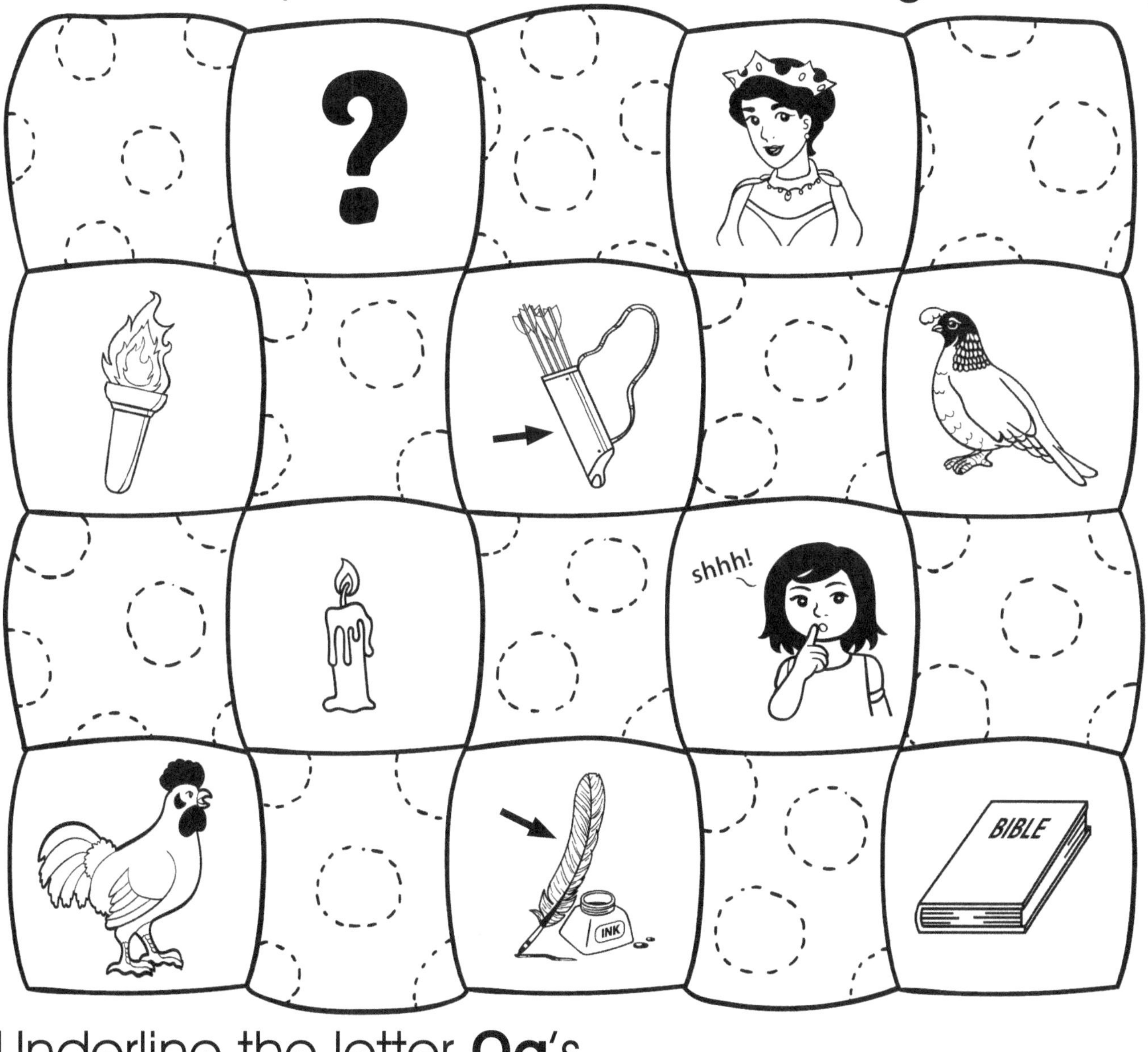

Underline the letter **Qq**'s.

Q   b   D   q   P   Q   q

G   Q   q   O   Q   q   g

Compare the sounds of the letters c, k, and q. Connect the pictures to the correct beginning letters.

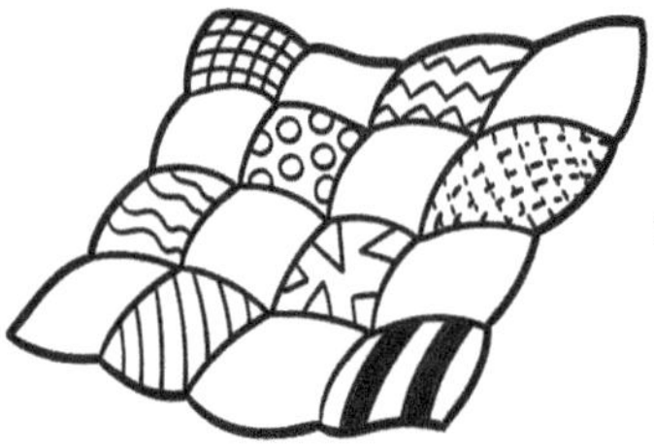

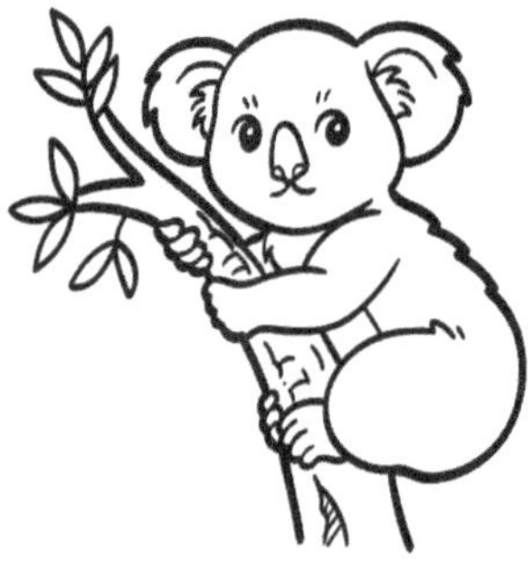

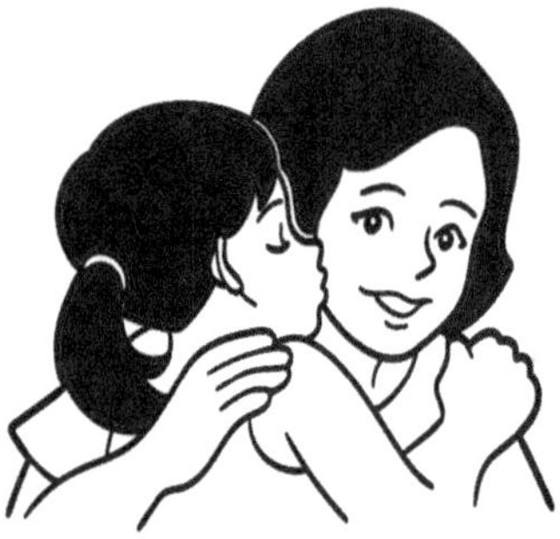

k

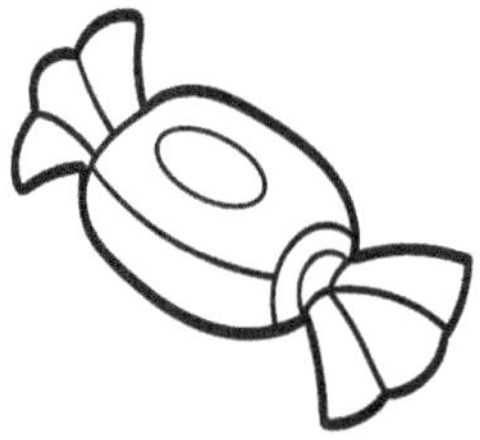

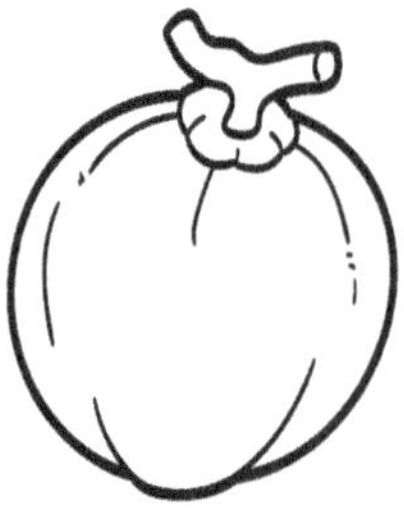

c

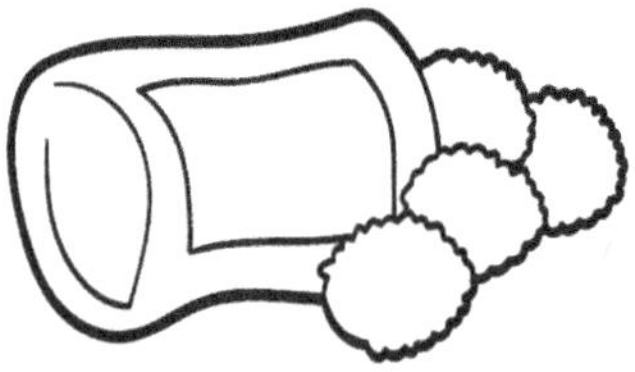

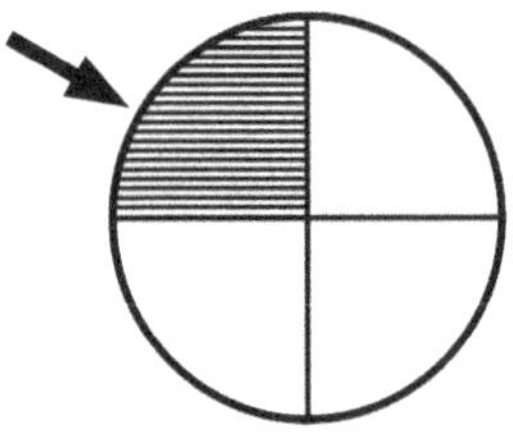

q

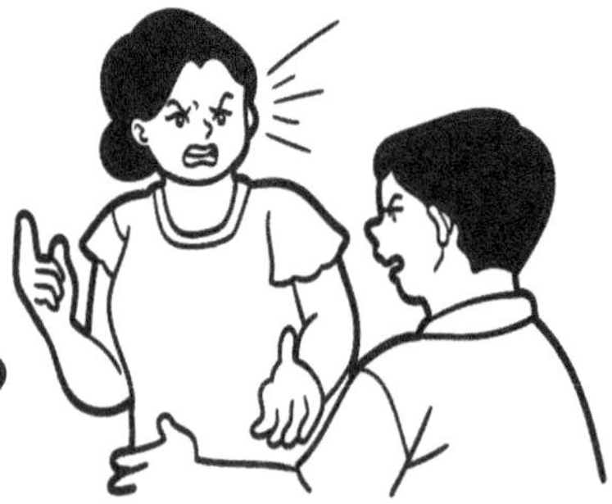

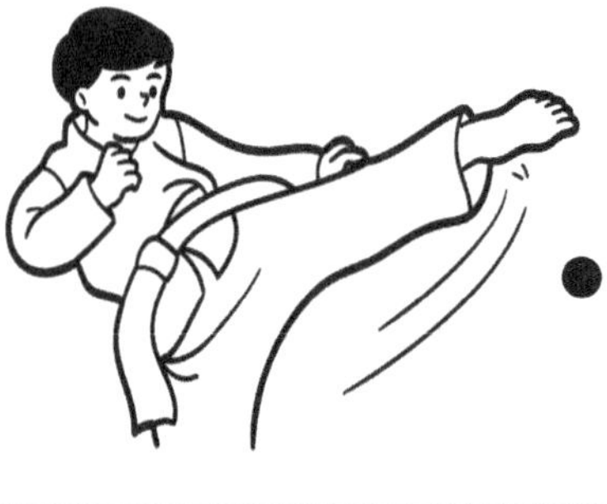

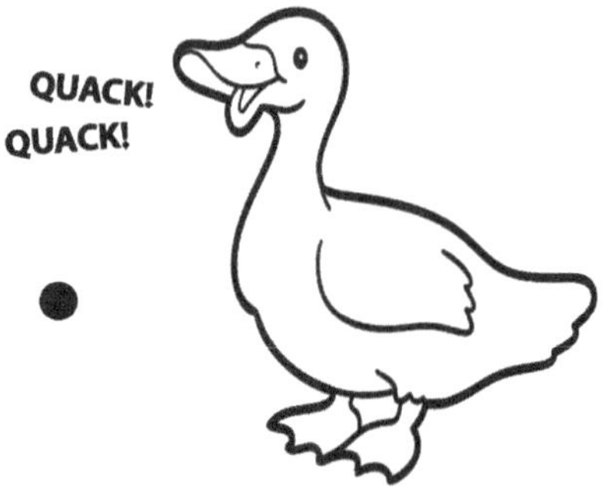

Rr
/r/

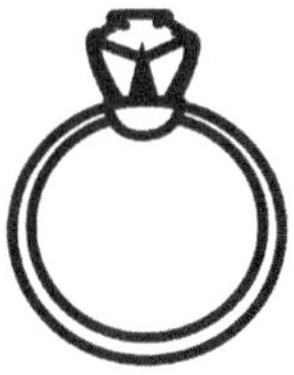

ring

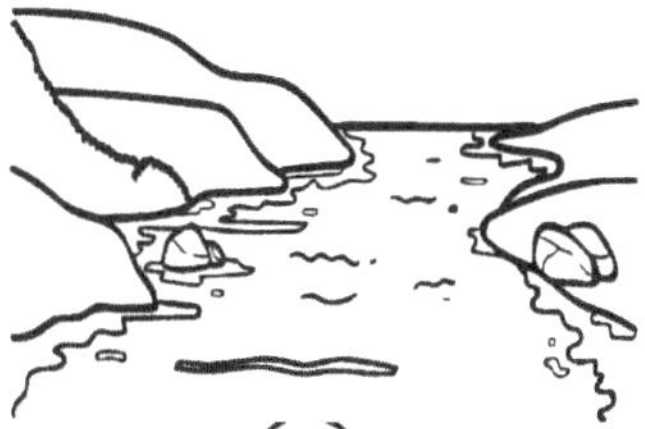

river

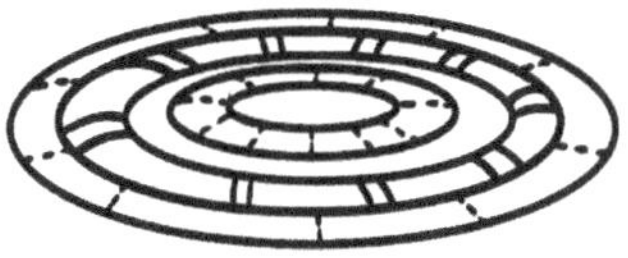

rug

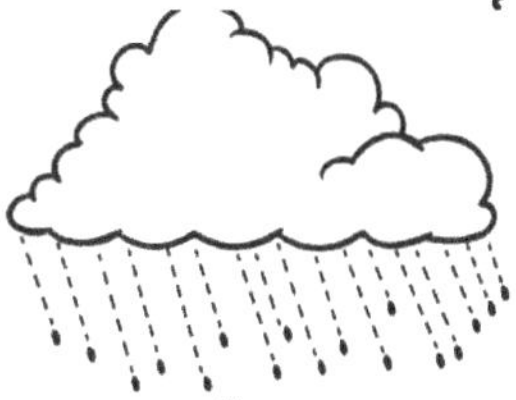

rain

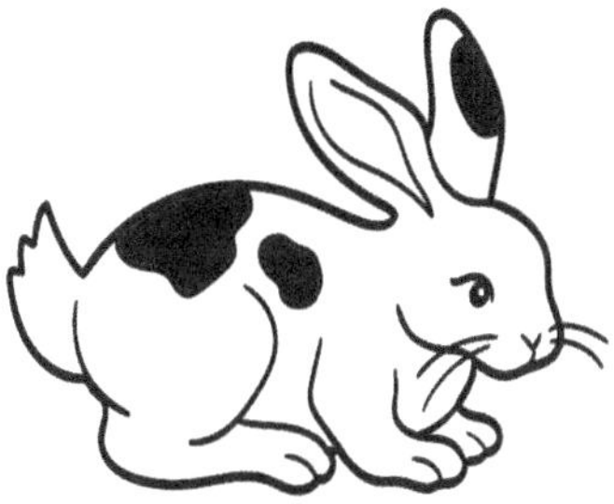

rabbit

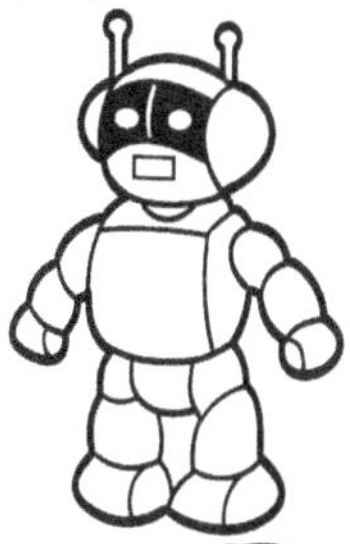

robot

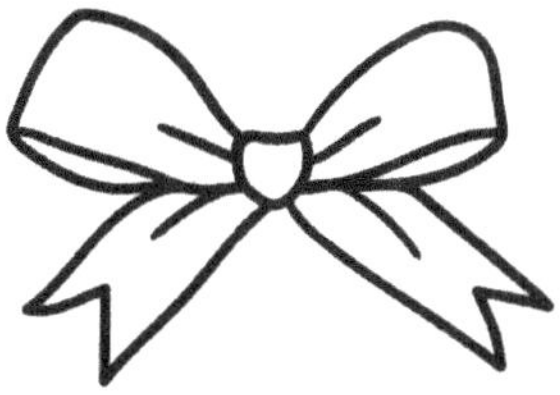

ribbon

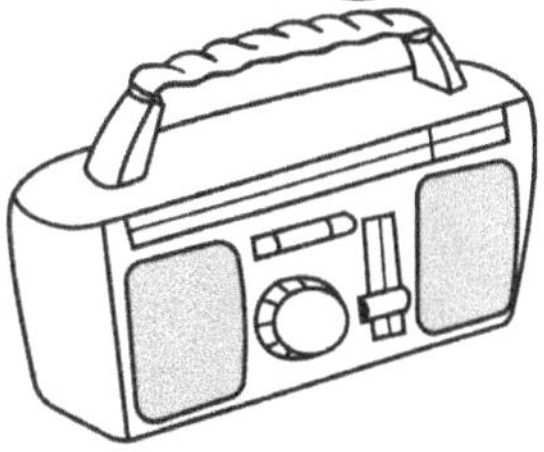

radio

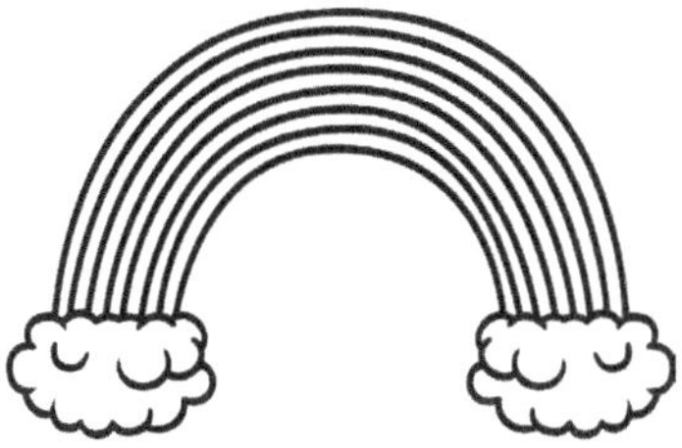

rainbow

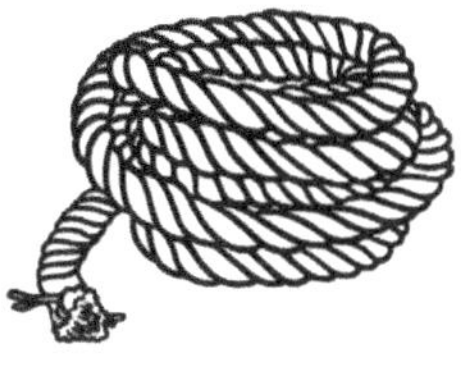

rope

Practice writing the letter **Rr**.

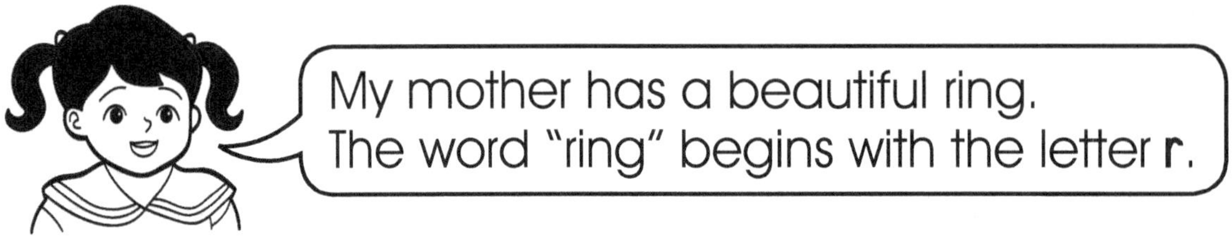

Connect the pictures whose names begin with **Rr** to the ring.

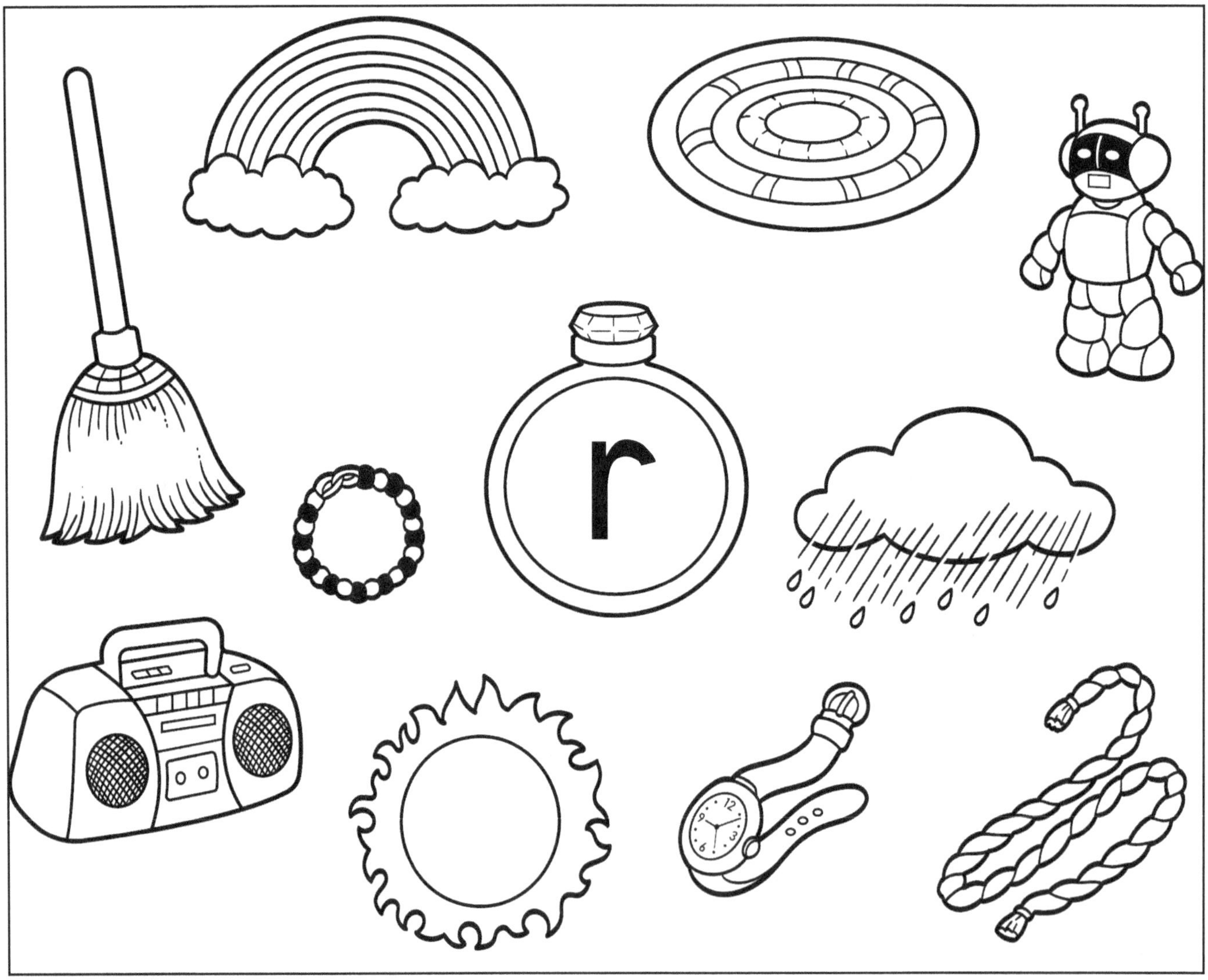

Box the letter **Rr**'s.

r	r	f	R	V	R	r
m	r	R	B	f	n	R

SCORE: _______

Cross out the picture whose name does not begin with the letter on the left.

p	
l	
h	
q	
r	

LESSON 15

Ss
/s/

slippers

seed

spider

sandwich

snake

socks

sand

snail

straw

school

Practice writing the letter **Ss**.

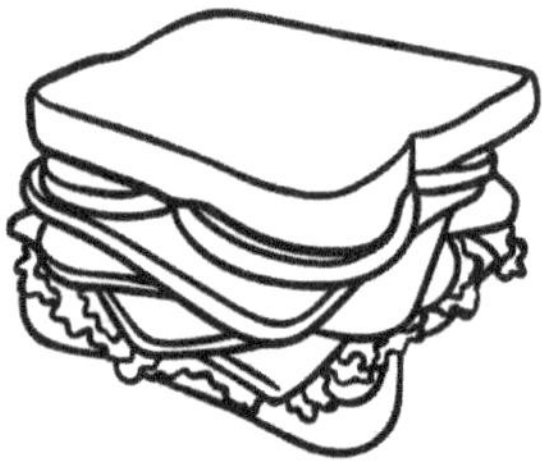

Ss

ACTIVITY 25

SCORE:________

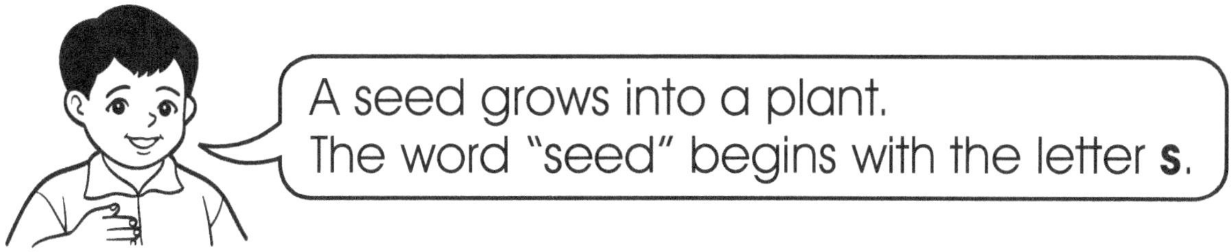

Color the pictures whose names begin with **Ss**.

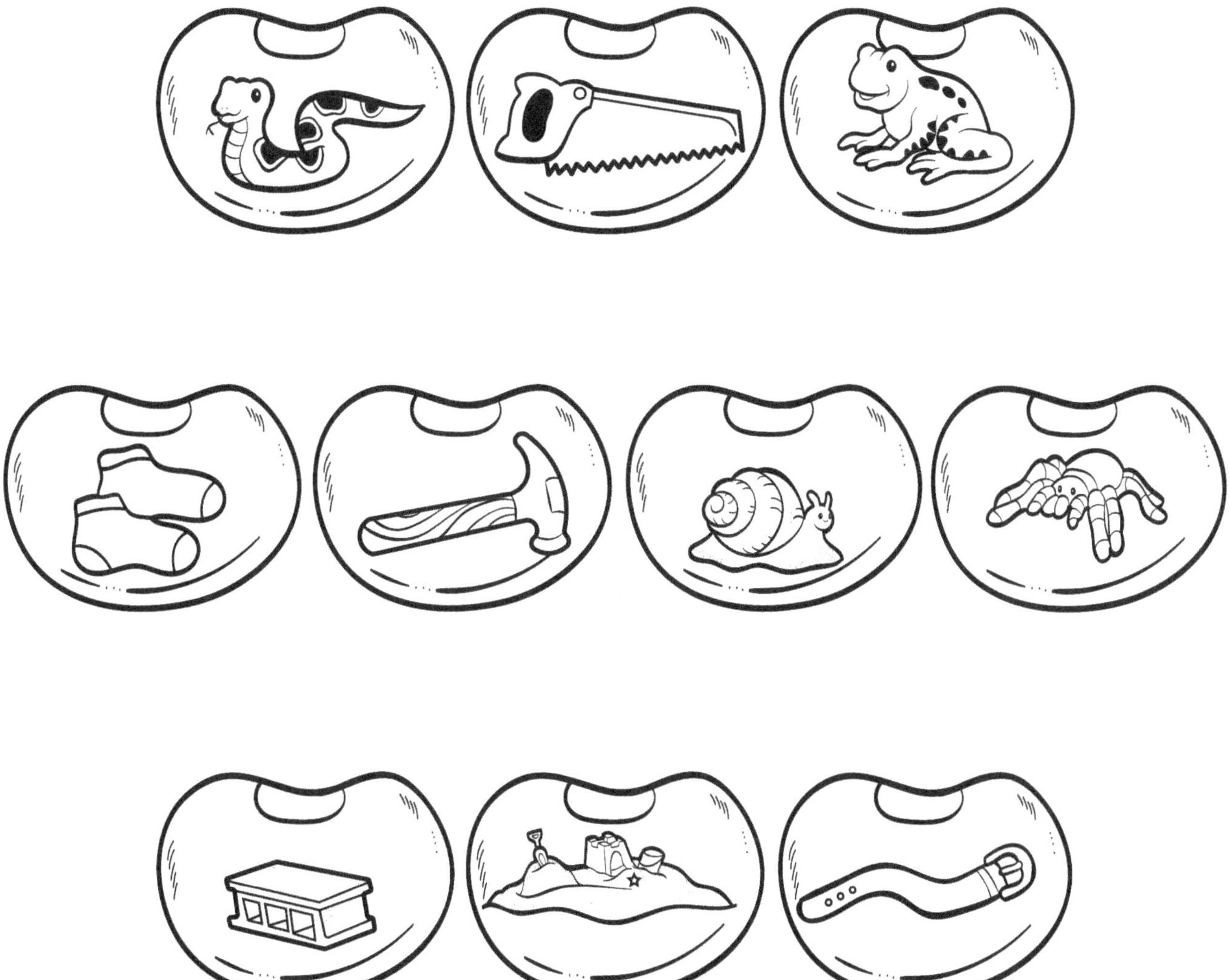

Draw a star on the letter **Ss**'s.

s   z   s   S   m   S   e

S   S   s   N   s   S   z   n

QUIZ NO. 8

SCORE: _______

Encircle the correct initial sound for each picture.

t / i		l / m	n / m	s / r
s / l		c / h	p / n	e / b
g / f		p / q	j / r	e / g
r / m		n / o	s / d	q / c
q / b		p / d	c / s	k / i

Tt
/t/

Guide: Bring in a medium-sized trunk filled with pictures of objects whose names begin with the letter **T**. Have the children take turns reaching into the trunk to take out a **T** picture. Have each child say the name of the picture.

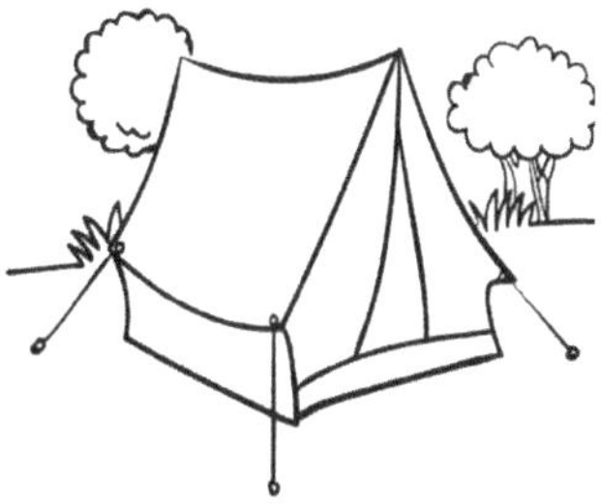

tent

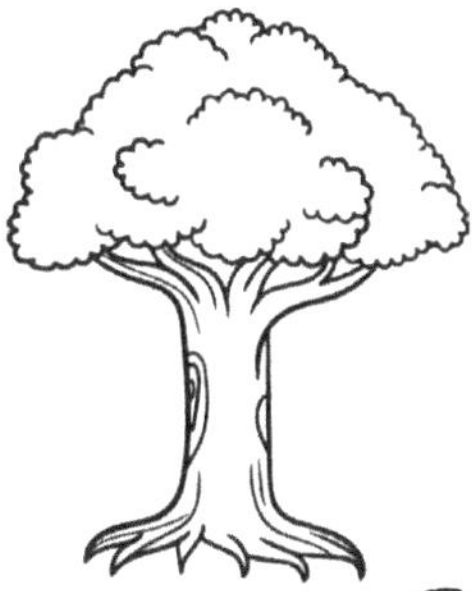

tree

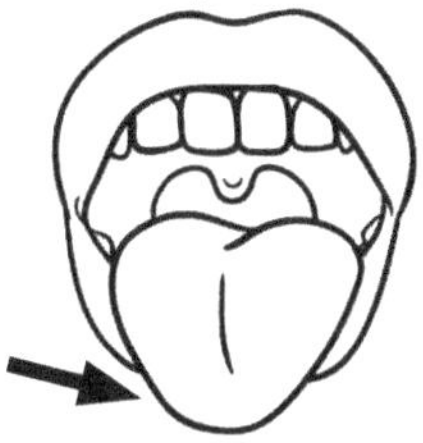

tongue

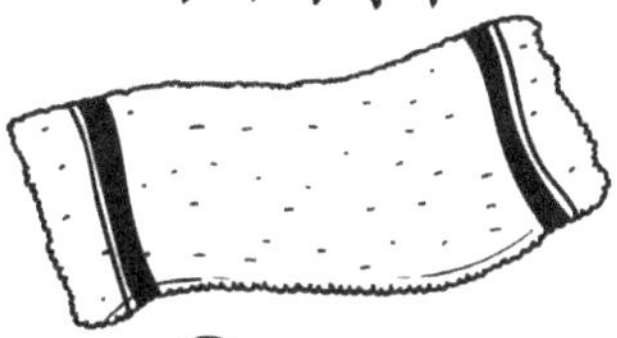

towel

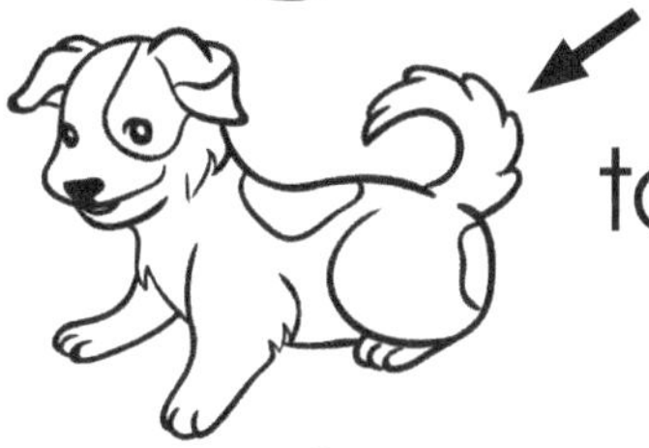

tail

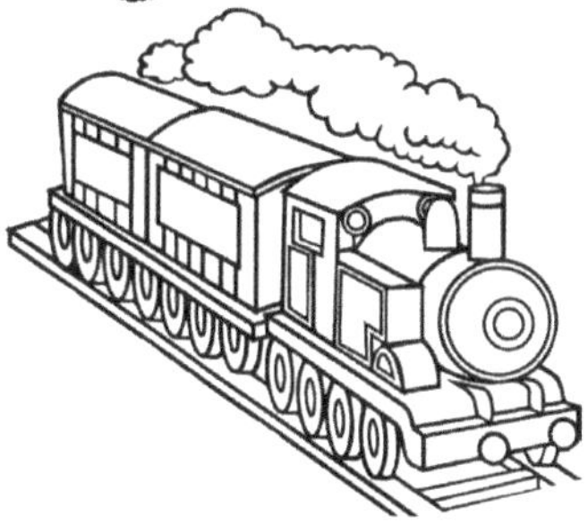

train

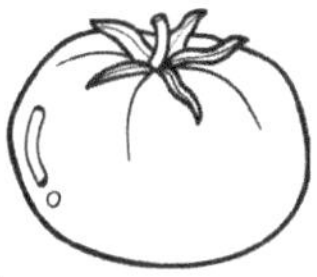

tomato

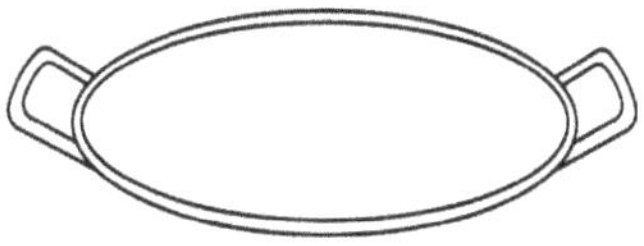

tray

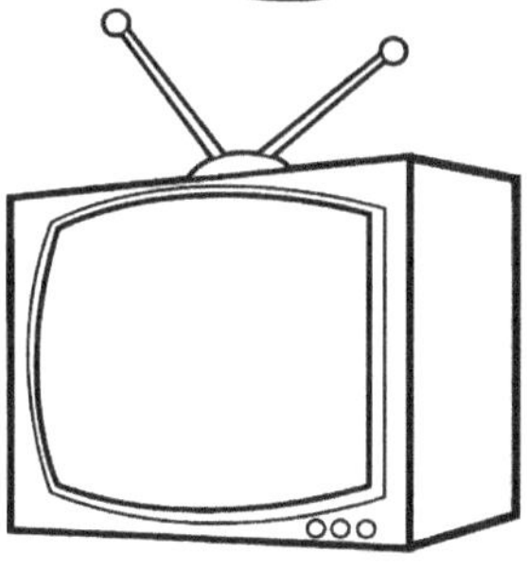

television

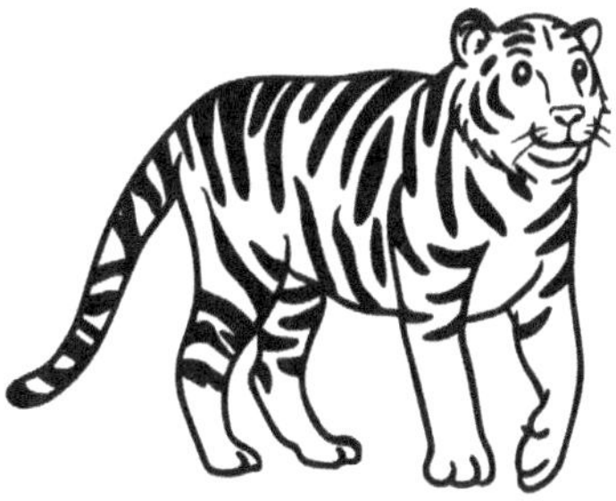

tiger

Practice writing the letter **Tt**.

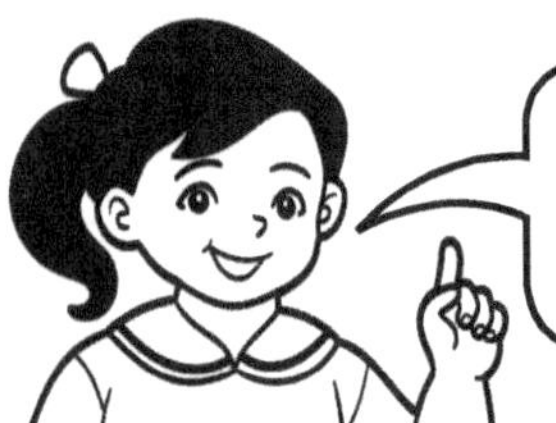

ACTIVITY 26 SCORE:______

We have a big flat screen television.
The word "television" begins with the letter **t**.

Shade the box before each picture whose name begins with **Tt**.

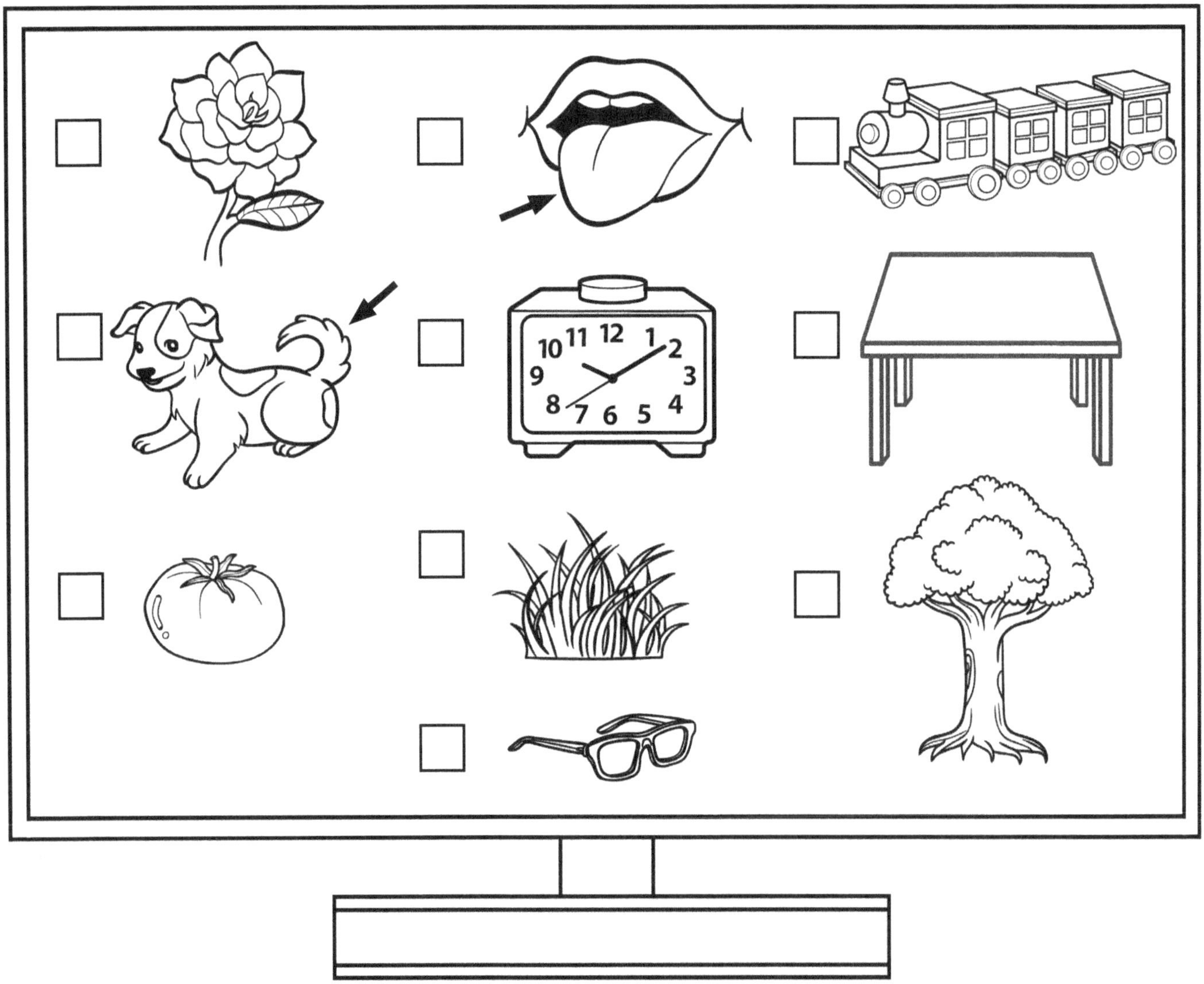

Encircle the letter **Tt**'s.

F	E	t	T	f	T	t
t	T	t	I	I	L	T

Color the correct initial sound of each picture.

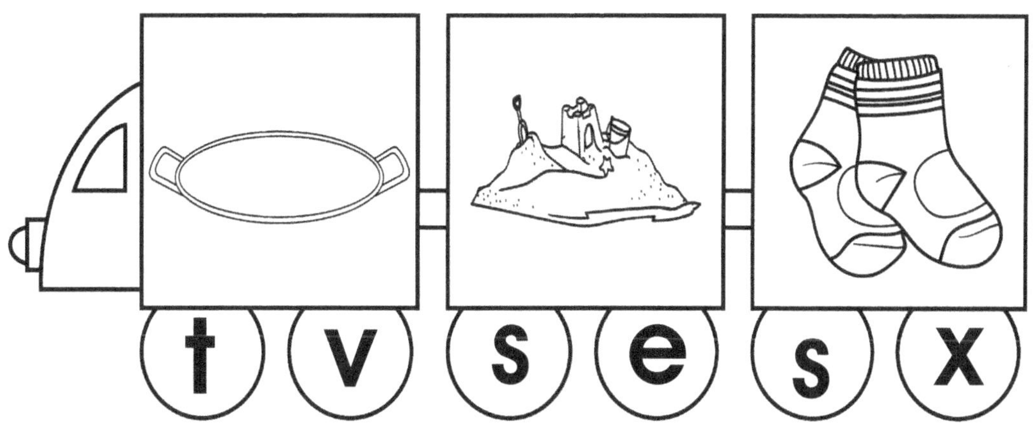

LESSON 17

Vv
/v/

Guide: Have the children pretend to be different kinds of vegetables. Then have them take turns describing what they look like. See if the other children can guess what type of vegetables they are. You may also make a box of **V** pictures for the children to learn. Include in the box pictures of veils, volcanoes, vases, vegetables, vests, vehicles, violins, and vans.

van

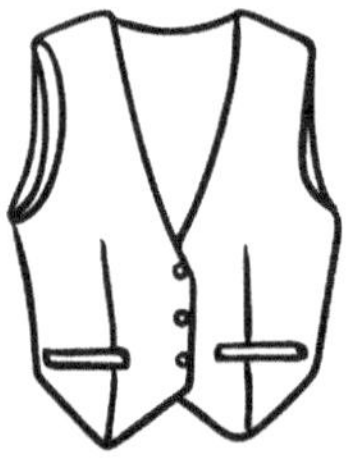

vest

veil

volcano

vegetables

violin

vulture

vine

vinegar

vase

Practice writing the letter **Vv**.

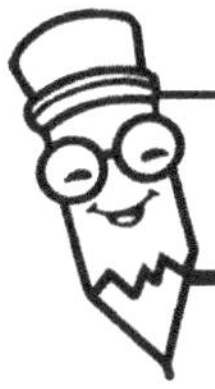

ACTIVITY 27 SCORE: ______

My grandmother loves to collect vases. The word "vase" begins with the letter **v**.

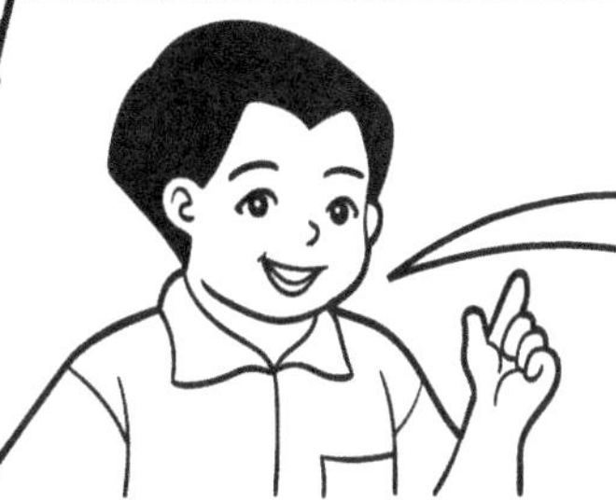

Box the pictures whose names begin with **Vv**.

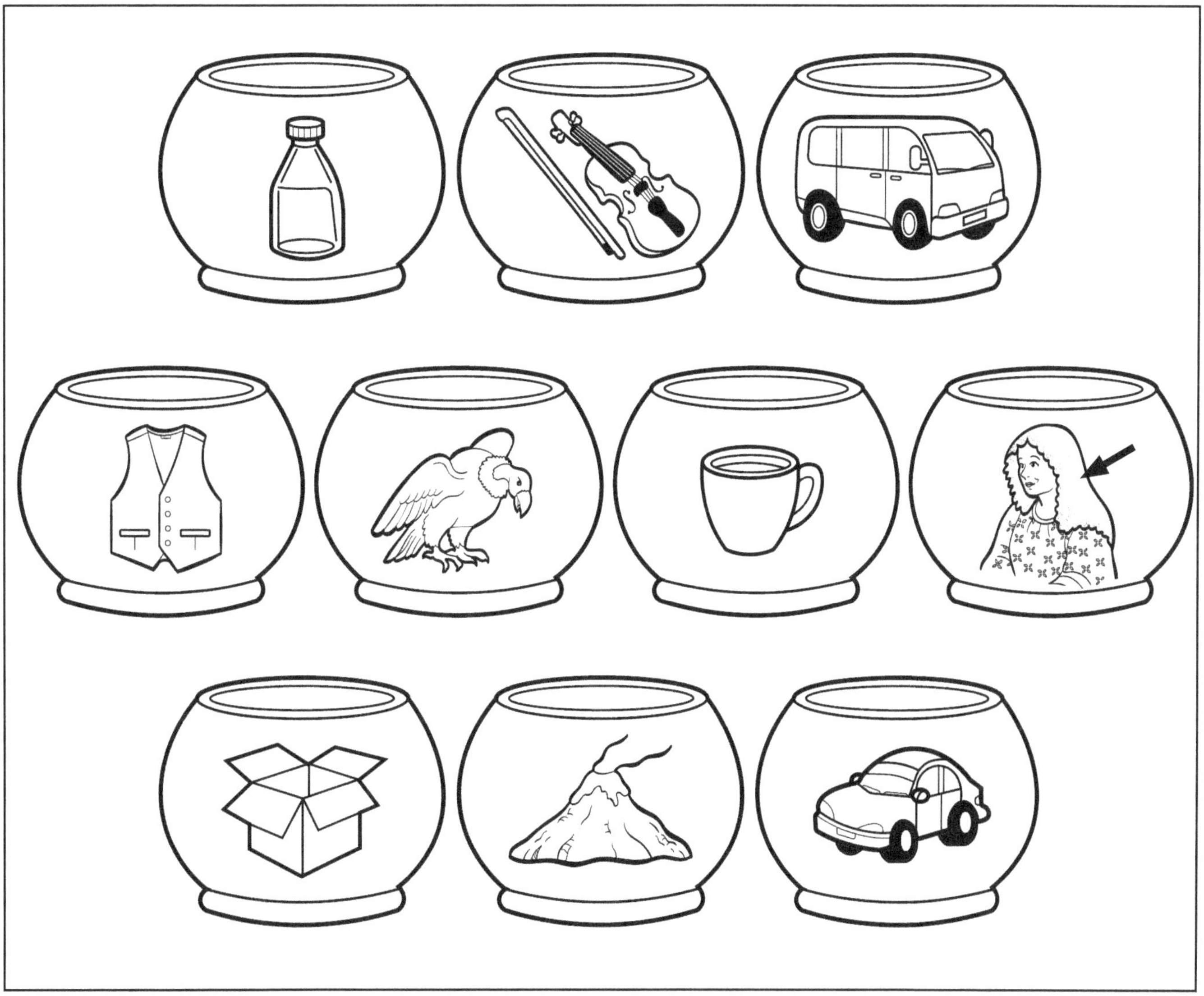

Check the letter **Vv**'s.

v	u	v	V	N	V	A
n	V	M	v	V	W	v

Cross out the picture in each group whose name does not begin with the letter on the left.

v				
s				
r				
p				
t				

Connect each picture to its initial sound.

p
v

s
t

   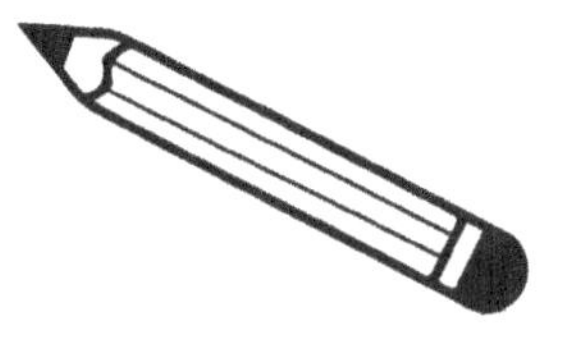

p
r

v
s

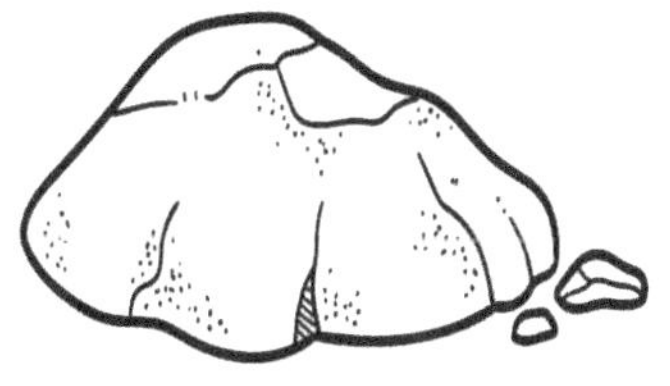   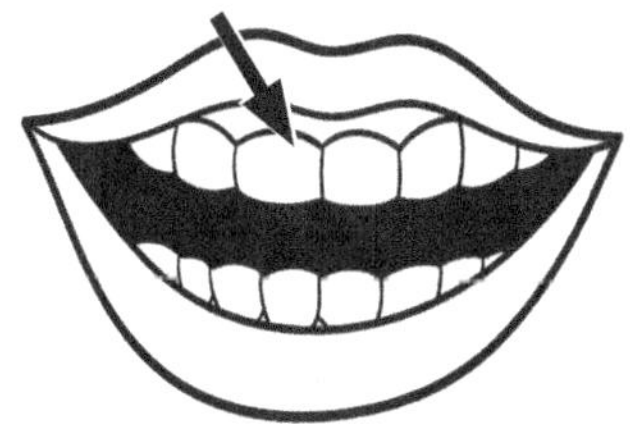

r
t

GAMES AND ACTIVITIES

Game/Activity	Learning Areas
Vegetable Guess Have the children pretend to be different kinds of vegetables. Then have them take turns and try to describe what they look like. See if the others can guess what type of vegetables they are.	* Physical Education and Health, Music, and Arts * Science * Language * Values Education and Social Studies * Mathematics
Voices Record a number of voices. Have the children guess to whom each voice belongs.	* Physical Education and Health, Music, and Arts * Language
Movement Games - Have the children fly around and pretend to be vultures. - Discuss how machines vibrate. See if the children can vibrate. - Let the children pretend to be "vehicles." Play a "stopping and starting" game.	* Physical Education and Health, Music, and Arts * Science * Language * Values Education and Social Studies
Erupting Volcano You will need modeling dough or clay, vinegar, baking soda, and red food coloring for the activity. First, have the children make a tall mountain from the clay. Make a hole at the top and fill it with a spoonful of baking soda. Finally, slowly pour in 1/4 cup of vinegar that has been mixed with red food coloring.Have them watch the erupting volcano.	* Science * Language
***V* Snacks** - raw vegetables - vanilla ice cream - vegetable soup - vanilla wafers - cucumber in vinegar	* Science * Mathematics * Values Education and Social Studies

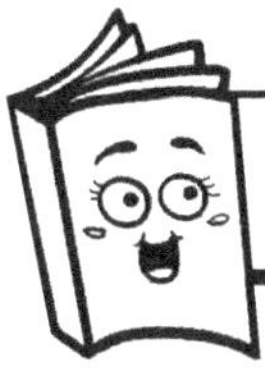

Ww
/w/

Guide: Have a wagon ready. Set some **W** pictures or real objects around the room. Have the children take turns pulling the wagon and placing a **W** picture or object into the wagon. Have each child bring the wagon back to the class and show his or her picture or object. Continue with other children until everyone has had a turn and has found something "**W**."

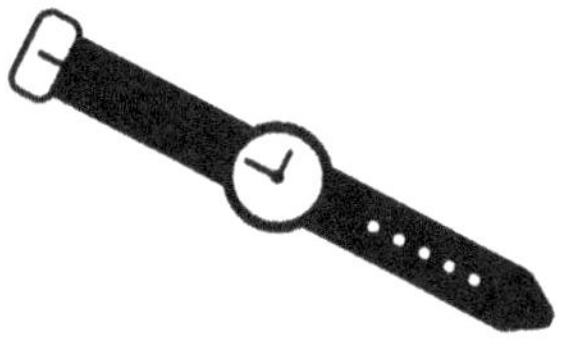

watch

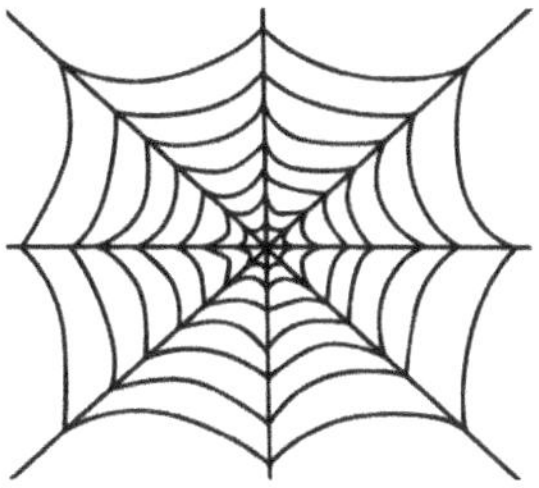

web

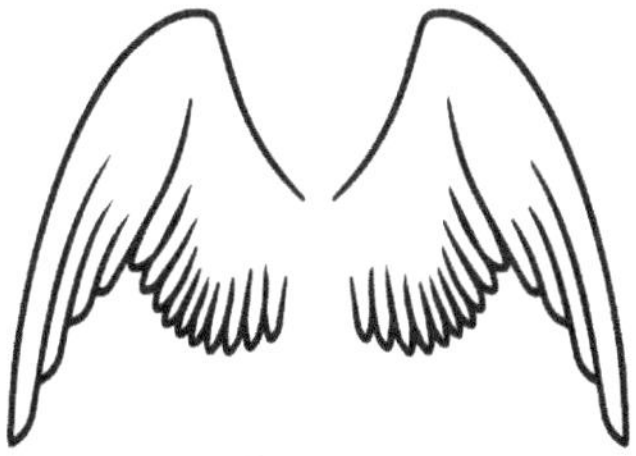

wings

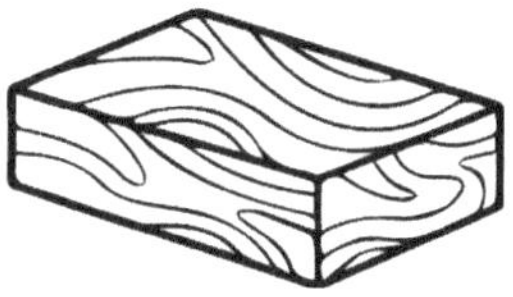

wood

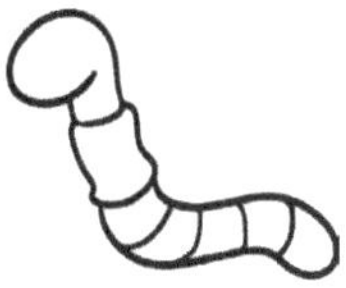

worm

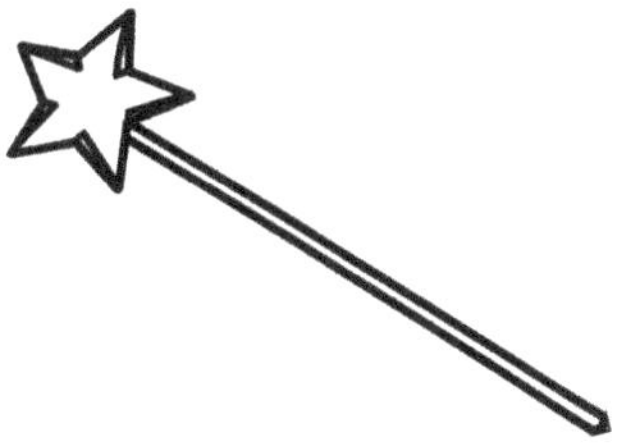

wand

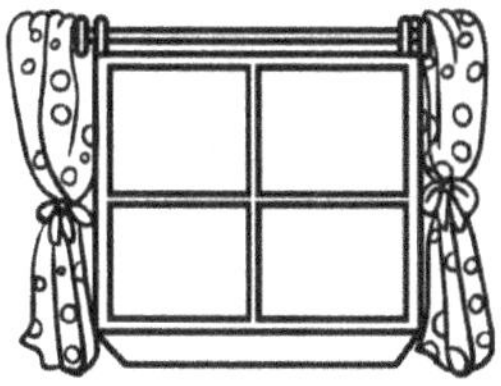

window

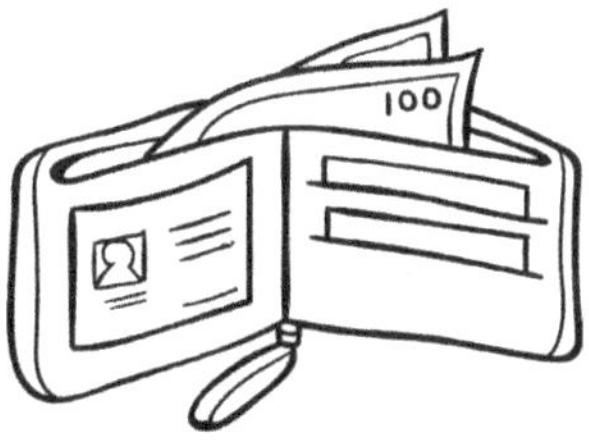

wallet

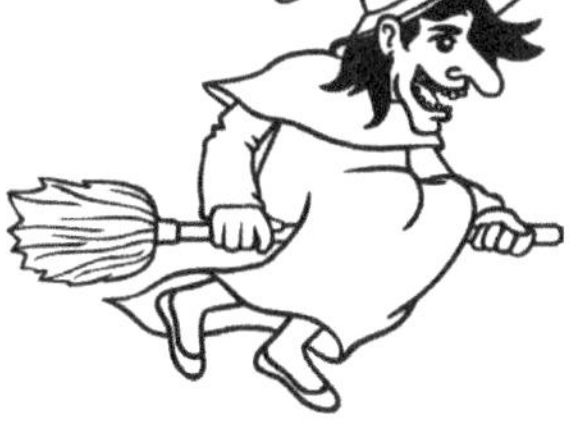

witch

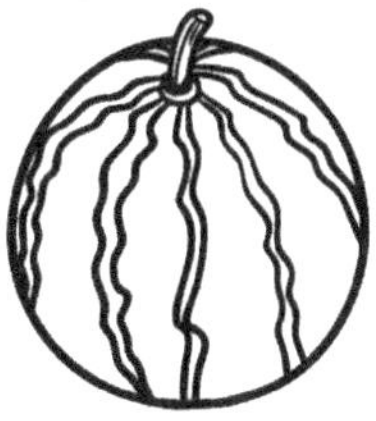

watermelon

Practice writing the letter **Ww**.

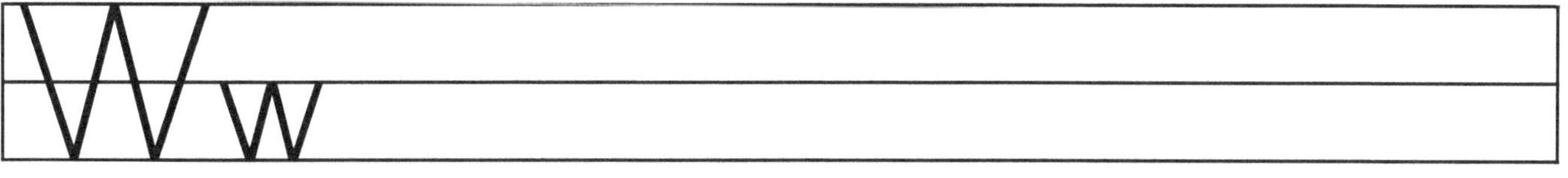

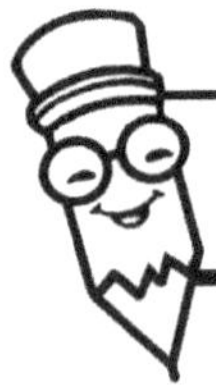

ACTIVITY 29

SCORE: ______

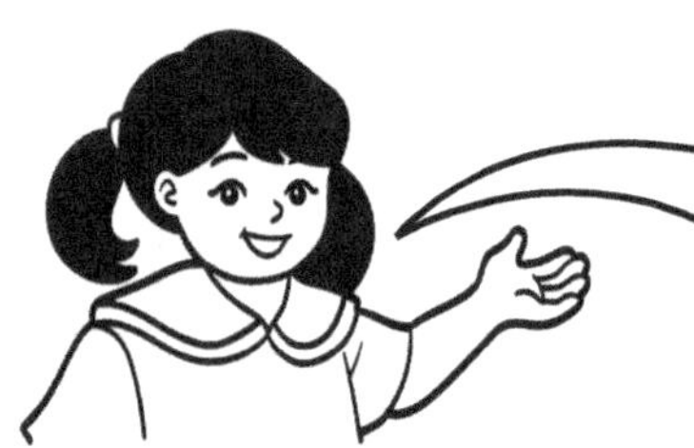

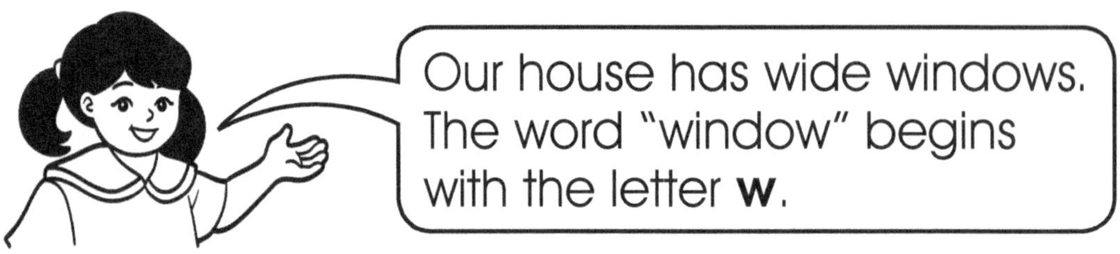

Encircle the pictures whose names begin with **Ww**.

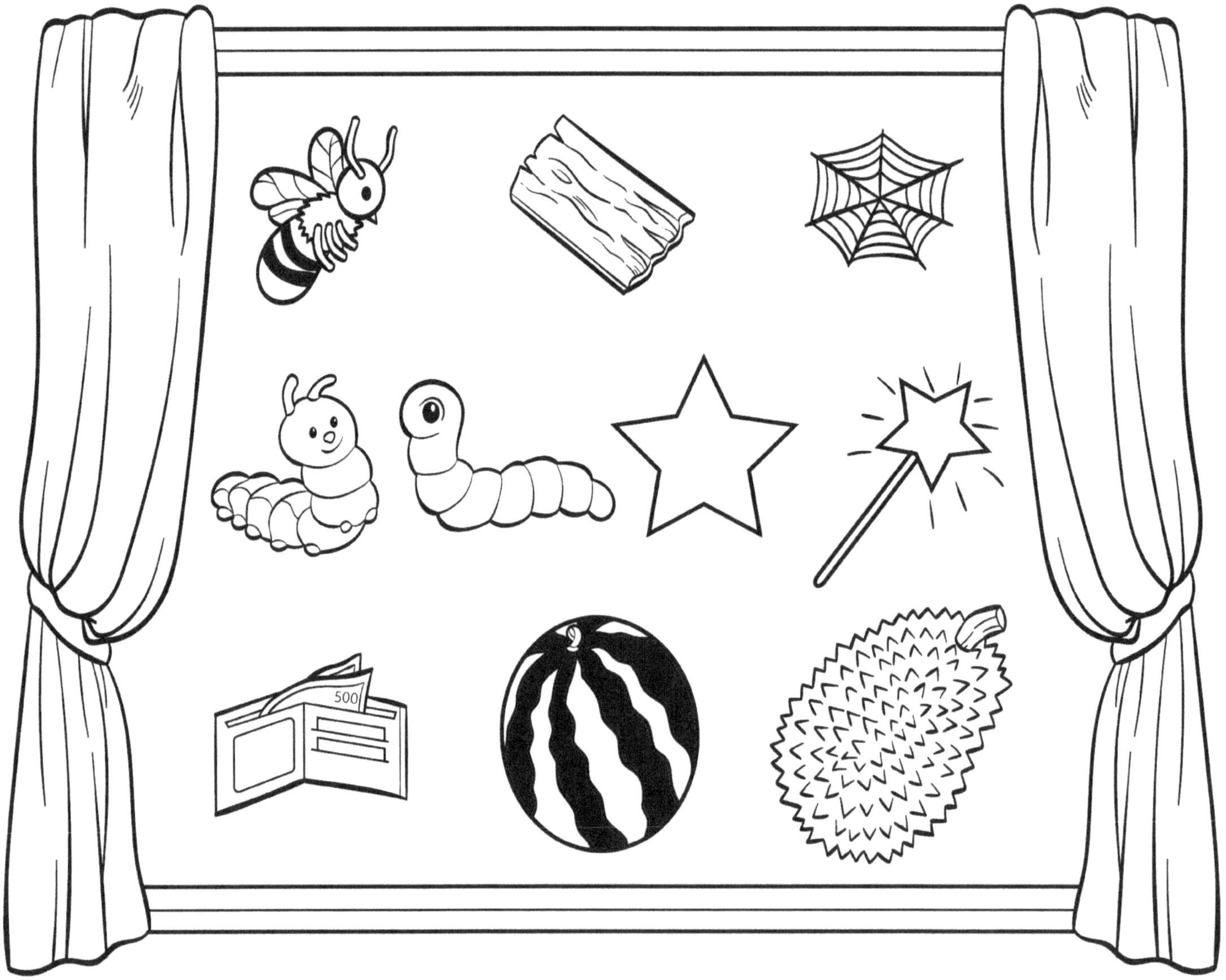

Underline the letter **Ww**'s.

w   m   w   N   W   r   W

V   w   W   M   w   W   v

Xx

/z/ as in *xylophone* /ks/ as in *six*

Guide: Form a musical band with your class. Have the children use xylophones made from recycled materials such as glass bottles filled with colored water. You may also play musical chairs with the children using a xylophone for music. Discuss other things whose names begin with the letter **X**.

Beginning Sound:

x-ray

xylophone

Ending Sound:

ax

six

box

mix

fix

fox

Practice writing the letter **Xx**.

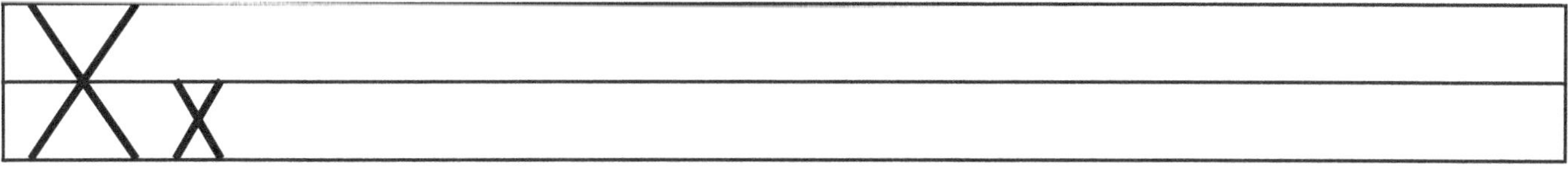

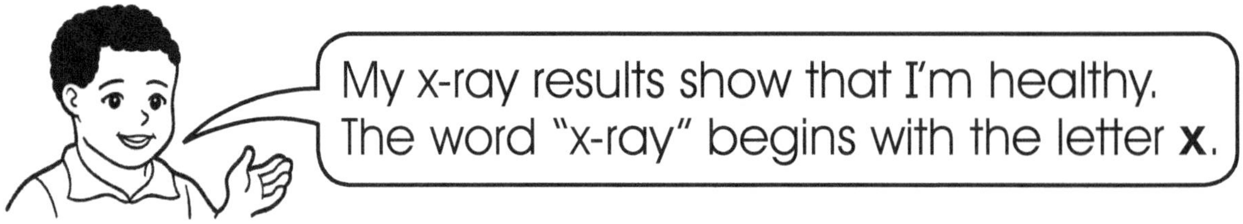

Check the pictures whose names begin with **Xx** and encircle the pictures whose names end with **Xx**.

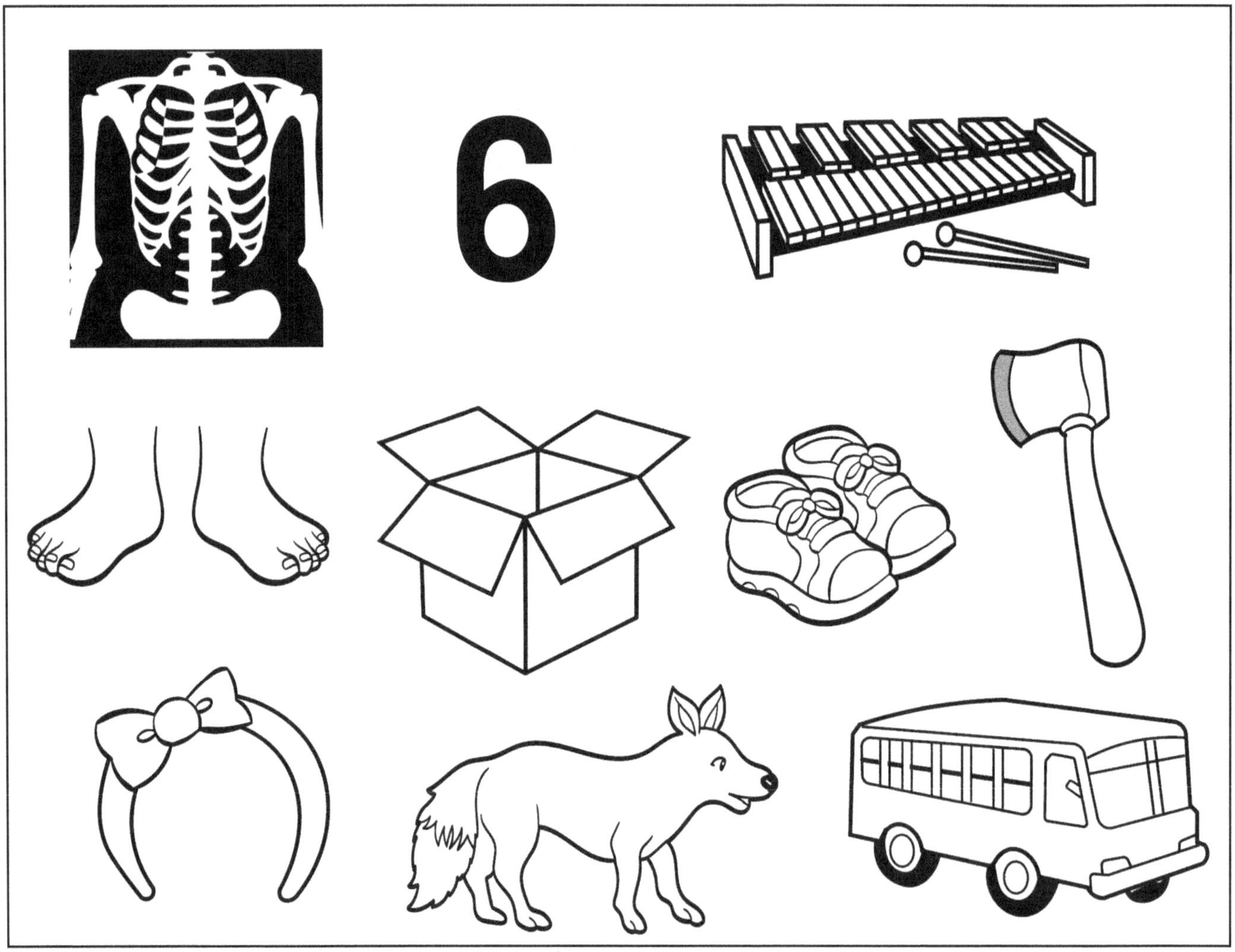

Box the letter **Xx**'s.

X	x	L	N	x	M	X
w	x	X	n	v	X	x

ACTIVITY 31   SCORE:_______

A. Box the letter that your teacher will tell you.

1.	l	v	b	p	t
2.	c	s	j	f	r
3.	m	k	h	w	q
4.	w	d	g	s	q
5.	t	v	x	n	r

B. Shade the oblong beside the letter that your teacher will sound out.

1. ◯ c   ◯ x   ◯ l   ◯ h   ◯ s

2. ◯ t    ◯ m   ◯ n   ◯ k   ◯ p

3. ◯ v   ◯ w    ◯ x   ◯ r   ◯ n

4.  ◯ r   ◯ n    ◯ j   ◯ g    ◯ m

5. ◯ d   ◯ q   ◯ f   ◯ b   ◯ p

Guide: A. Dictate the letters *t*, *s*, *w*, *q*, and *v*.
          B. Sound out the letters *x*, *m*, *r*, *n*, and *p*.

LESSON 20

Yy
/j/

Guide: Have a yoyo fun day with the children. Let them bring yoyos to class and play with them. Play a yoyo search game. Hide a yoyo for the children to search for. Then let the children hide the yoyo for you to find. Discuss other things whose names begin with the letter **Y**.

yoyo

yarn

yell

yawn

yak

yams

yacht

yolk

year

yard

Practice writing the letter **Yy**.

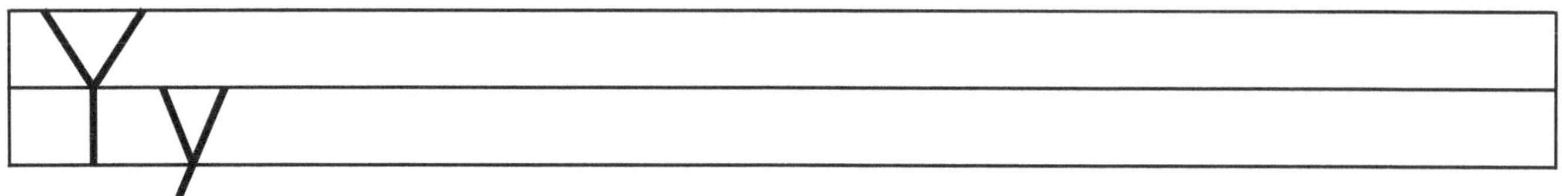

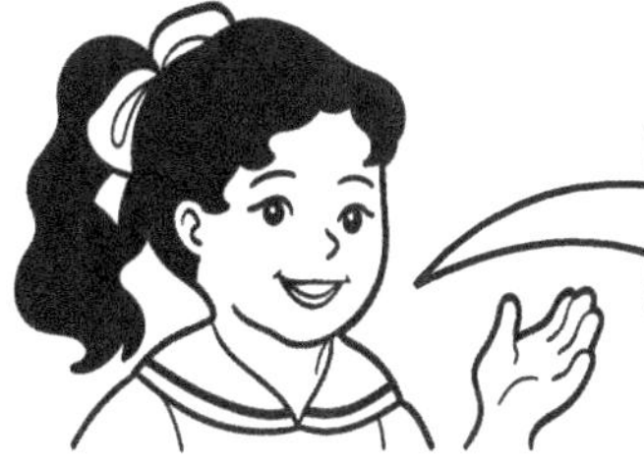

ACTIVITY 32 SCORE: ______

Boys love to play with yoyos.
The word "yoyo" begins with the letter **y**.

Box the pictures whose names begin with **Yy**.

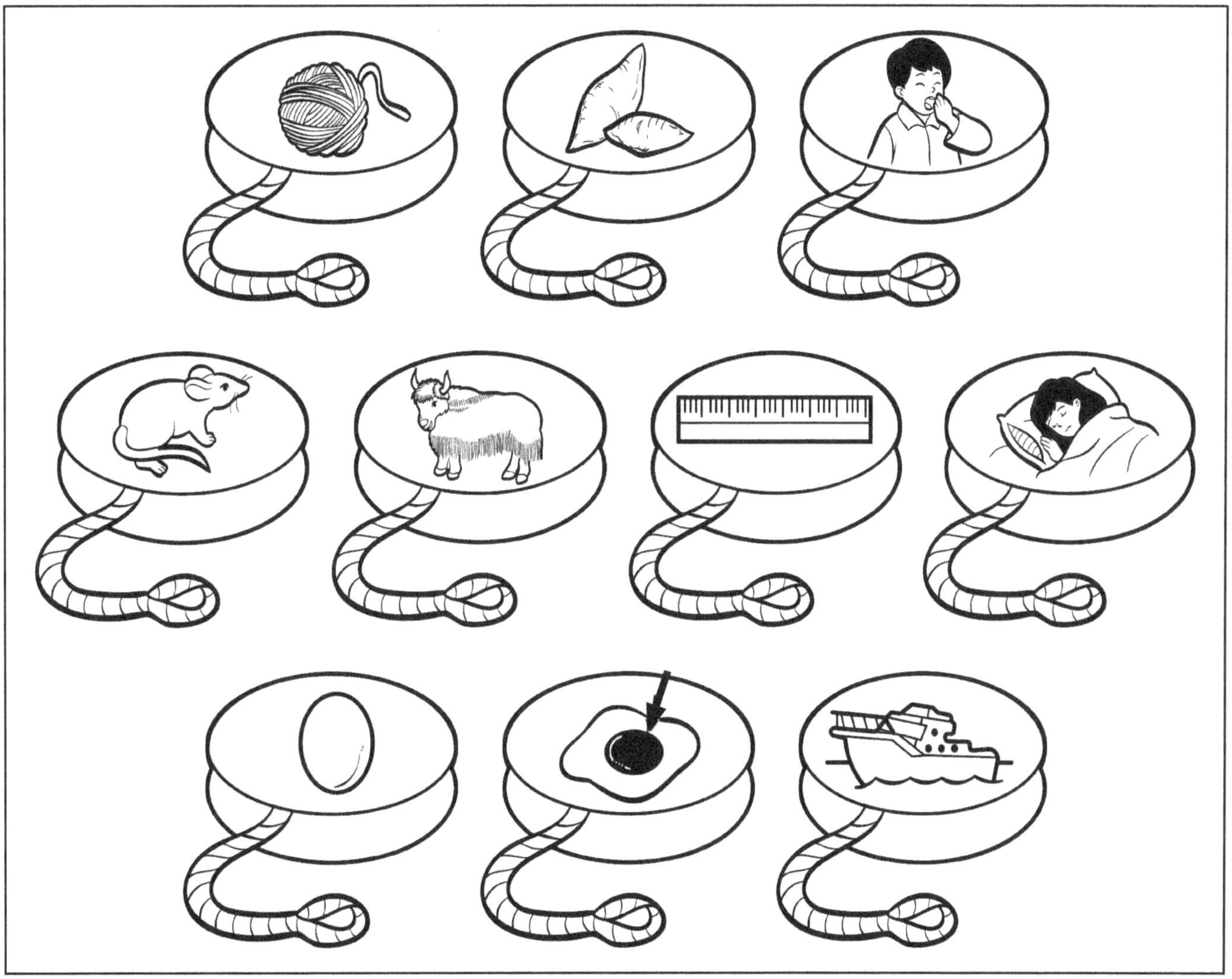

Draw a star on the letter **Yy**'s.

y Y P w y I Y

N y Y g y V Y

LESSON 21

Zz
/z/

Guide: Create a story about bees and the sound they make. Have the children fly and buzz around the classroom like bees. Discuss the sound of the letter **Z** and the things whose names start with it.

0 zero

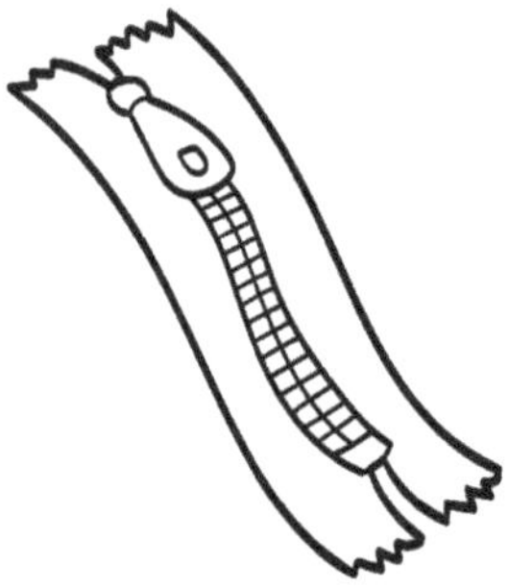

zipper

zebra

zigzag

zoo

zinnia

Practice writing the letter **Zz**.

Zz

ACTIVITY 33 SCORE: ______

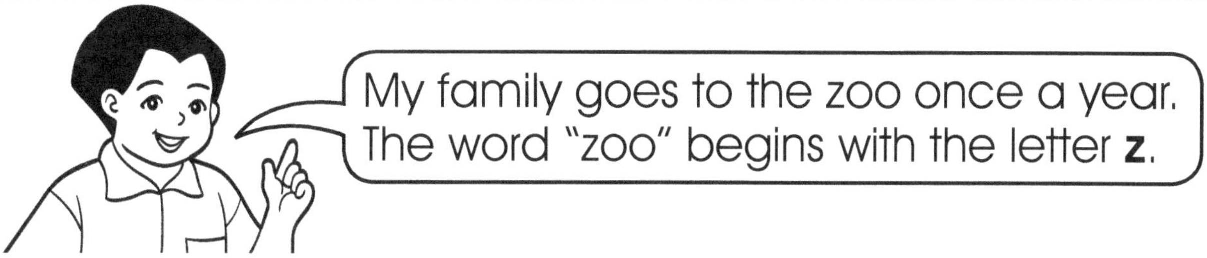

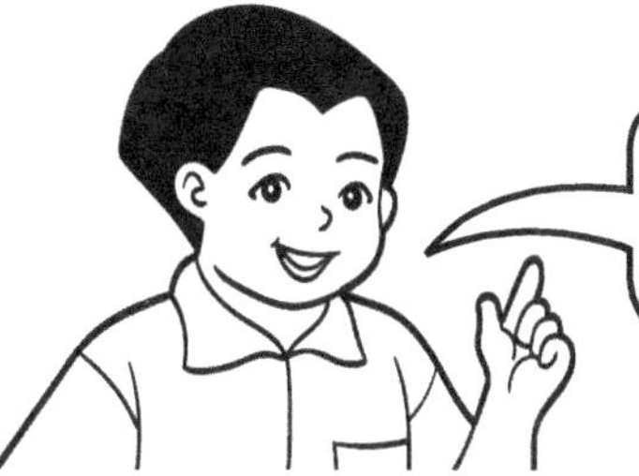

Check the pictures whose names begin with **Zz**.

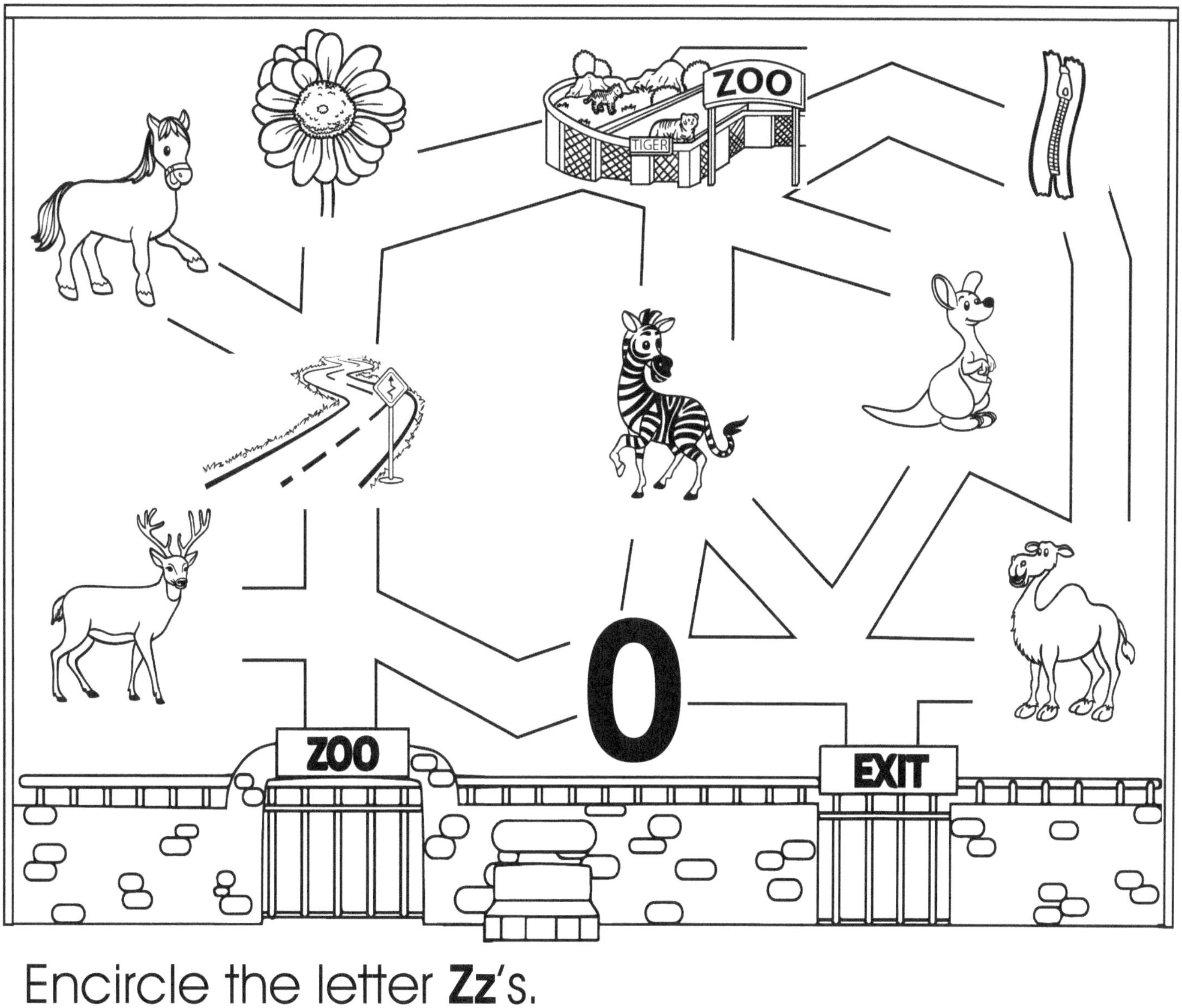

Encircle the letter **Zz**'s.

z	e	n	z	Z	l	Z
w	z	Z	v	z	N	Z

ACTIVITY 34

SCORE:_______

Choose the initial sound of each picture. Write only the numbers of your answers on the blanks.

| 1 - **Z** | 2 - **X** | 3 - **y** | 4 - **W** |

_______ 1.

_______ 2.

_______ 3.

_______ 4.

_______ 5.

_______ 6.

_______ 7.
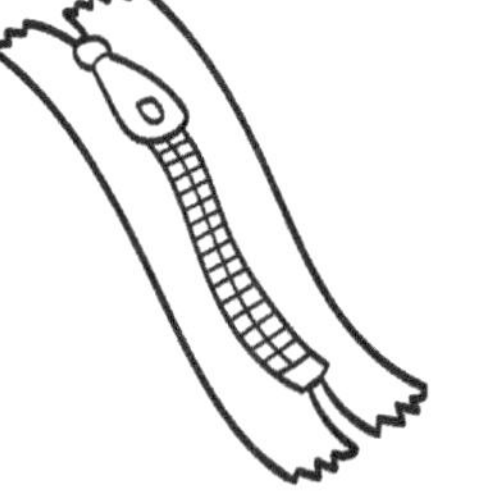

_______ 8.

_______ 9.

_______ 10.

ACTIVITY 35

SCORE: _______

Connect each picture to its initial sound.

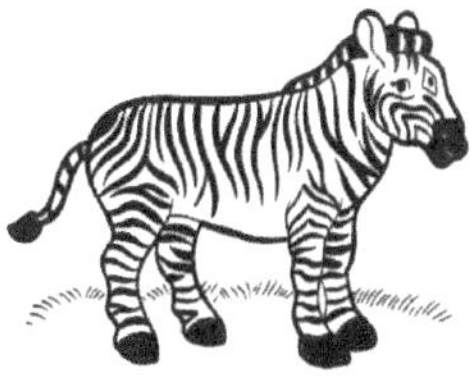

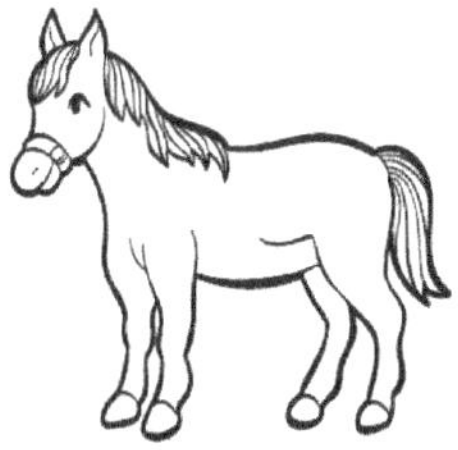

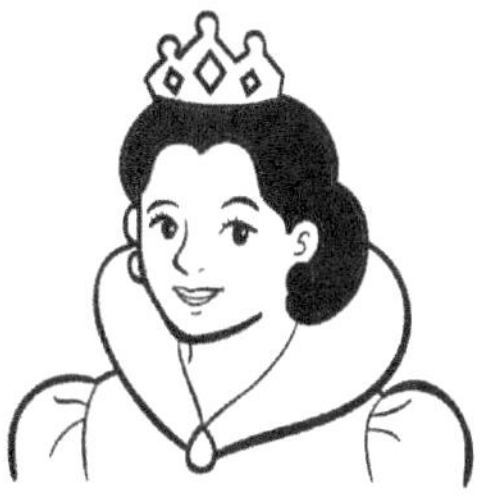

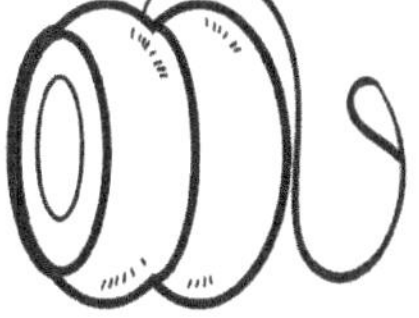

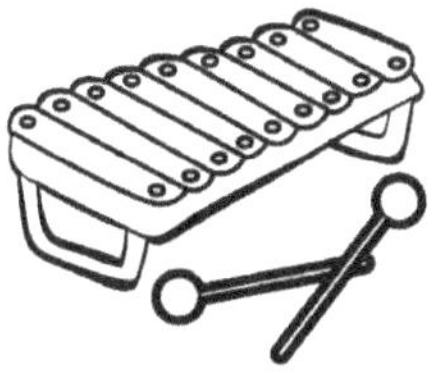

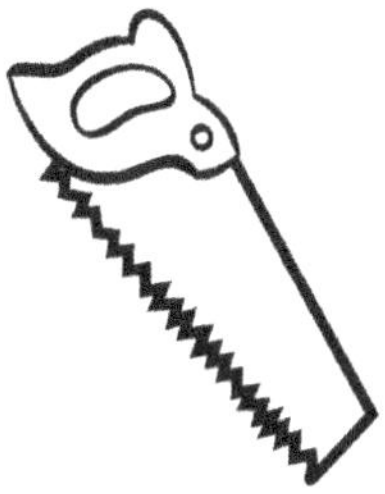

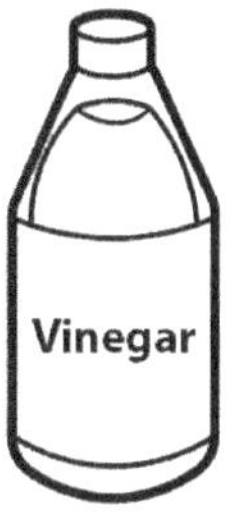

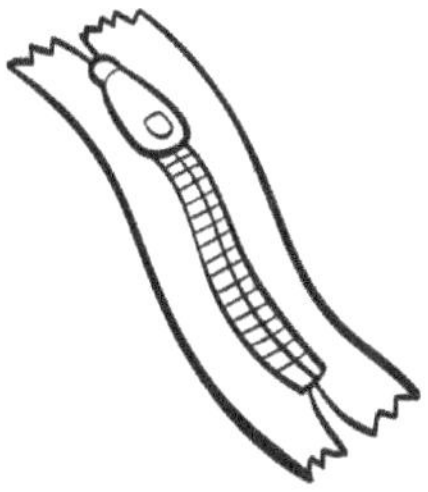

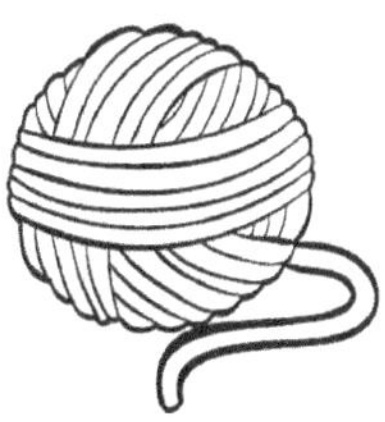

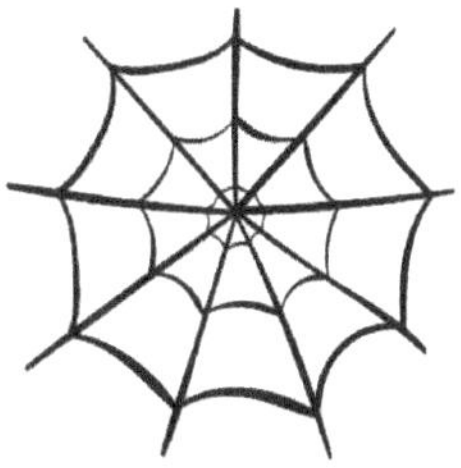

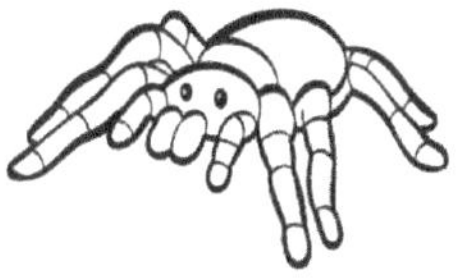

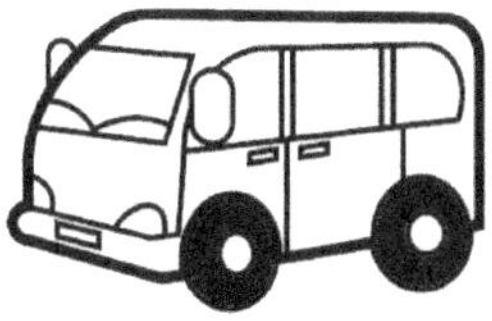

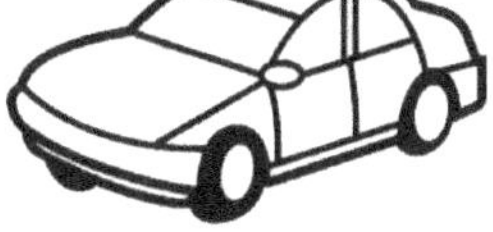

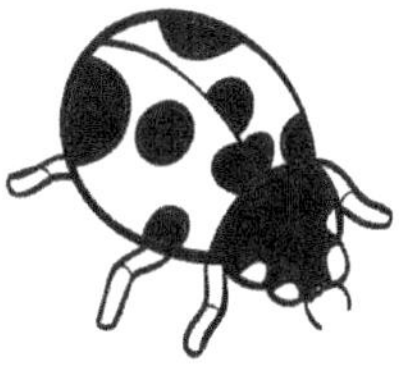

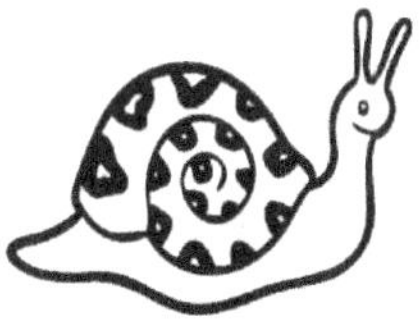

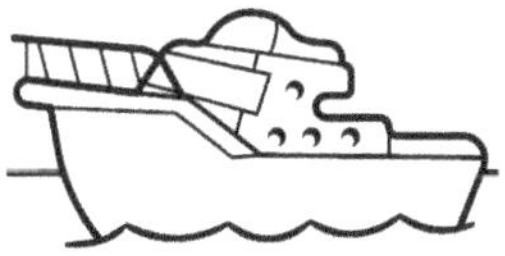

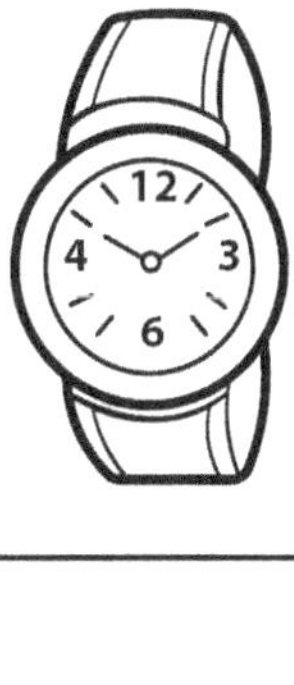

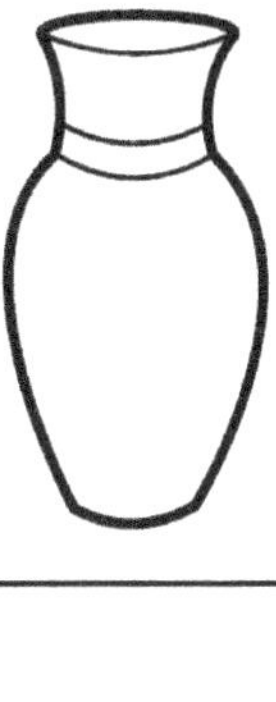

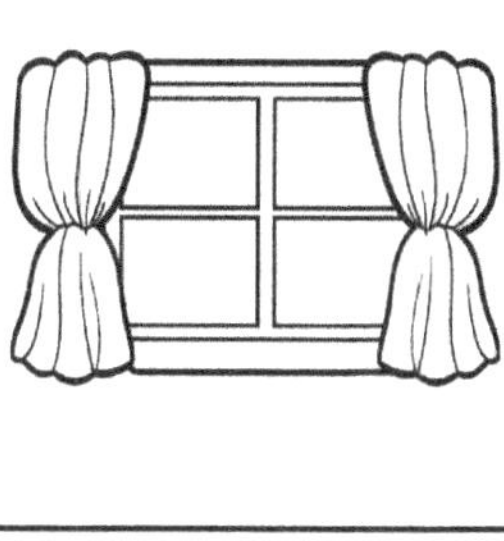

Complete the name of each picture by writing its initial sound.

1.  __ atch

2.  __ ueen

3.  __ ear

4.  __ iolin

5.  __ itch

6. __ ibbon

7. __ allet

8.  __ ray

9.  __ olcano

10. 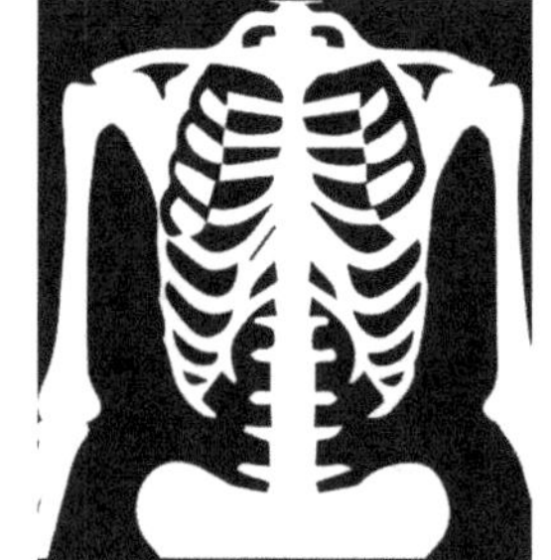 __ igzag

LESSON 22

THE LETTERS OF THE ALPHABET IN THEIR SEQUENCE

Aa   Bb   Cc   Dd   Ee

Ff   Gg   Hh   Ii   Jj

Kk   Ll   Mm   Nn   Oo

Pp   Qq   Rr   Ss   Tt

Uu   Vv   Ww   Xx   Yy

Zz

HOME ACTIVITY 7   SCORE:______

Write the letters of the alphabet in their correct sequence. *(15 points)*

ACTIVITY 36

SCORE:______

Connect the dots from *a – z* to form the mystery picture. (Teacher: Have the children draw a line from the sick boy to the hospital.) *(10 points)*

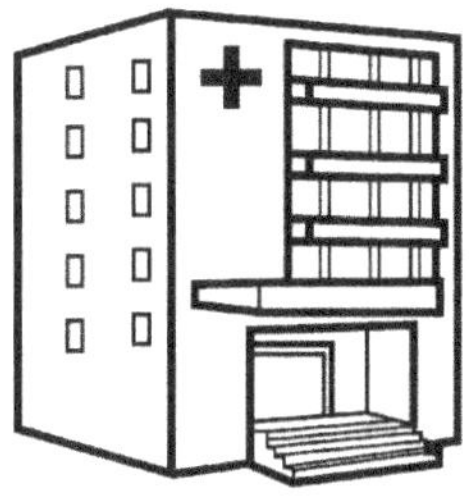

a b c

i j k

q r s

y z

t l d

h p x

w v u

o n m

g f e

Write the correct uppercase or lowercase letters of the following:

1.	B ___	11.	Q ___
2.	___ t	12.	___ d
3.	L ___	13.	P ___
4.	G ___	14.	___ j
5.	___ m	15.	___ y
6.	___ a	16.	E ___
7.	R ___	17.	___ k
8.	___ f	18.	N ___
9.	___ u	19.	H ___
10.	I ___	20.	___ w

Write the correct letter that comes after each letter below.

1.	v ____	9.	q ____
2.	l ____	10.	y ____
3.	i ____	11.	s ____
4.	o ____	12.	x ____
5.	f ____	13.	t ____
6.	d ____	14.	m ____
7.	g ____	15.	n ____
8.	c ____		

SECOND QUARTERLY TEST
(Review Guide for Parents and Teachers)

Name: ___________________________ **Score:** _________

Level: _________ **Date:** _________

I. Cross out the picture that is different in each
   group.

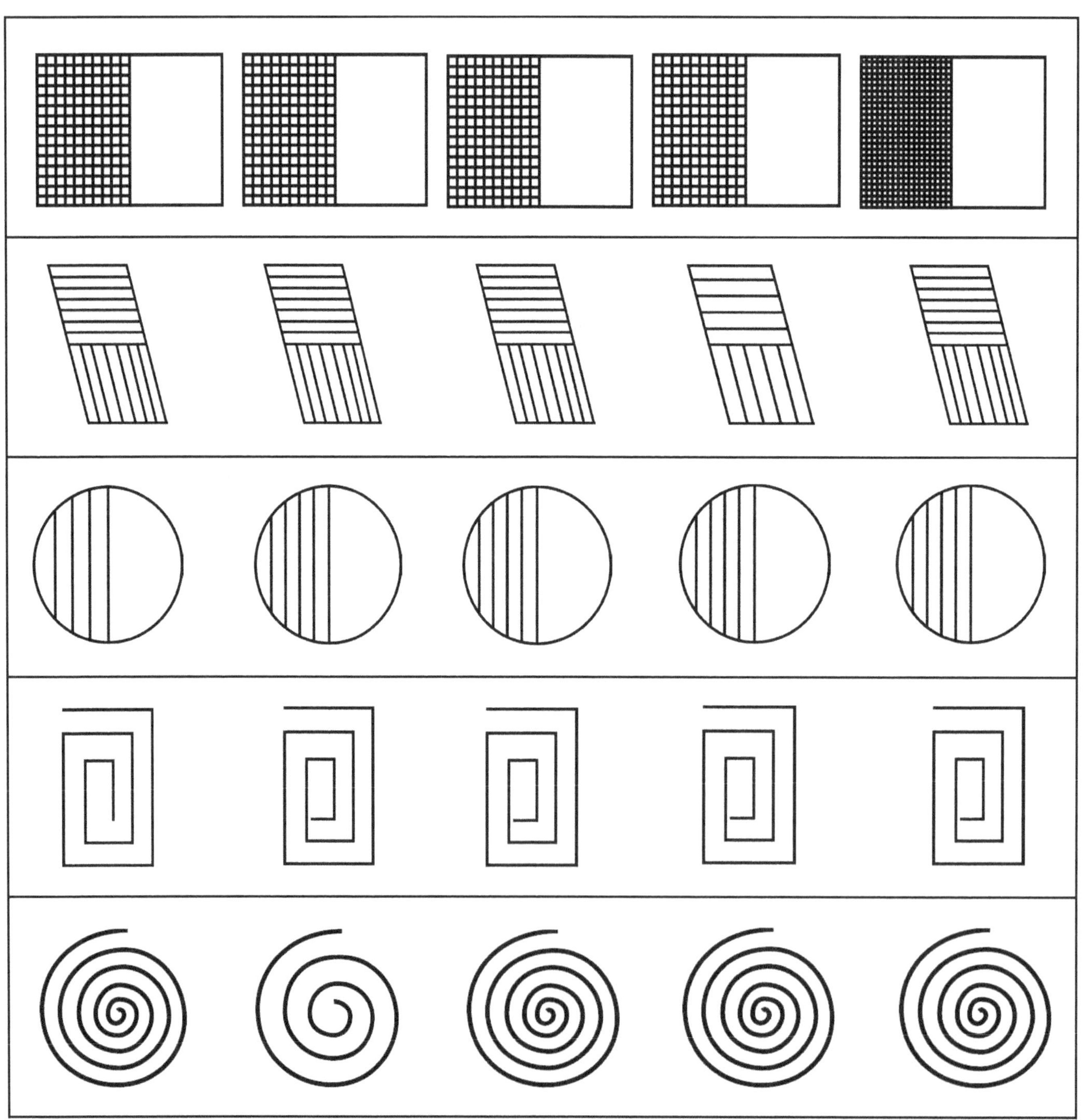

II. Write the missing uppercase and lowercase letters.

1.	I___	14.	Q___
2.	___b	15.	___u
3.	___f	16.	O___
4.	T___	17.	___x
5.	___g	18.	M___
6.	A___	19.	S___
7.	W___	20.	___l
8.	___z	21.	___r
9.	K___	22.	Y___
10.	___j	23.	___n
11.	___p	24.	V___
12.	E___	25.	C___
13.	___d	26.	___h

III. Write the letter that comes before or after.

Ll ____   Mm ____

____ Zz   Dd ____

____ Gg   ____ Oo

Ss ____   ____ Jj

____ Vv   Xx ____

IV. Write the missing letters of the alphabet.

Aa ____ Cc ____ ____

Ff ____ ____ Ii Jj

Kk Ll Mm Nn ____

Pp ____ Rr Ss ____

____ Vv ____ Xx Yy

Zz

V. Write the correct initial sound for each picture.

1.  _____guana

2.  _____ail

3.  _____ebra

4. _____ing

5.  _____ar

6. _____and

7.  _____eep

8. _____ylophone

9.  _____obot

10.  _____iolin

11.  _____ntidy

12. _____og

13.  _____ven

14. _____eed

15.  _____ish

16. _____uail

17.  _____olk

18. _____nt

19.  _____omato

20. _____rapes

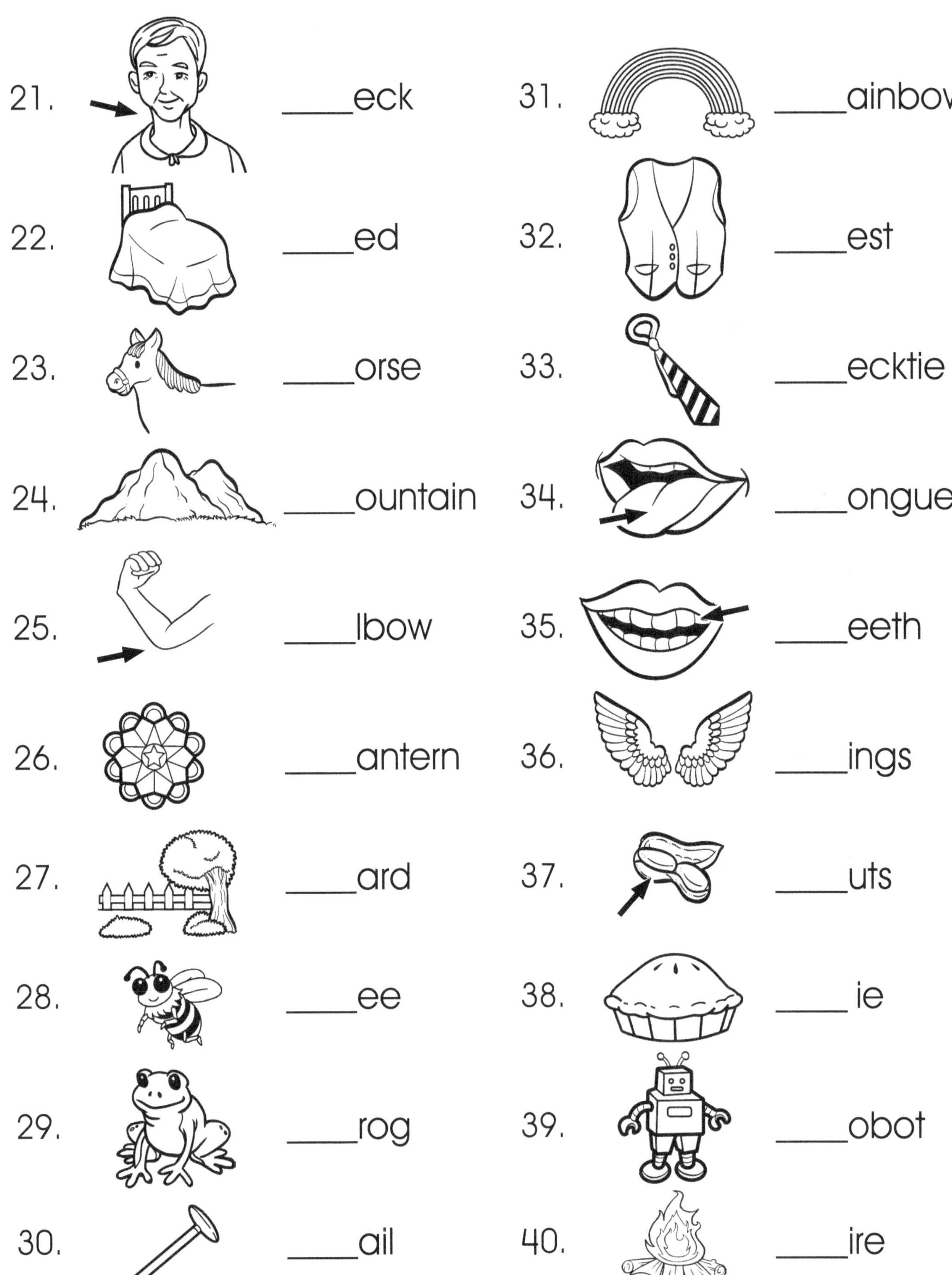

21. ____eck

22. ____ed

23. ____orse

24. ____ountain

25. ____lbow

26. ____antern

27. ____ard

28. ____ee

29. ____rog

30. ____ail

31. ____ainbow

32. ____est

33. ____ecktie

34. ____ongue

35. ____eeth

36. ____ings

37. ____uts

38. ____ie

39. ____obot

40. ____ire

PROGRESS CHART
SECOND QUARTER

Name: _______________________________   Level: __________

ACTIVITY	No. of Items	My Score	HOME ACTIVITY	No. of Items	My Score	QUIZ	No. of Items	My Score
1	10		1	10		1	10	
2	10		2	10		2	10	
3	10		3	10		3	10	
4	10		4	10		4	10	
5	10		5	10		5	10	
6	10		6	5		6	10	
7	10		7	15		7	5	
8	10		8	20		8	10	
9	10					9	10	
10	10					10	15	
11	5							
12	5							
13	15							

14	10							
15	10							
16	20							
17	10							
18	10							
19	10							
20	20							
21	10							
22	10							
23	10							
24	10							
25	10							
26	10							
27	10							
28	10							
29	10							
30	10							
31	10							
32	10							
33	10							
34	10							
35	20							
36	10							
TOTAL	385		TOTAL	90		TOTAL	100	

Parent's/Guardian's Signature   Teacher's Signature

THIRD QUARTER
BEGINNING READING

Teacher's Objectives and Student Evaluation				
Lesson	*At the end of the activities, the child should be able to:*	D	DD	WD
1	1. identify the ending sounds of objects			
	2. recognize objects whose names have the same ending sound			
	3. differentiate ending from beginning sound			
2	4. identify the middle sound of objects			
	5. recognize objects whose names have the same middle sound			
	6. differentiate middle from ending sound			
3	7. join letters to form blends			
	8. identify the missing blend			
	9. write the missing initial or final blend			
4	10. form blends with the letters *a, e, i, o,* and *u*			
	11. recognize the correct blend			
	12. tell the missing initial or final blend			
5	13. blend letters to form words			
	14. read three-letter words with the c-v-c pattern			
	15. tell the meaning of words read			
6	16. read other word families with short middle sounds			
	17. tell the meanings of words read			
	18. improve his or her vocabulary			

Legend:

D — Developing   D — Developed   WD — Well-Developed

LESSON 1

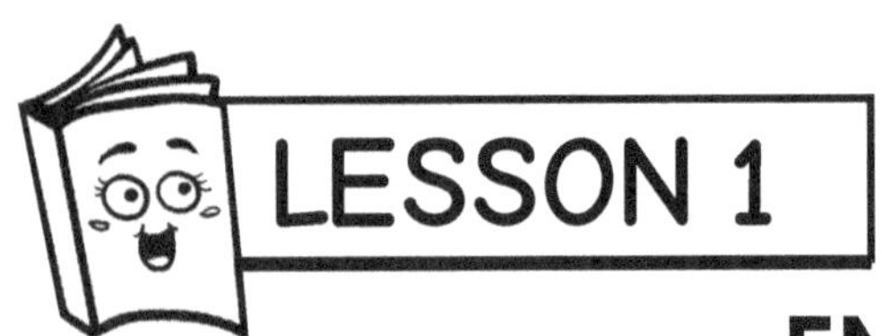

ENDING SOUNDS

Guide: Ask the children to close their eyes and listen to a sequence of three sounds. You may use rhythm band instruments for this activity. You may also tap a pencil, crumple paper, shake a rattle, etc. Let the children guess the sequence of sounds heard, giving emphasis on the last.

Ending sounds are the sounds you hear at the end of words. Let's practice sounding the letters.

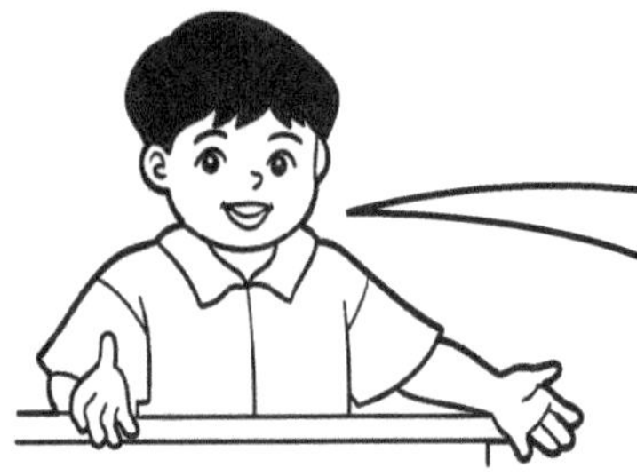

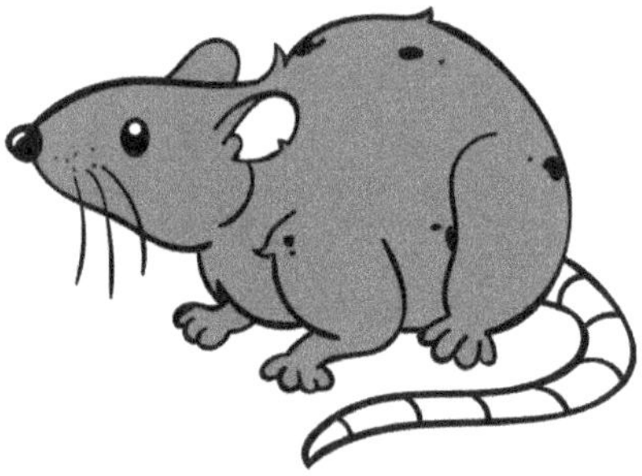

ra**t**

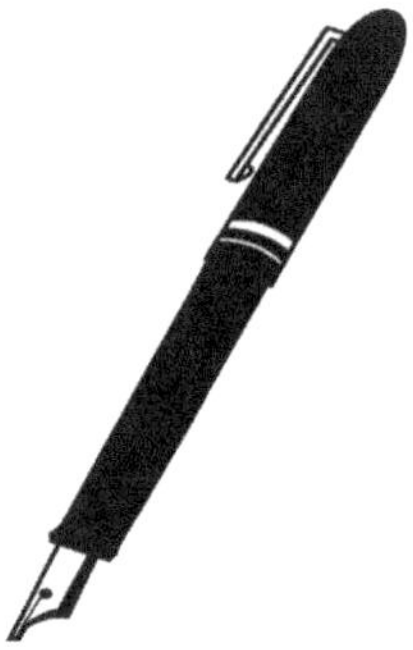

pe**n**

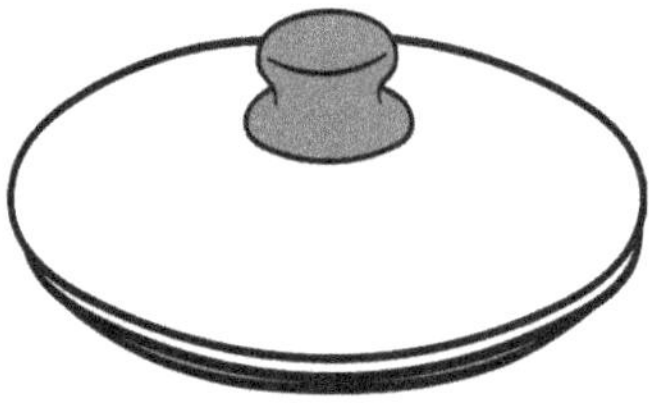

li**d**

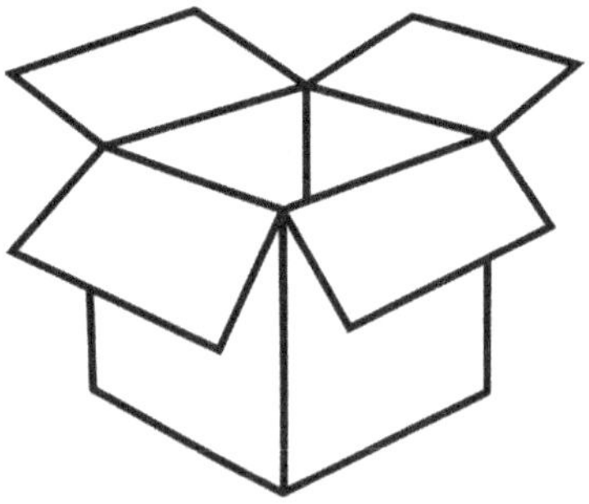

bo**x**

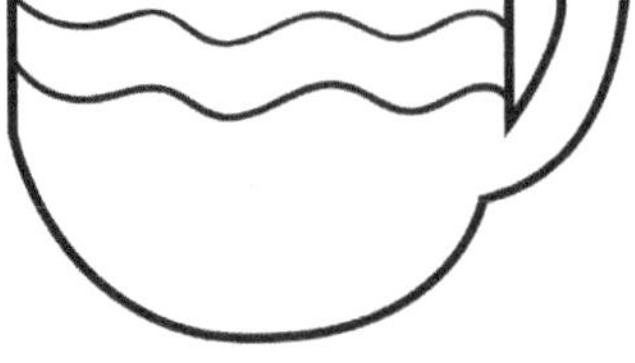

cu**p**

ACTIVITY 1

SCORE:_______

Box the pictures in each group whose names end with the letter on the left.

m				
x				
s				
b				
n				

ACTIVITY 2

SCORE:______

Connect the pictures to their correct ending sounds.

| w |
| g |
| t |
| n |
| k |
| l |
| d |
| p |
| a |
| r |

160

HOME ACTIVITY 1   SCORE:_______

Color the star beside the correct ending sound for each picture.

 (leaf) ☆ p ☆ f ☆ l	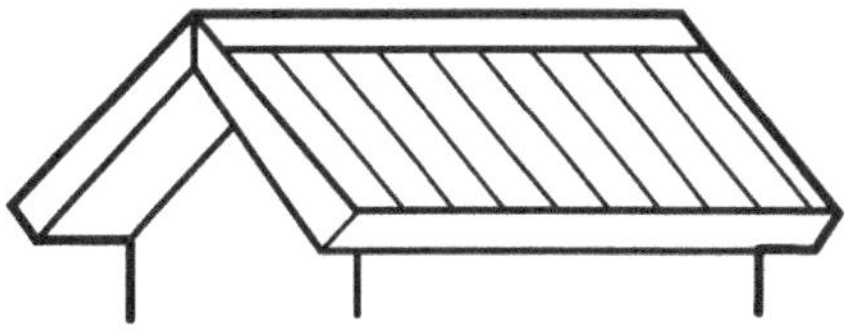 (roof) ☆ f ☆ r ☆ b
 (tomato) ☆ o ☆ d ☆ f	 (lamp) ☆ y ☆ s ☆ p
 (boy) ☆ g ☆ s ☆ y	 (hamburger) ☆ h ☆ r ☆ g
 (scarf) ☆ y ☆ f ☆ o	 (fox) ☆ x ☆ p ☆ d
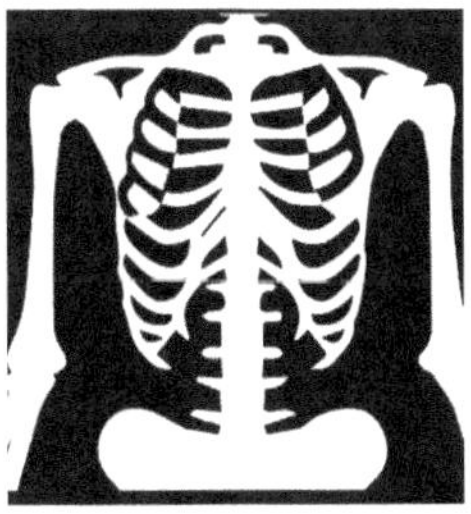 (x-ray) ☆ b ☆ l ☆ y	 (bus) ☆ p ☆ s ☆ j

161

Encircle the letter of the correct ending sound for each picture. Then write that letter on the blank to complete the name of the picture.

shoe ____	s x c	kiw ____	e i a
pizz ____	g o a	broo ____	n b m
hal ____	p f h	kangaro ____	o t u
cri ____	b d p	tra ____	x y g
har ____	b q p	pian ____	o a e

LESSON 2

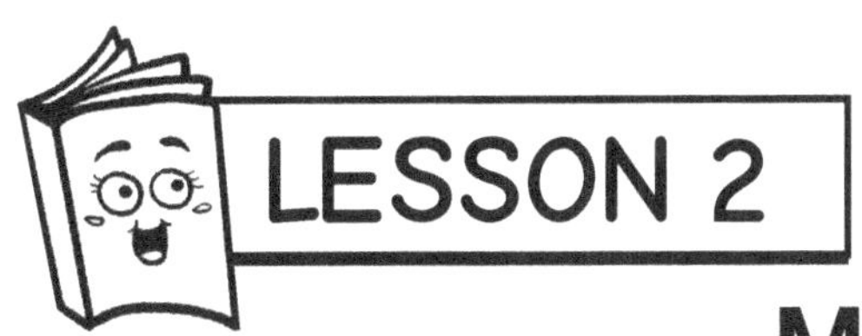

MIDDLE SOUNDS

Guide: Have the children create a clapping-snapping-tapping pattern. Record the pattern on an audio tape or a mobile phone. Play the recorded sound back. Have the children identify the sound at the middle of the pattern. Have them record other patterns such as snapping-clapping-tapping, tapping-snapping-clapping, etc.

Middle sounds are the sounds you hear at the middle of words.
Let's practice sounding the letters.

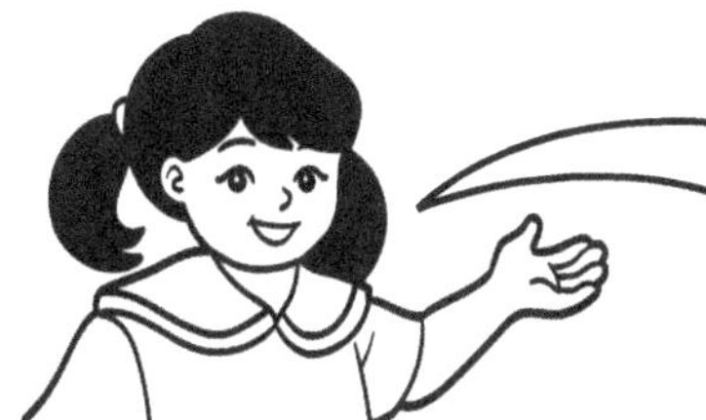

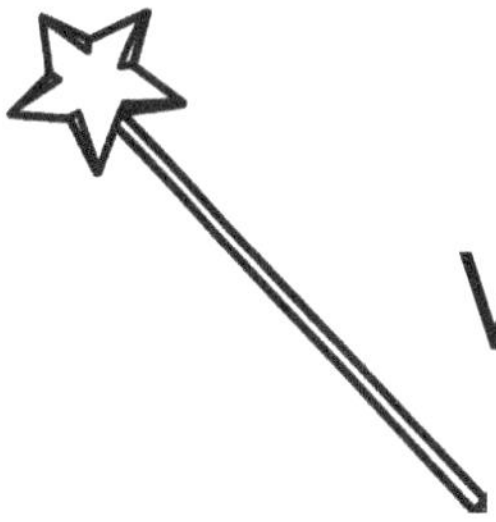

w**a**nd

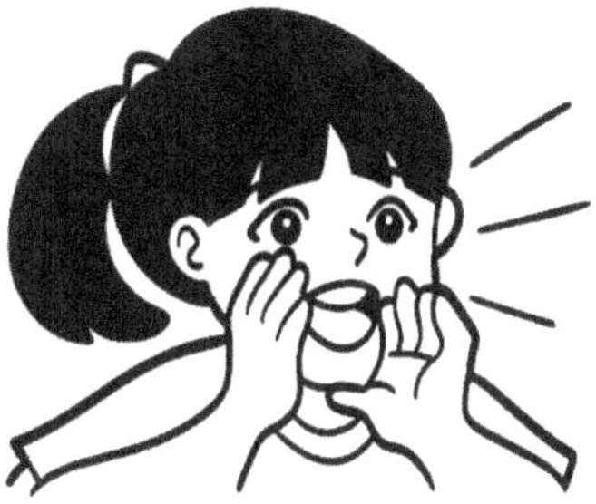

y**e**ll

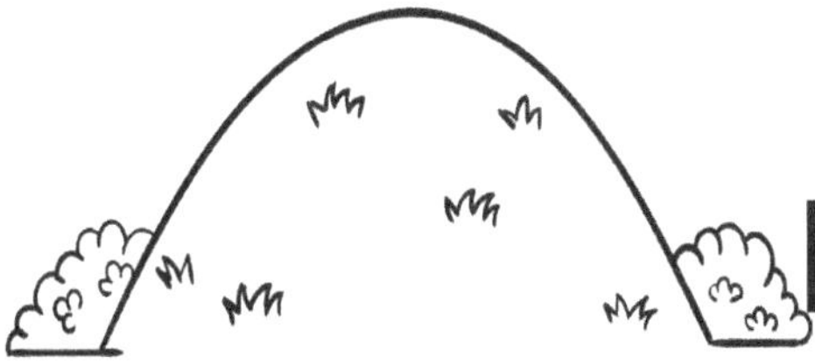

h**i**ll

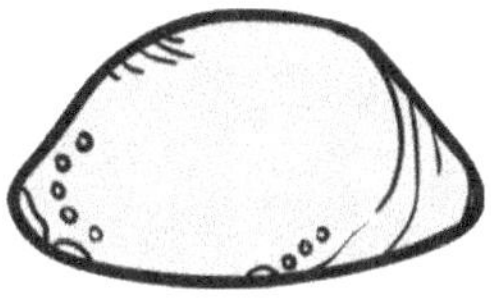

r**o**ck

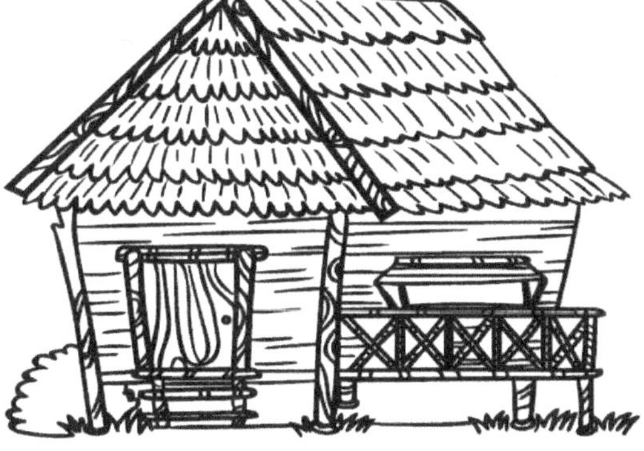

h**u**t

ACTIVITY 3

SCORE: _______

Underline the letter of the correct middle sound.

(house)	a o u	*(lock)*	u o a
(ring)	i e u	*(nest)*	e i o
(sandcastle)	a u o	*(doll)*	a u o
(king)	e i u	*(pants)*	u a o
(bell)	i a e	*(rose)*	e a u

164

ACTIVITY 4

SCORE:________

Draw a line to connect each picture to the letter of its middle sound.

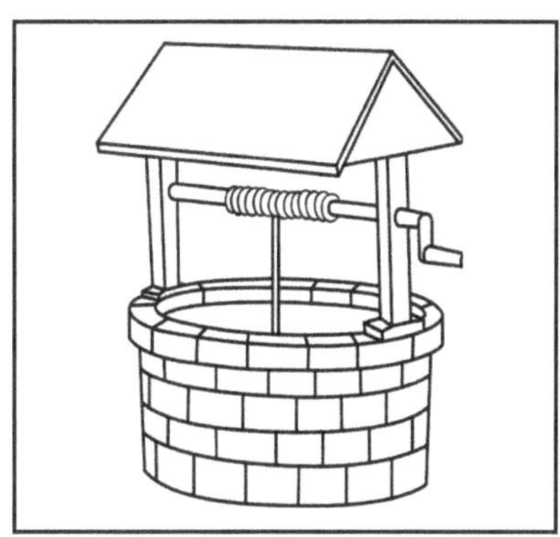

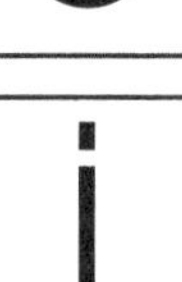

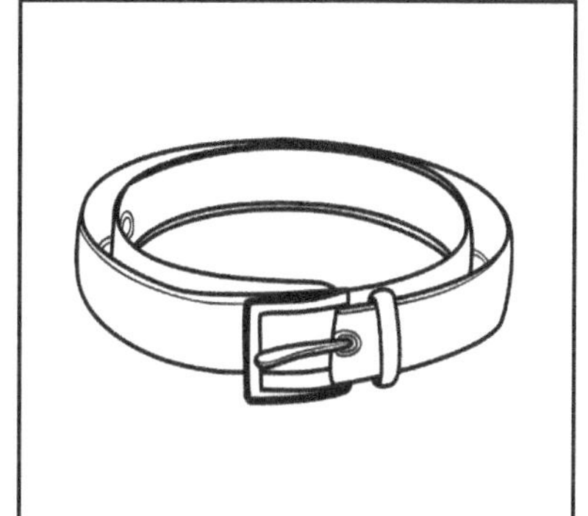

QUIZ NO. 2 SCORE: ______

Connect the pictures to the middle sounds of their names.

 e u 	 e i 
 i o 	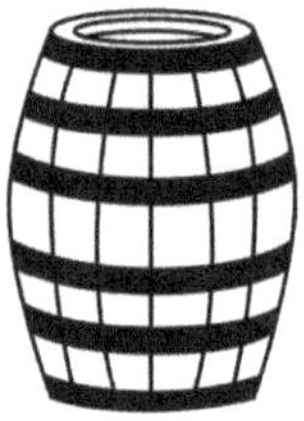 a e 
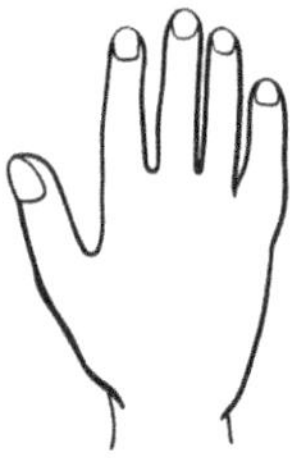 u a 	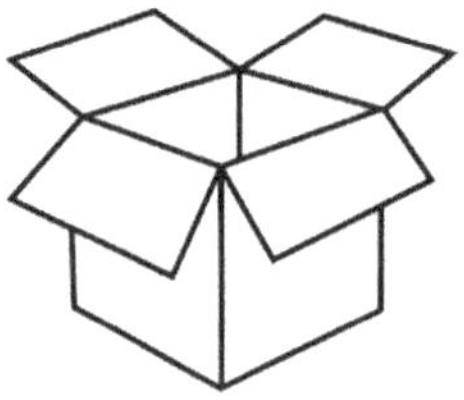 o i 
 i a 	 u a 
 o u 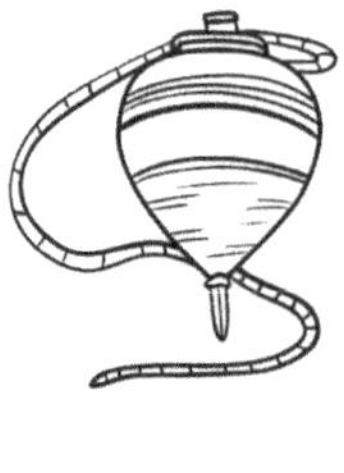	 e o 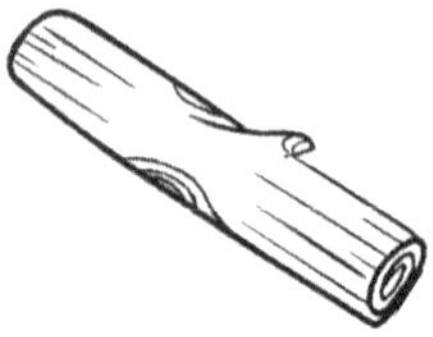

HOME ACTIVITY 2   SCORE:______

Write the beginning and ending sounds for each picture.

 ___ctopu___	 ___lbo___
 ___lowe___	 ___guan___
 ___mbrell___	 ___ai___
 ___nai___	 ___ar___
 ___lan___	 ___oal___

QUIZ NO. 3

SCORE: _______

Write the missing beginning, middle, or ending sound for each picture.

 n __ ck	 tomat __
 wol __	 ch __ ck
 __ nsects	 p __ nd
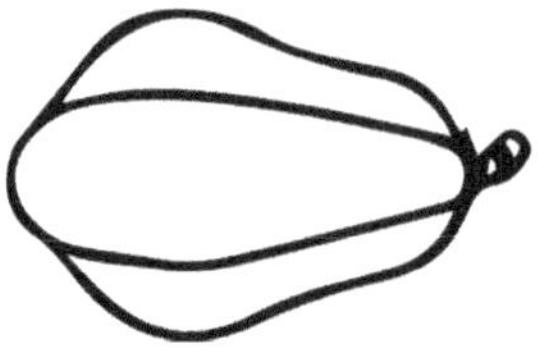 papay __	 bo __
 st __ r	 m __ g

LESSON 3

JOINING LETTERS TO FORM BLENDS

Guide: Prepare 26 alphabet flashcards. Separate the vowels from the consonants. Hang the letter "a" using yarn and clothespin. Have the children take turns hanging a consonant partner and blending the sounds formed. Do the same with the other letters.

r   a ⟶ **ra** ---- t

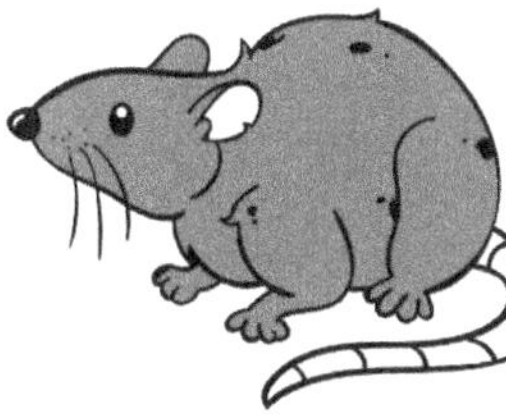

c   a ⟶ **ca** ---- r

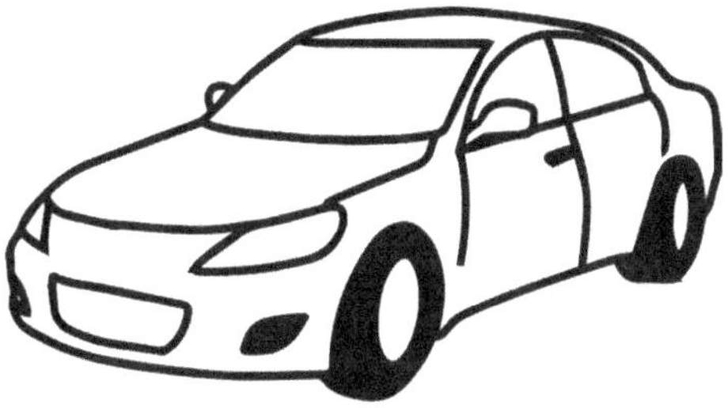

a   n ⟶ v --- **an**

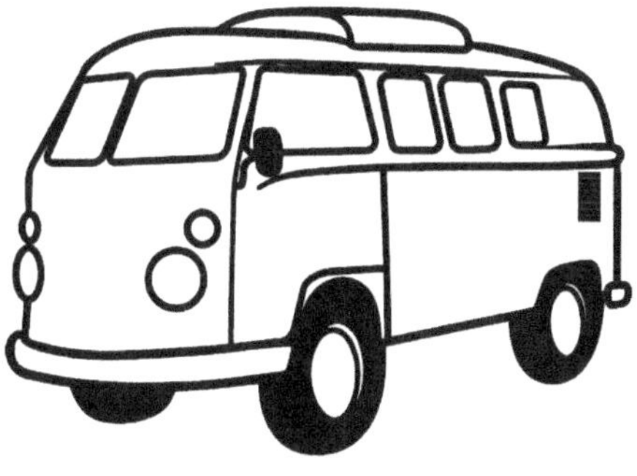

a   m ⟶ h ---**am**

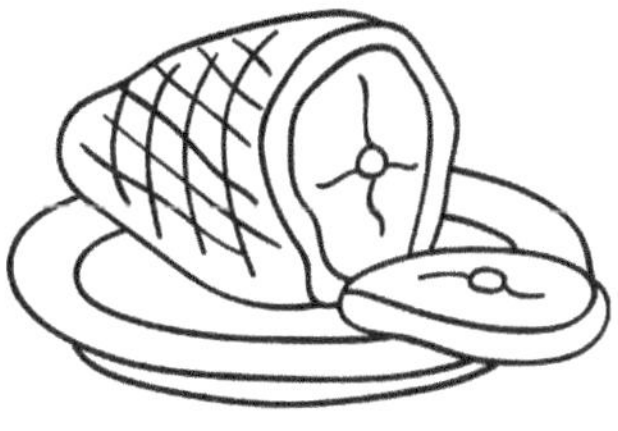

ACTIVITY 5

SCORE:________

Draw a triangle (Δ) around the initial blend for each picture.

	ja fa va		ca ra la
	pa ta ya		ya ma wa
	ma sa la		ta ja pa
	ba pa fa		ba pa va
	ra sa ta		ha ka la

ACTIVITY 6

SCORE:_______

Shade the box beside the correct final blend for each picture.

TAXI □ ag □ ab □ at	SHINING Floor □ ax □ as □ ac
□ at □ an □ am	□ ak □ at □ ax
WELCOME □ ap □ at □ as	□ ay □ af □ ap
GASUL □ ax □ as □ ab	□ an □ ab □ ad
□ ay □ an □ am	₱1.00 □ ag □ ay □ at

Write the missing initial blend to complete the name of each picture.

___lloon	___nce
___rlic	___ngaroo
___nny	___tch
___bbit	___ck
___ntern	___dpole

ACTIVITY 8

SCORE:______

Write the missing final blend to complete the name of each picture.

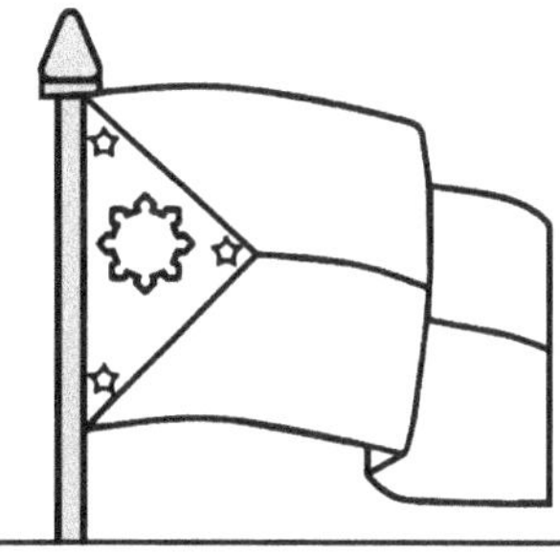 fl __ __	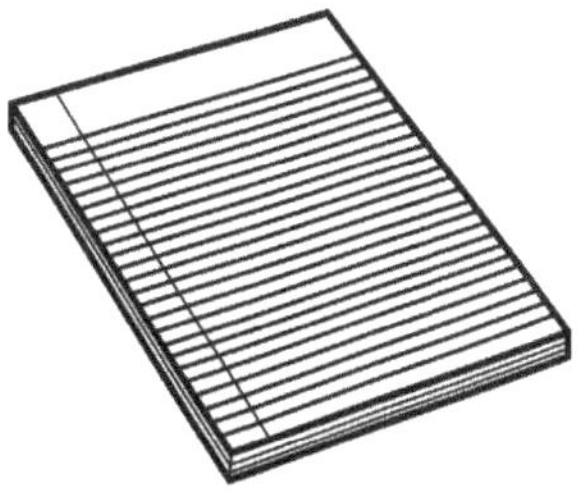 p __ __
 b __ __	 c __ __
 cr __ __	 c __ __
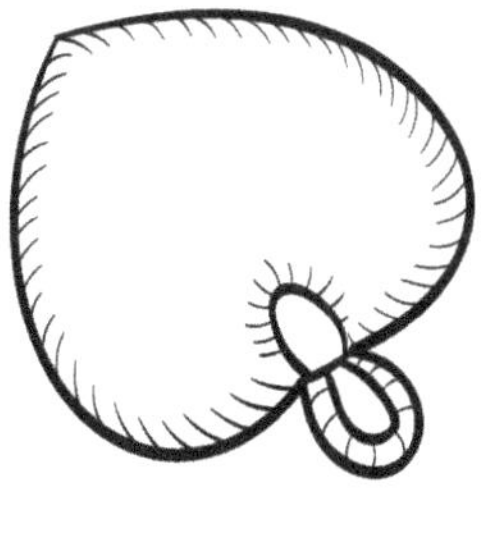 f __ __	 h __ __
 s __ __	 g __ __

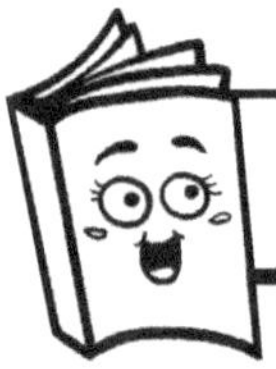

FORMING OTHER BLENDS

k e → **ke** ------ g

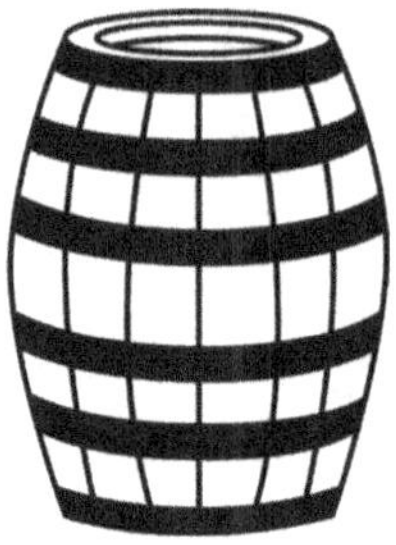

p i → **pi** ------ n

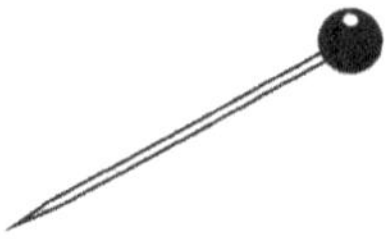

b o → **bo** ------ x

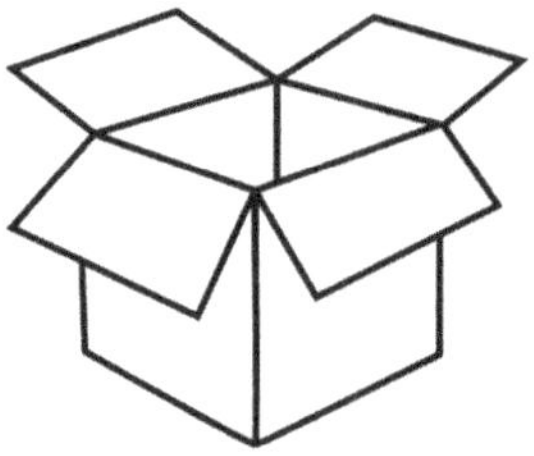

e t → n ------ **et**

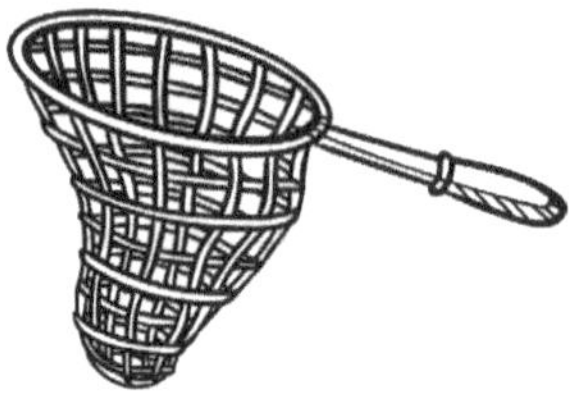

i d → l ------ **id**

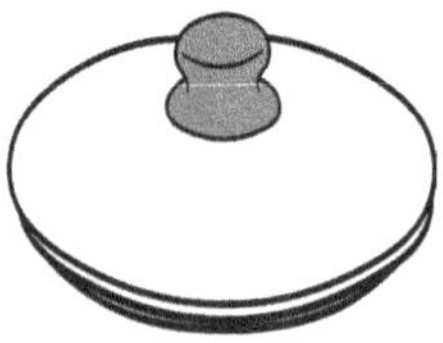

u p → p ----- **up**

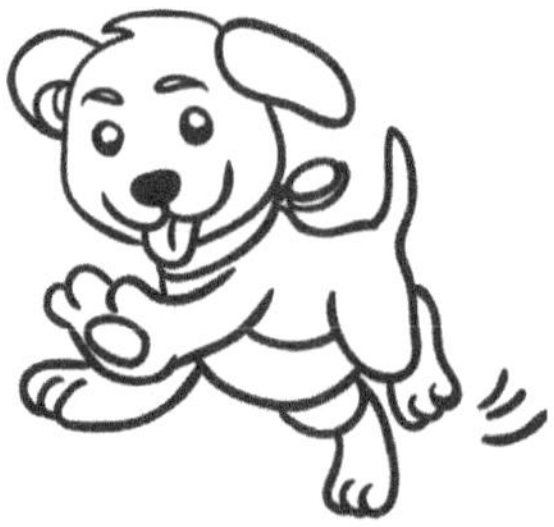

SCORE:_______

Connect the letter on the left to the correct letter on the right to form the initial blend for each picture.

(tent)	t	• i • e • u	(hanger)	h	• a • o • i
(mirror)	m	• i • e • u	(coconut)	c	• i • a • o
(jacket)	j	• u • o • a	(pencil)	p	• a • o • e
(nut)	n	• e • a • u	(duck)	d	• i • u • o
(domino)	d	• o • e • u	(zipper)	z	• e • i • a

SCORE:_______

Complete the name of each picture. Choose the blend from the box.

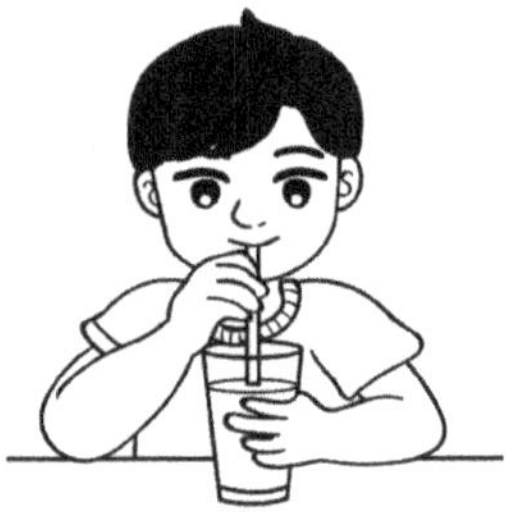

s __ __

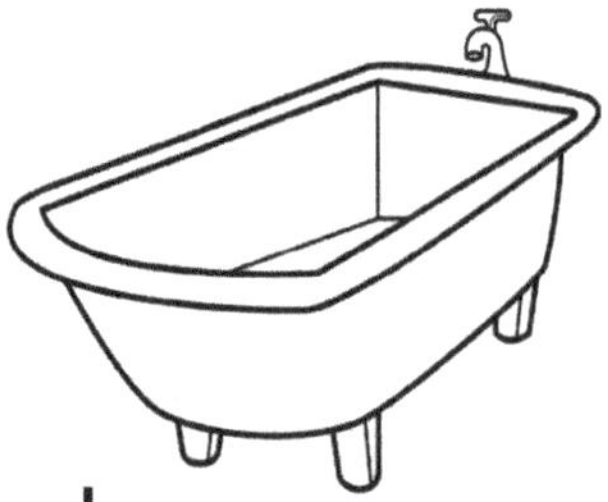

t __ __

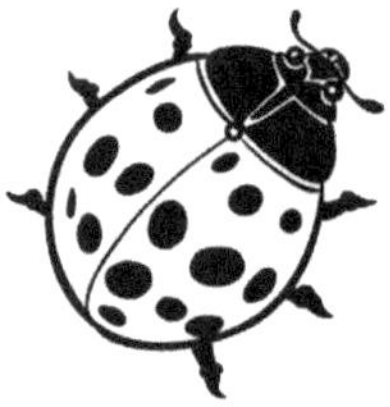

b __ __ __

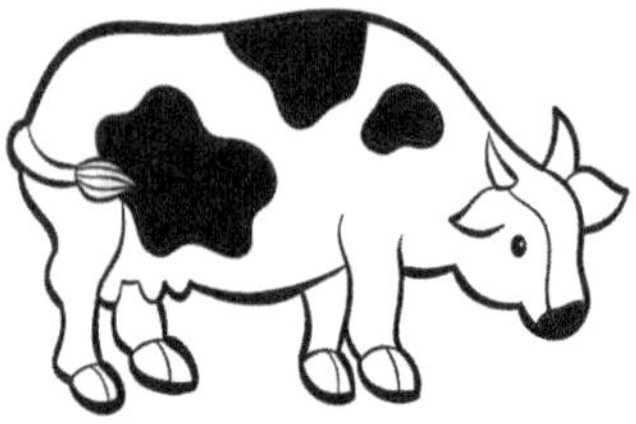

c __ __

ow   ed   ug

ip   ub   at   it

en   ar   ox

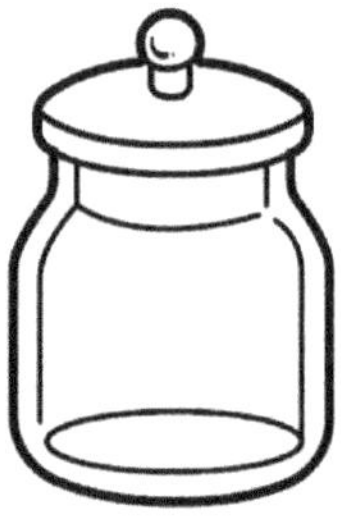

j __ __

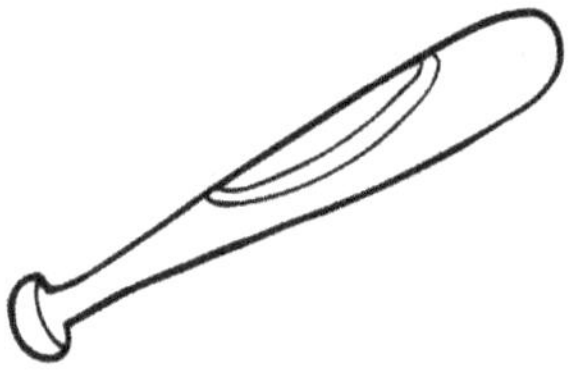

b __ __

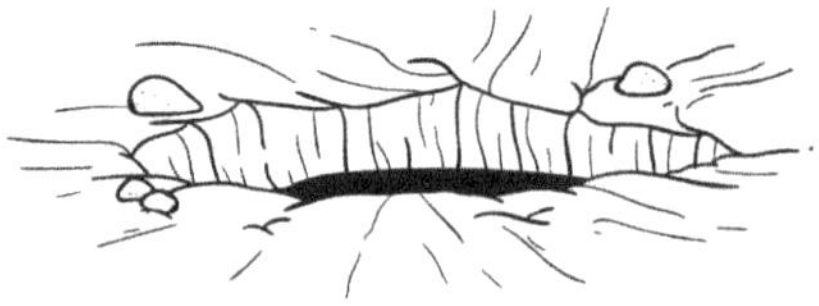

p __ __

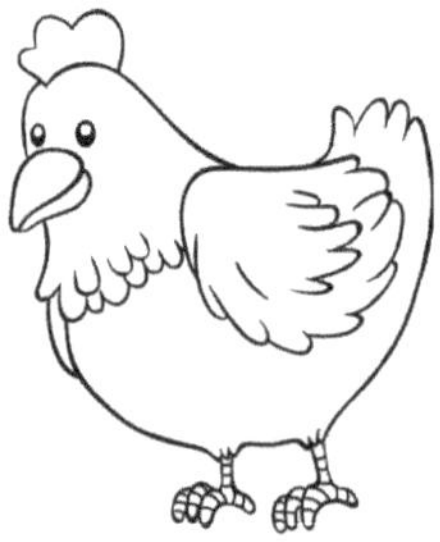

h __ __

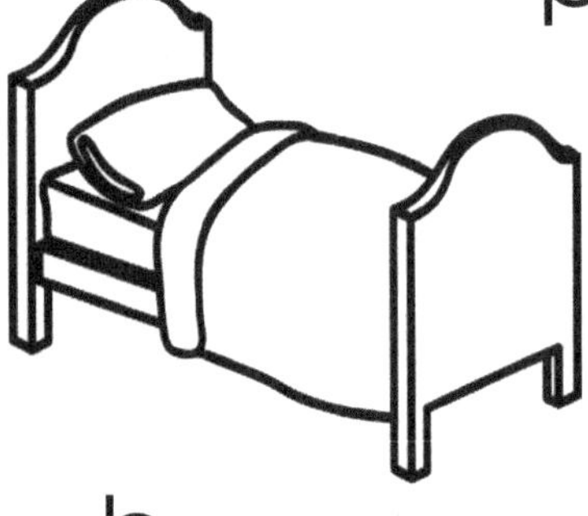

b __ __

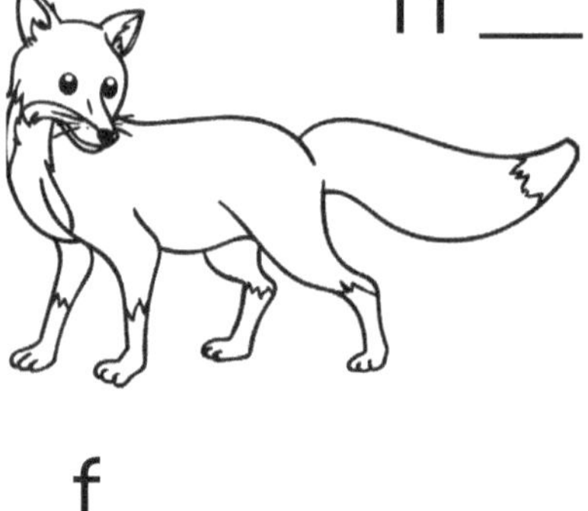

f __ __

HOME ACTIVITY 3   SCORE:______

Write the missing blend to complete the name of each picture. Look at the letters in the circles and copy them onto the boxes below to find the secret message.

1. ( )__mb

2. h( )__

3. ( )__st

4. t( )nt

5. b __( )

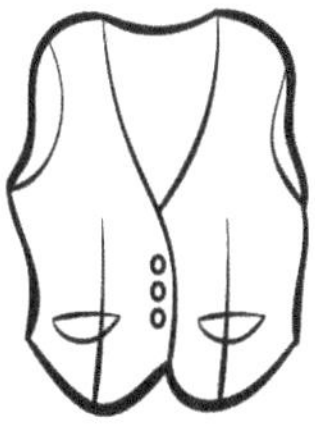

6. ( )__p

7. ( )__nd

8. volca__( )( )

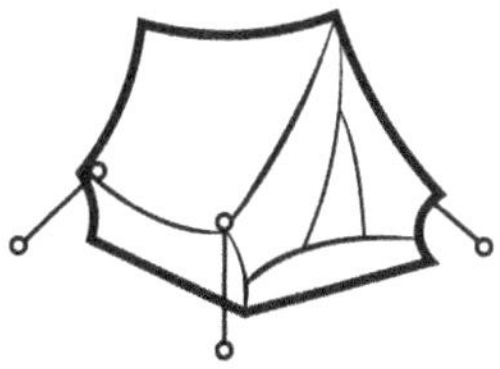

9. p( )__

10. ( )__ps

I [ ][ ][ ][ ] [ ][ ][ ][ ][ ][ ] !☺
  1 2 3 4   5 6 7 8 9 10

177

QUIZ NO. 4

SCORE: ______

Write the missing blend to complete the name of each picture.

ok __ __

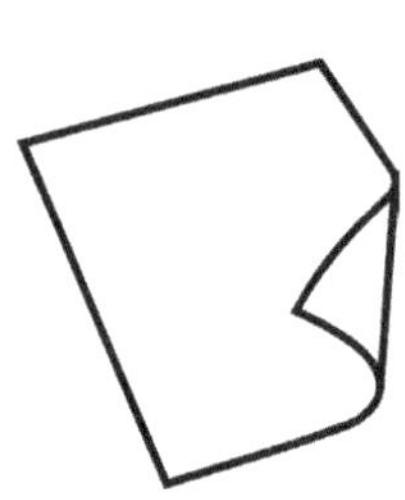

pap __ __

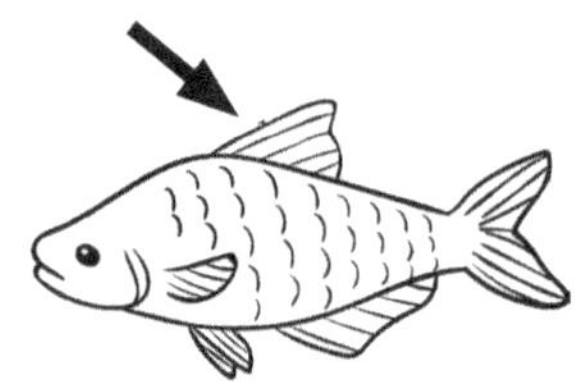

f __ __

pota __ __

__ __ ndor

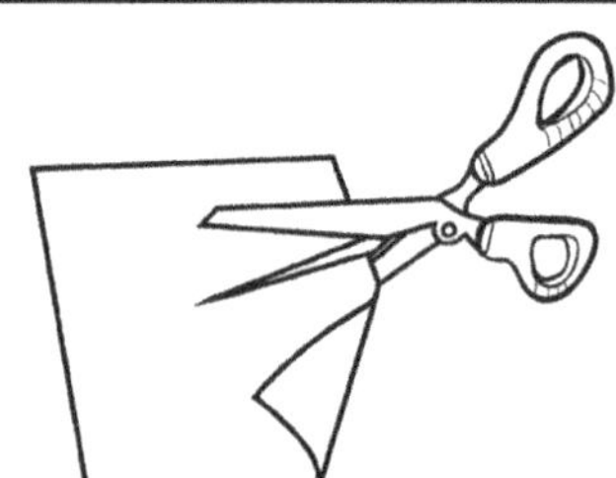

c __ __

__ __ lb

__ __ rachute

__ __ bot

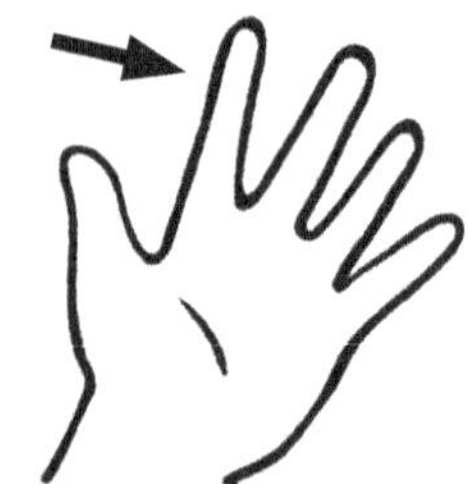

__ __ nger

ADVANCED GROUP

Write the missing initial or final blend for each picture.

	_ _ pper		mi _ _ _
	volca _ _		_ _ _ t
	_ _ ds		avoca _ _
	ki _ _		_ _ st
	bana _ _		pia _ _
	_ _ ll		gua _ _
	_ _ st		_ _ ail
	papa _ _		_ _ ll
	_ _ ft		_ _ ps
	piz _ _		kha _ _ _

LESSON 5

FORMING WORDS

<table>
<tr><td><u>Guide</u>:</td><td>Give the children scrabble letters or magnetic letters to make words. You may also write letters on round pieces of cardboard; punch holes on opposite ends, and encourage the children to string letters together to form words.</td></tr>
</table>

y → a → m **yam**

p → a → n **pan**

j → a → r **jar**

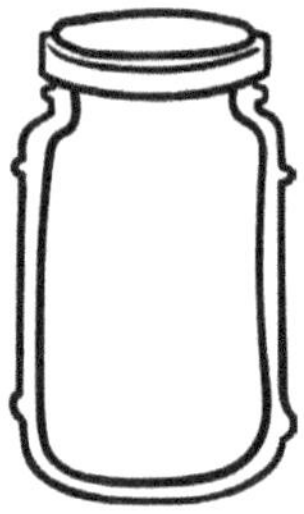

c → a → b **cab**

b → a → t **bat**

ACTIVITY 11

SCORE: _______

Write the missing initial and final letters to complete the name of each picture.

 __ a __	 __ a __
 __ a __	 __ a __
 __ a __	 __ a __
 __ a __	 __ a __
 __ a __	 __ a __

ACTIVITY 12

SCORE:______

Join the letters with the blend inside the box to form new words. Write the words formed beside each picture.

v

c [**an**] f

p   m

m   h

r [**at**] b

f

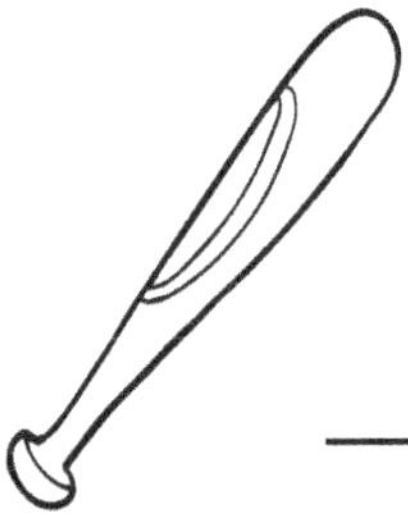

SCORE: _______

Connect the blend on the left to a letter on the right to form the correct word for each picture. Write the newly formed word on the blank.

Picture	Blend	Letters	Answer
(rag)	ra •	• p • g • y	_______
(angry face)	ma •	• d • p • t	_______
(map)	ma •	• n • t • p	_______
(fan)	fa •	• r • n • t	_______
(ham)	ha •	• m • n • v	_______
(saxophone)	sa •	• g • x • t	_______
(car)	ca •	• r • n • p	_______
(jar)	ja •	• r • m • n	_______
(tag ₱1.00)	ta •	• x • p • g	_______
(wave)	wa •	• d • y • g	_______

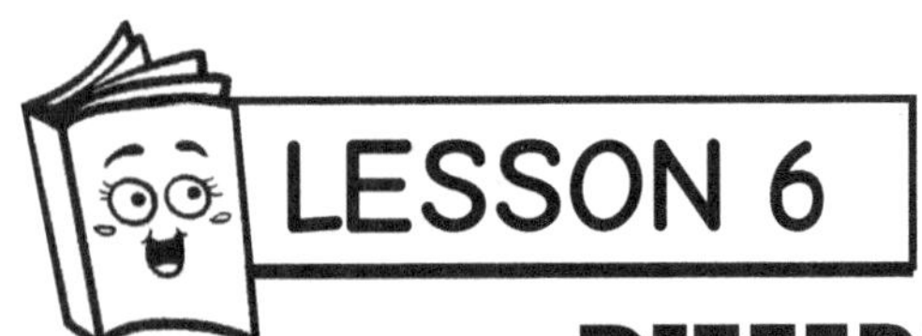

DIFFERENT WORD FAMILIES

Guide: Make word family wheels. Cut a "pie slice" out of a paper plate. Write a vowel-consonant blend on the plate and use a brad fastener to attach it atop a second plate. On the second plate, write the possible initial letters for that blend, so that the wheel makes new words as you turn the top plate around.

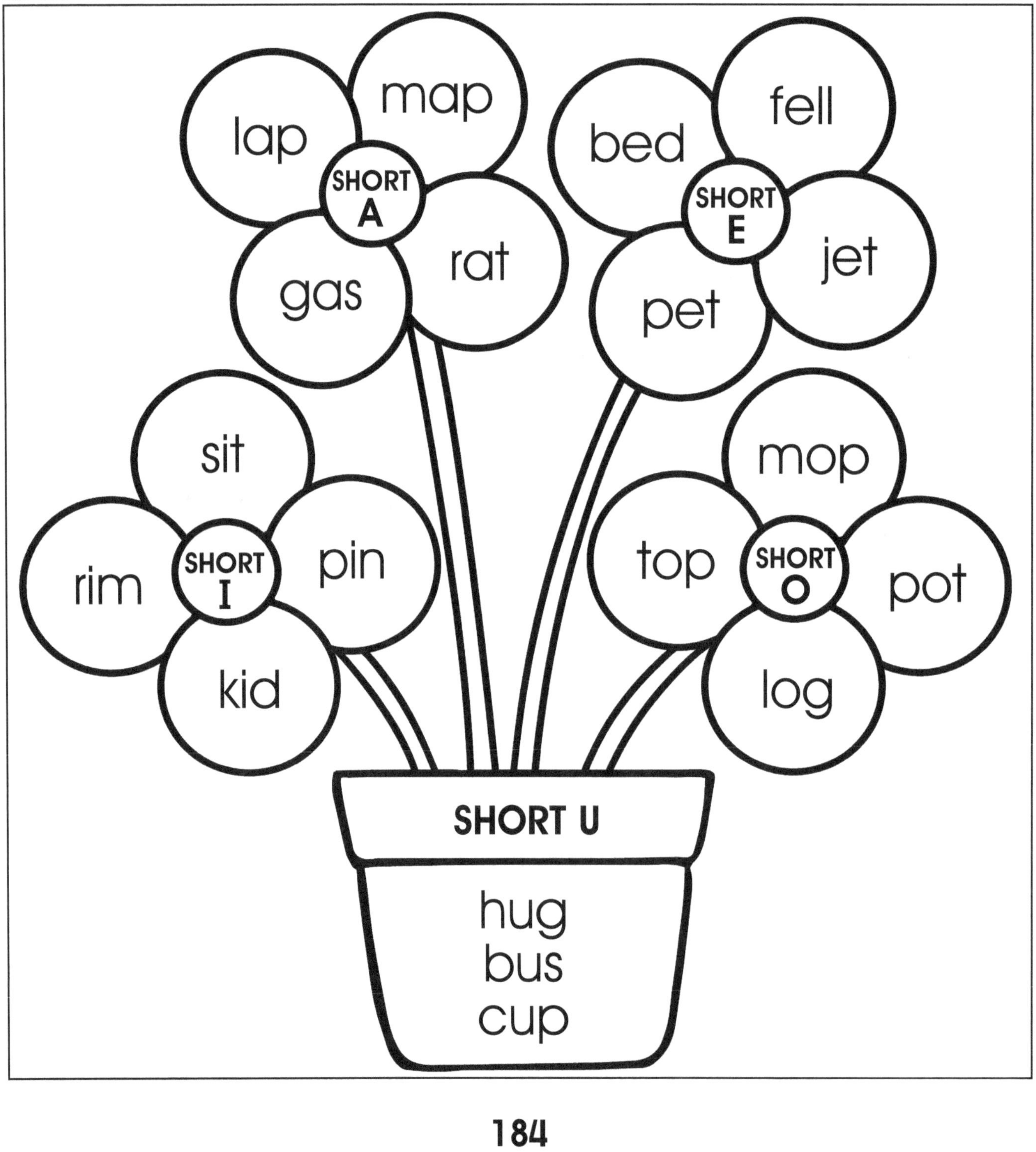

Aa Family

These are word families. Read the words and understand their meanings.

-ab	-ack	-ad	-ag
cab	back	bad	bag
dab	hack	dad	gag
gab	jack	fad	hag
jab	lack	had	lag
lab	pack	lad	nag
nab	rack	mad	rag
tab	sack	pad	sag
	tack	sad	tag
		wad	wag

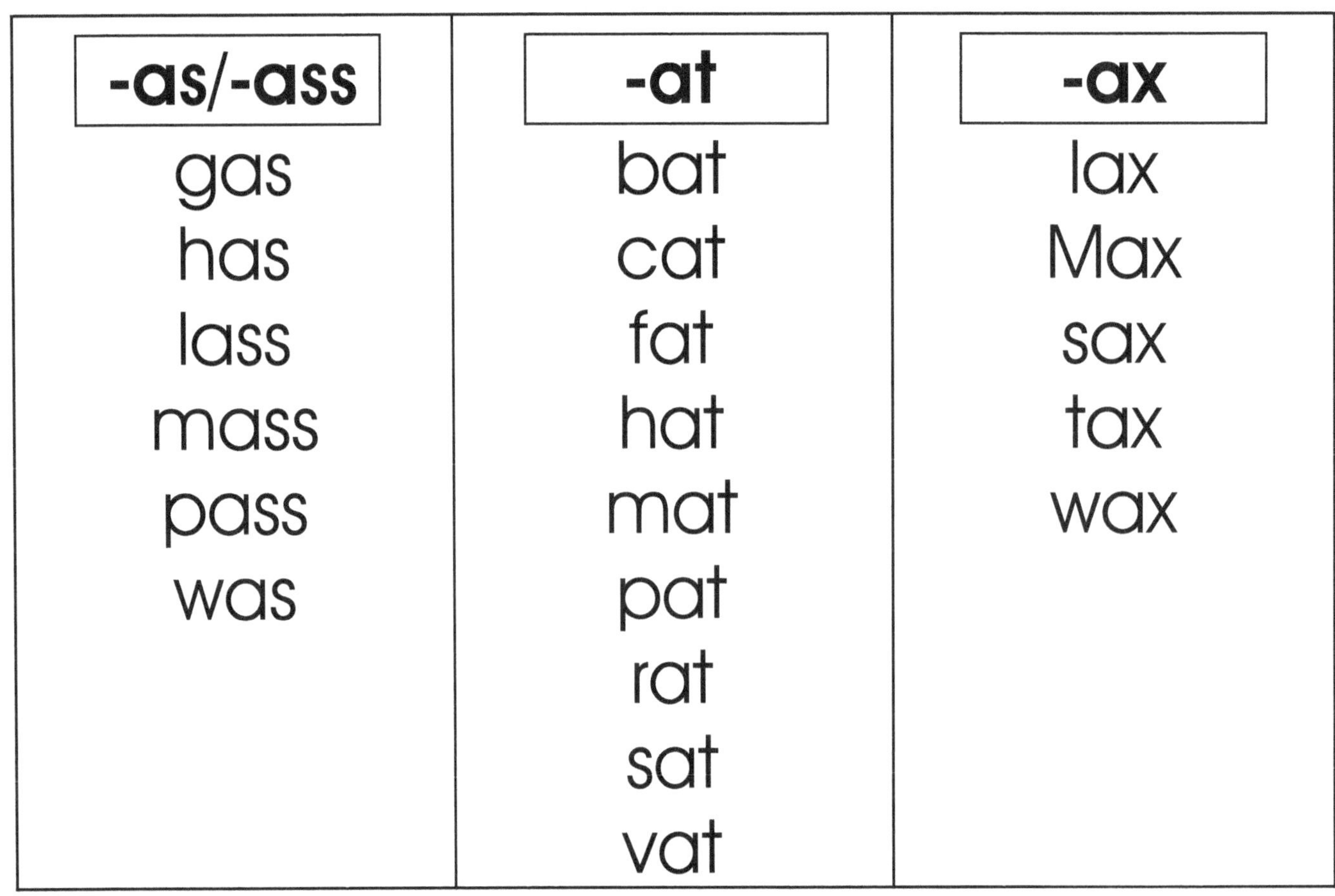

-am	**-an**	**-ap**	**-ar**
dam	ban	cap	bar
ham	can	gap	car
jam	Dan	lap	far
Sam	fan	map	jar
ram	man	nap	mar
Pam	pan	rap	par
yam	ran	sap	tar
	tan	tap	war
	van		

-as/-ass	**-at**	**-ax**
gas	bat	lax
has	cat	Max
lass	fat	sax
mass	hat	tax
pass	mat	wax
was	pat	
	rat	
	sat	
	vat	

bat	can	bad
cat	fan	dad
fat	man	lad
hat	pan	mad
mat	van	pad
pat		sad
rat		
vat		

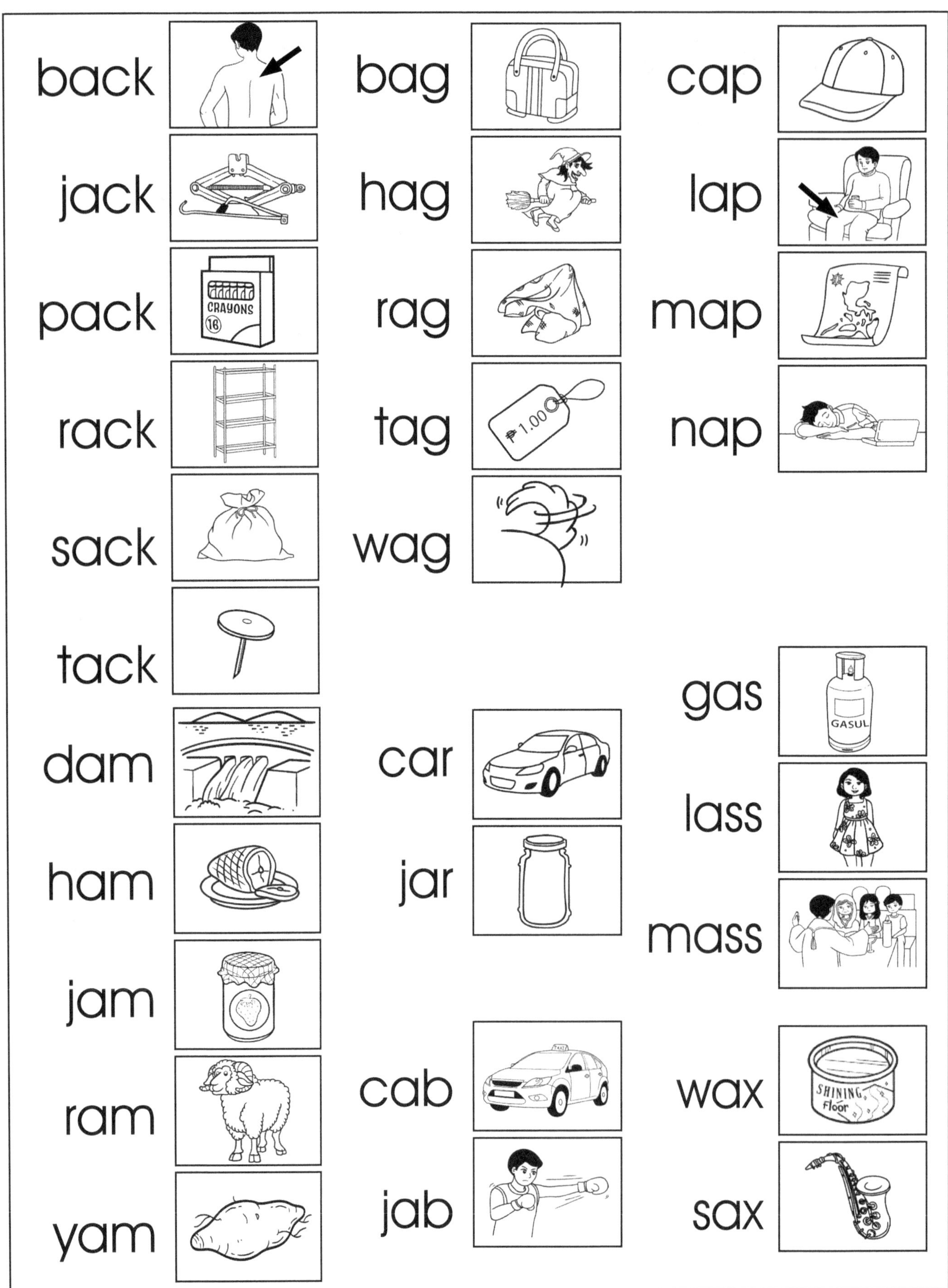

back
jack
pack
rack
sack
tack
dam
ham
jam
ram
yam
bag
hag
rag
tag
wag
car
jar
cab
jab
cap
lap
map
nap
gas
lass
mass
wax
sax
CRAYONS
16
₱ 1.00
GASUL
SHINING floor

ACTIVITY 14

SCORE: _______

Connect the words to the pictures.

hag

wag

pack

sack

cat

rat

lap

nap

can

pan

# ACTIVITY 15

SCORE:_______

Shade the box (☐) of the correct word for each picture.

☐ mat ☐ map ☐ man		☐ dam ☐ dab ☐ dad
☐ pat ☐ pan ☐ pad		☐ pad ☐ lad ☐ dad
☐ sag ☐ wag ☐ nag		☐ sax ☐ rag ☐ gas
☐ sad ☐ sack ☐ sax		☐ ram ☐ jam ☐ ham
☐ jack ☐ jar ☐ car		☐ lad ☐ lab ☐ lap

Read the words. Find the pictures that show the words. Color them. Then connect the names to the pictures.

cab •

jack •

mat •

fat •

rag •

bat •

can •

cap •

rat •

cat •

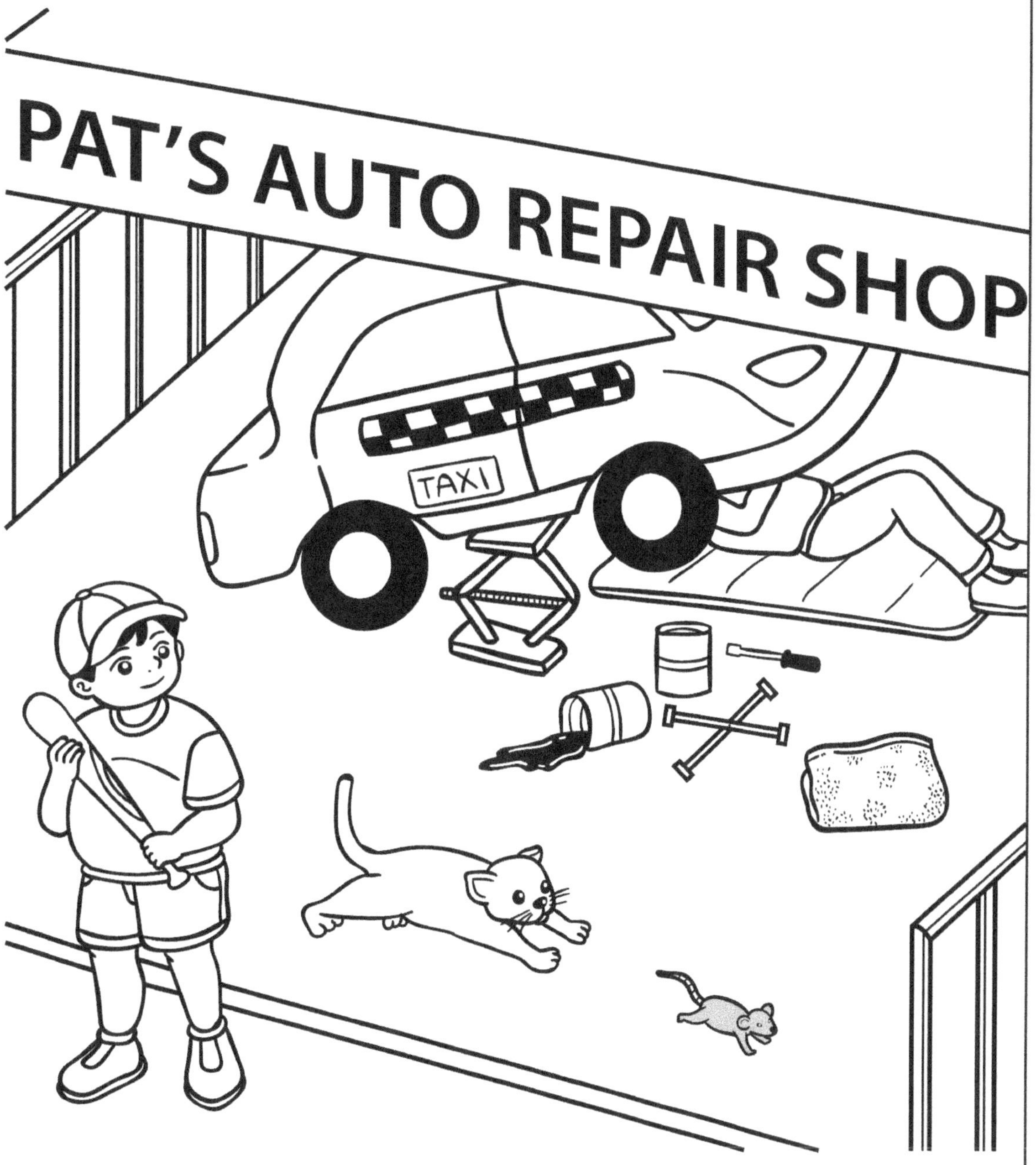

SCORE:_______

Match each word with its picture by writing its number in the circle.

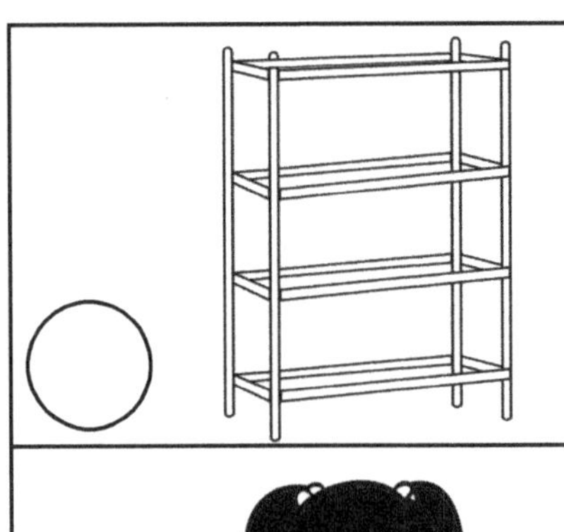

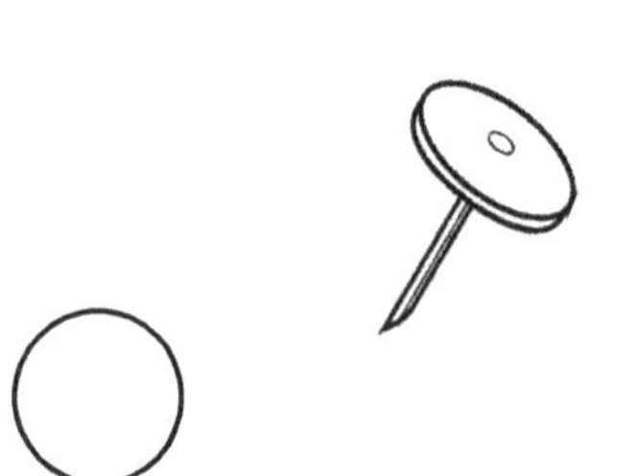

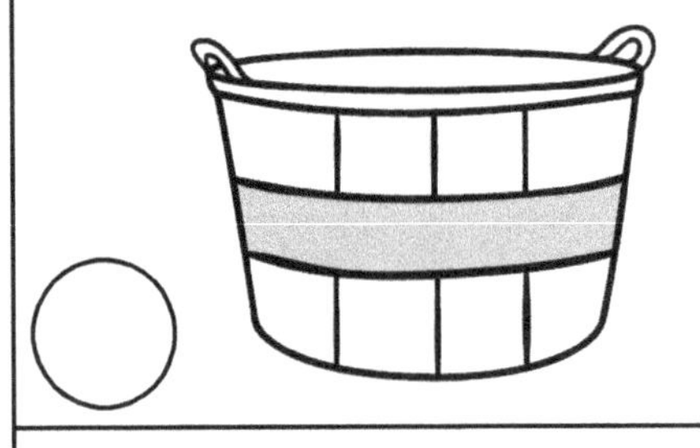

1. van

2. back

3. lass

4. vat

5. sad

6. rack

7. jab

8. car

9. mass

10. tack

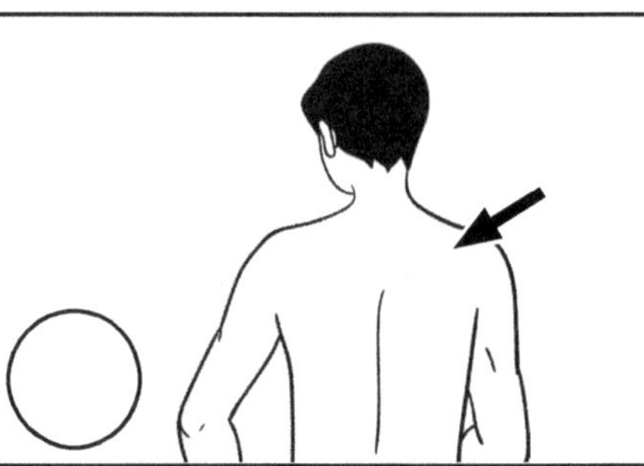

Ee Family

-ck	-ed	-eg
beck	bed	egg
deck	fed	beg
heck	led	keg
neck	Ned	leg
peck	red	Meg
	Ted	peg
	wed	Reg

-ell	-en	-et
bell	Ben	bet
dell	den	get
fell	hen	jet
hell	Jen	met
sell	men	net
tell	pen	pet
well	ten	set
yell	wen	vet
	yen	wet
		yet

bed	bell	egg
fed	dell	beg
wed	fell	keg
	sell	leg
	well	peg
	yell	
get	neck	den
jet	peck	hen
net		men
pet		pen
set		ten
wet		

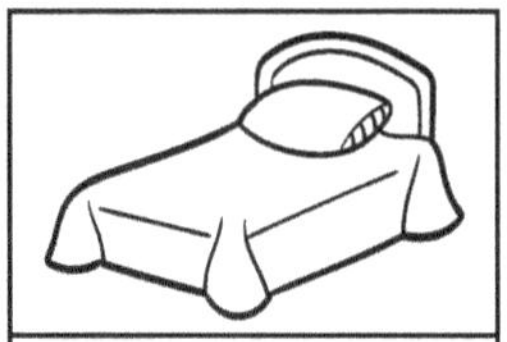

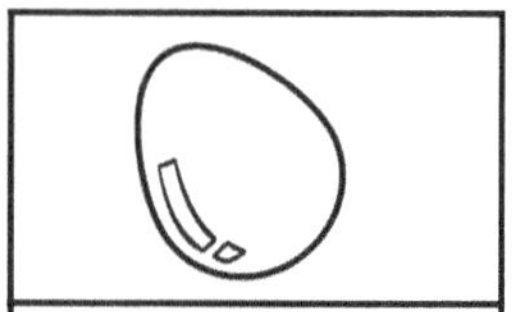

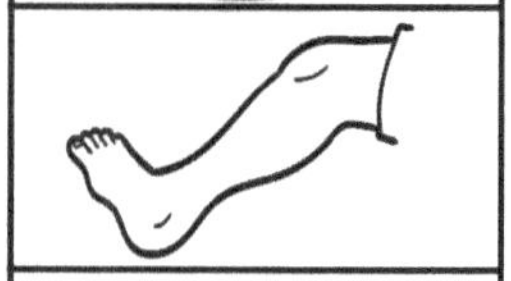

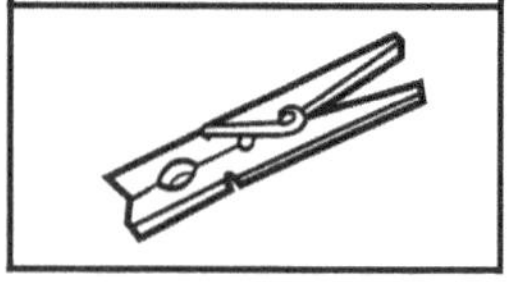

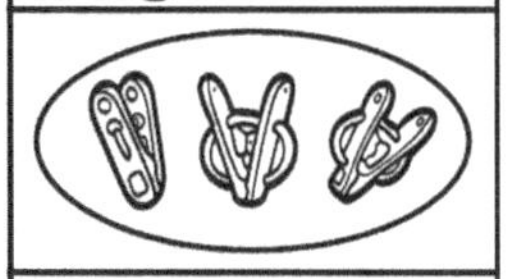

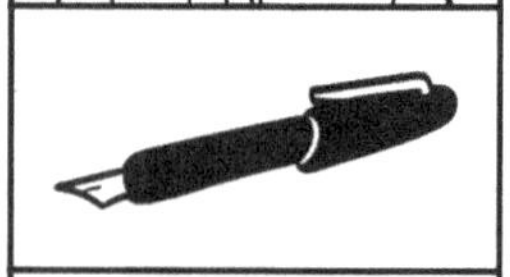

ACTIVITY 16

SCORE:______

Underline the correct word for each picture.

fed
bed

bet
get

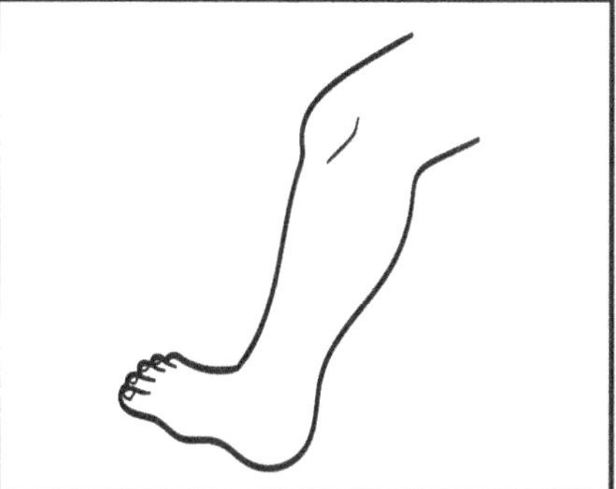

keg
leg

peg
beg

dell
tell

met
wet

wed
fed

den
yen

well
sell

set
pet

195

ACTIVITY 17

SCORE: _______

Encircle the star before the name of each picture.

☆ keg
☆ beg
☆ peg

☆ bell
☆ beck
☆ bet

☆ men
☆ pen
☆ ten

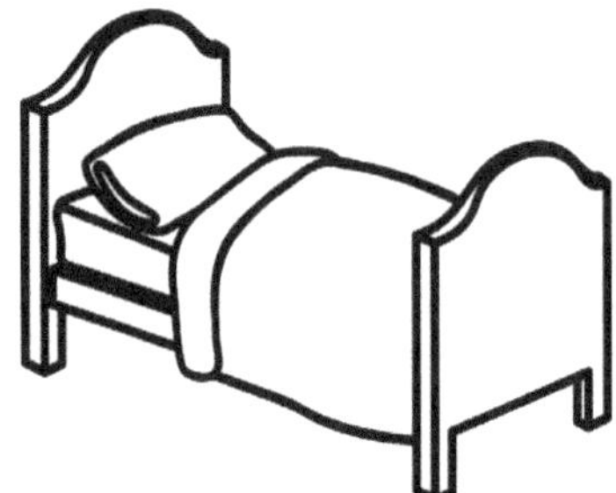

☆ bet
☆ beg
☆ bed

☆ egg
☆ leg
☆ keg

☆ pet
☆ get
☆ jet

☆ net
☆ neck
☆ nest

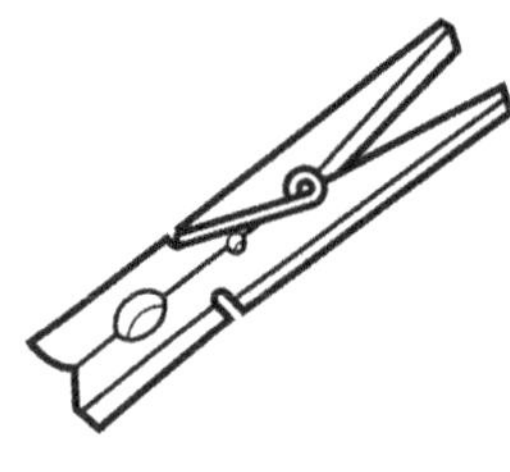

☆ peck
☆ peg
☆ ped

☆ vet
☆ met
☆ net

☆ wet
☆ well
☆ web

QUIZ NO. 6

SCORE: _______

Connect each word to the correct picture.

hand

hen

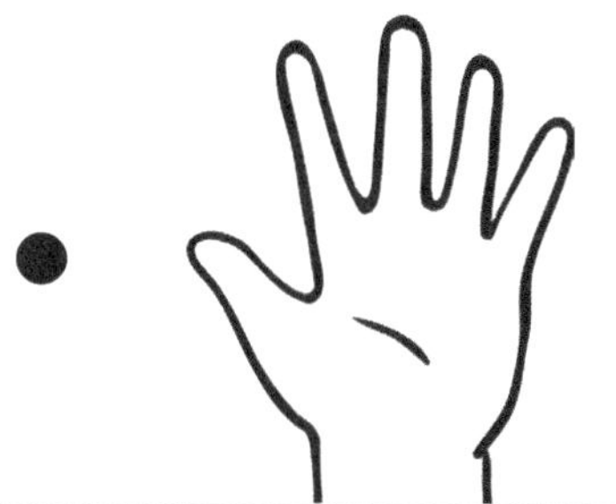

mat

met

peck

pack

pan

pen

pet

pat

Ii Family

-ick	**-id**	**-ig**	**-ill**
kick	bid	big	bill
lick	did	dig	fill
Nick	hid	fig	gill
pick	kid	gig	hill
Rick	lid	jig	Jill
sick	rid	Mig	mill
tick		pig	pill
wick		rig	sill
		wig	till
			will

-in	**-ip**	**-it**	**-ix**
bin	dip	bit	fix
fin	hip	fit	mix
kin	lip	hit	nix
pin	nip	kit	six
sin	pip	lit	
tin	rip	pit	
win	sip	sit	
	tip	wit	
	zip		

dip		kick		bill	
hip		lick		gill	
lip		pick		hill	
rip		sick		pill	
sip		tick		fin	
tip		wick		pin	
kit		fig		kid	
pit		pig		lid	
sit		wig		six	6

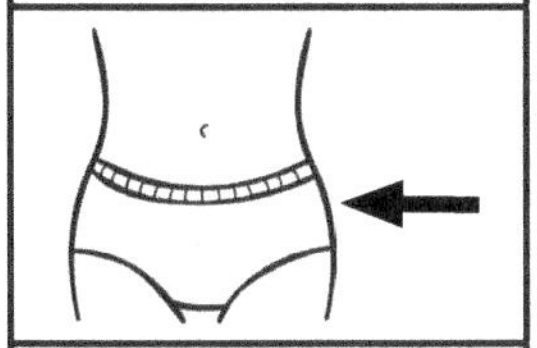

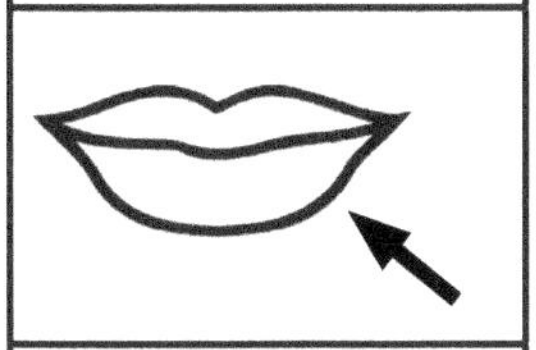

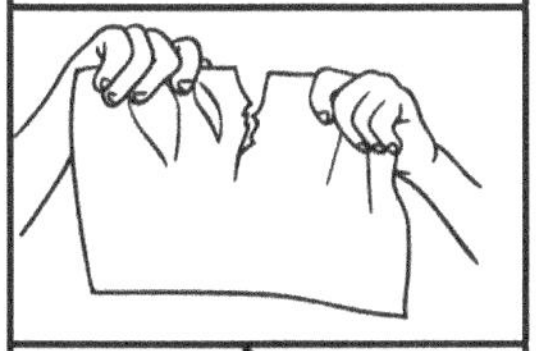

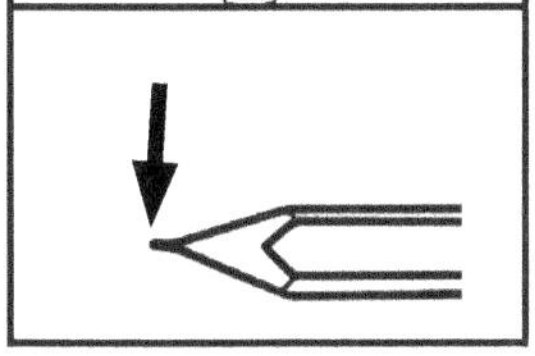

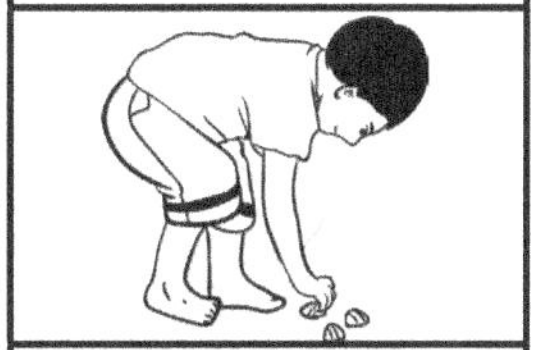

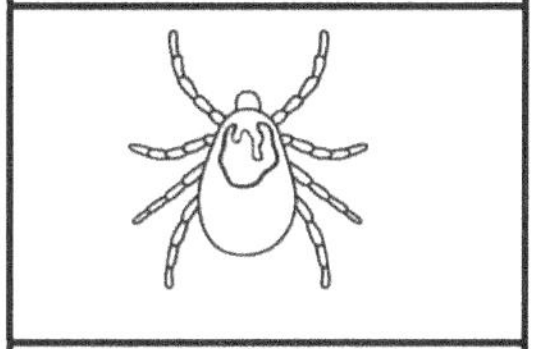

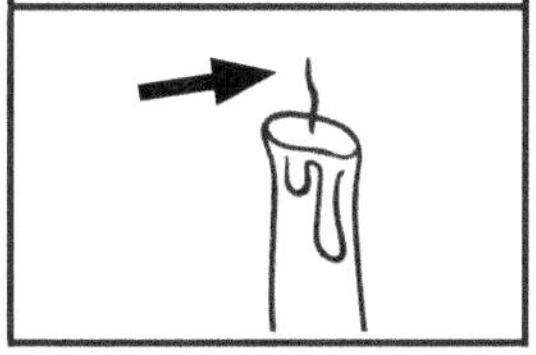

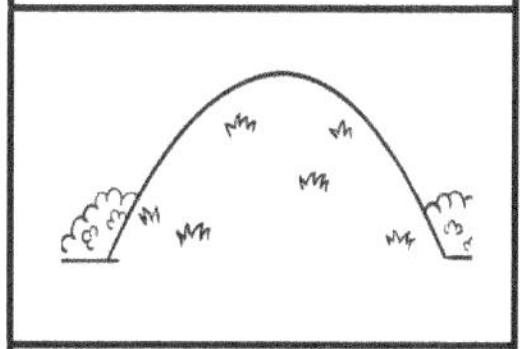

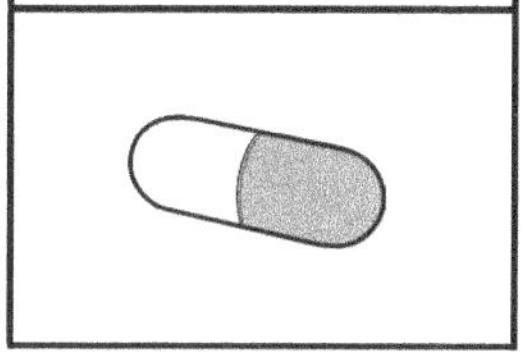

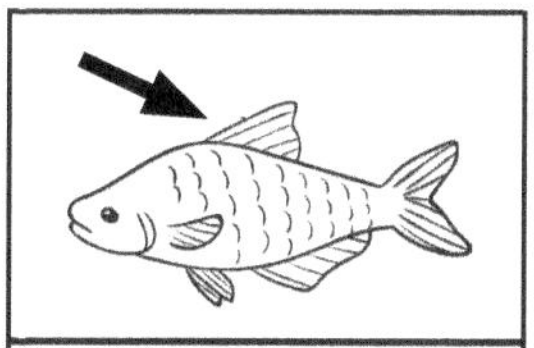

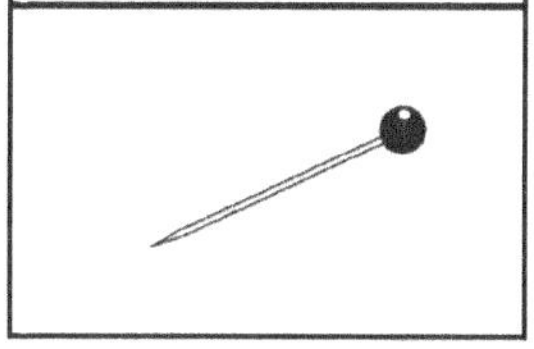

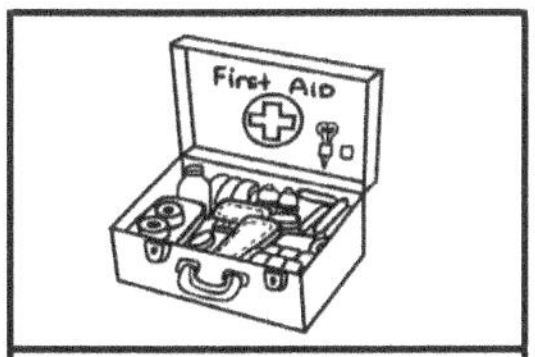

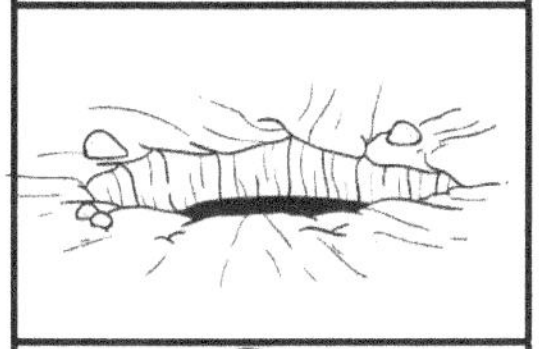

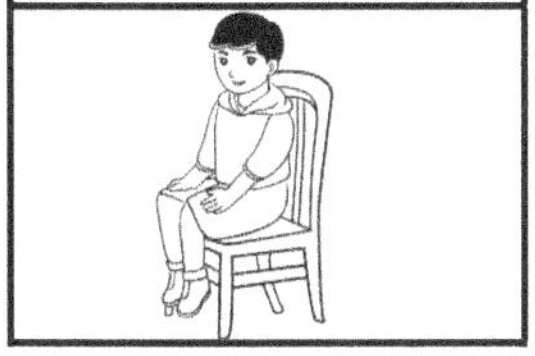

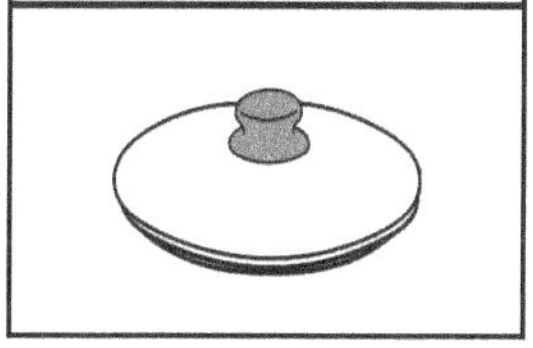

ACTIVITY 18

SCORE:＿＿＿＿＿

Supply the missing letters to complete the name of each picture.

200

ACTIVITY 19

SCORE:______

Put a check (✔) on the blank beside the picture that goes with the name on the left.

kick			
dip			
kid			
hill			
kit			
pin			
lick			
pig			
lip			
wig			

QUIZ NO. 7

SCORE: _______

Draw a moon (☾) beside the correct name for each picture.

___ tip ___ nip ___ rip	___ wick ___ wig ___ will
___ lip ___ tip ___ sip	___ pill ___ bill ___ hill
___ pit ___ bit ___ wit	___ sip ___ six ___ sit
___ sick ___ sit ___ sip	___ lit ___ lip ___ lid
___ pin ___ pill ___ pick	___ big ___ fig ___ pig

Oo Family

-ob	-ock	-od	-og
Bob	cock	cod	bog
cob	dock	God	fog
hob	lock	hod	hog
job	mock	mod	jog
mob	rock	nod	log
nob	sock	pod	
rob		rod	
sob			

-on	-op	-ot	-ow	-ox
Don	cop	cot	bow	ox
Ron	hop	dot	cow	box
son	lop	got	how	fox
ton	mop	hot	now	pox
won	pop	jot	wow	
	sop	lot		
	top	not		
		pot		
		rot		
		tot		

Let's study the new words learned.

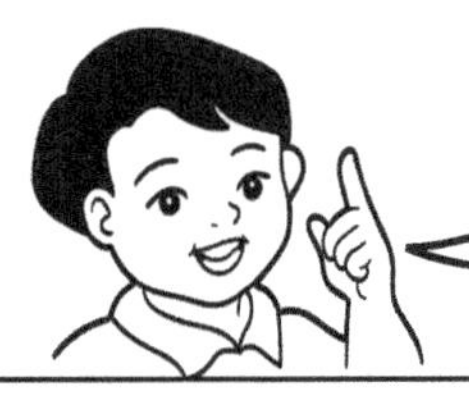

cot 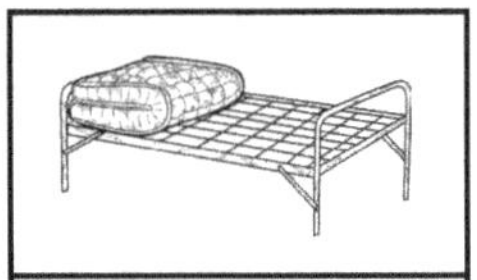

dot 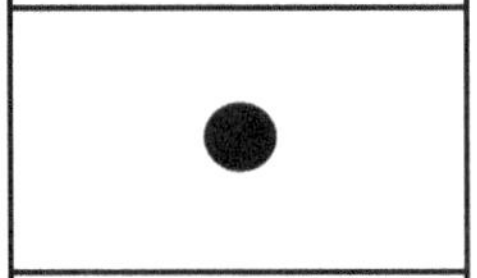

hot 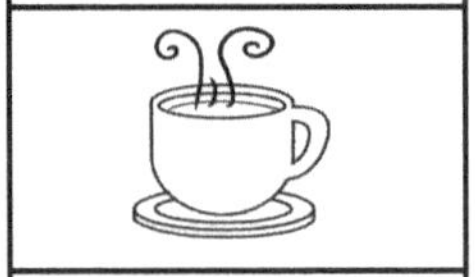

pot 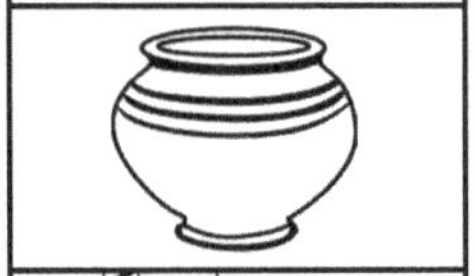

lot 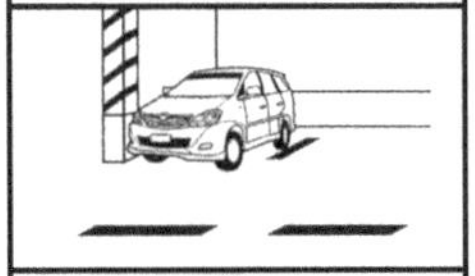

tot 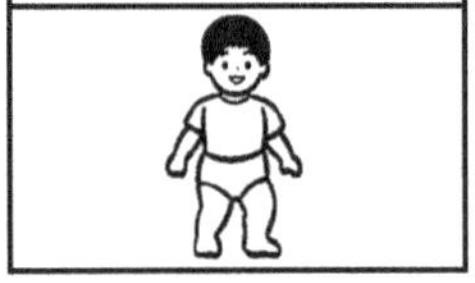

cop 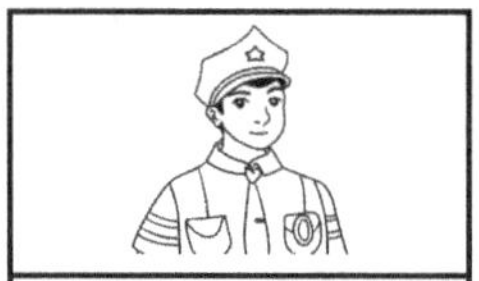

mop 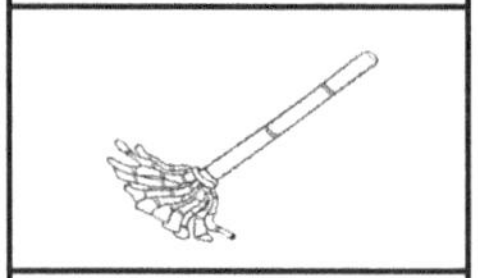

hop 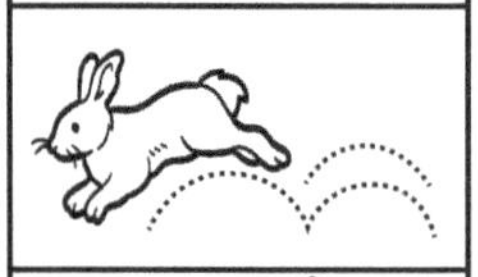

pop 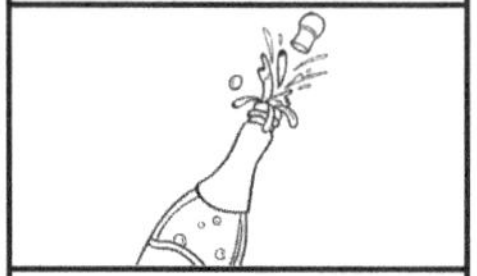

top 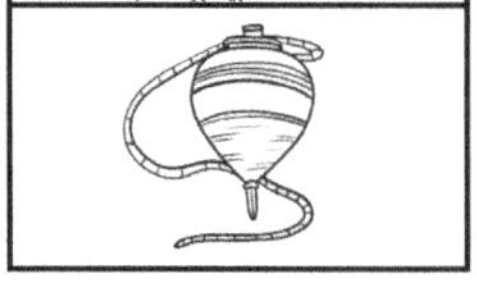

nod 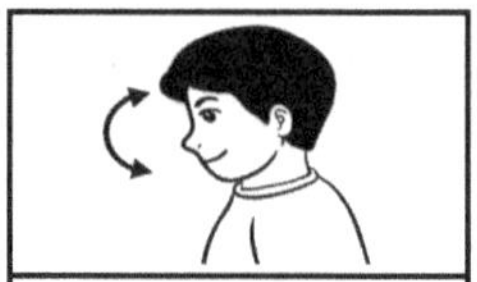

pod 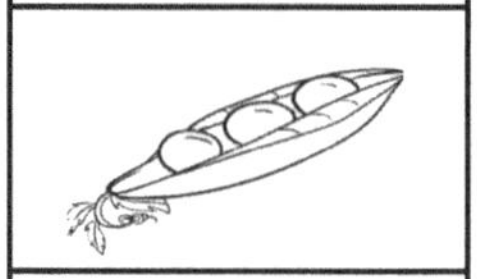

rod 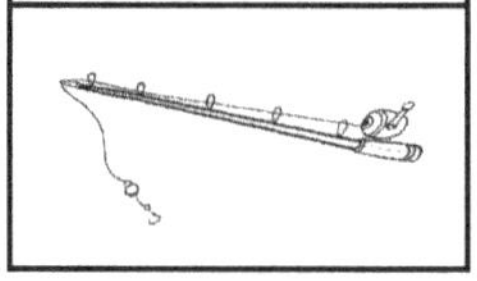

cob 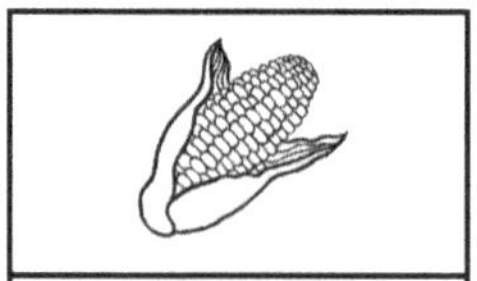

mob 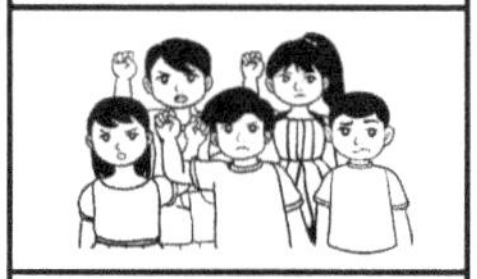

sob 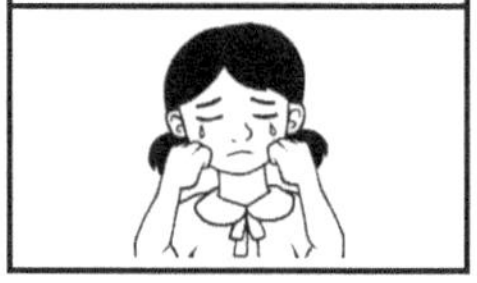

ox 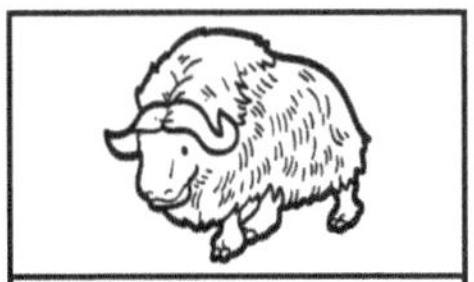

box 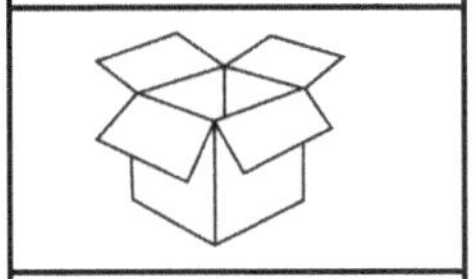

fox 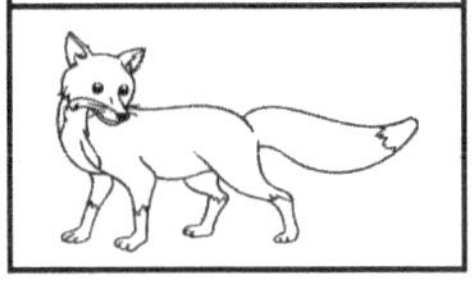

son 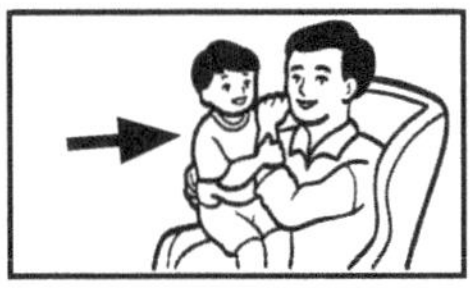

dock 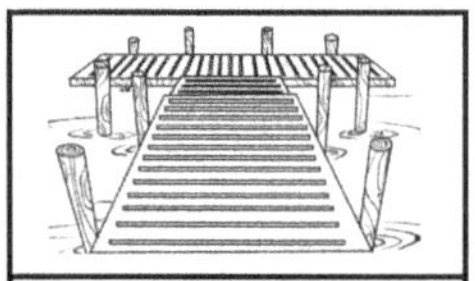

lock 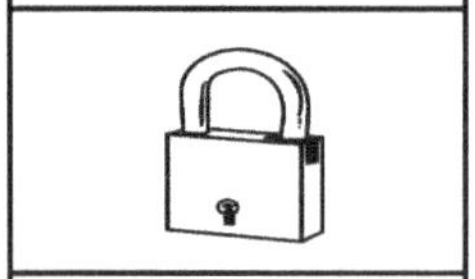

rock 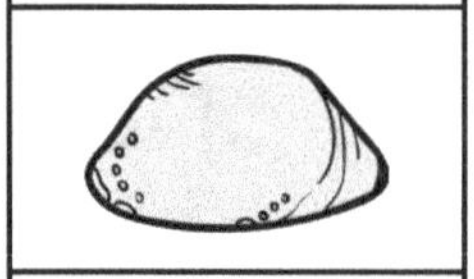

sock 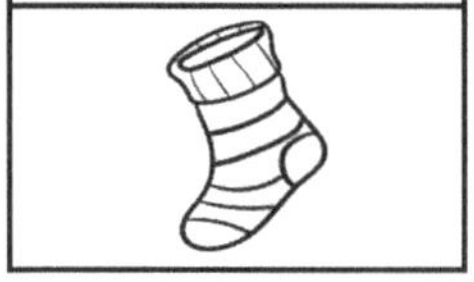

bow 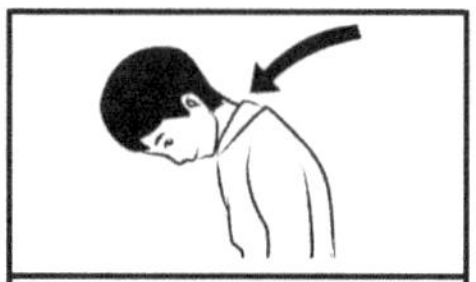

cow 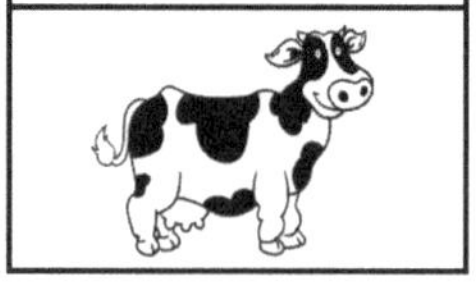

jog 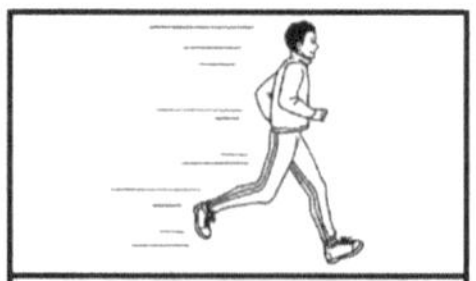

log 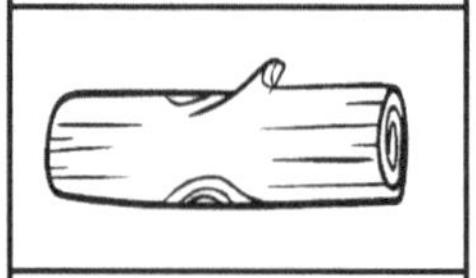

fog 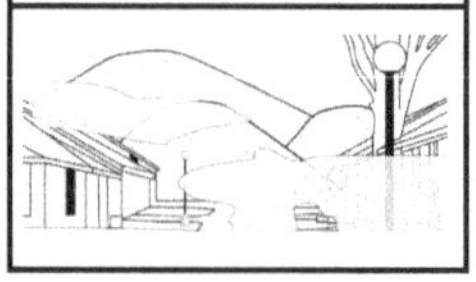

Read each word, then draw a line to match it with the correct picture.

mop •

pod •

dot •

sock •

box •

---

pot •

sob •

pop •

mob •

log •

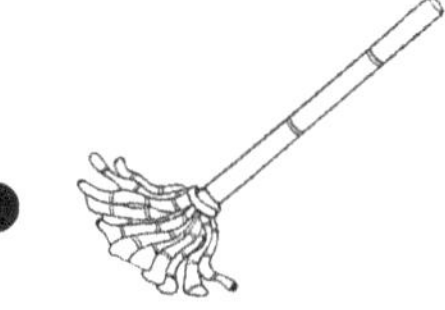

ACTIVITY 21

SCORE:______

Box the correct name for each picture.

hog hot hop		how bow cow
sock lock dock		cop cot cow
hot dot got		top mop cop
fox ox box		pod rod nod
job fox jot		fog log jog

Find the name of each picture in the puzzle and encircle it.

1. 

2. 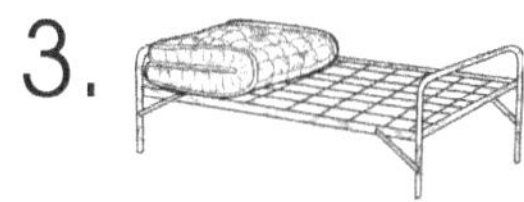

3. 

4. 

5. 

6. 

7. 

8. 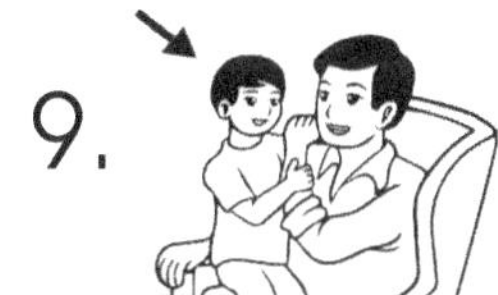

9.

10.

f	o	x	s	n
b	c	o	p	m
f	d	c	o	t
w	r	o	c	k
q	a	j	o	g
t	o	t	b	j
p	c	o	b	j
l	o	c	k	g
e	c	s	o	n
p	o	d	h	k

Uu Family

-ub	-uck	-ud	-ug
cub	buck	bud	bug
dub	duck	cud	dug
hub	luck	dud	hug
pub	suck	mud	jug
nub	tuck	suds	mug
rub			pug
sub			rug
tub			tug

-um	-un	-up	-ut
bum	bun	cup	but
gum	fun	pup	cut
hum	nun		gut
mum	pun	**-us**	nut
rum	run	bus	rut
sum	sun	pus	

cub 

tub

rub

bug 

hug

jug

mug

rug

tug

bun 

nun

run

sun 

cut 

hut

nut

bus 

duck 

suck

gum

sum

bud 

mud

suds

cup 

pup

ACTIVITY 22

SCORE: _______

Connect each word to the correct picture.

mug

cup

cub

bud

tub

tug

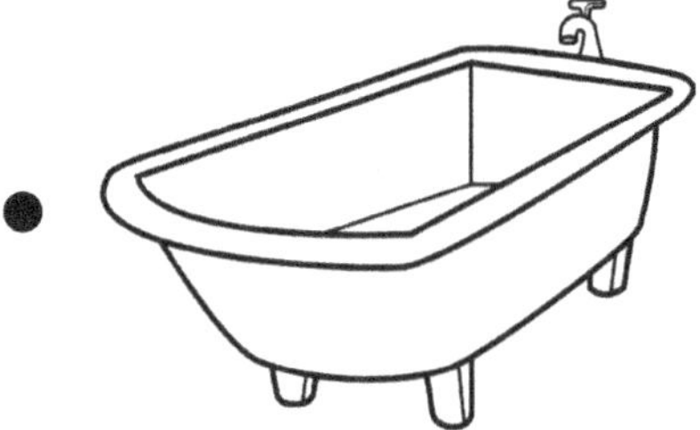

gum

bun

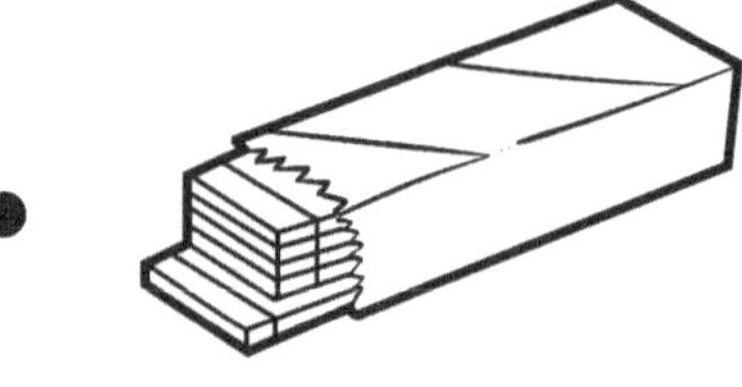

hug

hut

ACTIVITY 23

SCORE:_______

Choose the correct letters from the boxes and write them on the blanks to form the correct word.

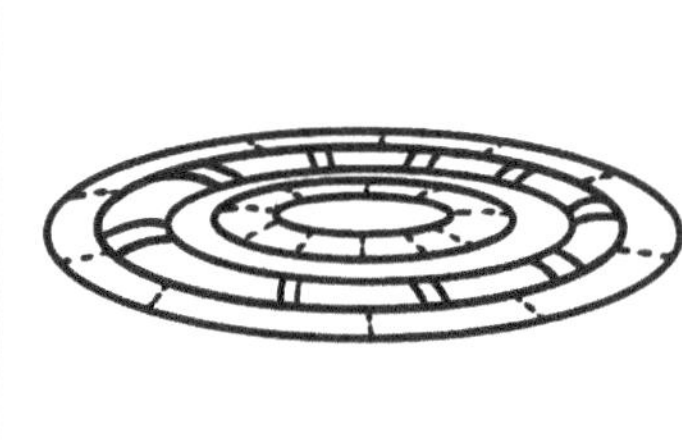

| b | g | r |

_ u _

| n | m | n |

_ u _

| c | p | t |

_ u _

| j | y | g |

_ u _

| k | s | l | c |

_ u _ _

| r | n | u |

_ u _

| c | b | s |

_ u _

| b | d | r |

_ u _

| n | s | x |

_ u _

| v | d | m |

_ u _

QUIZ NO. 9   SCORE: _______

Shade the circle beside the picture that goes with the name on the left.

sun	○ ☆	○ 🌙	○ ☀️
bug	○	○	○
sum	○	○ 1+2=③	○ **6**
cub	○	○	○
suds	○ ☹️	○	○ SOAP
duck	○	○	○
pup	○	○	○
mug	○	○	○
nut	○	○	○
bun	○	○	○

HOME ACTIVITY 5   SCORE:______

Look at the pictures, then write the correct letters to form a word chain.

ACTIVITY 24

SCORE: _______

Connect each picture to the correct name.

	bag **bug**	
	**rug** **rag**	
	**rack** **rock**	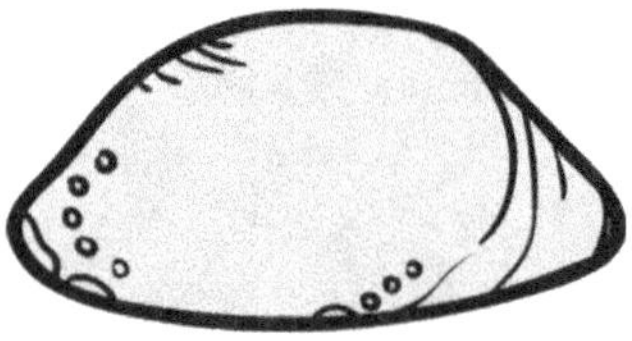
	**jog** **jug**	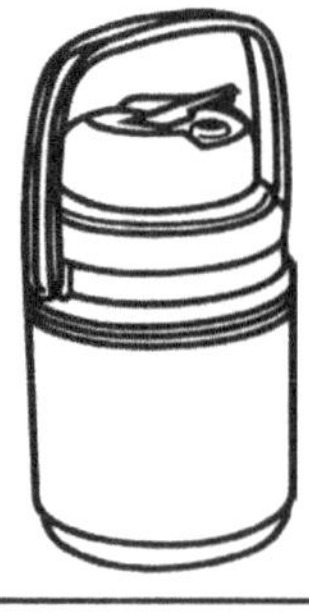
	**tag** **tug**	

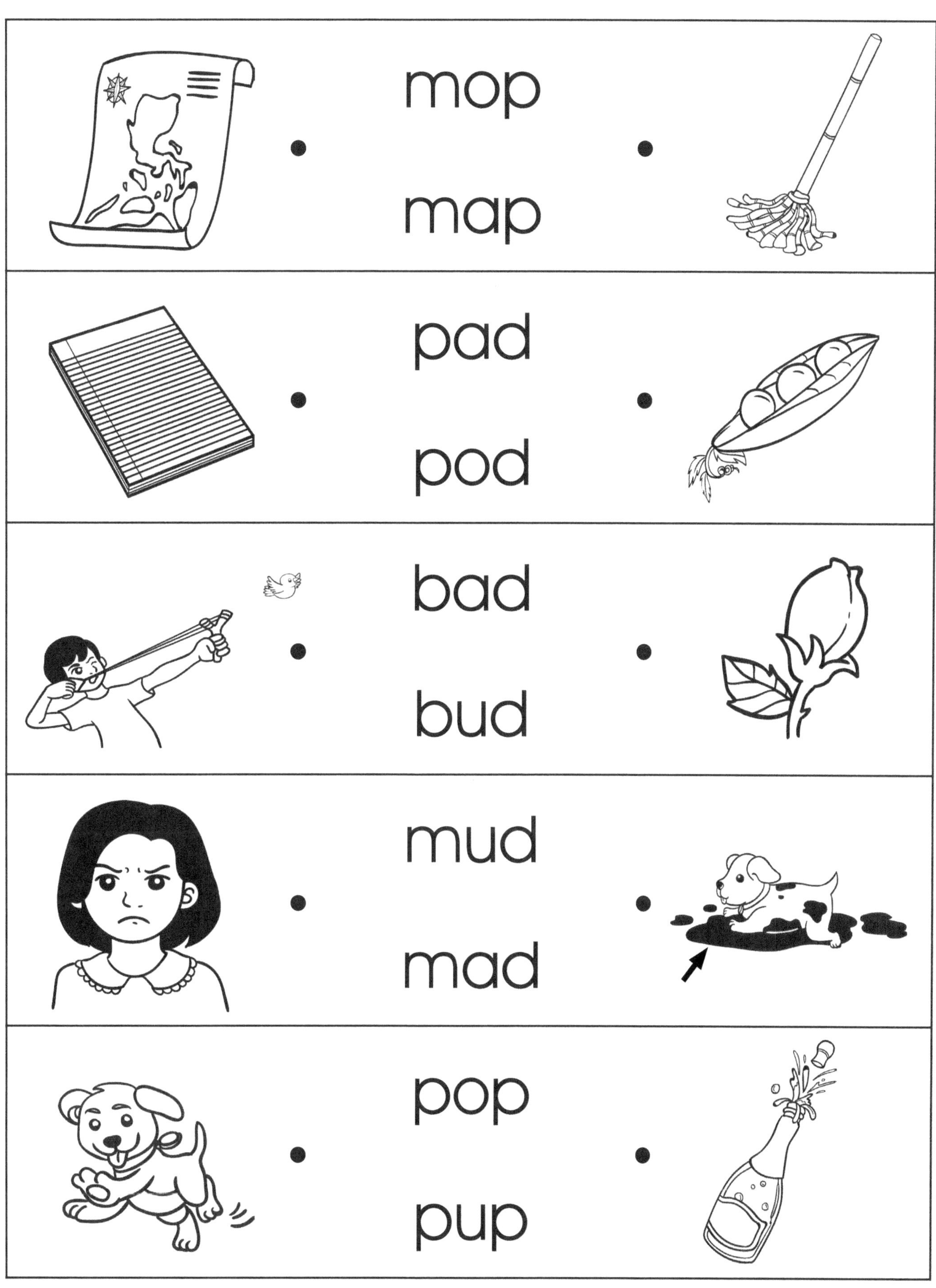
mop
map
pad
pod
bad
bud
mud
mad
pop
pup

ACTIVITY 25

SCORE: _______

Connect each word to the correct picture. *(20 points)*

hog

hag

hug

cab

cub

cob

cut

cot

cat

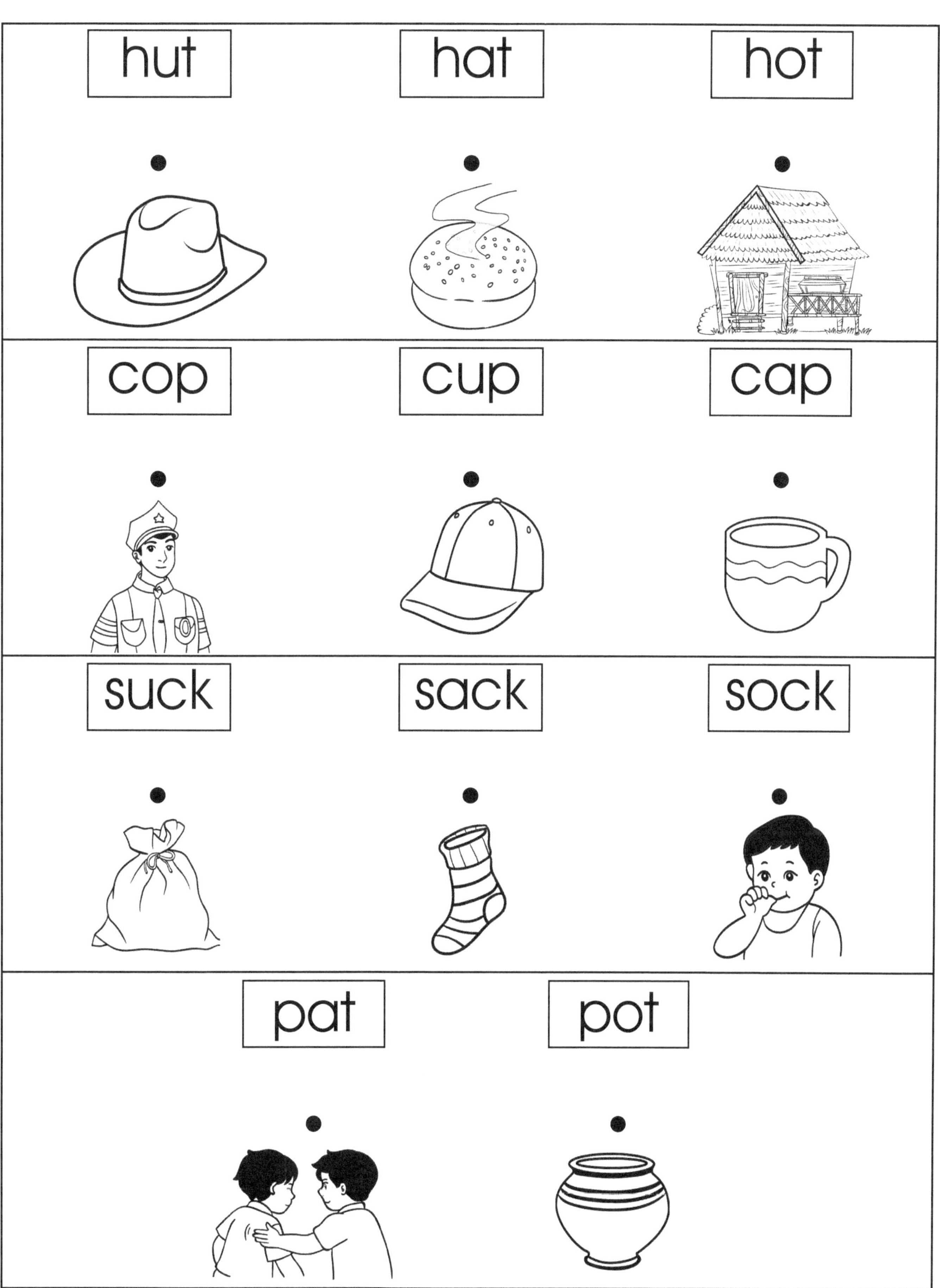
hut
hat
hot
cop
cup
cap
suck
sack
sock
pat
pot

QUIZ NO. 10

SCORE: _______

Cross out the extra letters that make each word incorrect. Write the correct word on the blank.

sticker	___________	blender	___________
stuck	___________	cracked	___________
clown	___________	sounds	___________
classes	___________	swells	___________
blocked	___________	finger	___________

THIRD QUARTERLY TEST
(Review Guide for Parents and Teachers)

Name: _________________________________ **Score:** _________

Level: _____________ **Date:** _____________

I. Shade the circle of the correct name for each picture.

1. **10** ◯ tin ◯ ten ◯ ton

2. ◯ lock ◯ dock ◯ rock

3. ◯ back ◯ lack ◯ tack

4. ◯ bill ◯ bell ◯ fell

5. ◯ tell ◯ well ◯ yell

6. ◯ mob ◯ mop ◯ mod

7. ◯ nut ◯ nun ◯ man

8. ◯ pack ◯ tip ◯ tack

9. ◯ hog ◯ hug ◯ hag

10. ◯ wick ◯ wet ◯ win

11.  ○ log   ○ lamp   ○ lock

12. 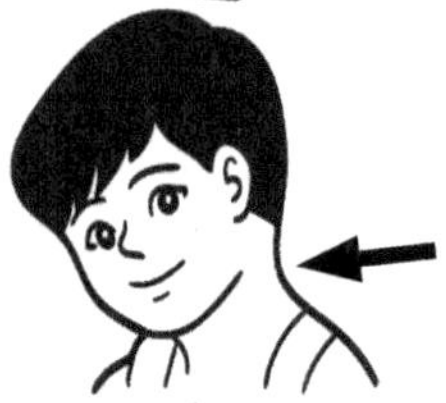 ○ back   ○ neck   ○ leg

13.  ○ cab   ○ cub   ○ cob

14.  ○ ham   ○ hat   ○ jam

15.  ○ luck   ○ lick   ○ lack

16.  ○ fig   ○ fin   ○ fish

17.  ○ far   ○ fan   ○ pan

18.  ○ peck   ○ pick   ○ deck

19.  ○ sick   ○ sock   ○ suck

20.  ○ cop   ○ top   ○ hop

II. Read and draw.

1. mug

6. bed

2. pin

7. sun

3. hat

8. box

4. jam

9. lock

5. hill

10. pen

Ⅲ. Write the name of each picture.

1.  __________

2. __________

3. __________

4. __________

5. __________

6. __________

7. __________

8. __________

9. __________

10. __________

11. 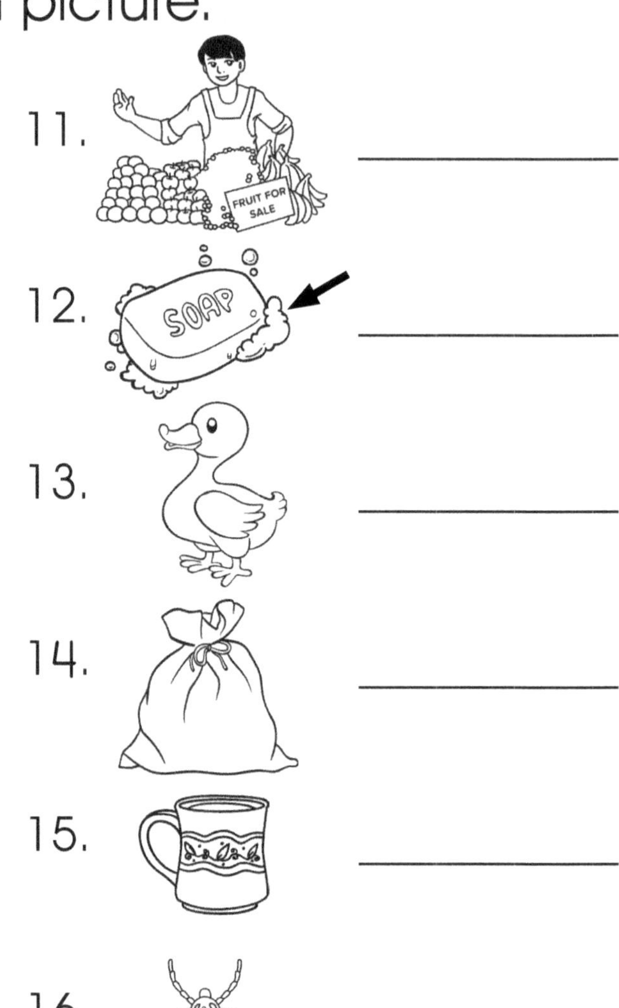 __________

12. __________

13. __________

14. __________

15. __________

16. __________

17. __________

18. __________

19. __________

20. 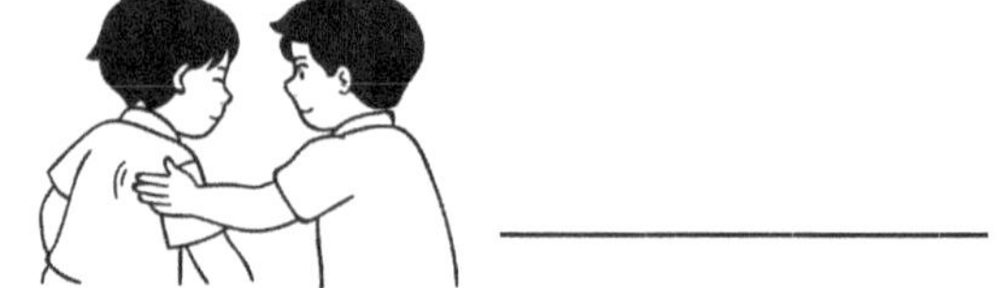 __________

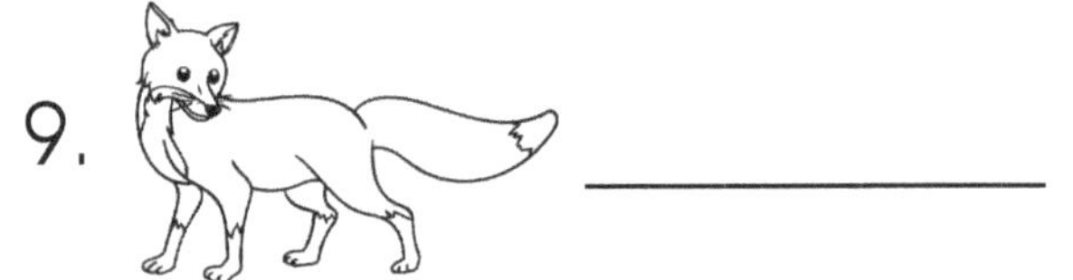

PROGRESS CHART
THIRD QUARTER

Name: _______________________________ Level: __________

ACTIVITY	No. of Items	My Score	HOME ACTIVITY	No. of Items	My Score	QUIZ	No. of Items	My Score
1	10		1	10		1	10	
2	20		2	20		2	10	
3	10		3	10		3	10	
4	10		4	10		4	10	
5	10		5	10		5	10	
6	10					6	10	
7	10					7	10	
8	10					8	10	
9	10					9	10	
10	10					10	10	
11	10							
12	10							
13	10							
14	10							
15	10							
16	10							
17	10							
18	10							
19	10							
20	10							
21	10							
22	10							
23	10							
24	20							
25	20							
TOTAL	280		TOTAL	60		TOTAL	100	

_______________________________ _______________________________
Parent's/Guardian's Signature   Teacher's Signature

FOURTH QUARTER
FUN WITH READING

Teacher's Objectives and Student Evaluation

Lesson	At the end of the activities, the child should be able to:	D	DD	WD
1	1. read high-frequency words			
	2. tell the meaning of high-frequency words			
	3. spell words correctly			
2	4. join words to form phrases			
	5. read and understand phrases			
	6. identify correct phrases for a given picture			
3	7. read and understand sentences			
	8. tell whether or not sentences make sense			
	9. answer questions about sentences read			
4	10. read more sight words			
	11. tell the meanings of words read			
	12. improve his or her vocabulary			
5	13. read and understand stories read			
	14. answer questions about stories read			
	15. retell stories to class			
6	16. identify objects whose names sound alike			
	17. name objects correctly			
	18. tell whether or not two objects have names that rhyme			
7	19. tell which of the given pictures should come first			
	20. arrange picture stories in their correct sequence			
	21. sequence events in stories heard or read			

Legend:

D — Developing   D — Developed   WD — Well-Developed

LESSON 1

SIGHT WORDS AND CONSONANT BLENDS

Guide: Play a memory game. Write the sight words on index cards (by pairs). The goal is to find sight words which are the same. Start the game by turning the cards over, so the sight words can't be seen. Spread the cards out and mix them all up. Have the children take turns in turning over two cards. If two sight words match, the pupil gets the cards. The pupil with the most number of sight words wins the game.

person	place	this	grass
tomorrow	often	shop	drink
goodbye	morning	nest	trap
hello	evening	they	clap
today	like	belt	he
never	love	mother	for
sometimes	animal	ball	shell
always	the	farm	flower
ring	milk	father	blast
mother	sister	post	plant
over	under	behind	beside
belt	old	grasp	pram
short	long	arms	new
with	that	she	those

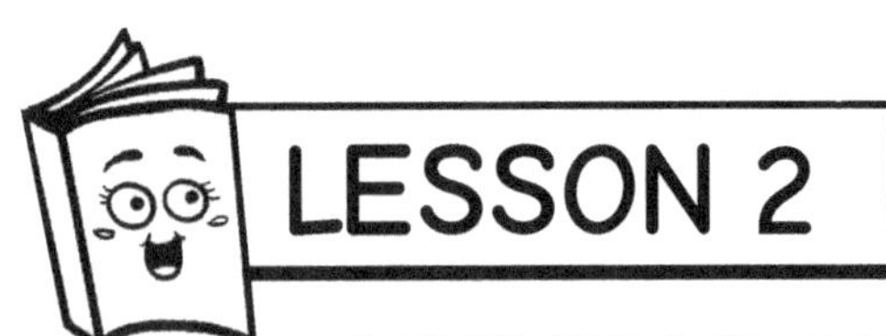

LESSON 2

JOINING WORDS TO FORM PHRASES

a fox in a box

a hen in the nest

a bat in a vat

six hot pots

a hog on the log

a tot on the cot

ten wet pups

a big fan

rat on the run

Check the correct picture for each phrase.

1. nap on the mat

2. cobs in a pot

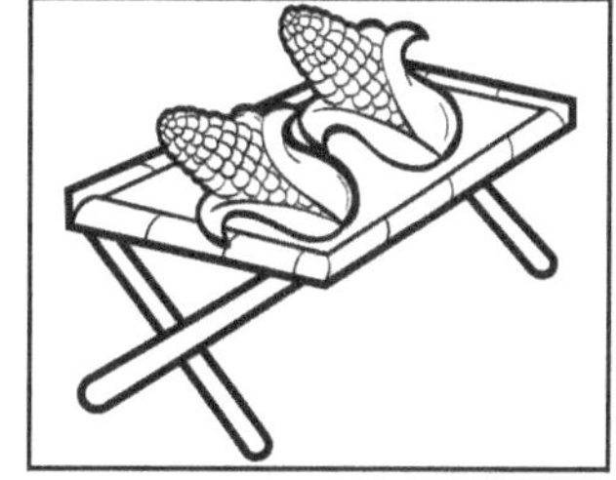 

3. fell in the pit

4. a bug and
   a bag

5. a fat cat
   on her lap

ACTIVITY 2

SCORE:______

Connect each phrase to the correct picture.

1. cups with tags ●

2. a kiss and a hug ●

3. a sack of yams ●

4. pups near the well ●

5. pick up the pins ●

6. king with a cape ●

7. a wet sock ●

8. two cows in the dell ●

9. fed the hens ●

10. books on a rack ●

QUIZ NO. 1

SCORE: _______

Write the letter of the correct picture in the circle beside the corresponding phrase.

◯ mob in the park

◯ a duck with a long bill

◯ walk to the hut

◯ hid behind the bed

◯ fill the jug with water

a.

b.

c.

d.

e.

QUIZ NO. 2

SCORE: _______

Color the box of the correct phrase for each picture.

	☐ sit on a big leg	☐ sit on a big log
	☐ boys in the van	☐ a boy in the van
	☐ lady with a pan	☐ lady with a fan
	☐ mud on the floor	☐ mug on the floor
	☐ a set of bags	☐ a set of bugs

QUIZ NO. 3

SCORE:______

Underline the phrase that tells about the picture.

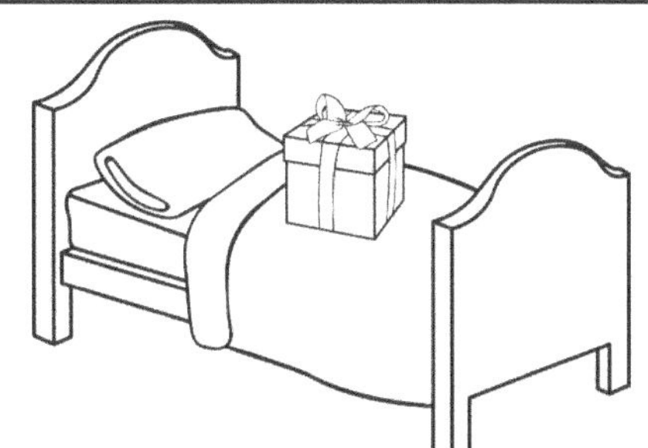

gift on the bed
gift on the keg
gift on the peg

ring the belt
ring the bell
sing the bell

blow the ball
roll the ball
throw the ball

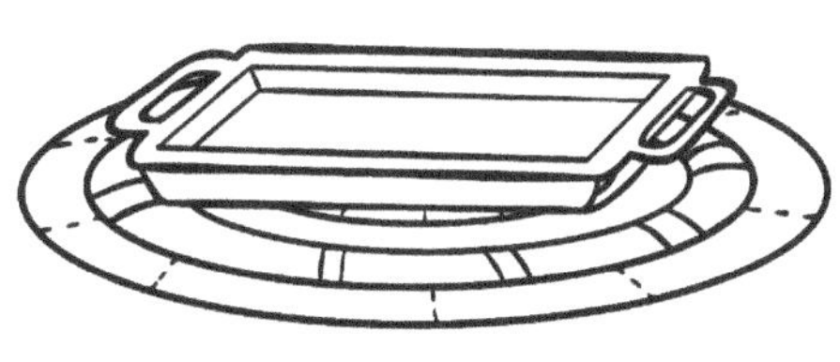

a tray on the rug
a tray on the mug
a ray on the rug

crabs in the pin
crabs in the pen
crabs in the pan

LESSON 3

READING SENTENCES

<table>
<tr><td><u>Guide</u>:</td><td>Provide sight words on index cards or have the children use their own collection of sight words to make sentences. You may also make up predictable sentences out of sight words. Take away a word. Let the children choose the correct word to put into the blank space.</td></tr>
</table>

The man has ten pigs.

She has a big garden.

This is my favorite dress.

Carmela sweeps the yard.

That stick hit my lips.

The children play with their toys.

Kael has seven hens.

They must sit on the rock.

The cat runs after the rat.

My mother cooks food for us.

Check the correct picture for each sentence.

1. The lad is sick.

2. Her socks are big.

3. Dad hugs the cub.

4. He jogs with his pup.

5. The girl has a small umbrella.

QUIZ NO. 5   SCORE: _______

Draw a ball (⚾) in the box beside the correct sentence.

	☐ Two men are in the car. ☐ Two men are in the can.
	☐ The fish has big fans. ☐ The fish has big fins.
	☐ There's a lock beside the box. ☐ There's a dock beside the box.
	☐ The pans are on the rack. ☐ The pans are on the rock.
	☐ The pig fell from the tree. ☐ The fig fell from the tree.

Put a check (✓) on the word that makes the sentence correct.

1. Lucas loves to (play, clay) with his pet.

2. I like banana (fake, cake).

3. Caylie has ten (red, bed) roses.

4. Gray and Gwen carry their (bags, tags).

5. She pats the (tack, back) of her friend.

6. Miggy reads his (hook, book).

7. I want to ride in a (ban, van).

8. We sleep in the (tent, tell).

9. Her new bag has a (lag, tag).

10. My pet dog (wags, nags) its tail.

Read the sentences and answer the questions that follow. Underline the letter of the correct answer.

Zara has ten ribbons in her bag.

1. Who has ten ribbons?

    a. Zara   b. Dara   c. Mara

2. Where are the ribbons?

    a. in her pocket   b. in her bag   c. in her shoes

The bird sits on the tree.

1. What sits on the tree?

    a. bee   b. frog   c. bird

2. Where is the bird?

    a. on the table   b. in the box   c. on the tree

The little boy has six balls.

1. Who has six balls?

    a. little girl   b. little boy   c. old man

2. What does the boy have?

    a. bag   b. books   c. balls

3. How many balls does the boy have?

    a. six   b. seven   c. five

236

The three toy cars are in the box.

1. What are in the box?

   a. rocks   b. pins   c. toy cars

2. Where are the toy cars?

   a. in the room   b. in the box   c. in the jar

3. How many toy cars are in the box?

   a. three   b. ten   c. nine

Two pigs play in the mud.

1. What play in the mud?

   a. ducks   b. pigs   c. hens

2. Where are the pigs?

   a. in the pen   b. in the garden   c. in the mud

3. How many pigs play in the mud?

   a. two   b. ten   c. seven

Jim has a jar of cookies.

1. Who has a jar of cookies?

   a. Joy   b. Jim   c. Jom

2. What is in the jar?

   a. cookies   b. sugar   c. candies

MORE NEW WORDS

Guide: Provide each child with several index cards to make a word bank. You can keep the cards in a shoebox, or punch holes in their top left-hand corners and bind the cards together using a ring clasp. Encourage the children to keep a running tab of all the words they are able to recognize by sight.

day	wait	there
find	pure	near
tell	ride	little
mass	want	happy
hook	tail	alone
cube	play	found
book	road	friend
pail	glow	become
seek	love	funny
cart	work	again
hold	then	away
pray	hard	swim
silly	food	women
fall	tight	around
very	sleep	together

LESSON 5

READING STORIES

<u>Guide</u>: Make a collection of short stories to read to the children. Have the children dramatize or roleplay the stories, substituting the words in the stories with their own version. Make paper plate masks for the children to use as they re-enact stories. Provide other simple props and recycled costumes, too.

The Bad Lad

The bad lad has a big backpack.
His backpack is full of tacks.
He pours the tacks onto the floor.
An old woman steps on the tacks.
The poor woman slips and falls on the floor.

QUIZ NO. 8   SCORE: _______

Encircle the letter of the correct answer.

1. Who has a big backpack?

a.    b.    c. 

2. What is in the backpack?

a. 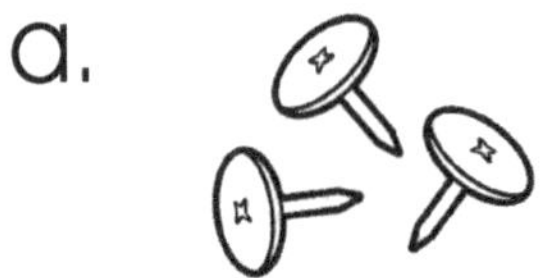   b.    c. 

3. Who steps on the tacks?

a.    b.    c. 

4. What happens with the old woman?

a.    b.    c. 

Denden and His Hens

Denden has ten hens.
The hens live in a big pen.
The hens lay many eggs.
Denden sells the eggs in the market.
Young men and women buy the eggs.

QUIZ NO. 9	SCORE: _______

Shade the circle of the correct answer.

1. What does Denden have?

2. Where do the hens live?

3. What does Denden do with their eggs?

4. Who buys the eggs?

Pink, the Silly Pig

Pink is a silly pig.
She loves to sleep on top of a hill.
She also loves to eat big figs.
She plays with a tick and a kid.
Then she sits to rest in a pit.

QUIZ NO. 10   **SCORE:** _______

Underline the correct answer.

1. Who is Pink?

| a pig | a cat | a kid |

2. Where does Pink love to sleep?

| beside a hill | on top of a pill | on top of a hill |

3. What does Pink play with?

| a tick and a kid | a tick and a lid | a pig and a kid |

4. Where does Pink sit and rest?

| on a rug | in a pit | in the mud |

Ronron, the Good Cop

Ronron is a good, old cop.
He works hard all day long.
He jogs with his brod to keep himself fit.
He also loves to cook food for his tot.
He sleeps tight on his cot each night.

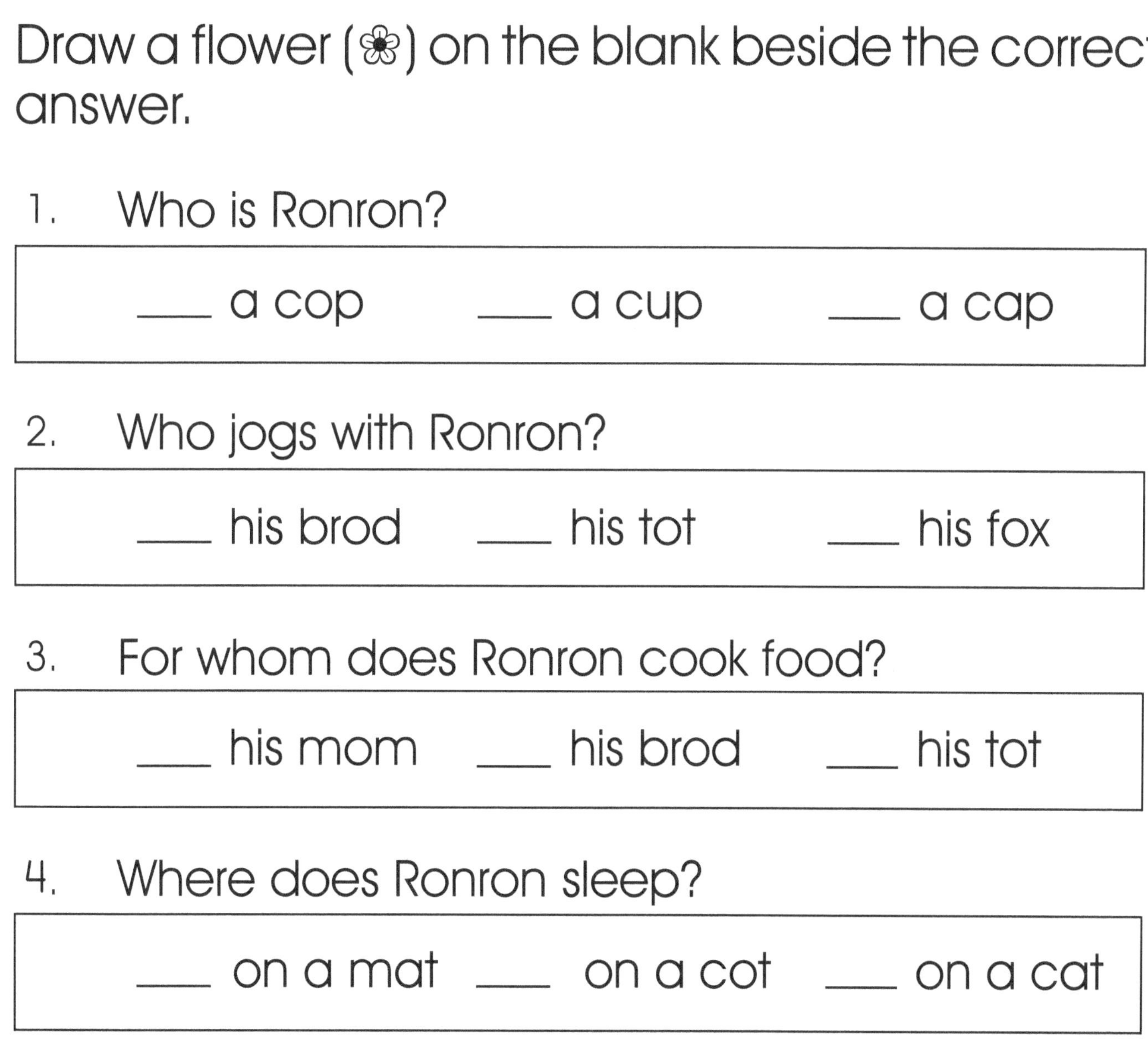

QUIZ NO. 11   **SCORE:** _______

Draw a flower (❀) on the blank beside the correct answer.

1. Who is Ronron?

    ___ a cop   ___ a cup   ___ a cap

2. Who jogs with Ronron?

    ___ his brod   ___ his tot   ___ his fox

3. For whom does Ronron cook food?

    ___ his mom   ___ his brod   ___ his tot

4. Where does Ronron sleep?

    ___ on a mat   ___ on a cot   ___ on a cat

The Nun in the Hut

There is a nun who lives in a hut.
She has four funny ducks and two cute pups.
The ducks love to swim in the mud.
The pups love to run under the sun.
The nun is happy living in her hut
with her ducks and pups.

QUIZ NO. 12   SCORE: _______

Put a check (✓) in the box beside the correct answer.

1. Where does the nun live?

| ☐ in a hat | ☐ in a coop | ☐ in a hut |

2. How many ducks does the nun have?

| ☐ four | ☐ two | ☐ five |

3. Who love to swim in the mud?

| ☐ the pups | ☐ the ducks | ☐ the nun |

4. What do the pups like to do?

| ☐ swim in the mud | ☐ run under the stool | ☐ run under the sun |

MORE FUN WITH STORIES

 ## Sam and Pam 

Sam and Pam are twins.  wears a blue .  wears a red . Together, they under a big shady  in front of their . plays with his toy . plays with her .

They like to be with each other every day, but they wish to have  to with, to with, and to share their with.

One day, a new  moves into the neighborhood. Their wish has come true. They meet new friends, Jim and Kim.

Now, they have friends to with, to with, and to share their with.

They get along very well. They play hide-and-seek, hopscotch, and tag every day.

ACTIVITY 3

SCORE:_______

Color the box of the correct answer.

1. Who wears a red hat?

2. Where do Sam and Pam sit?

3. Who plays with a toy train?

4. Who moves into the neighborhood?

5. What do Sam and Pam do with their friends?

Jim and Kim

Jim and Kim are siblings. Kim felt sad about leaving their old house and moving into a new neighborhood. She will miss her old friends. Jim, being the older brother, said, "Cheer up, little sister. We're going to meet new friends there, too!" Just then, Kim felt a little excited about moving into a new place.

As soon as they arrived in the new neighborhood, Kim saw two children playing under a big shady tree across their new house. She waved to the little girl who wore a red hat. The little girl waved and smiled back at her. Kim grabbed her dolls and went across the street.

Soon after, Jim followed her there. They laughed and played with their new friends under the big shady tree all afternoon.

ACTIVITY 4

SCORE:_______

Draw a star (☆) in the box of each picture that shows what happened in the story.

Encircle the letter of the correct answer.

1. Who was sad about leaving their old house?
   a. Tim   b. Jim   c. Kim

2. Who is Kim's brother?
   a. Tim   b. Jim   c. Pam

3. How many children did Kim see?
   a. one   b. two   c. three

4. Where did the kids play?
   a. under the big shady tree
   b. under the big thorny tree
   c. under the fig tree

5. Who waved and smiled back at Kim?
   a. the little girl with a hat
   b. the little girl with a cap
   c. the little girl with a map

Read the sentences. Arrange them according to their sequence in the story. Write the numerals *1* to *5* on the blanks.

________ 1. Kim ran across the street.

________ 2. The little girl waved and smiled back at Kim.

________ 3. Jim cheered up Kim.

________ 4. Kim was sad about leaving their old house.

________ 5. Kim waved to the little girl across their new house.

STORIES FOR FUN

Hungry Andy

Andy asks his aunt.
"Can I have an apple, please?"
His aunt answers, "Alright."
Andy bites the apple.
"Aahh! It tastes amazing!"
Then Andy asks for another.

Clever Ella

Ella is eleven years old.
She is in elementary.
Ella enjoys cooking.
She fries an eggplant with egg.
She uses an electric stove.
Excellent work, Ella!

Interesting Isha

Isha lives in India.
She is fifty inches tall.
Her favorite color is indigo.
Isha collects insects.
She also has a pet iguana.
Isha takes care of her infant brother.

The Zookeper

Oca works in a zoo.
He feeds onions to the ox.
He opens the ostrich cage.
He gives the orangutan a bath.
Oca walks on the overpass.
He waters the orchids there.

Uncle's Room

My uncle's name is Tuck.
He lives in the room upstairs.
Uncle's room is untidy.
His undershirt is on the chair.
His umbrella is under the table.
Even his underpants are on the floor!

ACTIVITY 5   SCORE:_______

Shade the circle beside the correct answer.

1. Who is hungry?

   ◯ Tuck   ◯ Andy   ◯ Isha

2. Who is the zookeper?

   ◯ Ella   ◯ Tuck   ◯ Oca

3. Who is interesting?

   ◯ Isha   ◯ Oca   ◯ Ella

4. Who lives in a room upstairs?

   ◯ Tuck   ◯ Isha   ◯ Andy

5. Who is clever?

   ◯ Oca   ◯ Ella   ◯ Andy

Answer the questions from the following stories.

Hungry Andy

Box the correct answer.

1. What does Andy eat?

   orange   apple   guava

2. Who gives Andy something to eat?

   his aunt   his uncle   his friend

3. How does the apple taste?

   sour   amazing   bitter

4. Does Andy like the apple?

   no   yes

5. Is Andy hungry?

   yes   no

Clever Ella

Encircle the letter of the correct answer.

1. How old is Ella?

   a. ten years old   b. six years old   c. eleven years old

2. What does Ella enjoy?

   a. cooking   b. dancing   c. singing

3. What does Ella fry?

   a. eggplant with   b. eggplant with   c. egg with onions
      cheese   egg

4. What does Ella use for cooking?

   a. electric stove   b. oven   c. charcoal

5. Who is clever?

   a. Eva   b. Ellen   c. Ella

<u>**Interesting Isha**</u>

Underline the correct answer.

1. Isha takes care of her (infant, old) brother.

2. Isha is (forty, fifty) inches tall.

3. Isha's favorite color is (red, indigo).

4. Isha's pet is an (alligator, iguana).

5. Isha lives in (India, Japan).

<u>**The Zookeper**</u>

Shade the box of the correct answer.

1. Where does Oca work?

☐ in the zoo ☐ in the park ☐ in the farm

2. What does Oca give to the ox?

☐ grass ☐ oats ☐ onions

3. What does Oca open?

☐ ostrich cage ☐ orangutan cage ☐ lion cage

4. What does Oca do with the orangutan?

☐ beat ☐ bathe ☐ pat

5. Where are the orchids found?

☐ in the underpass ☐ on the overpass ☐ on the tree

<u>**Uncle's Room**</u>

Write the correct answer on the blanks. Choose your answer from the box.

untidy	table	upstairs	undershirt	Tuck

1. My uncle's name is ________________.
2. My uncle lives in the room ________________.
3. Uncle's room is ________________.
4. Uncle's ________________ is on the chair.
5. Uncle's umbrella is under the ________________.

ACTIVITY 7   SCORE:________

Match the characters with the stories by writing the letters on the blank.

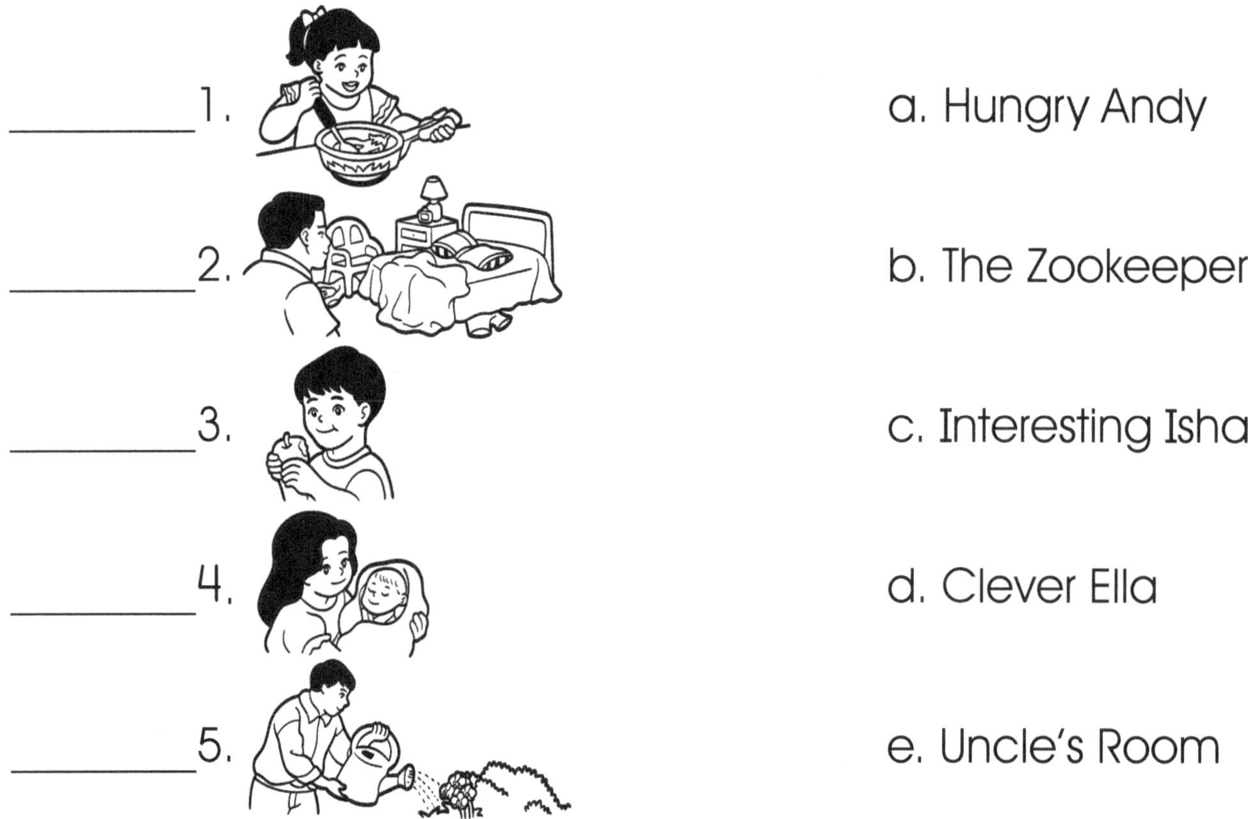

________ 1.   a. Hungry Andy

________ 2.   b. The Zookeeper

________ 3.   c. Interesting Isha

________ 4.   d. Clever Ella

________ 5.   e. Uncle's Room

HOME ACTIVITY   SCORE:______

Discuss the stories with your mother or your father, or any adult at home. Answer the questions that follow. (*Note: No score on this.*)

1. Which of the five stories did you enjoy reading most?

    ____

2. Who among the five characters do you like best? _______________Why? _______________________

3. If you were hungry like Andy, what would you eat?

    ____

4. Do you think Isha is a good girl? _______________
    Why? ____

5. If you were Tuck, what would you do with your room?

    ____

6. Why do Oca walks on the overpass?

    ____

7. What kind of girl is Ella?

    ____

LESSON 6

WORDS THAT RHYME

bat – cat	well – yell
net – pet	tong – gong
lip – dip	pale – tale
box – fox	hide – ride
bun – sun	cube – tube
pram – gram	dark – mark
trash – crash	cold – told
dish – wish	ring – sing

<table>
<tr><td>

ACTIVITY 8

</td><td>

SCORE:______

</td></tr>
</table>

A. Put a check (✓) before the pair of words that rhyme.

________ 1. pick – sick

________ 2. pan – pat

________ 3. kiss – hiss

________ 4. watch – catch

________ 5. top – tall

B. Choose a word that rhymes with the given word. Encircle it.

1. | clay | – play   train   toy

2. | west | – wear   nest   lass

3. | bent | – pant   part   tent

4. | lap | – lag   land   trap

5. | pink | – tack   sink   fund

Encircle the rhyming word-pair of the underlined word in each sentence.

1. <u>Joy</u> has a toy.

2. Jill is on the <u>hill</u>.

3. The <u>king</u> lost his ring.

4. They mix <u>six</u> bowls of flour.

5. <u>Meg</u> has a pain on her leg.

6. My car is parked too <u>far</u>.

7. Max knows how to play the <u>sax</u>.

8. The <u>vet</u> gives his pet a big hug.

9. The man with a coat rode on a <u>boat</u>.

10. I have so much <u>fun</u> whenever I run.

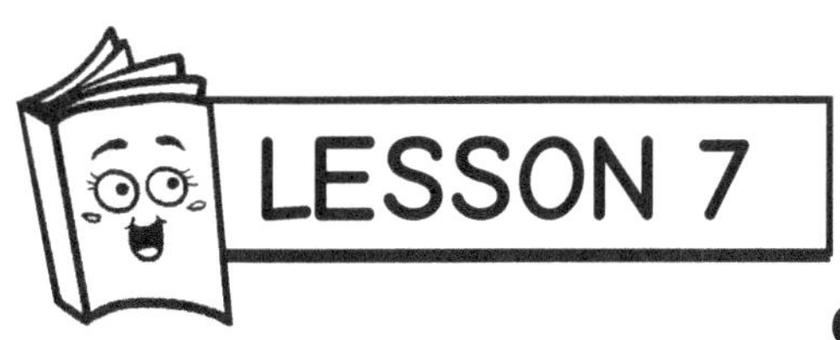

LESSON 7

SEQUENCING

Guide: Post colorful illustrations on the board. Encourage the children to tell a story out of the given illustrations. Let them arrange the illustrations based on their own story.

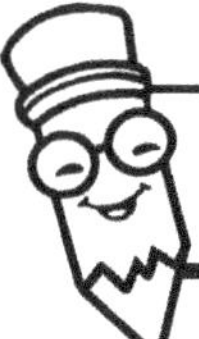

ACTIVITY 9 SCORE: ______

Write *1* or *2* beside each picture to show what comes first and last. *(10 points)*

______	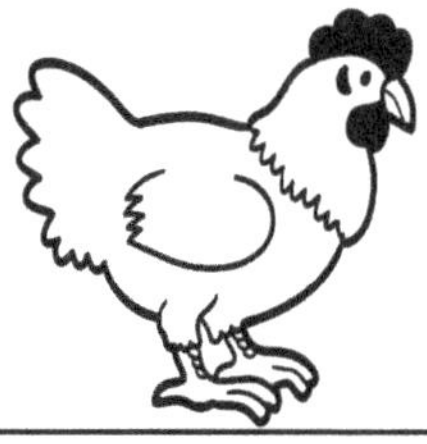	______	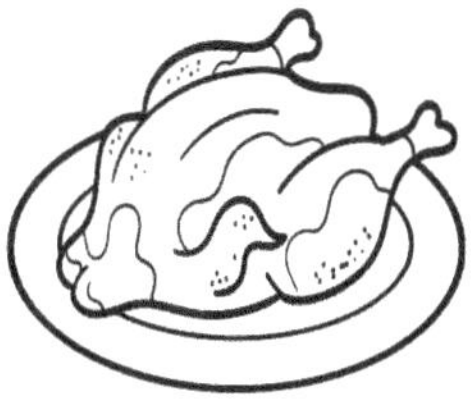
______	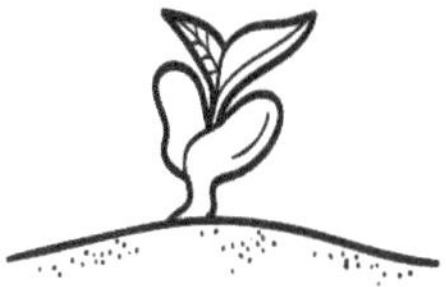	______	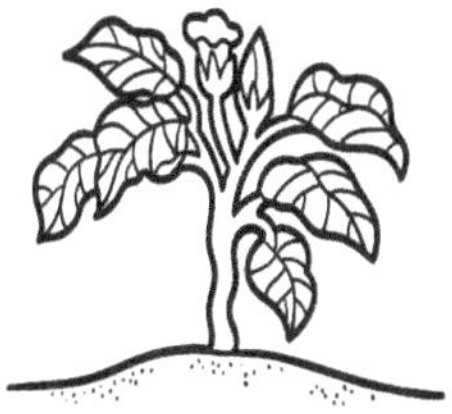
______	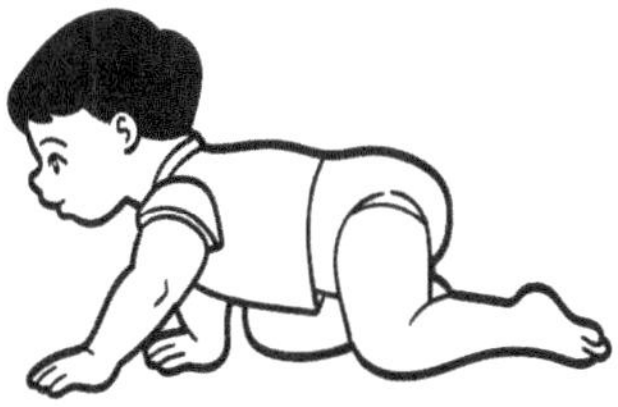	______	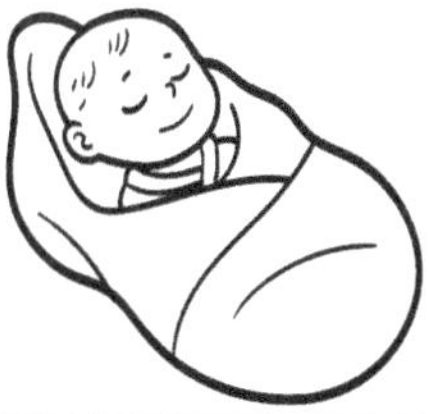
______	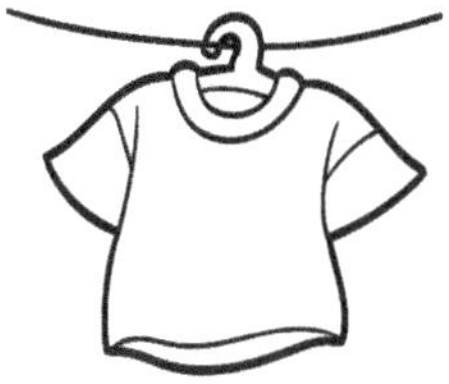	______	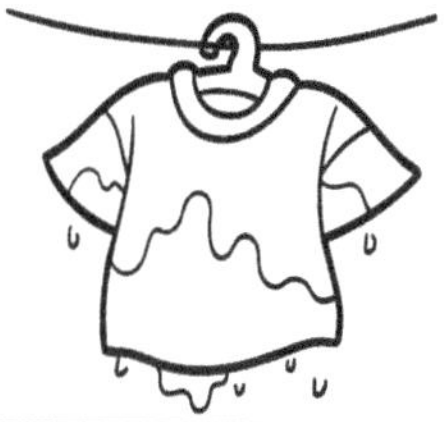
______	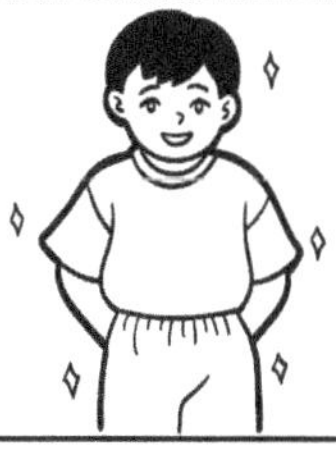	______	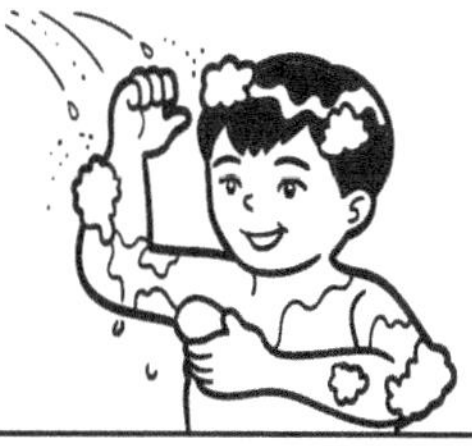

QUIZ NO. 16

SCORE: _______

Write 1 beside the picture that should come first.
Write 2 beside that which should come last.
(*10 points*)

FOURTH QUARTERLY TEST
(Review Guide for Parents and Teachers)

Name: _______________________________ **Score:** __________

Level: __________ **Date:** __________

I. Encircle the different picture.

1.	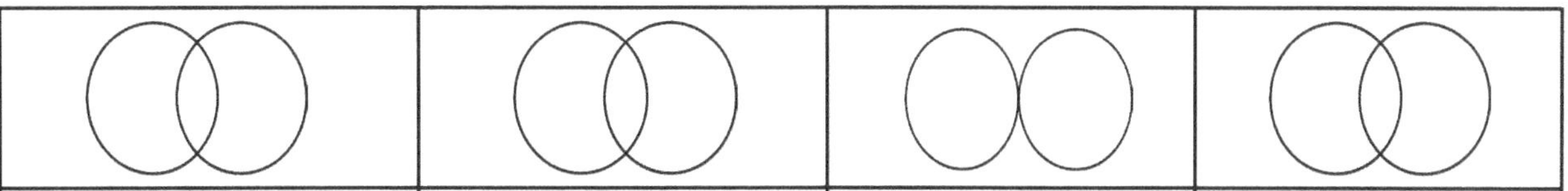			
2.	**838**	**833**	**838**	**838**
3.	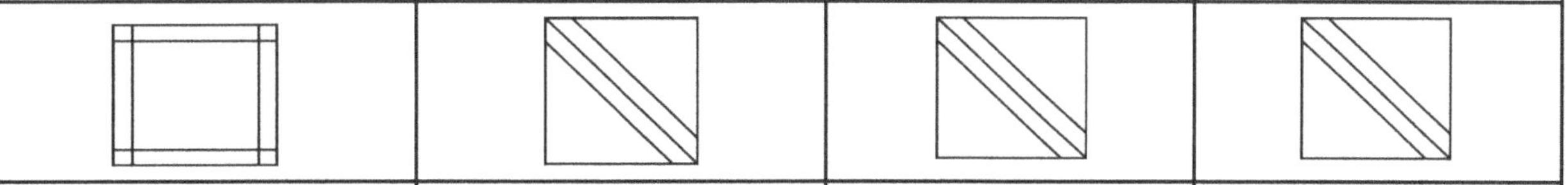			
4.	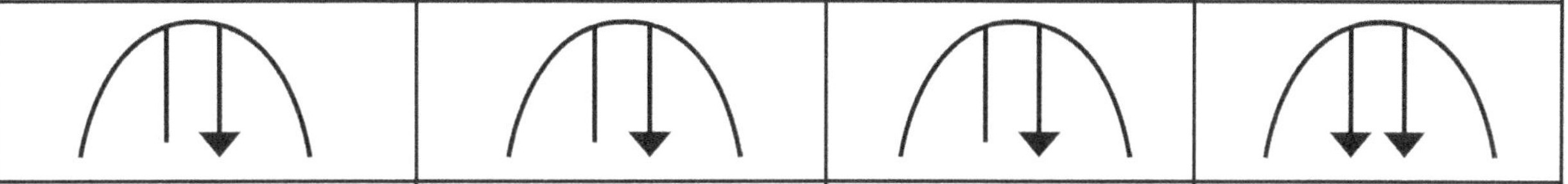			
5.	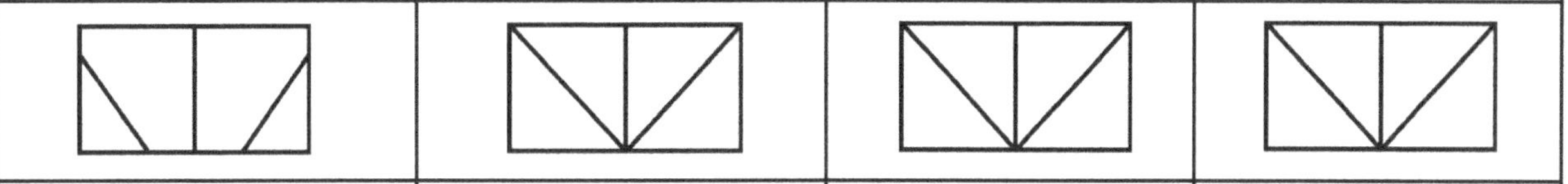			
6.	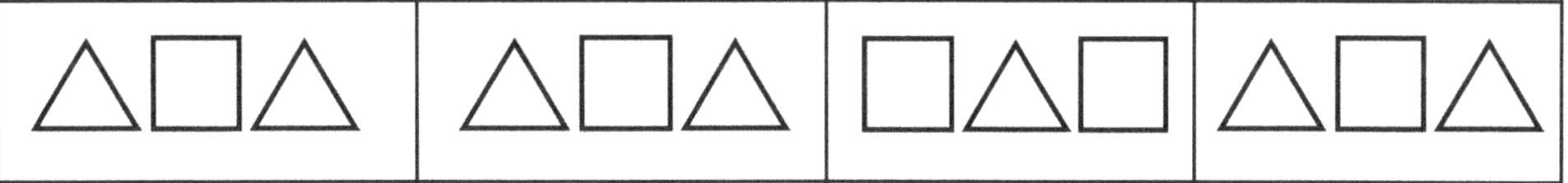			
7.	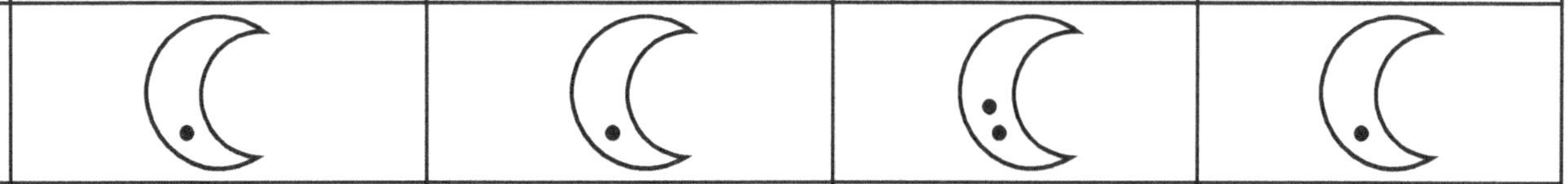			
8.	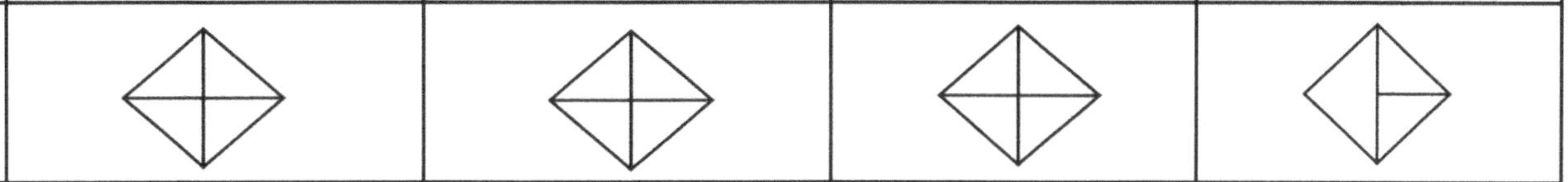			
9.	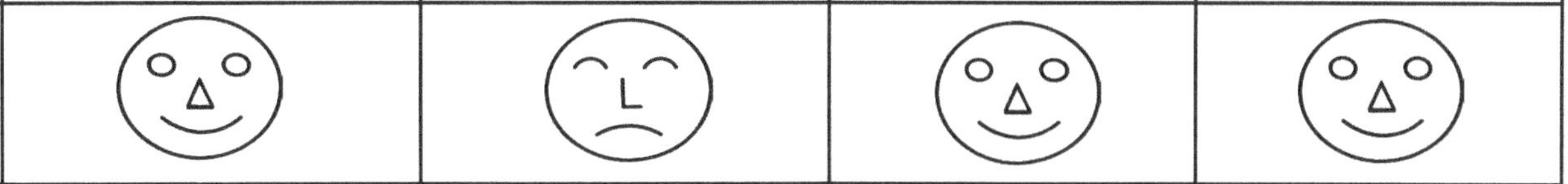			
10.	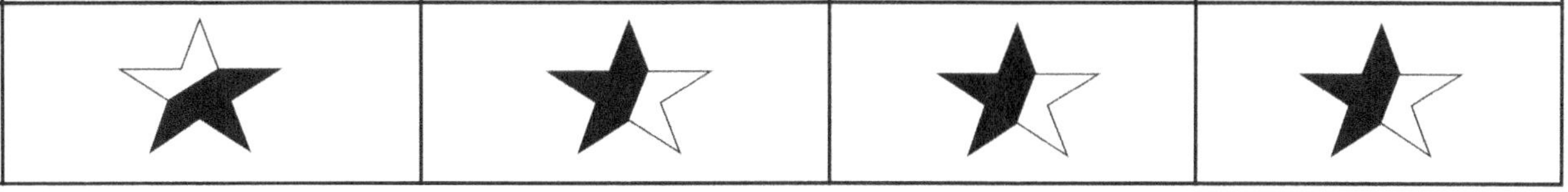			

II. Box the correct word.

1. My gift is a pink (dress, mess).

2. I (drink, wink) milk every morning.

3. Paper (clips, claps) can hold paper.

4. The (clock, cluck) tells time.

5. The bus is stuck in the (mud, mad).

6. We will sit on the (bench, bunch).

7. The (ship, sheep) sails on the sea.

8. Put the books on the (shell, shelf).

9. Jack is sad. He is (sick, sack).

10. The frog can (hop, top).

III. Put a ✓ if the sentence is correct and **X** if not.

______ 1. Man can run, walk, or jump.

______ 2. We use a spoon and a fork to eat.

______ 3. To sob is to cry.

______ 4. A lass is a young woman.

______ 5. We can eat a tack.

______ 6. A fig is a kind of pet.

______ 7. The opposite of "no" is "yes."

______ 8. Butterflies have two legs.

______ 9. A kid is a baby pig.

______ 10. A bill is a part of our body.

<u>IV</u>. Answer the riddles by encircling the correct answer.

1. I can be big or small.
    Tick-tock, tick-tock, as I call.
    Seconds, minutes, hours I can give.

| clock | duck | rock |

2. I am soft and smooth.
    After every meal, I can be of use.
    Your teeth and mouth, I take care of.

| pillow | hairbrush | toothbrush |

3. I am pure and white.
    Hot or cold I might be.
    Drink me any time you want.

| coffee | tea | milk |

4. I give you days and months,
    dates and years.
    Birthdates, events, anniversaries,
    and holidays each year.

| ticket | calendar | notebook |

5. I can hop, I can jump.
    I can also croak.
    Into the water, I let my body soak.

| frog | turtle | duck |

V. Follow the directions.

Color something that can croak.	  
Draw a heart inside the circle.	 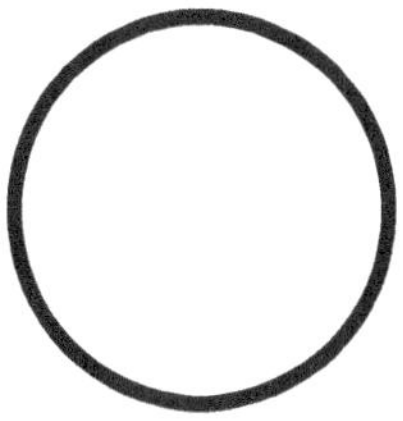
Check the one that rhymes with bill.	  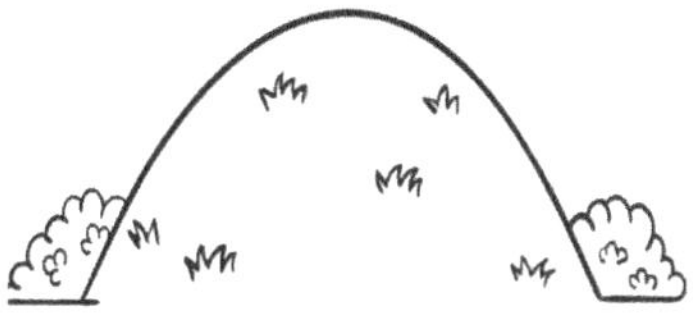
Cross out the thing that does not belong.	  
Underline the name of the person who takes good care of us.	mother pig baby

PROGRESS CHART
FOURTH QUARTER

Name: _______________________________________   Level: ____________

ACTIVITY	No. of Items	My Score	HOME ACTIVITY	No. of Items	My Score	QUIZ	No. of Items	My Score
1	5					1	5	
2	10					2	5	
3	5					3	5	
4	5					4	5	
5	5					5	5	
6	25					6	10	
7	5					7	15	
8	10					8	4	
9	10					9	4	
						10	4	
						11	4	
						12	4	
						13	5	
						14	5	
						15	10	
						16	10	
TOTAL	80					TOTAL	100	

___________________________   ___________________________
Parent's/Guardian's Signature   Teacher's Signature

HAZEL DOMINGO BABIANO

Hazel Domingo Babiano is the directress/owner of the Steppingstone Progressivist School. She leads a dynamic life in the education field as an Instructional Manager for the Department of Education ALS Division in the National Capital Region, an Educational Consultant for the Child Development Center of Sirkulo ng Kababaihan sa Pasig (SIKAPIN), Vice-Chairperson on Education, Urban Poor Institute for Community Building (UPICOB), official trainor/facilitator of BKP (Bagong Kulturang Pinoy) Philippines, and Educational Consultant of various private schools nationwide.

She finished both her degrees in Bachelor of Arts in Psychology and her Masters in Education major in Special Education from the University of the Philippines. Hazel loves to sing and dance, and her enthusiasm will surely make you join in the fun. She is the life of any party! To relax, Hazel plays games on her tablet, as well as dote on her grandson. She is also a mother to four energetic and naughty dogs.

DONOVAN DOMINGO BABIANO

Donovan Domingo Babiano took BA English Studies from UP Diliman, and is the Administrator of the Steppingstone Progressivist School. He is a former coach of Wilma Cruz Tapalla's Institute of Speech, Etiquette, and Image. Donovan writes poetry and songs, and during his downtime you can often find him playing imagination games (boardgames and D&D).

This mother-and-son tandem has worked together for a long time to bring tried-and-tested learning activities, as well as fresh ideas based on current experiences, to books that are relevant for the 21st century learner (and teacher).

ACKNOWLEDGMENT

Writing books is a formidable task, but we would like to thank the following people who turn it the other way around:
- Our family, our primary movers, and our source of inspiration — Alathea, Bohari, Adzel, and Aeden — for understanding our eccentricities;
- The STEPPINGSTONE Angels — Layra L. Del Rosario, Ofelieta O. Saladaga, Lizette Cadiente, Don, and Eva Mascariola — for taking charge of the school while we're busy writing books and conducting seminars;
- Our publishers — the fabulous Raymund and the alluring Isabel Catabijan — for believing in us and for the special bonding spiced with some "jokes";
- The magnificent sisters, Regine and Wowie — for guiding us through the digital aspects of book-writing;
- The staff and artists of Saint Matthew's Publishing — Sarah, Maricar, Janet, Josie, Gina, Jona, Darren, Orly, Gio, Eunice and, of course, Rollie — for all the fun and "kakulitan";
- The gorgeous agents and sub-agents — for their hard work and perseverance;
- All teachers — not only for helping us touch the lives of children, but also for making a difference in all the lives that we touch;
- All children — for inspiring us and helping us learn the greatest lessons in life;
- Our Almighty God, above all — for the good health and for the gifts of humor, wisdom, perseverance, resiliency, and extraordinary strength; and for the outpouring graces... thanks, Lord!